JOURNAL FOR THE STUDY OF THE NEW TESTAMENT
SUPPLEMENT SERIES

10

Executive Editor, Supplement Series
David Hill

Publishing Editor
David J.A. Clines

Department of Biblical Studies
The University of Sheffield
Sheffield S10 2TN
England

CHRIST
THE END OF THE
LAW

Romans 10.4 in Pauline Perspective

Robert Badenas

Journal for the Study of the New Testament
Supplement Series 10

To my parents, my first Bible teachers

Published by
JSOT Press
Department of Biblical Studies
The University of Sheffield
Sheffield S10 2TN
England

Printed in Great Britain
by Redwood Burn Ltd.,
Trowbridge, Wiltshire.

British Library Cataloguing in Publication Data

Badenas, Robert
    Christ the end of the law : Romans 10.4 in
    Pauline perspective.—(Journal for the study
    of the New Testament supplement series,
    ISSN 0143-5108; 10)
    1. Law (Theology)
    I. Title   II. Series
    241'.2   BT96.2

    ISBN 0-905774-93-0
    ISBN 0-905774-94-9 Pbk

CONTENTS

LIST OF ABBREVIATIONS

ACW	Ancient Christian Writers
AJT	*American Journal of Theology*
AnBib	Analecta Biblica
ANF	The Ante-Nicene Fathers
APOT	R.H. Charles (ed.), *Apocrypha and Pseudepigrapha of the Old Testament*
ASNU	Acta seminarii neotestamentici upsaliensis
ASTI	*Annual of the Swedish Theological Institute*
ATANT	Abhandlungen zur Theologie des Alten und Neuen Testaments
BAC	Biblioteca de autores cristianos
BAG	W. Bauer, W.F. Arndt, and F.W. Gingrich, *Greek-English Lexicon of the NT*
BDF	F. Blass, A. Debrunner, and R.W. Funk, *A Greek Grammar of the NT*
BEvT	Beiträge zur evangelischen Theologie
BFCT	Beiträge zur Förderung christlicher Theologie
Bib	*Biblica*
BJRL	*Bulletin of the John Rylands University Library*
BN	*Biblische Notizen*
BKAT	Biblischer Kommentar: Altes Testament
BR	*Biblical Research*
BSac	*Bibliotheca Sacra*
BTB	*Biblical Theology Bulletin*
BZ	*Biblische Zeitschrift*
CBQ	*Catholic Biblical Quarterly*
CCCM	Corpus Christianorum Continuatio Mediaeualis
CCSL	Corpus Christianorum Series Latina
CHB	Cambridge History of the Bible
ConcJ	*Concordia Journal*
CR	*Classical Review*
CSEL	Corpus scriptorum ecclesiasticorum latinorum
CTQ	*Concordia Theological Quarterly*
DiálEcum	*Diálogo Ecuménico*

DBSup	*Dictionnaire de la Bible Supplément*
EBib	Etudes bibliques
ErbAuf	Erbe und Auftrag
EstBib	*Estudios biblicos*
EstEcl	Estudios Eclesiásticos
ETL	*Ephemerides theologicae lovanienses*
ETR	*Etudes théologiques et religieuses*
EvQ	*Evangelical Quarterly*
EvT	*Evangelische Theologie*
ExpTim	*Expository Times*
FC	Fathers of the Church
FRLANT	Forschungen zur Religion und Literatur des Alten und Neuen Testaments
FoiVie	*Foi et Vie*
GCS	Griechische christliche Schriftsteller
Greg	*Gregorianum*
HBT	*Horizons in Biblical Theology*
HNTC	Harper's NT Commentaries
HTR	*Harvard Theological Review*
HTS	Harvard Theological Studies
ICC	International Critical Commentary
IDB	G.A. Buttrick, ed., *Interpreter's Dictionary of the Bible*
Int	*Interpretation*
JAC	Jahrbuch für Antike und Christentum
JB	*Jerusalem Bible*
JBC	R.E. Brown *et al.*, eds., *The Jerome Bible Commentary*
JBL	*Journal of Biblical Literature*
JES	*Journal of Ecumenical Studies*
JETS	*Journal of the Evangelical Theological Society*
JJS	*Journal of Jewish Studies*
JQR	*Jewish Quarterly Review*
JR	*Journal of Religion*
JSNT	*Journal for the Study of the New Testament*
JSS	*Journal of Semitic Studies*
JTC	*Journal for Theology and the Church*
JTS	*Journal of Theological Studies*
KD	*Kerygma und Dogma*
KExKNT	Kritisch-exegetischer Kommentar über Neue Testament
LB	*Living Bible*
LCC	Library of Christian Classics

LCL	Loeb Classical Library
LQ	*Lutheran Quarterly*
LTP	*Laval Théologique Philosophique*
LW	*Lutheran World*
MGWJ	*Monatsschrift für Geschichte und Wissenschaft des Judentums*
MTZ	*Münchener theologische Zeitschrift*
NASB	*New American Standard Bible*
NICNT	New International Commentary on the New Testament
NIDNTT	*New International Dictionary of New Testament Theology*
NJKA	Neue Jahrbücher der klassischen Altertums
NovT	*Novum Testamentum*
NovTSup	Novum Testamentum, Supplements
NRT	*La nouvelle revue théologique*
NOABA	New Oxford Annotated Bible with the Apocrypha
NPNF	Nicene and Post-Nicene Fathers
NTS	*New Testament Studies*
OTL	Old Testament Library
PG	J. Migne, *Patrologia graeca*
PL	J. Migne, *Patrologia latina*
PWSup	Supplement to Pauly–Wissowa, *Real-Encyclopädie*
RB	*Revue biblique*
RBén	*Revue bénédictine*
RechBib	Recherches bibliques
RE	*Realencyklopädie für protestantische Theologie und Kirche*
RevExp	*Review and Expositor*
RevMet	*Review of Metaphysics*
RevScRel	*Revue des sciences religieuses*
RGG	*Religion in Geschichte und Gegenwart*
RHE	*Revue d'histoire ecclésiastique*
RHPR	*Revue d'histoire et de philosophie religieuses*
RSPT	*Revue des sciences philosophiques et théologiques*
RSR	*Recherches de science religieuse*
RSV	*Revised Standard Version*
RTAM	Recherches de Théologie Ancienne et Médiévale
SC	Sources chrétiennes
ScrB	*Scripture Bulletin*
SE	Studia Evangelica I, II, III (= TU 73 [1959], 87 [1964],

	88 [1964])
SJT	*Scottish Journal of Theology*
SPC	Studiorum Paulinorum Congressus
ST	*Studia theologica*
Str-B	H. Strack and P. Billerbeck, *Kommentar zum Neuen Testament*
SVF	Stoicorum Veterum Fragmenta
TDNT	G. Kittel and G. Friedrich, eds., *Theological Dictionary of the New Testament*
TG	*Theologie und Glaube*
THAT	*Theologisches Handwörterbuch zum Alten Testament*
TLZ	*Theologische Literaturzeitung*
TS	*Theological Studies*
TSK	*Theologische Studien und Kritiken*
TWOT	R.L. Harris, G.L. Archer, and B.K. Waltke, eds., *Theological Wordbook of the Old Testament*
TZ	*Theologische Zeitschrift*
VC	*Vigiliae christianae*
VD	*Verbum domini*
WA	M. Luther, *Kritische Gesamtausgabe* (= 'Weimar' edition)
WTS	*Westminster Theological Journal*
WUNT	Wissenschaftliche Untersuchungen zum Neuen Testament
ZAW	*Zeitschrift für die alttestamentliche Wissenschaft*
ZNW	*Zeitschrift für die neutestamentliche Wissenschaft*
ZPPK	*Zeitschrift für Philosophie und philosophische Kritik*
ZST	*Zeitschrift für systematische Theologie*
ZTK	*Zeitschrift für Theologie und Kirche*

PREFACE

Unless otherwise indicated, biblical quotations in English are taken from the Revised Standard Version (*New Oxford Annotated Bible with the Apocrypha* [New York: Oxford University Press, 1973]). Where the Greek text is cited, the source, in the NT, is *The Greek New Testament* (by K. Aland *et al.*, eds., 3rd edn [New York: United Bible Societies, 1975]), and in the OT, the *Septuaginta Vetus Testamentum Graecum* (Auctoritate Academiae Scientiarum Gottingensis editum [Göttingen: Vandenhoeck & Ruprecht, 1974]). Where the Hebrew text is cited, the source is the *Biblia Hebraica Stuttgartensia* (K. Elliger and W. Rudolph, eds. [Stuttgart: Deutsche Bibelstiftung, 1977]). Unless another source is indicated, the translations of classical sources are those of the Loeb Classical Library (edited by T.E. Page *et al.* [Cambridge, Mass.: Harvard University Press, 1932-1962]).

It should perhaps be noted that some quotations from ancient and foreign languages have been left untranslated. This was done in cases where nuances of meaning would be lost or obscured by translation. Translations into English are given, however, where they would aid the reader's understanding of the quotation's relation to the point this study is attempting to make.

References to τέλος and τέλος νόμου have been located, in cases where lexica and indexes were not available, through the services of Wordsearch, a computerized research facility offered by the Department of Classics of the University of North Carolina (U.S.A.)

Ancient sources are mentioned and abbreviated according to the following criteria: H.G. Liddell and R. Scott, *A Greek-English Lexicon with a Supplement* (Oxford: Clarendon Press, 1973) and N.G.C. Hammond and H.H. Scullard, eds., *The Oxford Classical Dictionary* (Oxford: Clarendon Press, 1970) for classical Greek literature; G.W.H. Lampe, ed., *A Patristic Greek Lexicon* (Oxford: Clarendon Press, 1961) for Greek Patristic literature; A. Sauter *et al.*, *Oxford Latin Dictionary* (Oxford: Clarendon Press, 1968) for Latin classical literature; A. Blaise, *Lexicon Latinitatis Medii Aeui*

(CCCM; Turnhout: Bregoli, 1975) for the Latin Medieval literature. For the Pseudepigrapha, J.A. Charlesworth, *The Pseudepigrapha and Modern Research* (Missoula: Scholars Press, 1975); for Philo, *Studia Philonica* 1 (1972), p. 92, and for the Dead Sea Scrolls, Talmudic, Mishnaic, and other rabbinic works, *JBL* 95 (1976), pp. 336-38.

It would be remiss to complete this work without an acknowledgment of those who aided in its accomplishment. Many thanks are given to Drs Abraham Terian, Yvan Blazen, and Gerhard Hasel, for their precious help in the elaboration of my thesis; to Drs Leona Running, Joyce Jones, and Jon Paulien, for their assistance in the proper expression of the English; and to Drs Robert Jewett and Bruce D. Chilton, for their skillful orientation, suggestions, and counsel in the publication of this work.

INTRODUCTION

We owe to Paul the shape of many of the most common and oft-repeated expressions of our theological language. Some of them beautifully convey, in a minimum of words, the basic concepts of Christianity, and are so concisely and successfully worded that they have become axiomatic in current theological speech. But, as is commonly known, phrases frequently repeated become so common-place that they sometimes lose not only their force but also their original meaning.

This seems to have happened with the statement 'Christ is the end of the law' (Rom 10.4). There are few Pauline statements more used and abused than this one. Utilized either as an easy caption[1] or as a stereotyped slogan,[2] the phrase 'Christ is the end of the law' is too often used without any specification of its meaning, which is either assumed—generally in the sense that 'Christ has put an end to the law'[3]—or taken for granted—in whatever sense—as absolutely self-evident.[4]

Paradoxically, there are few Pauline statements more ambiguous and controversial than this one. Although Rom 10.4 seems, at first glance, an 'easy text'—no textual variants, no special problems of grammar, no *hapax legomena*—it has exercised exegetes of all times and has been considered 'one of the most hotly debated passages in the Pauline epistles'.[5] The uncertainty of its meaning is due, partly, to the confusing ambiguity which surrounds Paul's use of the term 'law' (νόμος), but principally to the perplexing polysemy of the word 'end' (τέλος). Thus, although there is also some difficulty in the translation of νόμος,[6] the main problem of Rom 10.4 centers around the meaning of τέλος, which seems to be the determinant element for the understanding not only of the phrase τέλος νόμου, but of the whole verse, and possibly even of the whole passage.[7]

However, since νόμος is a *theologoumenon* of extremely great importance in Paul's theology it has monopolized the interest of exegetes of Rom 10.4 and attracted the attention of scholarship to the question of the law. Depending on the particular place of the law in the theology of each scholar, τέλος has been translated in a positive or in a negative way. Not being a theological term *per se*, and playing only an auxiliary role in Paul's theological language, τέλος has been given very little attention thus far.

Yet, even lesser words may have been used by Paul in certain statements with a very important theological intention. They may significantly modify key sentences and introduce into them some particular nuances revealing profound aspects of Paul's thought. The contention of the present study is that τέλος in Rom 10.4 is one of these words, and that the determination of its meaning is crucial for the understanding of the whole passage.

The problem of the interpretation of Rom 10.4 is a long-unresolved question. Moses Stuart, 150 years ago, already called Rom 10.4 'a long agitated and much controverted text'.[8] In spite of all the efforts which have been devoted to the exegesis of this verse, the endless debate around the meaning of τέλος not only has never ceased, but 'has always been a focus of exegetical discussion'.[9] Notwithstanding the considerable amount of literature recently dedicated to the problem of Rom 10.4, including three doctoral dissertations,[10] the 'never-ceasing controversy'[11] still goes on. The question of the meaning of τέλος has not been resolved, and Rom 10.4 is still today a 'much disputed and notorious crux'.[12]

The polysemy of τέλος[13] has given rise to an incredibly wide spectrum of interpretations, covering practically the whole range of meaning of the Greek word, namely: 'termination',[14] 'terminus',[15] 'limit',[16] 'cessation',[17] 'abrogation',[18] 'abolition',[19] 'conclusion',[20] 'consummation',[21] 'completion',[22] 'culmination',[23] 'climax',[24] 'fulfillment',[25] 'aim',[26] 'goal',[27] 'purpose',[28] 'object',[29] 'intent',[30] 'Final Cause',[31] 'sense and meaning',[32] and even 'toll'.[33]

On the basis of the numerous meanings of τέλος and the various nuances of νόμος, Rom 10.4 has been interpreted in such different ways as: 'Christ means the end of the struggle for righteousness-by-the-law',[34] 'Christ has brought the era of the law to an end',[35] '(in Christ) the Jewish religion is superseded',[36] 'The law is set aside as a way of salvation by the Christ event',[37] 'Christ has superseded the law',[38] 'Christ is the climactic development of the law',[39] 'Christ has brought the law to completion',[40] 'The law finds its fulfillment in Christ',[41] 'Christ is the end that the law had in view',[42] 'Christ is the goal to which the law pointed',[43] or 'Christ has completed the purpose of the law'.[44]

Although some of the above interpretations deserve to be treated separately, they may conveniently be summed up into three categories corresponding to the three main shades of meaning which have been traditionally attributed to τέλος in Rom 10.4: (1) temporal/terminal; (2) perfective/completive; and (3) teleological. The controversy and debate centers particularly on the opposition between the temporal and the teleological interpretations,[45] although there is increasing interest in a mediating position which defends the compatability of both interpretations.

The supporters of the temporal interpretation contend that τέλος must be translated in Rom 10.4 by 'end' in the sense of 'termination', 'cessation', or 'abrogation'. Since they generally approach Rom 9.30–10.21 from the hermeneutical perspective of law versus gospel (or works versus faith), they interpret the phrase 'Christ is the end of the law' in the sense that 'Christ has put an end to the law', implying by it that the law is no longer binding for Christians.[46] Thus, as Rhyne has rightly observed, 'more than any other text Rom 10.4 has become the *locus classicus* for expressing the discontinuity between the Church and the Old Testament'.[47] Explained in several different ways,[48] the temporal interpretation is the prevailing one in modern Pauline scholarship.[49]

However, the temporal interpretation is not the earliest nor has it been universally accepted. The Early Fathers, the Reformers, and many among their theological heirs have claimed for τέλος the basic meaning that was common to this word in classical Greek. Thus, understanding τέλος either as 'goal', 'object', or 'fulfillment', they have interpreted Rom 10.4 as one of the basic statements of the continuity between the Hebrew Scriptures and Christ, meaning that in Christ the law (understood as the law of God, as the Jewish Torah, or as the Old Testament) has reached its purpose, completion, or fulfillment.[50] So we face the surprising situation that the same text is used to support two opposite views of the relationship between the law and Christ, both by those who see a total rupture between the Old Testament and Christianity, and by those who see a harmonious continuity between the two.

But, equally surprising, we find that Rom 10.4 has also become the most important rallying point for those who attempt to mediate between the extremes of discontinuity and continuity! For a growing number of scholars[51] the temporal and the teleological meanings of τέλος are not exclusive, but complementary. Thus, they contend that somewhat opposing meanings of 'goal', 'fulfillment', and/or 'termination' are simultaneously possible in the word under discussion.

So, the inevitable question is: What is the real meaning of τέλος in Rom 10.4? Is it temporal ('Christ has abolished the law'), completive ('Christ has fulfilled the law'), teleological ('the law pointed to Christ'), or all of these at the same time? Is there a way of removing the ambiguity of this perplexing phrase, or must we conclude, with John W. Drane, that 'the ambiguity was intentional on Paul's part'[52] and, therefore, resign ourselves never to know what Paul meant?

The importance of these questions cannot be disputed, for, as Cranfield has rightly observed, Rom 10.4 represents 'one of the fundamental theses of Pauline theology as a whole, since, in whatever way it is taken, it is obviously a decisive statement concerning the relation of Christ and the law'.[53] Getty argues that 'an interpretation of this verse in its context is crucial for understanding the religious problem of the relation between Christianity and Judaism'.[54] J.A. Sanders states that Rom 10.4 'summarizes the central belief of the early church',[55] and Kirk affirms that this verse is 'an epigram summarizing the gospel'.[56] The fact that such great importance is accorded to Rom 10.4 and that it is used in support of such different theological positions is sufficient to prove the importance of determining the meaning of this verse and to show the existence of a semantic/exegetical problem which needs to be solved.

The heart of the problem seems to be the lack of methodological criteria for determining the sense of τέλος. This lack is primarily due to the fact that a comprehensive study of the meanings and usages of τέλος in biblical literature has not yet been produced. Consequently the interpreters depend almost exclusively on the context for finding out the sense of this word. Yet the context of Rom 10.4 (9.30–10.21) is one of the most difficult passages in Paul, more often avoided as an additional source of problems than interpreted as an aid for clarification. Therefore, the exegesis of this passage is often governed and controlled by the only criteria easily available to would-be interpreters, namely, their own theological convictions. And thus, as H.A.W. Meyer rightly observed, 'the understanding of 10.4 depends on decisions that one has made elsewhere'.[57] This is made particularly evident in the survey of the history of the interpretation of this passage which constitutes the first chapter of the present study.

The contention of the present study is that Rom 10.4 needs, first of all, lexical and exegetical clarification. This passage is far more eagerly used than explained. In most cases, τέλος, the key word of the passage, is either ambiguously translated by 'end', without any explanation of what is meant, or interpreted in the sense of 'termination', 'fulfillment', or 'goal' without any convincing rationale for the choice of meaning. Sometimes two, three, or even more of the above-mentioned meanings are proposed as simultaneously valid. It is clear that, even though several translations are theoretically acceptable, all of them cannot be equally probable, nor simultaneously possible—unless the ambiguity was intended by Paul himself, and even in that case it would need to be proved. Therefore, a more comprehensive lexical study of the use of τέλος is needed, in order to provide a better basis—if there is any—for the interpretation of Rom 10.4.

In spite of the many excellent studies on Rom 10.4 and its context that have been published thus far, and in spite of their extremely valuable contribution to the understanding of this verse, it must be acknowledged that Rom 10.4 has almost exclusively been approached from the perspective of law theology in its relation to the 'law-gospel' debate. The thrust of the passage has been largely disregarded, as well as the relation of Rom 10.4 to its immediate context (Rom 9–11) and to the purpose of the Epistle.

In order to enhance research in some of the basic areas where it is needed, the present study aims:

1. To survey and evaluate, in Chapter 1, the most representative interpretations of Rom 10.4 from the early Church to our days, in order to provide the necessary background for a correct appreciation of the current trends in their historical perspective.

2. To provide, by means of a semantic study of the use of τέλος, and, especially, of the meaning of the phrase τέλος νόμου and related expressions in biblical and cognate literature, in Chapter 2, some objective criteria for the determination of the meaning of τέλος νόμου in Rom 10.4.

3. To interpret Rom 10.4 in context (9.30–10.21), and, with due consideration to the thrust of the section (chs. 9–11), and to the main purpose of Paul in the epistle to the Romans, to pay particular attention to Paul's view of Scripture, and to the relationship between Χριστός and νόμος obtained through Paul's hermeneutical perspective, in order to discover whether Paul's view of that relationship is basically 'temporal' or 'teleological' (Chapter 3).

Since the object of the present research is only to ascertain the meaning of τέλος in Rom 10.4, it is limited to the field of biblical studies, and, as far as possible, avoids the problems pertaining to systematic theology. Thus, it does not deal with the concept of 'end'—which could hardly be limited to a single word—nor with the theological question of the 'end of the law'—which would imply that the meaning of τέλος in Rom 10.4 had already been decided. This is, then, only an exegetical approach concentrated on a single word in a single passage. Its object is to provide—as a groundwork intended for clarification—a modest but hopefully useful contribution to a further and more encompassing study on Paul's view of the law in its relation to Christ. The reason for this limitation is not that the exegetical approach is considered more important than the systematic, but the literature on the subject is so vast that a thorough study of both areas would go far beyond the scope of the present undertaking. In any case, the stated limitations do not imply a total disregard for doctrinal questions.

Chapter 1

HISTORY OF THE INTERPRETATION OF
ΤΕΛΟΣ IN ROMANS 10.4

According to Basil Hall, 'the history of biblical exegesis is one of the most neglected fields in the history of the Church and its doctrines', and it would be necessary to review it seriously to 'change for the better some fixed patterns of interpretation'.[1] Although this chapter does not pretend so much, it does aim, since no comprehensive survey on the exegesis of Rom 10.4 has heretofore been produced,[2] to review the history of the interpretation of this passage and thus provide the necessary background for the understanding of the origins and developments of the different trends of interpretation. Scholarship on Romans is so extensive that an exhaustive review of literature is virtually impossible. The present survey is limited to a brief but representative review of the main contributions. As a conclusion to this historical survey, a short summary of the main interpretations and a synthesis of the principal issues involved in the current debate is given.

From the Early Church to Scholasticism

A complete reconstruction of the history of the interpretation of Rom 10.4 from the early church to the rise of scholasticism is not easy. During these fourteen centuries, a mass of exegetical material on the writings of Paul had been produced. However the commentaries on Rom 10.4 which have not been lost have reached us in widely scattered or fragmentary documents so that it has become difficult even to obtain a complete list.[3] Nevertheless, the important commentaries of the period have been so carefully copied, so systematically quoted, and so abundantly plagiarized and paraphrased that it is still possible to reconstruct a fairly accurate picture of the leading trends of interpretation during this evasive period in spite of the above-mentioned difficulties.

The earliest documented interpretations

One probably must renounce knowing the first commentary on Rom 10.4 and even the first commentary on Romans. During the first 150 years of our era, the greatest part of Christian exegesis was that of the OT. Its main concern was to prove that the Hebrew Scriptures had been fulfilled in Jesus the Messiah.[4] The emphasis on the continuity between the OT and Christ was paralleled by an emphasis on the discontinuity between Israel and the Church.[5] Both of these simultaneous features should be kept in mind in order to understand the earliest interpretations of Rom 10.4. Some commentaries may already have existed by the middle of the second century.[6] But the earliest known commentary on the Pauline epistles seems to be the Marcionite *Antithesis*,[7] in which Marcion intended to demonstrate, among other things, the radical discontinuity between the OT and Christ and the absolute opposition between Law and Gospel.[8]

In the early Church, the controversy with the Jews turned on the interpretation of the OT, and the controversy with the Marcionites and Gnostics turned on the interpretation of the NT.[9] The issue was that of continuity and discontinuity between the OT and Christianity. Most Christians regarded the OT Scriptures as their Bible and treated them with the same respect with which they treated the apostolic writings of the New Testament. They had many problems, however, with some legal passages of the OT that they could not take as literally binding. The response to this dilemma took several forms.[10] Gnostics proposed an allegorical interpretation of all Scriptures. Marcion (d. c. 160) proposed the more drastic solution of abandoning the OT altogether.[11]

Unfortunately, only a few fragments of Marcion's exegetical work have come down to us.[12] What remains of his commentary on Romans is very incomplete.[13] Among the passages of Romans omitted by Marcion is 3.31–4.25, for the thought of 'establishing the law' and the references to Abraham were intolerable to him.[14] The same motif may be assumed for his rejection of all but a few verses in chs. 9–11. Though the quotation of Rom 10.4 by Marcion is attested, we do not know what interpretation he gave to the verse, for the entire passage from 10.5 to 11.33 is missing.[15] What we do know is that Marcion was rejected by the church, which saw itself—in spite of its anti-Jewish sentiments—in continuity with the OT.[16] The church understood Christianity as the crown and climax of revelation, and, consequently, appropriated the OT as its own sacred Scripture.[17]

Its 'new' Scripture was conceived 'not as replacing the Old but as complementing and consummating it'.[18]

The first Latin writer of the early Church, Tertullian (c. 160–c. 220), in his refutation of Marcionism (*Adversus Marcionem*)—one of the best pieces of Scriptural interpretation in Christian antiquity—quoted Rom 10.4 to support the unity of the Bible and the continuity between Christ and the OT. Tertullian understood *finis* as 'plenitude' or 'fulfillment', equating *finis legis* with *consummationem legis*.[19]

Gnosticism and the anti-Gnostic reaction

The other most influential trend within the Church in the second century was Gnosticism.[20] Though in contemporary NT scholarship Paul is considered the chief opponent of Gnosticism,[21] the Gnostic exegetes of the second century claimed Paul's writings as sources of Gnostic theology.[22] This fact must be taken into consideration when studying the interpretation of Paul at that time, since the 'orthodox' interpretation certainly defined itself in opposition to heresy.[23] The Gnostic interpretation of Rom 10.4 is not well attested. However, we can have an approximate idea of it by the argumentation against Heracleon and the Valentinians found in Origen's commentaries. According to Gnostic 'spiritual' exegesis, Gentiles and Jews in the epistle to the Romans are to be understood allegorically as 'psychic' and 'pneumatic' Christians. According to Valentinian exegesis the 'psychic' Israelites, though zealous (10.2), are ignorant that salvation comes from a superior knowledge of God, and they seek 'the righteousness of the law' (10.5) on the teachings of 'Moses the demiurge'. The Valentinians apparently inferred from 10.10 that Paul intended to discriminate between the two groups, distinguishing between those who 'confess with their mouth' and those who 'believe in their hearts'.[24] The interpretation of 10.4 was probably antinomian, since Origen argues against Heracleon, saying that 'if Christ came to fulfil the law (πληροῖ ὁ σωτὴρ τὸν νόμον) our faith cannot abolish the law, but strengthen it (οὐ γὰρ καταργοῦμεν νόμον διὰ τῆς πίστεως, ἀλλὰ ἱστάνομεν δι' αὐτῆς)'.[25] The emphasis on the validity of the Law in the early church may be related to the anti-Gnostic and anti-Marcionite controversies.[26]

The first documented interpretation of Rom 10.4 we possess comes from the anti-Gnostic Irenaeus (c. 130–202), but unfortunately it has come to us only in a Latin translation. Irenaeus explains *finis* in relation to *initium* saying that Christ is both the beginning and the end of the law, in the sense that he embodies it.[27] The context shows that *finis* translates τέλος in a completive/teleological way, for it goes on to say that 'the law remains permanently with us receiving by means of His [Christ's] advent in the flesh, extension and increase, but not abrogation'.[28] Thus, in the first attempts of proving by the NT that there is continuity and discontinuity between the Old Scriptures and Christ, Rom 10.4 is quoted as a proof-text for the *continuity*, and τέλος (*finis*) is understood in a teleological/completive sense.

In *Strom.* 2.9 (cf. 2.45.5) Clement explains τέλος νόμου Χριστός in Rom 10.4 by appealing to the prophetic role of the Law (ὑπὸ νόμου προφητευθείς).[29] In *Strom.* 4.21, after referring again to the prophetic role of the law pointing to Christ, he paraphrased τέλος νόμου Χριστός of Rom 10.4 as πλήρωμα νόμου τὸν Χριστόν, giving to τέλος a clearly teleological meaning.[30] If we add to this the fact that Clement described Christ in his relation to the law in terms of τελείωσις[31] and that he called Christ 'τέλος' in a most philosophical way,[32] we have a clear picture of what τέλος in Rom 10.4 meant for Clement: 'fulfillment', 'culmination', 'fullness' or 'perfection'. This teleological view of the Old Scripture 'leading to Christ' may also be found in *Strom.* 1.5, where we read that 'as philosophy is a schoolmaster leading the Greeks unto Christ, the Law had the function of directing the Hebrews to Christ'.[33]

The interpretation of Rom 10.4 as a statement of the prophetic character of the law is common in other early writings, but probably the most explicit quotation that can be found is the one given by Eusebius of Caesarea (260–c. 340) in his comments on Matt 5.17.[34] Eusebius understands νόμος as a prophetic corpus and τέλος as fulfillment in a sense close to πλήρωμα. The substitution of τέλος by πλήρωμα in Rom 10.4 is a common feature among Greek Christian writers. A significant example of this understanding of Rom 10.4 is given by Hippolytus (c. 170–c. 236) in his commentary on Matt 3.15.[35] Only if τέλος had a meaning really close to πλήρωμα are these apparent 'misquotations' of Rom 10.4 understandable.

The first of the Fathers that may be regarded as primarily a biblical exegete,[36] Origen (c. 185–c. 254) also understood τέλος in a sense akin to πλήρωμα and τελείωσις. In his commentary on Rom 10.4—known only through the Latin version made by Rufinus of Aquileia—[37] τέλος is rendered by *perfectio*.[38] This understanding is confirmed in several other undisputed passages where Origen deals

with the relationship between Christ and the OT law. Thus, in *Princ.*
4.1, Origen states that 'by the law of Christ, that is the precepts of the
Gospel, all things [of the Old Testament] are brought to perfection'.[39]
Origen's understanding of the relation νόμος-Χριστός and of the
unity of the Scriptures seems to reflect the general belief held by the
early church.[40]

The fourth century and the Antiochene School
The Christological controversies of the fourth century produced a
renewal of literal exegesis.[41] This fact, however, did not introduce
any substantial change in the interpretation of Rom 10.4. Athanasius
(c. 296-372), the most representative theologian of the anti-Arian
controversy, appeals to Rom 10.4 when he wants to prove the
prophetic character of the OT as pointing to Christ, and when he
wants to state that the law has *not* been abolished.[42]

The great authority of the Antiochene School, Theodore of
Mopsuestia (c. 350-428), with his characteristic concern for literal
and historical interpretation, offers in his commentary on Romans
one of the best examples of contextual exegesis of Rom 10.4 in
Patristic literature. For Theodore τέλος meant 'purpose' and could
be explained by the word σκοπός. For him the passage meant that
the righteousness taught and required by the law is obtained only
through its intended way (νόμου σκοπός), through faith in Christ
(διὰ τῆς ἐπὶ τὸν Χριστὸν πίστεως). When we accept Christ through
faith, the purpose (τέλος/σκοπός) of the law is fulfilled in us (ὁ νόμου
πληροῦται σκοπὸς ἐν ἡμῖν.[43]

Some of the elements of Theodore's interpretation of Rom 10.4 are
also found in the work of Chrysostom (c. 354-407). But in his *Hom.
17 in Rom. 11*, where he deals at length with this text and context, he
does not interpret νόμος as the OT Scripture but as a code to be
observed and treats τέλος in a way which may have at the same time
final and temporal connotations.[44] The thrust of the passage is that
Christ has taken, for the Christian believer, the place of the law: ὁ δὲ
τὸν Χριστὸν ἔχων, κἂν μὴ ἡ κατωρθωκὼς τόν νόμον, τὸ πᾶν
εἴληφε. The double meaning of τέλος is made evident and explained
with the analogy of the relation between medicine and health: τὸ γὰρ
τέλος ἰατρικῆς ὑγεία. The purpose of the medicine is to bring health.
But when health comes the medicine is no more needed.[45]

The dual function of τέλος in Rom 10.4, both teleological and
terminal, appears also in other passages, as in *Hom. 3 in Phil. 9.1*,[46]

where the law is presented under the image of a bridge that leads us to Christ, but is no more needed when one is 'in Christ'. The teleological function of the law is apparently considered primary: 'The law, if you use it aright, sends you to Christ' (παραπέμπει σε πρὸς τὸν Χριστόν), 'for since its aim (σκοπός) is to justify man, and it fails to effect this, it remits us to Him who can do so'.[47] The auxiliary, temporal, role of the law seems to be a consequence of the first: 'the law is still necessary for the confirmation of the gospel ('ὡς καὶ νῦν ἐπὶ βεβαιώσει τοῦ Εὐαγγελίου δεῖ νόμου').[48]

However, in *Hom. 16 in Mt. 2*, Chrysostom rejects emphatically the idea that the law has been abrogated. In order to prove that the fact that 'Christ fulfilled the law' does not mean that he abolished it but rather that he made its requirements full (οὐ μόνον οὐκ ἐναντιουμένου ἦν, ἀλλὰ καὶ συγκρατοῦντος αὐτήν), he quotes as proof texts Rom 10.4 and 3.31.[49] Chrysostom obviously perceived the tension between the OT and Christ, but it is interesting for our study to note that he did not use Rom 10.4 for resolving that tension in the sense of discontinuity or abrogation (*Jud.* 8).

The fifth century and the last great Greek Fathers
Probably the best examples of a teleological interpretation of Rom 10.4 are to be found in Cyril of Alexandria (c. 370-444). Though an heir of the Alexandrian exegetical tradition, Cyril introduced a new emphasis and dealt with an exegetical question which is particularly interesting for the present study, namely the question of the purpose (τέλος-σκοπός) of Scripture.[50] In his interpretation of Rom 10.4[51] Cyril uses both πλήρωμα and σκοπός for explaining τέλος as the 'purpose' of Scripture. That Cyril understood νόμος in Rom 10.4, meaning 'Scripture' (as revelation) and not 'law' (as code), is made clear enough by his consistent way of 'misquoting' Rom 10.4 with the phrase τέλος νόμου καὶ προφητῶν ὁ Χριστός.

In *Ador.* 1.5 Cyril explains the phrase Χριστὸς τέλος καὶ πλήρωμα νόμου by saying that 'every prophetic and legal oracle looks towards him and is turned towards him'.[52] In *Adv. Jul.* 9 Cyril retorts to Julian, who invoked Rom 10.4 as a proof of Christian inconsistency regarding the law (*Gal.* 319 E), that Paul's statement must be understood as indicating that 'the law was given to the ancients in order to teach them Christ's mystery and to show them the truth by means of figures'.[53]

With Cyril of Alexandria ends a period of exegesis in the Greek

Church. There is little new after him. Even Theodoret of Cyprus (393-458), the most famous of the last fathers, has little originality in his commentaries.[54] His interpretation of Rom 10.4 is heavily dependent on Theodore, Chrysostom and Cyril. He is worth mentioning here, however, because his commentary summarizes well how this passage was understood in the Greek-speaking era of the Church: Faith in Christ is not in opposition to the law, but rather in harmony with it (οὐ γὰρ ἐναντία τῷ νόμῳ ἡ εἰς τὸν Χριστὸν πίστις, ἀλλὰ καὶ μάλα σύμφωνος); the law had the purpose of leading one to Christ (ὁ γὰρ νόμος ἡμᾶς πρὸς τὸν Δεσπότην Χριστὸν ἐποδήγησε). In fact, the law already announced salvation by faith (διὰ τοῦ νόμου ὁ θεὸς τὴν πίστιν ἐπηγγείλατο). Therefore, in those who accept Christ the purpose of the law is fulfilled (τὸν τοῦ νόμου τοίνυν πληροῖ σκοπὸν ὁ πιστεύων τῷ Χριστῷ).[55]

The Latin Fathers

The Latin fathers generally followed the exegesis of the Greek fathers, and gave to *finis* the same spectrum of meanings as τέλος. Some, such as Paulinus of Nola (354-431)[56] and Gregory of Elvira (d. after 392),[57] interpreted *finis* in the sense of σκοπός and saw in Rom 10.4 a statement of the teleological and prophetic character of Scripture as pointing to Christ. But most often *finis* was understood in a completive/perfective sense, near to *perfectio* and *plenitudo*, as by Ambrose (c. 339-397)[58] and Zeno Veronensis (326-375).[59] This 'plenitude' was interpreted by Ambrosiaster (d. 375)[60] in the sense that Christ 'embodied' the law and took its place.

After Marcion doubtless the most discussed interpreter of Paul in the early church was Pelagius (c. 380–c. 450). His insistence on the law and his emphasis on its fulfillability attracted against him the attacks of Augustine as an enemy of the grace of God, and of Jerome as a heretic defender of the doctrine of sinlessness.[61] In his interpretation of Rom 10.4 Pelagius states that faith in Christ is practically (*quasi*) synonymous with observance of the law.[62] But at the same time, the law of Moses can only be properly understood in the light of its *finis*, namely, when Christ is believed.[63] Only thus can the believer pass from 'the time of the law' to the 'time of grace'.[64] Some of the features of Pelagius's interpretation were accepted in later Christianity, through interpolated texts of Ambrosiaster and Jerome.[65]

Jerome (c. 345–c. 419) was, next to Augustine, the greatest biblical authority of the Latin Church.[66] Because of Jerome's deep concern

for the original languages of the Bible, his interpretation of Rom 10.4
is important to us, as a reliable witness of how this passage was
understood in his time. It is worth noting that Jerome, following the
Greek Fathers, always interprets Rom 10.4 in a prophetic way: in
Christ the times foretold by the Law are fulfilled.[67]

Augustine (354-430) represents the culmination of several centuries
of Christian thought.[68] He too interpreted Rom 10.4, at times, as a
statement of the prophetic-Christological character of the OT,
pointing to Christ as its 'end' and 'fulfillment'.[69] In *Enarrationes in
Psalmos* (where Rom 10.4 is quoted more than thirty times) Augustine
always interprets *finis* (τέλος) in the teleological sense that this term
had taken in Aristotelian and neo-Platonic philosophy,[70] namely, as
'purpose' and 'final cause'. Augustine explicitly denies that *finis* in
Rom 10.4 may imply abrogation: 'non quia consummit, sed qui
perficit'.[71]

It is only when he is commenting on Josh 24.10[72] that Augustine
quotes Rom 10.4 in a context where the OT law is presented as
superseded by the NT. Though Rom 10.4 is not explained, it may be
assumed that *finis* is here meant in the sense of 'cessation'. This
temporal interpretation was probably related to the anti-Pelagian
controversy.[73] Yet the Augustinian interpretation of Rom 10.4 that
prevailed was not the temporal one but the teleological. Only in the
post-Reformation era did the authority of Augustine begin to be
invoked in support of the temporal interpretation.

At the end of the Patristic period interpretation became tradition.
The commentaries became more and more dependent on the greatest
authorities of the past. In all the attested instances Rom 10.4 is
interpreted either as a statement of the fact that the OT Scriptures
pointed to Christ or as a statement of the fact that Christ has
'fulfilled', i.e. 'made full' or 'perfected', the OT[74] or a statement of
the fact that Christ is the 'purpose' or the 'goal' of Scripture.[75] Thus,
the term *finis* is consistently interpreted with prophetic, completive,
perfective, final, or teleological connotations, but never in the sense
of 'abrogation' and very seldom in the sense of 'supersession'. The
theological problem of the so-called antithesis between the law and
Christ is so completely absent from these writers that in some
instances, when they interpret Rom 10.4 they drop the word 'law'![76]
For the abolition of the law they used other texts.

The Early Middle Ages

After Gregory the Great (d. 604) biblical interpretation lost its force and originality. The exegesis of this period is characterized by its sense of tradition and its dependence on Patristic interpretation. Though the Bible was the most studied book in these centuries, biblical exegesis remained almost reduced to the compilation of excerpts from the writings of the Fathers,[77] most of which are found in collections of commentaries called *catenae*.[78]

The interpretations of Rom 10.4 in the Greek *catenae*[79] closely followed the Fathers.[80] Τέλος was understood either as 'purpose' or 'intention' (as synonymous with βούλημα),[81] as 'goal' and 'aim' (identified with σκοπός),[82] or as 'fulfillment' and 'completion' (associated with πλήρωμα and related terms).[83] Νόμος is understood primarily as the OT (νόμος καὶ προφῆται).[84] And so Rom 10.4 was taken as an affirmation of the continuity between the OT and Christ. The idea of 'abrogation' or 'cessation' was explicitly rejected.[85] Only in a commentary attributed to Severian of Gabala (d. c. 400) and in a quotation by Photius of Constantinople (c. 810–c. 895) is νόμος interpreted as an ethical code, and Christ is said to be 'the end of the Law' both because he fulfilled it (ἐχρήσατο) and made it to cease (ἔπαυσεν).[86] Bede the Venerable (d. 735), the most outstanding scholar of his time, quotes Rom 10.4 every time he wants to point to the christological import of the Old Testament.[87] For him *finis legis* refers either to the fulfillment of the law (as prophecy)[88] or to the fulfillment of its purpose (*intentionem legis*),[89] as in Patristic times.

From the second half of the eighth century on, as a result of the Carolingian 'renaissance', biblical exegesis flourished and several commentaries on the epistles of Paul were produced. Rom 10.4 is consistently quoted as stressing the 'perfective' role of Christ vis-à-vis the Law, as by Ambrosius Autpertas (d. 778/9).[90] For Haymo of Halberstadt (d. 778), 'dicitur Christus finis esse legis, non consumptio, sed completio et consummatio legis et Prophetarum, ad justitiam omni credenti.'[91] Rabanus Maurus (c. 776-856), the leading scholar of his time, adds to this 'prophetic' explanation of *finis legis* a purposive one: the object of the law—understood as *tota lege et prophetis*—is fulfilled in Christ, and by faith, this purpose is also fulfilled in the believer, for 'perfectionem legis habet qui credit in Christum'.[92] Florus of Lyon (d. c. 860) equated *finis legis* with *intentio legis*.[93] Atto II of Vercelli (c. 885-961) stressed the notion of *perfectio*.[94] But Lanfranc, Archbishop of Canterbury (c. 1005-1089), retained *implementum, intentio,* and *perfectio.*[95] Most commentators in fact, gave to *finis* in Rom 10.4 a multiple meaning (generally *consummatio, intentio, completio,* and *perfectio,* or related terms), due to the medieval-idea of the fourfold sense of Scripture.[96] However, among the various meanings conceded to *finis* very seldom may be found that of 'termination'.[97]

In the exegetical milieu of the schools of the cathedrals, the old *catenae* developed into *glossae,*[98] which consisted of new personal interpretations added to the commentaries of the Fathers.[99] The *Glossa Ordinaria,* attributed to Walfrid Strabo (c. 808-849) but due in its final form to Anselm of Laon (d. 1117),[100] interpreted Rom 10.4 in a traditional way, but related this passage to the doctrine of salvation by faith versus legalism.[101] Though the exegetical value of the *Glossa* cannot be discussed here, suffice it to say that it became the handbook and standard commentary for the last three centuries of the Middle Ages, and therefore it played a decisive role in medieval scholarship.

The twelfth century

The twelfth and the thirteenth centuries are the most significant in the whole history of medieval exegesis. The cathedral schools gradually organized themselves into universities and in these centers of high scholarship Scripture was read (*lectiones*), examined (*quaestiones*), and discussed (*disputationes*) in a scholarly manner.[102] The new interest for exegesis was accompanied by an emphasis on literal and contextual interpretation.[103] The commentaries on Romans, which are very numerous,[104] became more and more doctrinally oriented.[105] Theological terms and concepts were carefully defined and analyzed,[106] and the patristic texts which had been transmitted almost *ad litteram* in the *glossae* began to be questioned. Exegesis became more personal, though not yet independent.[107] Good examples of the new trend are Hugh of St Victor (1096-1141)[108] and Robert of Melun (d. 1167),[109] who explains Rom 10.4 in its context in a very stimulating discussion on salvation by grace.

The interpretation defended by Peter Abelard (1079-1142) shows a significant autonomy from the authority of the Fathers. It presents three new features: (1) *lex* is interpreted as *legalia opera* (i.e. 'legalism' or even 'righteousness by works') rather than as the OT, as had been customarily done; (2) *Christus* is explained as *fides Christi*; and (3) *finis* is given a clear nuance of 'termination'.[110] Furthermore, the whole passage is approached from the perspective of Paul's law theology in Galatians, and, therefore, with an emphasis on the discontinuity between the law and Christ which departs considerably from the medieval interpretations of Rom 10.4,[111] and which was only picked up and generalized in the post-Reformation era.

The school of Abelard, however, did not seem to have been especially affected by the new interpretation of Rom 10.4.[112] In the 'digest' of Hervaeus Burgidolensis (d. 1150),[113] as well as in the *Magna Glossatura* attributed to Peter Lombard (d. 1160), the interpretation of Rom 10.4 follows the traditional medieval pattern. In fact, the *Magna Glossatura* may be considered as the best summary possible of all the interpretations known at that time.[114] *Lex* is both the OT (as prophecy) and the law (as moral code); *finis* is explained both as perfective (*perfectio*) and purposive (*intentio*); and the passage is treated as a main statement for the continuity between Christ and the law, and at the same time, as a statement of salvation by grace versus salvation by works. Peter Lombard's work became the textbook of Scholasticism.[115]

The thirteenth century

The thirteenth century, with its emphasis on Aristotelian philosophy, its universities and secular masters marked a new era in biblical studies. The main interest shifted from exegesis and theology to philosophy. The principal concern of scholasticism was to relate faith and reason, to recapture 'ancient philosophy under the control of ecclesiastical doctrine'.[116] The point of interest was less to discover than to formulate, to furnish theology with an apparatus of scientific nomenclature.[117] And since scholastic exegesis was less interested in the text than in apologetics, dogmatics remained during all the scholastic period the key to interpretation.[118]

Thomas Aquinas (c. 1225-1274) interpreted Rom 10.4 on the basis of Aristotelian teleology.[119] For him, *finis* meant 'the ultimate end', 'the final cause', 'the goal in view of which an agent acts, the intrinsic fulfillment and completion of a process'.[120] And so, Christ is *finis legis* in the sense that he fulfills the ultimate end of the law (understood philosophically).[121] The purpose (*intentio*) of the law is to make man good, but man cannot reach this purpose because he is unable to keep the law by his own effort; therefore the ultimate purpose of the law is reached by man only when he receives the undeserved divine grace from Christ through faith. Thus, although

Aquinas stressed elsewhere the discontinuity between the law and Christ,[122] he quoted Rom 10.4 only for the purpose of stressing the teleological relation of the OT to Christ.[123]

The Late Middle Ages

After Thomas Aquinas, the current approach for expounding the Bible was dialectic, not exegetical.[124] The Bible was so much neglected that there are very few commentaries on Romans of that time which deserve to be mentioned.[125] Even the *Postillae* of Hugo of St Cher (d. 1263) did not add to the *Glossae* anything of particular interest.[126]

Only Nicholas of Lyra (1265-1349) may be considered an important exegete during this period. Called 'doctor plenus et utilis' for his emphasis on the literal, contextual sense of the Bible,[127] he interpreted *finis* in Rom 10.4 as *intentum* (intent, object, purpose) taking this verse as a main statement of salvation by faith,[128] in a rather 'protestant' way. After the death of Nicholas of Lyra there were practically no important additions to the study of Scripture till the dawn of the Reformation.

Summarizing the history of interpretation of Rom 10.4 from the Early Church to the end of the Middle Ages, several conclusions may be listed:

1. The word τέλος/*finis* was interpreted in two main ways: (a) perfective/completive (πλήρωμα, τελείωσις, *perfectio*, *consummatio*, *impletio*) and (b) teleological (σκοπός, βούλημα, *intentio*), very seldom with temporal/terminal connotations.

2. Νόμος/*lex* was generally understood as the Hebrew Scriptures (ὁ νόμος καὶ οἱ προφῆται, *lex et prophetae*), though in a few instances it was also seen as an ethical code.

3. Consequently, the phrase τέλος νόμου Χριστός (*finis legis Christus*) was most often explained either as a statement of the predictive character of the OT as pointing to Christ, or as a statement of the purpose of the law as fulfilled in Christ.

4. Very often, especially in the late Middle Ages, there was a *multiplex intelligentia* of the passage, with τέλος/*finis* explained simultaneously in several senses. But even in these cases indications of 'termination' are rare.

It may be concluded that, in spite of the strong anti-Jewish and antinomian sentiments which prevailed, Rom 10.4 was not invoked for supporting the discontinuity between the law and Christ.[129]

Taking into consideration the importance that biblical interpretation has had ever since the Reformation, it is remarkable that the study of its history has not aroused more interest among scholars.[130] In this period the NT takes the supremacy, and the epistles of Paul—especially Galatians and Romans—which had already been prominent in the Middle Ages now come to the forefront.[131]

The Humanists

The Renaissance, with its interest in philology and history, had significant repercussions on biblical exegesis. In reaction to the allegorical and mystical exegesis of the Middle Ages, as well as to the philosophical and dogmatic interpretation of Scholasticism, there was a new philological approach to the Bible, interested in what the text itself had to say and not in how the church interpreted it.[132] The interpretation of Rom 10.4 by John Colet (1466-1519) is a good example of the new exegetical approach. Colet did not deal with the elements of the passage in an atomistic way but interpreted them in context, trying to find the relation of the parts to the whole. Thus, he explained Rom 10.4 in relation to 10.5-8—a relation that had been systematically ignored or overlooked in most medieval commentaries. As a result, he exegeted the passage in the following terms: 'Since Christ is the end of the Mosaic law, and since all that Moses wrote points to Christ, he [Moses] appears, while speaking of his own law, to have prophesied also of the law of Christ, and of faith'.[133]

Desiderius Erasmus (1467-1536)—called by many the founder of modern biblical criticism[134]—represents a real return to the sources. When compared to the rationalism and dogmatism of late Scholasticism, his *editio princeps* of the Greek NT (1516) is to be considered as a turning point in the history of NT exegesis.[135] The discovery of the *Collationes* of Lorenzo Valla (1406-1457) provided Erasmus with the basic elements for his commentary on the epistle to the Romans.[136] From his *Annotationes* (1502) to his *Paraphrases* (1523-1524) Erasmus shows himself the master of Patristic literature on Paul.[137] Erasmus defended his perfective interpretation of τέλος in Rom 10.4 on philological grounds.[138] His view of Christ as *perfectio* of the Mosaic law is clearly intended to support the idea of the superiority of the NT Scripture over the OT. But for Erasmus Christ, the new lawgiver, supersedes the law of Moses only in the sense that he fulfills

completely what the Mosaic law could achieve only partially, so that
Christ does not cut away what existed before so much as he fills up
what was partial and brings it to perfection.[139]

The Reformers
Martin Luther (1483-1546) made a new start in the field of exegesis
against the current positions of Scholasticism. His hermeneutical
principle of *Scriptura Scripturae interpres* advocated the self-
sufficiency of the Bible for its own interpretation, opposing biblical
authority to church authority and divine revelation to human
reason.[140] For Luther, then, Scripture became the sole foundation of
faith.[141] Avoiding the arbitrariness of allegorism and the rigidity of
the literal interpretation of Nicholas of Lyra, Luther 'worked his way
towards a historical-Christological interpretation that was to be the
core and center not only of his teaching, but also of his preaching and
living'.[142]

Luther explains Rom 10.4 by saying that the whole Bible everywhere speaks alone of Christ when we regard its real meaning, even
when the words, outwardly considered as a picture and image, may
sound differently. For this reason we also read, 'Christ is the end of
the law, for righteousness . . . that is *everything* (in Scripture) *points
to Christ*'.[143]

Notice that Luther's interpretation of Rom 10.4 is essentially
teleological. Even though he translated τέλος as *Ende* in his German
Bible, he did not use Rom 10.4 as a statement of the abolition of the
Law, but as a statement of the teleological and Christological
character of the OT as announcing and prophesying Christ.[144]

Luther's followers applied to Rom 10.4 the negative viewpoint on
the law presented by Luther in other contexts,[145] and therefore,
reading this verse from an antinomian perspective, filled it with a
content which Luther did not see here.[146] But what matters at this
point is that Luther did not use Rom 10.4 to support the antinomian
elements of his theology.

Philip Melanchthon (1497-1560)—'the teacher of the Reformation'[147]—interpreted Rom 10.4 in the sense that Christ fulfills the
purpose of the law, namely, to make us righteous.[148] Taking support
from the context, Melanchthon stressed the teleological interpretation
and explicitly rejected the exegesis of *finis* as abrogation.[149] With
different emphasis and nuances, but in a trend close to Luther and
Melanchthon, worth mentioning are the interpretations of Huldreich

Zwingli (1484-1531),[150] Martin Bucer (1491-1551),[151] Heinrich Bullinger (1505-1575),[152] Joannis Oecolampadius (1482-1581),[153] Juan de Valdés (1500-1541),[154] and others.

John Calvin (1509-1564), considered as 'the greatest exegete and theologian of the Reformation',[155] in his interpretation of Rom 10.4 followed Erasmus and Bucer. He translated *finis* as *complementum*, though he did not discard the validity of the interpretation of *finis* as 'purpose'.[156] Calvin saw, like Luther, the essential meaning of the relationship between the law and Christ in this passage in the fact that 'every doctrine of the Law, every command, every promise, always points to Christ (*ad hunc scopus collimet*)'.[157]

In spite of being in a certain sense the successor of Calvin, Theodore Beza (1519-1605) interpreted *finis*-τέλος in Rom 10.4 in a purely teleological way,[158] against the completive-perfective interpretation of Erasmus[159] which Calvin had at least partially followed. The Reformers then, as we have seen, understood Rom 10.4 as a statement of the fulfillment in Christ of the purpose of the law, interpreting τέλος-*finis* either as 'fulfillment' or as 'purpose'. Although they held the conviction that Christ had somehow superseded the law, they did not appeal to Rom 10.4 to support that conviction.

The Catholic interpretations after Trent

In Catholic Counter-Reformation exegesis, the literal sense, which better served apologetics among the Protestants, also received special attention, as may be specially perceived in the exegesis of Cardinal Sadoletus (1477-1547)[160] in his efforts to reconcile the Protestants with Rome. The menaces of the Inquisition against any heretical interpretation made inevitable, however, a recrudescence of the so-called 'spiritual' (moral and allegorical) senses.[161] As a natural consequence to this, the interpretation of Rom 10.4 in the post-Reformation era did not depart significantly from the medieval ones.

Probably the most representative exegeses of Rom 10.4 in this trend are those of Cardinal Cajetan (1469-1534) and Cornelius a Lapide (1567-1637).[162] The Catholic traditional principle of a coexistent plurality of senses shaped a fourfold interpretation of Rom 10.4. Willem Hessel von Est (Estius) (1542-1613) went even further, giving to *finis* the sixfold meaning of *scopus, causa finalis, impletio, consummatio, perfectio,* and *plenitudo*.[163] Catholicism did not produce any original exegesis until recent times.[164]

From Protestant Scholasticism to Protestant Heterodoxy

In reaction to the dispositions of the Council of Trent and the Catholic Counter-Reformation, and as a result of the numerous heresies and controversies among Protestants, the period between the mid-sixteenth and the mid-seventeenth century was an age of creeds, symbols, confessions, theological systems, rigid formulae, but of little exegesis. There were many polemicists and dogmatists, but few exegetes.[165] In this period of bitter dogmatism doctrinal positions became the controlling factors of exegesis.[166] Dogmaticians looked specially for passages which could be usefully brandished for controversial purposes, and the search for *loca probantia* took the place of real exegesis.[167]

This new attitude paved the way for a significant shift in the interpretation of Rom 10.4. This shift of emphasis is almost imperceptible at the beginning, and it has to be traced back through a long and discontinuous process, parallel to the development of the 'law-gospel' debate. It took different forms in the different theological traditions. In Lutheran circles, where the law was regarded as an entity in radical opposition to the gospel and understood as 'that which attacks and accuses man in his self-sufficiency' the 'end of the law' of Rom 10.4 began to be explained in terms of abrogation.[168] In Reformed milieus, where the law was understood primarily as the 'eternal will of God' and his standard of demands and prohibitions, Rom 10.4 began to be explained in terms of cancellation, because of Christ's substitutionary fulfillment.[169]

The emphasis on the doctrines of the abrogation of the law (either superseded by the Gospel or fulfilled in our stead) and of justification by faith made it easy to shift from the completive and teleological interpretations to the temporal and antinomian one.[170] Soon Rom 10.4 began to be interpreted not according to the Reformers' exegesis, but according to the theological positions of the Confessions of Faith, and attention was paid more to doctrinal convictions than to contextual and philological data.

Of all the parties which developed from the Reformation the Anabaptists were among those who regarded most highly the law and the OT.[171] However, in their radicalization many tended to look at the NT as superseding the OT and tended to adopt antinomian positions, rejecting 'the letter' and claiming only 'the spirit'.[172] The followers of Calvin were accustomed to defend a more positive relationship between the Testaments, but they also engaged in hot debates regarding the relation of law to grace.[173] Hugo Grotius (1583-1645), the most famous commentator, interpreted Rom 10.4 in a classical teleological way: the law pointed to the gospel as its goal (*meta*).[174] Johannes Cocceius (1603-1669) gave to the Calvinist tradition the shape of what is called 'covenant theology', according to which the law of Moses reflects a covenant of works—terminated by Jesus—and the gospel consists in a covenant of grace—initiated by Christ.[175]

In reaction against the rigidity of dogmatic orthodoxy, Pietism brought a new emphasis on the Bible—though primarily for ethical and devotional purposes—which led to a renewal of authentic exegesis. The best exponent of Pietistic interpretation of Rom 10.4 is J.A. Bengel (1687-1752). For him, 'the end of the law' has to be understood in a completive-final way.[176] It has been said that 'Bengel's text and critical apparatus of the New Testament (1743) mark the beginning of scientific work in this field'.[177]

Puritanism and the English trends

To a great extent, England remained isolated from the theological controversies that tore Protestantism in the Continent. Puritan preaching gave great popularity to the Bible and produced new interest in biblical studies among scholars and laymen alike.[178] Puritan tradition interpreted Rom 10.4 generally in a teleological way. John Owen (1616-1683), who is generally considered the greatest Puritan interpreter, explained Rom 10.4 in a purposive way, very similar to that of the Reformers, emphasizing the fact that the purpose of the law is the righteousness which only Christ can give.[179] This basic interpretation was shared by Anthony Burgess[180] and preserved in the vogue of paraphrases and commentaries that characterize the seventeenth and eighteenth centuries in England.[181] John Wesley (1703-1791) explained τέλος as 'scope and aim', giving to Rom 10.4 an interpretation which remained traditional in classical Methodism.[182] However, not all Puritans, nor their religious heirs, understood Rom 10.4 in the same way. Their interpretation of this verse depended on their theology of the law. For the Antinomians Rom 10.4 meant that the law has been abrogated, for the Baxterians, that the law has been modified, and for the traditional Puritans, that the law has been established.[183] The discussion in Reformed circles about the meaning of Rom 10.4 is still unsettled.[184]

The Eighteenth Century: From Dogmatism to Rationalism
The sevententh century marked the beginning of a decisive change in
attitude towards the Bible. The controversies and extreme positions
of some Lutheran and Reformed trends had paved the way for
English deism, French rationalism, and German 'enlightenment'.
Against the rigidity of dogmatic orthodoxy, its narrow and dictatorial
concept of inspiration and its immobilism, Rationalism was an
attempt to make of Christianity a religion whose principles could be
explained by reason, rather than by a church or even a biblical
authority.[185] In this reaction, shaped by skepticism,[186] the seventeenth and the eighteenth centuries, as a whole, did not bring any
significant change in the interpretation of Rom 10.4. But the
extended attitude of reducing to a minimum the biblical principles
which are of eternal value against those superseded as temporary and
Judaic contributed to the growing tendency of interpreting Rom 10.4
as a statement of the abolition of the law.

With the new liberal mentality a new theology came into being.
'Abandoning the fixed creeds and traditions, and dedicated to the
modern ideal of freedom of thought, it interpreted and restated the
Christian religion in terms of modern civilization.'[187] The subjectivism of Immanuel Kant (1724-1804), with his emphasis on the
conscience, had the effect of reducing Christianity, for many, to its
moral aspects. Friedrich Schleiermacher (1768-1834)—the most
influential theologian of Protestant liberalism—with his emphasis on
intuition and feeling (*Anschauung und Gefühl*) rather than on an
objective revelation, interpreted the phrase 'Christ is the end of the
law' in the sense that 'He so animates us that we ourselves are led to
an even more perfect fulfilment of the divine will'.[188]

The Nineteenth Century: The Liberal School and Historicism
Trying to draw the study of Paul out of the bounds of Protestant
dogmatics, Ferdinand Baur (1792-1860), leader of the so-called
'Tübingen School', applied to it the perspectives of the Hegelian
dialectic of history.[189] His dialectical approach was adopted by the
liberal school of NT criticism and had important repercussions on
the interpretation of Rom 10.4. So, D.F. Strauss (1808-1874) interpreted 'the end of the law' on the basis of the progressive and
evolutive character of human history.[190] The natural consequences
of this trend were the rejection of the unity of the Bible and the view
of the NT as superseding the Jewish religion. The liberal relativiz-

ation of the Bible, the optimistic view of history as evolution and progress, and the increasing confidence in the results of human research and science favored an anti-OT and antinomian interpretation of Rom 10.4. The new trends were soon popularized in many commentaries on Romans, among which undoubtedly the most influential was H.A.W. Meyer's (1800-1873).[191] Meyer paraphrases Rom 10.4 in the following terms: 'The validity of the law has come to an end in Christ, in order that every believer may be a partaker of righteousness'.[192] The translation of τέλος as 'fulfillment' is rejected because 'it is contrary to the meaning of the word', while the teleological one, though 'linguistically faultless', is rejected as 'not corresponding to the context', since the relation between Christ and the law can only be viewed in temporal terms.[193] The subordinate view of the OT in relation to the NT was expressed in its extreme form in the works of Adolf von Harnack (1851-1930). Rather than *lex aeterna*, the OT law is for Harnack just something which came between the times, pertaining only to a particular stage in the evolutive process of the history of mankind, as a part of a historical dispensation now superseded.[194] Harnack explains Rom 10.4 by saying that for Paul 'the end of the law' meant that the coming of Christ revealed 'the merely temporary validity of the Law and therewith the abrogation of the Old Testament religion'.[195]

For the English-speaking world a 'new era into the study of Romans was opened by the commentary of Sanday and Headlam'.[196] This critical commentary popularized the interpretations that had been accepted in liberal NT criticism. Rom 10.4 was explained by means of Galatians, Eph 2.15, Col 2.14, and a theology of the supersession of the OT law by the NT: 'Law as a method or principle of righteousness has been done away with in Christ'.[197] This kind of exegesis required a negative understanding of νόμος, either as 'a way of attaining righteousness by works', which came to an end in Christ,[198] or as 'a controlling factor that cursed us', and from whose dominion Christ has removed us.[199] Taking also for granted that *Christ* and *law* are mutually exclusive realities, the interpretation of τέλος in Rom 10.4 as 'termination' seemed, indeed, the only possible one.

The 'temporal/terminal' interpretation of τέλος in Rom 10.4 began to prevail around the middle of the nineteenth century. Of course, it took a long time to displace the completive and teleological interpretations and they were never really discarded completely. It is perplexing that the first statement indicating that the interpretation of τέλος as 'termination/abrogation' was held by 'the majority of commentators' appears in Meyer's commentary on Romans published in 1832,[200] while his contemporaries Tholuck (1824), Stuart (1832), Hodge (1835), *et al.*, still defended the teleological interpretation and considered themselves to be doing so with 'the majority of commentators'.[201] Moreover, according to Alford (1855), Meyer was among the first modern supporters of the temporal interpretation![202] In any case, this interpretation was, indeed, the prevailing one by the end of the century.[203]

However, not all the commentators adopted the temporal/terminal interpretation of τέλος. Some, since 'there is nothing unreasonable in supposing that all of them may be intended by the apostle', listed several meanings without choosing any.[204] Taking a mediating position between the Reformers and the new historicist trends, F. Godet (1812-1900) proposed an exegesis of τέλος which has been followed by many after him, taking the meanings of 'aim' amd 'termination' as necessarily simultaneous and inseparable.[205]

In spite of the new trends not a few retained teleological interpretations. So for F.A.G. Tholuck (1799-1874) 'the law impels men to Christ'.[206] For T. Chalmers (1780-1847) 'we should have a more precise understanding of the verse by taking the word *end* as equivalent to *purpose*'.[207] For A. Barnes 'design and purpose' is the given meaning here.[208] For Moses Stuart 'there remains no good reason to doubt that *telos* may mean here *exitus, the end, final object, the result*'.[209] And for H.C.G. Moule Rom 10.4 means that 'the law's End, its Goal, its Final Cause in the plan of redemption, is Christ'.[210]

Summarizing the history of the interpretation of τέλος in Rom 10.4 from the Reformation to the end of the nineteenth century, we can draw two main conclusions. First, during the Reformation era, with the progress of the studies of biblical Greek brought by the Renaissance and with the new emphasis on literal and contextual exegesis, the completive/perfective/teleological interpretations flourished. Second, after the Reformation era, with the Protestant emphasis on the 'law'-'gospel' antithesis and with the emphasis of liberal theology on historicism, biblical criticism, the superiority of Christianity over Judaism, and the discontinuity between the OT and the NT, the temporal/terminal/antinomian interpretations of Rom 10.4 began to prevail.

Contemporary Trends

For several reasons the last period of the history of interpretation of Rom 10.4 is difficult to evaluate. The complexity of some new positions, the multiplication of literature on the subject, and the difficulty of comprehending movements and trends which have not yet attained their full development and shape are among the main obstacles to a complete and objective survey.

The Interpretation of Rom 10.4 on the Basis of Pauline Backgrounds

With the turn of the century a certain consensus seemed to have been reached by modern criticism on the meaning of Rom 10.4 as an affirmation of the abolition of the law by Christ.[211] However, since there still remained wide disagreement on the interpretation of 'the end of the law', the debate shifted from the meaning of τέλος to that of νόμος.[212] For a long time the spectrum of significations given to νόμος in Rom 10.4 still went from 'the Law of God', and 'the Mosaic law'[214] to 'law as a principle' and 'legalism'.[215] In this new search for objective criteria, the diverse statements of Paul about the law that had been explained in terms of different stages in the development of Paul's Christian experience,[216] or in terms of a differentiation between the ethical and the ceremonial aspects of the law, now began to be explained on philological bases, namely, by the use of the article with νόμος.[217] Thus, νόμος with the article was said to mean the Mosaic law—which Paul respected—while νόμος anarthrous was said to mean legalism—which Paul rejected. Though these distinctions were soon challenged and generally discarded,[218] they showed the necessity for taking the discussion out of the limits of dogmatics to the text itself, to grammar, philology, and historical exegesis, thus setting the new directions of research in the twentieth century.

Attention turned first to the possible backgrounds of Paul's view of the law.[219] Jewish scholarship entered into the discussion and brought to it new insights and viewpoints. Departing from the traditional doctrinal approaches,[220] the so-called 'Pauline emancipation from the law' began to be explained on historical bases, either as a product of Jewish Hellenistic and heterodox influences,[221] or as the natural conclusion of rabbinic belief that the end of the law would come in the Messianic Age.[222]

Τέλος *and eschatology*

On the basis of some rabbinic texts, such as Niddah 61b,[223] Rom 10.4 began to be explained through the rabbinic apocalyptic notion of the two successive aeons: the 'old age' (interpreted as the realm of the law) and the 'new age' (interpreted as the realm of Christ). Thus, Christ ends the 'era of the law' and brings about 'the Messianic era'.[224] Albert Schweitzer's (1931) interpretation of Paul's theology from this eschatological perspective brought a new approach to the exegesis of Rom 10.4; according to him, this verse simply states 'the logical conclusion from the fact that the law ceases when the Messianic Kingdom begins'.[225]

Among the most influential contributions to the new trend was that of W.D. Davies. He explained Paul's law theology in the light of Jewish expectations of the role of the Torah in the Messianic age.[226] Comparing Paul's thought with rabbinic Judaism, Davies concluded that Paul was a sincere Pharisee who accepted Jesus as the Messiah and believed, therefore, that in the Messianic age which had come the Messiah was supposed to supersede the old Torah and give to the world a new Torah.[227] Although Davies was reluctant to interpret Rom 10.4 eschatologically,[228] it is evident that his view influenced subsequent exegesis of this passage.[229]

Building on slightly different premises, H.J. Schoeps argued that Paul's 'antinomian' theology was due to his misunderstanding of Judaism and Jewish Torah theology. Being an unorthodox Diaspora Jew,[230] Paul shared the 'widespread opinion' that 'in the Messianic era the old Torah will cease together with the evil impulse, but that God will give a new Torah through the Messiah'.[231] Since Schoeps supposes that 'the abolition of the Law is a Messianological doctrine in Pauline theology',[232] he assumes that Paul interpreted Rom 10.4 on the basis of that doctrine. This messianic-eschatological interpretation of Paul deeply influenced Pauline scholarship of all trends and affected the exegesis of Rom 10.4.[233]

Τέλος *and teleology*

Bringing the investigation into the field of philology and philosophy, E. Stauffer produced a most stimulating work on Paul's teleological thinking.[234] Stauffer's studies were based on Paul's use of τέλος and related terms, but more particularly on Paul's abundant use of ἵνα in final sentences. Although Stauffer did not produce any specific study on Rom 10.4, he showed that teleological categories were extremely important in NT thought and should be taken into consideration when dealing with Paul's hermeneutic.

After Stauffer, other studies on Pauline teleology were published, but specially focused on the ethical ideas of the Judeo-Hellenistic world.[235] Unfortunately the teleological theme does not seem to have attracted the attention of current scholarship on Rom 10.4. Although several scholars have interpreted this verse 'teleologically', only a few, such as C.F.D. Moule, have even contemplated the possibility of understanding Paul's view of Torah in teleological categories.[236] Therefore, and surprisingly enough, this field of research is still practically untouched.

Only Karl Barth brought into the discussion on Rom 10.4 a new 'teleological' element. He interpreted τέλος in analogy to (and even perhaps as a translation of) the rabbinic concept of the כלל 'as a comprehensive formula for the manifold content of the Law, as a designation of the common denominator . . . or ontically as the substance, the be all and end all of the Law, or practically, as its meaning . . . '[237] So, for Barth Christ is τέλος νόμου in the sense that he is 'the meaning, the authority, the fulfiller and the way of fulfillment of the Law'.[238] However, it is surprising to realize that, in spite of the enormous influence of Barth's work on contemporary theology, his interpretation of Rom 10.4 has been ignored, or at least overshadowed by most commentators.[239]

Τέλος *and philology*

The difficulties of determining the sense of τέλος in Rom 10.4 ask for philological help. But the first studies treating the subject at some length appeared only after 1950. The first and best-known study is certainly G. Delling's article on τέλος in the *TDNT*. Following the procedures of this famous dictionary, Delling reviews the use of τέλος in biblical and cognate literature. Very valuable as a list of references, Delling's work is, in fact, not much more than that. Concerned, as it is, more with a certain theology than with the philological data, Delling's interpretation of Rom 10.4 does not depart from current Lutheran tradition.[240]

More comprehensive is the survey of P.J. Du Plessis on τέλος and cognate terminology. On the basis of an interesting etymological and literary study, Du Plessis concludes that the fundamental connotations of τέλος 'are never indicative of mere cessation, discontinuation, or suspended action'.[241] Though his interpretation of τέλος in Rom

10.4 as 'turning point' is disputable, Du Plessis's thesis may be considered a landmark in this field of research.[242]

In his brief but important article, 'Christus, des Gesetzes τέλος', Felix Flückiger revalued, on philological bases, the purposive interpretation of τέλος in Rom 10.4. For him, the translation 'goal' (*Ziel*) is needed not only because it is the normal meaning of τέλος but also because it is the only one which does justice to the race-track imagery of the context.[243] At the same time, Flückiger has proposed a challenging explanation for the fact that τέλος is used in biblical literature in temporal expressions much more often than in classical Greek. He argues that the clear distinction maintained in secular Greek between the temporal field of meaning (expressed by τελευτή) and the teleological field (expressed by τέλος) is not maintained in the Bible because in the Bible time itself is understood teleologically.[244] Therefore, concludes Flückiger, in the NT, even where τέλος can be translated by 'end', its fundamental meaning of 'goal' is still retained.[245]

Recent scholarship depends considerably on the studies mentioned and some lesser philological contributions.[246] A comprehensive study of τέλος in biblical literature is still needed.

The Interpretation of Rom 10.4 on the Basis of Theological Principles
Rudolf Bultmann, in his article entitled 'Christus des Gesetzes Ende',[247] introduced into the discussion on Rom 10.4 an existential approach. For him 'the end of the law' means the existential liberation which takes place in the life of the believer when he surrenders to God in faith and enters into a new and real relationship with God.[248] This subjective interpretation of Rom 10.4, however, did not differ essentially from those of Lutheran orthodoxy, since both interpreted τέλος as termination. The only difference was that the end of the law was transferred by Bultman from history to personal experience.[249] Once again the discontinuity between the law and Christ was stressed, but now on the basis of the experiential faith of the believer.[250]

The new perspectives introduced by the eschatological and Bultmannian interpretations were rapidly assimilated and integrated into Pauline scholarship of all trends but did not affect substantially the current Protestant approaches to Rom 10.4. The almost universal agreement is that Rom 10.4 teaches that Christ has put an end to the law as a way of salvation.[251]

Though the interpretations of Rom 10.4 by various scholars differ from each other in many nuances, they have, particularly in Lutheran scholarship, a common denominator: their methodology.[252] Their pattern of interpretation moves consistently from systematic theology to exegesis, and from Galatians to Romans, on the assumption that Paul is saying the same thing in both places.

E. Käsemann, a representative example of this trend, explains Rom 10.4 as an antithesis between Christ and the law, in parallel with the antithesis between Christ and Adam in 5.12ff., 'in the contrast and contradiction of the old and new aeons'.[253] Rejecting all the teleological explanations,[254] which he sees as influenced by a wrong, 'pedagogical' understanding of Gal 3.24, he gives to τέλος 'a plainly temporal and not a final sense': 'The Mosaic Torah comes to an end with Christ because man now renounces his own right in order to grant God his right'.[255]

On the other hand, some scholars, particularly from the Reformed tradition, interpret τέλος in Rom 10.4 as 'fulfillment', in a completive/ perfective way.[256] For them this verse says that Christ has fulfilled the law and brought it to completion and perfection. Most of the supporters of this interpretation rejoin the conclusions of the supporters of the interpretation of τέλος as 'termination'. It is only that they explain the 'end' in a slightly different way. For example, Ladd says that 'Christ has brought the era of the Law to its end because He has fulfilled all that the Law demands'.[257] Consequently Rom 10.4 would mean that Christ makes the believer *heilsgeschichtlich* free from the law so that righteousness comes to him because Christ's perfect obedience is imputed to those who believe in him.

The implication in both trends is that Christ put an end to the law. Trying to resolve the 'abolition problem' presented by the prevalent interpretations, some scholars have explained Christ's abrogation of the law in terms of transformation: under the gospel the law either 'loses its form of external law and becomes an internal principle of life',[258] 'is replaced by Christ',[259] or 'from γράμμα becomes πνεῦμα'.[260] Others speak of a partial abrogation: Christ ends the legal or ceremonial aspects of the law, but not its ethical and revelatory aspects, which still remain valid for Christians.[261]

In spite of its particular presuppositions and hermeneutics, the standard dispensationalist interpretation of Rom 10.4 does not differ essentially from the liberal ones: the Mosaic law is temporary and ends with Christ. It belongs to the 'covenant of works' (with Israel) and, therefore, it does not apply to the Church, which is under a 'covenant of grace'.[262]

Catholic scholarship, which has traditionally followed an interpretation of τέλος as polysemous (mainly in perfective, completive, and teleological senses), today seems to incline towards Protestant positions, emphasizing the meaning of 'termination' over the traditional ones of 'fulfillment' and 'completion'.[263] However, the tendency is to include in τέλος the senses of 'termination' and 'goal' and/or 'fulfillment' as complementary.[264] Some scholars, however, manifest their preference for the teleological sense.[265]

Reviewing the results of current scholarship on this point, P. Stuhlmacher, in an article in which he focuses on the problem of 'the end of the law' from a systematic-theological perspective, concluded that contemporary theology of the law—especially in the Lutheran sector—needs 'a serious revision'.[266]

Recent Studies on Romans 10.4

Most of the studies dealing specifically with Rom 10.4 have appeared only in the last two decades. It is significant that—in general—the studies which are more exegetically oriented interpret τέλος in a teleological way, while the more systematic approaches interpret the term temporally. Since a growing number of scholars who defend the temporal approach have begun to acknowledge also the purposive connotations of τέλος it has become difficult to speak of 'schools' or trends of interpretation, and each of the current positions deserves to be considered separately.

As a result of the exegetical and theological problems related to the temporal/terminal interpretation, and probably also as a result of philological research on τέλος, a growing number of scholars are shifting towards teleological interpretations of Rom 10.4. Not satisfied with the interpretation of τέλος as 'termination' or 'abrogation', but without rejecting it, they are claiming for τέλος a multiple meaning, simultaneously temporal and completive, perfective, or teleological.[267]

From a temporal/terminal perspective, Mary Ann Getty (1975) has produced a very comprehensive study. Although the subject is approached from the angle of historical theology and is specially intended to challenge the Bultmannian existentialist interpretation defended by U. Luz,[268] it provides also an exegesis of Rom 10.4 and context, in which special attention is devoted to demonstrating the relation between Rom 10.4 and the theme of the epistle.[269] Excellent as a refutation of the existentialist interpretation, Getty's dissertation may be considered as a culminating point in the eschatological trend. It explains the 'end of the law' from a salvation-historical perspective in the sense that the Christ event has brought to an end the era of the law.[270] Since Getty's thesis takes for granted the consensual meaning of τέλος as 'termination', it does not dedicate any attention to the question of τέλος, and, therefore, does not bring any significant element to the subject of the present undertaking.

Ragnar Bring has particularly emphasized the culminating signification of τέλος, stressing the importance of the race-track imagery in the context (Rom 9.30–10.4), and arguing that τέλος 'signifies the winning-post of a race, the completion of a task, the climax of a matter'.[271] Bring argues that, since 'the goal of the law was righteousness', the law acted as a παιδαγωγός directing men to Christ, the only one who can give righteousness, and consequently Rom 10.4 must be understood in the sense that Christ is the eschatological fulfillment of the Law.[272]

The translation of τέλος by 'goal' has been championed in the English-speaking world by C.E.B. Cranfield. For Cranfield Rom 10.4 means that 'the Law has Christ for its goal, is aimed at, directed towards, Him, bears witness of Him',[273] and that Christ is 'the intention, the real meaning, and the substance of the Law'.[274] Paying more attention to the thrust of the passage and context, G.E. Howard also advocates a purely purposive interpretation of τέλος in Rom 10.4, arguing that 'Christ is the goal of the law to everyone who believes because the ultimate goal of the law is that all be blessed in Abraham'.[275]

The lengthiest treatment of this passage from a teleological perspective comes from J.E. Toews (1977).[276] He interprets τέλος teleologically 'on linguistic and contextual grounds'.[279] However, since Toews approaches this passage from a perspective of personal salvation, which disregards the thrust of the section, his theological presuppositions lead him to see, as the main teaching of the passage, a simultaneous and equally valid double way of salvation—one via the observance of the Law and the other via faith in Christ.[278]

More recently, C.T. Rhyne has published a stimulating dissertation on Rom 3.31 in which he deals also with the interpretation of Rom 10.4.[279] Rhyne's study has the particular merit of showing the theological links between Rom 10.4 and 3.31.[280] Although his teleological interpretation of τέλος is supported only on theological grounds, it represents a positive contribution to a more consistent understanding of Paul's view of the relationship between Christ and the law in Romans. In this same teleological trend, it is worth mentioning, among others, the interpretations of D.P. Fuller, P.W. Meyer, J.A. Sanders, and U. Wilckens.[281]

Summary

This detailed survey of literature has hopefully provided the necessary historical perspective to summarize, in a few sentences, the major developments in the interpretation of Rom 10.4. The period from the Early Church to the end of the Middle Ages is characterized by a *multiplex intelligentia* of τέλος with an absolute predominance of the teleological and completive meanings. The Greek-speaking church understood and explained τέλος in Rom 10.4 by means of the terms σκοπός, πλήρωμα, and τελείωσις, seeing in it the meanings of 'purpose', 'object', plenitude', and 'fulfillment'. Νόμος was understood as the Holy Scripture of the OT (often rendered by νόμος καὶ προφῆται). Consequently, Rom 10.4 was interpreted as a statement of the fulfillment of the OT, its prophecies or its purposes, in Christ. In the Latin Church *finis* took practically all the meanings given by the Greek Church to τέλος. It was explained by the terms *perfectio*, *intentio*, *plenitudo*, *consummatio*, or *impletio*. In extremely rare instances (e.g. Augustine) *finis* was given temporal connotations.

The Patristic interpretations were followed without any special change during the Middle Ages, with the particularity that the manifold meanings of τέλος/*finis* were accepted as simultaneously present in Rom 10.4. The emphasis was, however, more on the completive/perfective nuances than on the purely purposive ones. The temporal/terminal possibilities of *finis* were seldom (e.g. Abelard) contemplated. Rom 10.4 was interpreted, therefore, as a statement of Christ's bringing the OT law to its plenitude and completion. The Reformation, with its emphasis on literal exegesis, preserved the Greek and Latin meanings of τέλος/*finis*, giving to Rom 10.4 both teleological (e.g. Luther) and perfective (e.g. Calvin) interpretations. After the Reformation era the doctrinal influence of the antithesis between 'law' and 'gospel' and the theological emphasis on the discontinuity between the OT and the NT, favored, particularly in Lutheran circles, an antinomian interpretation of Rom 10.4. The overwhelming influence of German liberal theology in the nineteenth century, with its emphasis on historicism, biblical criticism, and developmentalism, caused the temporal/terminal/antinomian interpretation of Rom 10.4 to prevail.

As for the present situation concerning the interpretation of Rom 10.4 there may be discerned four different—though not always easily definable—trends revolving about the meaning of τέλος:

1. Τέλος *as temporal*. For those who interpret τέλος as 'termination', 'cessation', or 'abrogation', Rom 10.4 is a main statement of the discontinuity between the Law and Christ.[282]

The principal arguments advocated in favor of this interpretation are: (1) the assumed antithesis between νόμος (understood as 'works') and Χριστός; (2) the assumed negative view of the law by Paul in Rom 9–10 (based on Pauline statements in Galatians, 2 Cor 3 and Phil 3); and (3) the assumed negative eschatological relation between the OT and Christ in salvation history. Other arguments invoked are: (4) the Pauline use of τέλος as 'termination';[283] (5) the thrust of the context of Rom 10.4, interpreted as dealing with the opposition between 'law' and 'faith' as ways of righteousness;[284] and (6) a presumed Pauline theology that supposes the abrogation of the law.[285]

Within the group of the supporters of the temporal/terminal interpretation, there are two main trends corresponding to two different approaches: (1) the messianic-eschatological view of the 'end', as with Schweitzer, Davies, and Schoeps; and (2) the salvation-historical view, as with Conzelmann, Gutbrod, and others. In a mediating position, which may be considered as a representative synthesis of both trends, stands Käsemann. Although all the supporters of this line of interpretation take τέλος somehow as 'termination', there is disagreement on what that termination means. In order to resolve the ambiguity and give sense to the phrase 'Christ is the end of the law', the word νόμος is interpreted as standing for something more than 'law'—which must consequently be supplied: 'the *validity of the observance of the OT* law', 'the law *understood as legalism*', 'the law *era*', 'the law *in its ritual aspects*', etc. Each interpretation seems to solve some problems, but at the same time has to face some important questions.

The majority of scholars interpret Rom 10.4 as the '*end of the law as a way of salvation*'. Whether this 'end' is explained in a historical or in a subjective way, the result is very similar. This interpretation not only seems to contradict a main theme of Romans, namely, that salvation has always been by grace through faith (see especially ch. 4)[286]—and so Christ could hardly put an end to what did not exist— but it postulates a temporal meaning for τέλος and a negative meaning for νόμος,[287] which still have to be proved.

The interpretation of Rom 10.4 as '*end of the law aeon*', in spite of its great success,[288] is much questioned in recent scholarship. The texts invoked as evidence for this view are not only too late as acceptable sources or witnesses of Paul's law theology, but, in fact, they do not really support the doctrine of the abolition of Torah in the Messianic age.[289]

Although the idea that the law somehow 'ends' for those who live God's will by faith is certainly Pauline, the interpretation of Rom 10.4 as '*the end of the law as an existential experience*'[290] presents the problem that there is no hint in Rom 10.4 and context for supporting this 'subjective' interpretation.[291]

With slight variations, the same objection may be made against the interpretations of 'end' as *partial abrogation*[292] or as *transformation*.[293] These explanations may be theologically correct, but they are exegetically unacceptable. Though Paul could speak of the moral and ceremonial aspects of the law separately, there is no indication in the context which allows one to interpret τέλος as '*partial* abrogation' or νόμος as '*ceremonial* law'.[294]

2. Τέλος *as teleological*. For those who translate τέλος as 'goal', 'purpose', 'aim', or 'object', Rom 10.4 is a main statement of the Pauline belief in the continuity between the law and Christ, or between the OT and Christianity.[295] The principal arguments advocated in favor of this interpretation are the following: (1) the basic meaning of τέλος in Greek;[296] (2) the flow of the context (9.30–10.21) and the thrust of the section (Rom 9–11);[297] (3) Paul's law theology in Romans;[298] and (4) the theological assumption of the unity of divine revelation and action.[299]

3. Τέλος *as completive/perfective*. For those who interpret τέλος as 'fulfillment', 'climax', 'plenitude', or any other completive/perfective expression, Rom 10.4 may express either/both the continuity and the discontinuity between the OT/law and Christ/Christianity.[300] The arguments invoked for each of the possibilities mentioned vary according to each interpreter and may be a combination or selection of the arguments listed above under trends 1 and 2. The specific nuances of each position make it impossible to file every case in a

particular and clearly delimited trend. The interpretation of τέλος as '(substitutory) fulfillment'—i.e. by fulfilling the law in our stead Christ put an end to it—not only does not fit the context of Rom 10.4 and shares the problems of the temporal/terminal interpretations, but runs counter to the theology of Romans, where the law is presented as fulfilled, yet in force; 'weak' and 'unable to justify', but 'holy and good' and still binding for Christians.[301]

4. Τέλος *as polysemous*. Finally, for those who see the temporal/ completive and/or teleological meanings of τέλος as not mutually exclusive but complementary, Rom 10.4 may mean any of the already reviewed interpretations.[302] Putting aside for the moment the problem of ambiguity—whether intentional or accidental—of the Pauline statement, and the problem of the logical and linguistic possibility of such a multiple understanding, this exegesis shares with the temporal ones a similar burden of proof: both involve some contradiction in Paul's exposition of his law theology in Romans, leaving unexplained why 3.31 says that the Christian faith *establishes* the law while Rom 10.4 declares that Christ has *abrogated* it. The fact of giving to τέλος a temporal and a teleological/completive *double entendre* does not resolve the irreconcilable antithesis between *establishing* and *abrogating*.

In conclusion, in spite of undeniable progress, the interpretation of Rom 10.4 is still a 'bone of contention'.[303] The relation between gospel and law has dominated the theological discussion in modern times and focused the attention of exegetes on Paul's law theology as the decisive criterion for the understanding of this passage. The divergent recent studies which have been here surveyed witness to the contemporaneity of the debate on Rom 10.4 and to the need of better criteria and approaches for the interpretation of such a controversial text. Two areas of research appear to need special clarification: the terminology of the verse and the role of this passage in its context. First of all, a lexical study of the use and meaning of the word τέλος and the phrase τέλος νόμου in biblical and cognate literature is needed in order to provide, if possible, an objective, philological basis for the interpretation of Rom 10.4. Then, an exegesis paying due attention to the contextual setting of Rom 10.4 is also necessary. These are the tasks of the next two chapters.

Chapter 2

THE USE OF ΤΕΛΟΣ IN BIBLICAL AND COGNATE LITERATURE

Among the reasons which would explain the present disagreement over the interpretation of Rom 10.4, the most consistently neglected is, indeed, the deficient use of factual criteria for determining the sense of the phrase τέλος νόμου. As the survey of literature in Chapter 1 has shown, the meaning of Rom 10.4 has generally been decided on the basis of theological inference, while little or no attention has been paid to terminological substantiation. Furthermore, a comprehensive study of the meanings and uses of τέλος in biblical and cognate literature has never been done. The best available studies, namely, the works of Delling and Du Plessis, though extremely valuable, are nevertheless defective and incomplete.[1]

The object of the present chapter, then, is to further existing semantic research and to provide a philological contribution to the areas of more specific need. These areas include: the particular connotations which τέλος received in the Hellenistic period, the use of τέλος with a noun in genitive, and, especially, the meaning of the phrase τέλος νόμου and similar expressions.

The Use of τέλος in Classical Greek Literature

The word τέλος is used in Greek literature with a surprisingly wide range of meanings.[2] This plurality of significations—already found in the earliest writings—perplexed even the ancient Greek lexicographers: Philemon the Grammarian (c. AD 200) observed that τέλος πολυσήμαντόν ἐστιν,[3] and a Homeric scholion (of earlier date)[4] listed six different meanings for τέλος.[5]

Etymological considerations
Modern scholarship has a challenging task to try to find out the

common origin of such apparently unrelated meanings as 'fulfillment', 'authority', 'issue', 'goal', and 'tax'.[6] G. Curtius supposed two distinct words which in classical Greek were confused, one derived from the root *tel- (related to τέλλω), originator of the meanings 'duty', 'office', etc., and the other derived from the root *ter- (related to τέρμα), meaning 'to propel (towards an object), impel, traverse', which was the source of most of the current meanings of τέλος.[7] For Curtius, then, τέλος meant basically 'that which has reached its destination' (hence, 'end').[8]

The etymology proposed by Curtius very strongly influenced subsequent scholarship on τέλος.[9] A. Walder, however, regarded as the most probable derivation the root *tel(a)-, 'to hold out, to endure' (cf. Latin *tollo).[10] For Walder this single stem would also give reason for the notion of 'turning', and, therefore, would explain the use of τέλος as 'tax, payment, customs' on the one hand, and as a 'telic' concept on the other.

Following Walther Prellwitz a probable derivation from the root *quel- has been widely supported.[11] This root (in Greek τελ-/πελ-)[12] is supposed to carry the basic meaning of 'turn, turn around, wheel, swerve, etc.'; hence τέλος would mean, originally, 'turning point, where one makes a U-turn in the course of a process'.[13] So, says J.B. Hofmann, the original root is still preserved in the verb πέλω (πέλομαι), 'to come into existence', 'to become', but the closest word to τέλος—apparently a poetic form of it—would be τέλσον, which means 'headland, land where the plough turns'.[14] Accordingly— explains Du Plessis—the original verb τελεῖν would be indicative of 'an activity directed towards a point where movement is reverted', as in the case of the ploughman who reaches the end of his furrow and then retraces his steps. The turning point is the τέλος, which may as well be the object of the action concerned or its conclusion.[15]

For D. Holwerda, however, the original meaning of τέλος would not be 'headland' but 'scales' or 'beam of a balance'.[16] By means of a very well-documented analysis of an impressive list of Greek refer- ences, Holwerda shows that this origin fits better the Indo-European root *quel- with its basic meaning of 'in qua torquendi vel vertendi inest vis'.[17] If the verb τελεῖν meant originally 'to weigh, value, judge, determine, decide', it is easy to understand that it came to mean, by simple extension and derivation of meaning, 'to solve, accomplish, complete, finish, pay'. Consequently, from its basic meaning of 'deciding point', all the other meanings of the noun τέλος could be easily derived, even its apparently more divergent senses such as 'tax' and 'aim, goal, end, purpose, or momentum'.[18] Thus, οἱ ἐν τέλει are 'those who have the deciding power' (the magistrates),[19] and the adjective τέλειος came to mean 'perfect' because it meant 'decided' rather than 'accomplished'.[20] H. Frisk discussed Holwerda's hypothesis, and though he did not reject it entirely, he proposed as the basic notion for τέλος not 'turning' but 'lifting', supporting his view with the meaning of τελαμών, ἀνατολή, and other examples.[21]

E. Boisacq, followed by other scholars,[22] preferred to explain the polysemy of τέλος by the conflation of at least two different roots: *quel- ('tourner, accomplir, exécuter, réaliser, achever', cf. πέλομαι), and *tel- ('supporter, soulever, lever', cf. τέλθος). The first root would explain the meaning of τέλος as 'result, issue, outcome, aim, purpose, etc.', and the second root would explain the meaning of τέλος as 'tax, custom, group', etc.

This 'multiple-roots' theory has been challenged by Z.P. Ambrose in a work which has not received due attention thus far, and which concurs with the results of Holwerda's hypothesis of a single origin for the different meanings of τέλος. After an exhaustive study of the use of τέλος in Homeric and related ancient Greek literature, Ambrose concludes that all τέλος groups of meanings appear to derive from the single root *kwel-. From the original verb τελεῖν ('to bring a thing fully into existence', or 'to complete fully an action') the basic and original meaning of τέλος as 'accomplishment' (completion and fulfillment) is broad enough—says Ambrose—to suggest itself as the source for the variety of meanings which this word enjoyed in classical Greek.[23] Τέλος, then, in its multiple senses, would simply have widened its semantic potential without losing its primitive and basic meaning.

A hypothesis which would take into consideration the more solid aspects of the thesis of Holwerda and Ambrose would seem to work in a reasonable direction. However, the definitive elucidation of such a hard question falls outside of the limits of the present study.

Cognates and derivatives

The basic meaning of τέλος is borne out when compared with its numerous derivatives and cognates. Their common semantic import is so evident that we do not need here to do more than recall some of the most important words of the τέλος group by way of reminder. The most relevant for our survey is the verb τελέω, because the noun τέλος shares with the verb τελέω not only a common root but also a basic semantic content.[24]

All the dictionaries agree that the meaning of τελέω is 'to carry out', 'complete', 'execute', 'fulfill', 'bring to an end', and 'accomplish'.[25] Sometimes it also means 'to bring into accordance with the object in view', 'to comply with the requirements of', 'to make effective', and therefore, 'to pay'.[26] In the Hellenistic era it came to be used for the performance of religious ceremonies, and became the technical verb for the expression of intitiation. As Du Plessis says, 'It is scarcely possible to mistake the dominant implication of *completion*'.[27]

Τελέω with objects of time or referring to handiwork means 'to complete and bring fully into existence'.[28] Used with concepts indicating plan, intention, command, request, ordinance, prayer, promise, assurance, threat, prophecy, omen or prediction (i.e. μῦθος, αἶνος, λόγος), it means 'to accomplish', or—in the words of Ambrose— 'to bring that concept (plan, command, prayer, promise, or prophecy) to fulfillment in deed'.[29]

It is noteworthy that τελέω used with νόμος and synonyms like ἐντολή always means 'to carry out the demands of the law' or 'to keep the law'.[30] The compound forms of τελέω more often used, ἐπιτελέω and συντελέω, are generally emphatic forms of τελέω.[31]

According to Buck (p. 979), the original sense of τελευτή (from τελευτάω) was also 'turning point'. But as a statistical comparison clearly shows, the words of the root τελευτ- were soon used to indicate termination. In accordance with this specialization of meaning the verb τελευτάω was almost always used for the end of life as a euphemism for 'to die'. The noun τελευτή appears almost exclusively for 'the end of life' (death).[32] The less common adjective τελευταῖος appears with the meaning of 'end' in temporal and local senses.[33] It seems that in the Hellenistic period there was a clear distinction of meaning between τέλος, generally used with teleological and completive connotations, and the words of the τελευτ-group, used with terminal and temporal force.[34]

The noun τελείωσις[35] (from the adjective τέλειος 'whole', 'complete', 'perfect', and the verb τελειόω 'to make or to become τέλειος', 'to bring to completeness', 'to make perfect', 'to fulfill') is a *nomen actionis* denoting the act or the result of completing, making perfect, etc. It is used in Greek classical literature for 'development', 'completion', 'perfection', 'conclusion', 'fulfillment', sometimes as a synonym of τέλος. In the NT it is used only in Luke 1.45 and Heb 7.11.

The noun συντέλεια[36] (from συντελέω) is another *nomen actionis*. Originally the preposition σύν gave to it the nuance of 'common accomplishment or performance' (hence 'taxes', or 'performance of sacrifices'), but it was soon used also as an emphatic form of τέλος, meaning 'execution', 'completion', 'full realization', 'consummation'. In the LXX (Daniel) it is used for the apocalyptic end, and in the NT for 'the consummation of the age'.[37] In general the words derived from τέλος or formed from the same root share a common, basic notion of culmination and completion.

Basic meaning and semantic range

To ask for the basic meaning of such a polysemic word as τέλος is probably not only unrealistic but also linguistically inconsistent. However, the task has been undertaken by some, and their results are worthy of being taken into consideration. For W. Wachsmuth τέλος should not be thought of as the 'end of something' but rather (by virtue of its derivation from τέλλω) as 'the power to fulfill'.[38] For J.H.H. Schmidt, τέλος means basically 'culmination and fulfillment', and secondarily 'goal and purpose'.[39] For M.A. Bayfield the basic meaning of τέλος might have been 'authority'.[40] As we have already seen, for Du Plessis τέλος is a *nomen actionis* meaning 'turning point'.[41] Ambrose, however, denies that τέλος is basically a *nomen actionis* and states that 'the *télos* is a state of being which fulfills the attributes which define it or are required to it'.[42]

Whether τέλος is essentially a *nomen actionis* or not the words with which it is used must determine its precise meaning. Since the semantic content of this term is not the event itself but its outcome, the context indicates whether the issue of the action is to be viewed as preceding or subsequent.

1. When the issue of the action is viewed as preceeding, τέλος is necessarily prospective, propulsive, directional, inceptive, and denotes either the direction of the action,[43] or its outbreak, its coming to pass. Τέλος is here the object, goal, purpose, or aim towards which the action is directed and is used for the winning-post of a race,[44] the prize or reward following a performance,[45] a personal goal,[46] or an ethical purpose.[47] In this use the closest Greek synonym would be σκοπός.[48]

2. When the issue of the action is viewed subsequently τέλος is completive, and it denotes either the conclusion or attainment of a previous purpose, or the state resulting from such attainment. Τέλος

is here the performance, the outcome, the result, the consummation, the final point of an action or state, and is used to designate the fulfillment of a thing that was promised, prophesied, or desired,[49] the result of events leading up to a climax, the attainment, achievement, or completion of something.[50] In this use the closest Greek synonym would be πλήρωμα.[51]

Summarizing this brief survey, the following conclusions on the meaning of τέλος may be suggested:

1. Though τέλος was a word with various meanings, these meanings do not seem to represent a series of homonyms, but diversifications of a single word.[52]

2. Originally τέλος seems to have been used to designate a concrete 'highest point' (headland, etc.) or 'turning point' (fulcrum, etc.). From this original basic notion (whatever it may have been) of highest point or deciding point, τέλος passed to be used in an abstract and metaphorical sense.

3. As *nomen actionis* (certainly in relation with its cognate the verb τελέω), τέλος was used for designating both the action towards the crucial point, and the result or consequence of reaching that point. The basic notion of τέλος is then not temporal but related to the notions of 'intention' and 'completion'.

If this conclusion is correct, it may likely explain the three fundamental qualifications of τέλος which we find in Greek literature (so little perceptible in the common English translation 'end'), namely (1) 'apex', 'climax', etc.; (2) 'aim', 'goal', 'purpose', etc.; and (3) 'attainment', 'completion', 'fulfillment', etc.

The special meanings of τέλος in use during the Hellenistic period deserve much lengthier treatment than is possible here. This cursory survey deals only with those which may have an import for the understanding of Rom 10.4.

According to Du Plessis 'perhaps the most significant characterization of τέλος would be to describe it as *that which forms the deciding factor in any issue*'.[53] In fact, many times τέλος would be well rendered in English by 'the issue concerned', 'the crucial factor', 'the main feature', 'the center', etc. Aristotle gives an excellent example in *Resp.* 480 B19: τοῦ ζῆν καὶ μὴ ζῆν τὸ τέλος ἐστὶν ἐν τῷ ἀναπνεῖν ('the *decisive difference* between living and not living is breathing').

The notion of *completion* is so dominant that τέλος may mean 'totally' in the cases when by the attainment of its τέλος something becomes total. This use is common in adverbial expressions such as εἰς τέλος ('totally'), διὰ τέλους ('through to the end'), and ἀπ' ἀρχῆς μέχρι τέλους or similar ἀρχή-τέλος expressions.[54]

Because of its strong denotations of 'highest point', 'decisive factor', etc., the word τέλος was chosen in philosophical language to designate the highest ideal, the ultimate purpose, the final cause, and the supreme good (Lat. *summum bonum*). This use became so important in the Hellenistic period that it deserves to be treated separately.[55] Suffice it here to observe that only because the dominant connotations of τέλος were qualitative and not temporal could this word have been used for conveying such a philosophical notion.[56]

Τέλος may convey the idea of termination when the attainment of what has been brought to completion implies the termination or consummation of it, i.e. a period of time.[57] But—as Du Plessis has shown—'τέλος is not primarily the *moment* of desistance, or the *point* of cessation, but the *centre* of an activity: the hinge'.[58] Therefore, in the phrases where the action or the process is indeed suspended, the basic meaning of culmination is kept as the resultant, the preconceived end, or the issue of the matter.[59] 'Here the important fact to recognize is that the final notions of τέλος are never indicative of mere cessation, discontinuation, or suspended action. When finality is incurred, it is accompanied by a hint of innate fulfillment.'[60]

The terminal connotations depend on the words with which τέλος is constructed: a completed action ceases to exist, while a completed thing, by contrast, remains in existence. The basic culminative qualification of τέλος is essential to keep in mind as far as its terminal associations are concerned. Ambrose has argued very convincingly that τέλος designates 'the point at which full genesis of something is achieved instead of the point at which an activity is terminated'.[61] And Du Plessis has demonstrated that because of its 'innate sense of completion' τέλος expresses basically 'culmination but not ultimation'.[62]

In all the etymological studies of τέλος the notion of 'termination' is absolutely secondary and the notion of 'abolition' is completely alien to the semantic content of τέλος and other words of its same root. The temporal and terminal connotations that τέλος may take in certain contexts represent an extension of the original meaning and come from the context in which this word is used rather than from τέλος itself.[63]

A categorical statement on the non-terminal character of τέλος is given by Aristotle. In a crucial passage where he defines the meaning of τέλος, he explicitly says that 'τέλος does not mean any kind of termination, but only the best (βούλεται γὰρ οὐ πᾶν εἶναι τὸ ἔσχατον τέλος, ἀλλὰ τὸ βέλτιστον)'.[64] It is certainly not coincidental that the ancient scholiasts and the earlier lexicographers did not list the meaning of 'termination' as one of the basic meanings of the τέλος.[65]

The temporal 'end'is generally designated in Greek by the word ἔσχατον, referring to any kind of reality.[66] For the 'end' of man's life, i.e. his death, the common term is τελευτή.[67] For the idea of spatial (and often also temporal) terminus, the Greek has the words τέρμα, τέρμων (meaning usually 'limit'), πέρας, and ἄκρον.[68]

Besides its basic and most common meaning of 'attainment-fulfillment-completion', τέλος is also used for 'tax-tribute',[69] 'group-horde',[70] and 'sacrifice-initiation rite'.[71] Since the last two meanings are not attested in the NT they are omitted from discussion. And since most instances where τέλος means 'tax', 'tribute' or 'toll' are very clearly explicated by their contexts and do not present any theological difficulty, they are also disregarded in the present study, which concentrates on the first, basic, and more numerous group of meanings.

As a word of conclusion concerning the semantic range of τέλος it may be said that the basic meaning of 'performance' or 'realization' seems broad enough to take in context the perfective nuances of 'fulfillment' and 'completion' (hence the popular use for 'tax'—fulfillment of the civic duties—and for 'cultus'—fulfillment of the religious duties), the teleological significations of 'aim' and 'goal' (hence the philosophical meanings of 'purpose', 'final cause', or *summum bonum*), and the temporal sense of 'end' as 'conclusion' or 'termination'. Being such a polysemous word, the determination of its meaning in any specific case depends in a decisive way on the context in which it is used.

The use of τέλος νόμου *and similar expressions*

Since the main concern of the present study is to determine whether the phrase τέλος νόμου in Rom 10.4 may have predominant temporal connotations or not, a survey of the meaning of other phrases where τέλος is constructed with a noun in genitive is of particular importance.

In about half of its occurrences τέλος is defined by a genitive, whose function needs to be determined in every case for a proper understanding of the sentence. In some instances—as in Rom 10.4—the meaning of the genitive is also a problem, since this case can express several different kinds of relationships, not always easily definable.[72]

According to Ambrose, with expressions indicating activity or duration, τέλος may indicate termination, but with abstract nouns 'there is no connotation of cessation or termination, except perhaps for the negative notion of the termination of a state of incompleteness'.[73] Thus, the phrase μύθου τέλος does not mean 'the end of the myth or story', but rather its 'essential point, the sum or substance'.[74] Consequently, the sentence ἀτὰρ οὐ τέλος ἵκεο μύθων (Hom. *Il.* 9.56) does not mean 'you have not yet *finished* your story', but 'you have not yet reached *the point* of your argument'.

In the same way the phrase τέλος γάμου never is used for denoting the 'dissolution of marriage', but rather its *consummation*.[75] For Plato (*Mx.* 249 A) ἀνδρὸς τέλος does not mean 'a man's end or death', but 'a young man's attainment of maturity'. Even the phrase τέλος βίου is abundantly used in respect of plants, animals, and human beings with no implications of discontinuity or cessation, but rather implying aim or purpose.[76] In a few instances τέλος βίου is used referring to the death of someone, but it is very likely that the word is intended to describe less the *fact* of the death than the *fate* or the *consummation* of life.[77]

Some constructions of τέλος with genitive, when referring to the deities, are very often indicative of 'authority'.[78] Thus, in Hom. *Od.* 10.412, the phrase τῶν θεῶν τέλος means 'the supreme authority of the gods'. If τέλος had terminal (or temporal) connotations, some of these expressions would have been very difficult to understand, especially the formula τέλος ἀθανάτων (cf. Hes. *Op.* 667), which clearly refers to the 'power of the immortal ones' (namely the gods), rather than to their 'end'.

Plutarch in *Amatorius* 750 E furnishes us with a perfect example of how a phrase using τέλος with an abstract noun in genitive was understood around the end of the first century AD. The phrase τέλος γὰρ ἐπιθυμίας ἡδονή corresponds grammatically word by word to the phrase τέλος γὰρ νόμου Χριστός in Rom 10.4. The structure of the sentence and the syntactical function of every word are absolutely identical in both passages:[79]

1. predicate (nom. sing.)	2. conjunction	3. complement of noun (gen. sing.)	4. subject noun (nom. sing.)
τέλος	γὰρ	ἐπιθυμίας	ἡδονή
τέλος	γὰρ	νόμου	Χριστός

In both cases the verb ἐστιν is omitted, as it normally is in purely nominal sentences.[80] All the translators of Plutarch agree that the phrase is not temporal and that it means 'the object of desire is pleasure'.[81] The grammatical and philological burden of proof is therefore upon those who translate Rom 10.4 a temporal-terminal sense.

As W. Jaeger says, the construction of τέλος with genitive does not mean 'the time when things end, but the ideal end contemplated in action'.[82] Therefore the expressions featuring 'the end of (τέλος)' and a noun in genitive, even when the reality described by the noun is capable of having a temporal end, are not intended to denote termination, but any other of the basic meanings of τέλος which have been mentioned.[83]

In the few instances where τέλος is put in reference to laws (or similar concepts), we have not found any occurrence of τέλος meaning 'cessation' or 'abrogation', but rather 'object', 'purpose', or 'fulfillment'. Thus, Plato's phrase τέλος τῶν νόμων means 'the object (or the goal) of the laws', not their cessation.[84] And Plutarch's statement, δίκη μὲν οὖν νόμου τέλος ἐστι, obviously means that 'justice is the aim (object) of the law' (*Moralia* 780 E).

The dynamic character of τέλος is made strikingly evident in the fact that it may be used even for the *ratification* of a law.[85] Thus, to bring to its τέλος a law, or a word, is to make it come true, to carry out what has been previously stated.[86] So the wish expressed by Cleinias to the Athenian visitor in Pl. *Epin.* 980 B, εἰ γάρ σοι τοῦτο τέλος εἴη τῶν νόμων means 'thus may you be able to fulfill the laws', not 'to make them cease'. Aeschylus' statement, ἐντολὴ Διὸς ἔχει τέλος, means 'the order (or commandment) of Zeus is binding'.[87] A passage in Diogenes Laertius shows that this meaning was still the common one several centuries later, and that τέλος and τελέω applied to νόμος did not mean cessation. In *Vita Platonis* 3.96 we read:[88]

> There are four ways in which things are completed (διαιρεῖται τὸ τέλος τῶν πραγμάτων εἰς τέτταρα εἴδη): the first is by legal

enactment (ἕν μὲν κατὰ νόμον τέλος τὰ πράγματα λαμβάνειν), when a decree is passed and this decree is confirmed by a law (ὁ νόμος τελέσῃ).

The phrase τέλος νομοθεσίας refers to the conclusion of the elaboration of a legislative code, and ἡ νομοθεσία τέλος ἂν ὑμῖν ἔχοι means 'your task of legislation has nearly come to an end' in the sense that the elaboration of the laws is almost finished.[89] By τέλος ἁπάσης πολιτείας Plato means 'the culmination of the legislative task' (*Lg.* 1.632). Something similar may be said of the phrase τέλος παιδείας.[90]

For expressing 'end' in the sense of 'cessation', 'discontinuation', 'suspension of activity', 'abolition', or 'abrogation', the Greek language used phrases constructed with terms such as ἀπαλλαγή (from ἀπαλλάσσω, 'putting an end'), 'removal'; κατάλυσις (or any form of the verb λύω or καταλύω), 'destruction, loosing, release'; ὄλεθρος, 'destruction'; or any phrase with the verbs τελευτάω (generally referred to 'death'),[91] καταστρέφω ('to overturn or supersede'),[92] or other compounds of στρέφω, ἀφανίζω ('to make disappear or cease'), καταργέω ('to abolish, nullify'),[93] ἀθετέω ('to reject, reduce to nothing'), ἐξουδενέω ('to reject'), etc. These terminological facts need to be kept in mind for the interpretation of Rom 10.4.

Special Use of τέλος in Greek philosophy

Among the various uses of τέλος there is one which became particularly important in the Hellenistic period: the use of τέλος for the philosophical last end, final cause, supreme goal, or *summum bonum*. According to Dillon the question of the τέλος became 'the first issue'[94] in ethical and theological controversies among the Hellenistic philosophers by the time when the NT was written. On the assumption that Paul was not unaware of such a τέλος question, and taking into consideration the possibility that he could have chosen his terminology from among the most significant words that were available to him for conveying his theological notions, it seems justified to retrace the history of the τέλος controversy from its origins to the NT era. Since the notions conveyed by this particular use of τέλος are essentially related to the discussion of teleology, this survey on τέλος follows the history of the developments of the teleological concepts in Greek philosophy.

First of all it must be said that the question of τέλος and teleology is not a traditional Greek issue. Greek philosophers were primarily interested in the ἀρχή of the cosmos. Only in a later step did they ask for the meaning and aim of existence. In pre-Socratic philosophy the teleological possibility is at best hinted at[95] in some fragments of Anaxagoras of Clazomenae (c. 500–c. 428 BC),[96] Diogenes of Apollonia (c. 440),[97] and his contemporary Leucippus.[98]

Although some pre-Socratic philosophers asked themselves about the meaning of life,[99] they do not seem to have used any special *terminus technicus* for what in later philosophy would be called the τέλος.[100] It seems that the use of τέλος for the 'aim of life' had its origin with Socrates (469-399 BC).[101] According to Jaeger the search for 'the end of life' in an age of widespread skepticism 'was a brand new idea' which 'changed the history of the human spirit'.[102] 'It is Socrates' idea of the *aim of life*', adds Jaeger, 'which marks the decisive point in the history of *paideia*.'[103] Unfortunately we do not know anything with certainty about Socrates' teachings. It seems that his trend of thought was followed in this area by his disciple Plato.

Plato (c. 429-347 BC) was among the first to manifest his disagreement with the Greek classical explanation of things as restricted to their mechanical causes. In *Lg.* 10.889 B-C Plato strongly rejects the prevailing opinion that everything has to come into existence by merely physical causes. From his contemplation of the ordered cycles of the cosmos, Plato concluded that the world and everything which it contains must be the result of an intentional conscious working, a τέχνη, a νοῦς, a God.[104] For Plato this teleological view of nature is a fundamental postulate, essentially grounded on the principle of a rational will (God) at the origin of all.[105] In the *Timaeus* Plato defends the absolute precedence of purpose over mechanism and necessity.[106]

The question of the goal of human life depends for Plato on his teleological view of nature.[107] Since the universe (κόσμος) is directed by a superior intelligence for purposes that are good, there is no superior criterion for human behavior than striving for the best (*Lg.* 10.903 B-D).[108] For Plato the τέλος of man is what he emphatically calls 'the good' (Lat. *summum bonum*):[109] τέλος εἶναι ἁπασῶν τῶν πράξεων τὸ ἀγαθόν (*Grg.* 499 E). All the other aims (which he generally calls not τέλος but σκοπός) are but parts of the supreme aim of life, the good *per se*.

Plato is not only the first philosopher who gave to the question of the τέλος a great importance for human ethics but also the first to point to the question of a goal of human life beyond man himself.[110]

In *Th*. 176 B Plato defines the *summum bonum* in terms of ὁμοίωσις θεῷ, a formula that became very famous in later Platonism.[111] In *Lg*. 4.716 CD Plato explains the reason for aiming at the likeness of God (ὁμοίωσις θεῷ) as the supreme τέλος of man by stating that 'the measure of all things for us is first of all God, not man',[112] which is quite a new idea for a Greek philosopher.[113]

Aristotle (384–322 BC), following Plato, also reacted against the classical mechanistic theory.[114] As a man does not act without an aim—says Aristotle—so in nature nothing happens without purpose (*Ph*. 2.199 A 8-18). In the instinct-like nature of events (φύσει), in the bird's building of a nest or the plants' driving their roots into the ground (199 A 26-29), the purposeful cause (τέλος) is included (199 A 29-32). Nature is essentially matter (ὕλη) and form (μορφή), but it is moved by the τέλος, the goal for the sake of which everything happens (199 A 30-32). Everything in nature moves constantly toward its final purpose until it reaches it. To substitute the purpose (or τέλος) by 'chance' would be to destroy nature (199 B 14-17). Things do not come just by necessity (ἀναγκαῖον). They always come for the sake of their purpose (200 A 7-11).

For his teleological explanations Aristotle uses the word τέλος where Plato still preferred σκοπός. And he used it so profusely and systematically that he consecrated it as the *terminus technicus* for the final cause. Aristotle defined the τέλος in several different—though closely related—ways: as 'the end or purpose for the sake of which a process is initiated, its final αἰτία or cause';[115] 'that which always appears as the final result of a development . . . and in which the process attains completion';[116] 'that for the sake of which a thing is done';[117] 'the perfect result at which processes tend to arrive' (*Phs*. 2.8.199). Summarizing, for Aristotle 'the telos of anything is its full actualization'.[118]

Aristotle's ethical concept of τέλος, contrary to what happens in Plato, is little related to his doctrine of natural teleology.[119] In the *Ethics* Aristotle restricts his concept of τέλος to the general assumption that each human action and decision aims at what man considers 'the good' (*EN* 1.1 1094 A). The highest value at which one aims for its own sake is the good *per se* or *summum bonum*, which he calls the τέλος.[120] This τέλος, however, which Aristotle identifies sometimes with ἀρετή (*EN* 1.6 1098 A) and sometimes with εὐδαιμονία[121] is totally immanent and man-centered.[122] There is nothing in Aristotle comparable to the ὁμοίωσις θεῷ of Plato. What

Aristotle wanted primarily to state was that natural processes are only adequately understood when their outcomes and ends are understood. Or in the very words of Aristotle, that 'everything is only understood in the light of its τέλος'.[123]

In spite of all its weaknesses the Aristotelian teleological system is still the most logically grounded and explained in the ancient world. Its influence is seen in Peripatos, Simplicius, and Philoponus, and above all—though with several modifications—in the Stoa. However, teleological explanations never were well accepted in Greek philosophy, which remained predominantly mechanist or skeptically unconcerned about the question of the final end.[124]

From Aristotle onwards the question of the τέλος became so important in the philosophical debate that a whole series of writings appeared under the title περὶ τέλους.[125] In the first of them Epicurus (341-270 BC) attacks the teleological explanations and defines the τέλος of man in terms of εὐδαιμονία, understood as 'ἡδονή of the body and ἀταραξία of the soul' (D. L. 10.128). What Epicurus understood by that remained a very much discussed matter in antiquity.[126] The Stoics, in particular, vehemently criticized the Epicureans on the ground that their τέλος was not just 'pleasure and happiness' but 'lust'.[127] The sure fact is that the Epicureans rejected any kind of teleology. Lucretius attacked final causes at length. Since the world is manifestly imperfect—he argued—design is not a feature of the cosmos, and therefore there is no purpose which the world as a whole, things in general, or man in particular are designed to fulfill.[128]

The question of the τέλος became a fixed *topos* in Stoicism.[129] The discredited teleological explanations of nature were picked up by Zeno (335-263 BC), the founder of the Stoa, and his disciples. They developed the principle that 'everything comes into being according to a plan',[130] and, therefore, that 'nature always works purposefully'.[131] The lowest beings exist for the sake of the higher,[132] and the whole plan of nature has man as its goal.[133] Accordingly, human existence itself has to have a supreme goal also.[134]

The famous Stoic definition of the τέλος was 'life according to nature' (τὸ ὁμολογουμένως τῇ φύσει ζῆν),[135] worded sometimes as 'life according to virtue (ἀρετή)'[136] or 'according to reason (Λόγος)'.[137] In later Stoicism the τέλος formulations acquired striking religious connotations. Thus, for Posidonius 'τέλος is the life in contemplation of truth and order'.[138] For Cleanthes it is 'life in obedience to the universal law of God'.[139] Similar definitions may be found in Chrysippus[140] and Antipater of Tarsus.[141] While the Stoic teleological explanations of nature were strongly contested,[142] the Stoic ethical concept of τέλος powerfully influenced the philosophical thinking of the Hellenistic world.

The τέλος question in the Hellenistic period

Next to Christianity Platonism was the most influential trend of thought in the Hellenistic period. According to Dillon, among the dominant themes of Middle Platonism 'the first issue is, naturally, the purpose of life, or, as it was termed, "the end of goods" (τέλος ἀγαθῶν)'.[143] Although the Middle Platonists followed primarily the teachings of Plato, they also adopted from Aristotle and the Stoics many ethical conceptions, including their philosophy of the purposefulness of all created beings.[144]

Antiochus of Aschalon (c. 130–c. 68 BC), the head of the school and, with Philo, its most representative character, taught that the universe is governed by the providence of God,[145] which he related to the supreme τέλος.[146] The main question in Antiochus's thought is the inability of human nature for carrying man's desire to the attainment of the supreme good, or final purpose of life (τέλος). This basic incapacity is the source of the problem of evil in the world. Therefore, an external aid is required for man's reaching his τέλος. For Antiochus this aid could only come from Platonic philosophy (Cic. *Fin*. 5.24–71).

Among the Middle Platonists three τέλος formulas were specially common: Plato's 'withdrawal of the soul from the things of the body' (*Phd*. 64 E); the Stoic 'concordance with nature' (Cic. *Fin*. 2.34); and especially the definition of τέλος as 'likeness to God (ὁμοίωσις θεῷ)', derived from Plato (*Tht*. 176 B).[147] Though Antiochus adopted as his personal definition of the τέλος the old Stoic formula, he added to it some non-Stoic nuances. So 'the τέλος of man is life in accordance with nature [understood as "human nature"], *developed to its full perfection and supplied with all its needs*'.[148] Antiochus's feeling of the impossibility of reaching the τέλος in this life is made evident in his insistence on the distinction between the 'happy life' (βίος εὐδαίμων) and the 'happiest life' (βίος εὐδαιμονέστατος).[149]

The identification of the τέλος with the ὁμοίωσις θεῷ became a feature of the Middle Platonists. Plutarch of Chaeroneia (AD 50–120) defined this 'likeness to God' as 'in some sort an assimilation to

Himself (ἐξομοιῶσιν . . . πρὸς αὐτόν), accessible to all who can follow God . . . through copying and aspiring to the beauty and goodness that are God's'.[150] The reaching of the τέλος through the *imitatio Dei*[151] was an aspiration later adopted and adapted by Christian thinkers.[152]

In a related sphere of thought, another issue widely discussed among the Platonists was the question of the σκοπός of the ancient writings.[153] The possible influence of this trend on the Jewish debates about the *skopos*/τέλος of the law[154] should be further explored.

The importance of the τέλος discussion in the Hellenistic period may also be perceived in the repercussions it had on the Latin thinkers. Cicero (106-43 BC) wrote a whole treatise on that question, entitled *De finibus bonorum et malorum*, which is, according to the best commentators, 'the most elaborate of Cicero's philosophical writings'.[155] In this work Cicero discusses the definition of τέλος (cited very often in Greek as a generally accepted *terminus technicus*) according to the different schools of philosophy of his time, mainly Epicurean, Stoic, and Platonist. The term itself is defind by Cicero as follows: 'That which is not itself a means to anything else, but to which all else is a means, is what the Greeks term the *Telos*, the highest, the ultimate or final Good' (*Fin.* 1.42; 3.26).

The Latin understanding of the Greek τέλος (which was translated by either *finis* or *summum bonum*) connoted, as H. Rackham has observed, 'not only "aim", but "completion" . . . extreme point . . . of an ascending scale of goods'.[156] The Stoic Seneca (c. 4 BC–AD 65) dealt also with the question of the τέλος in his moral essay entitled *De vita beata*. He defined the *summum bonum* in terms of 'seeking virtue' (4.2), 'following God' (15.6), and 'obeying God' (15.7). The Latin concept of τέλος seems to have kept all the connotations that this word had in Greek.

This short survey shows that the τέλος question was at the center of philosophical discussions during the NT era. By that time τέλος had become a *terminus technicus* for designating the ideal end, the ultimate purpose, the goal of life, the final cause, or the *summum bonum*. However, the Hellenistic world as a whole, in spite of the growing influence of Platonism and even Judaism, remained skeptical of teleological questions at the dawn of the Christian era. The main body of Greek philosophy did not accept any transcendent τέλος either for the cosmos or for human life,[157] and in general the mechanistic view of nature always predominated.

At the end of this brief review of the meanings and uses of τέλος in Greek literature, some conclusions impose themselves for our consideration.

1.   The first undeniable fact is the perplexing polysemy of τέλος, which may be traced all through the history of Greek literature back to Homer. Etymological research has not yet succeeded in ascertaining the original meaning at the source of such diversification. The lexicographical data seem to point, however, towards the conclusion that 'highest point' or 'turning point' could be close to the original meaning of τέλος. This basic meaning likely explains the fundamental qualification of τέλος as designating at the same time the crucial point ('end', 'climax', etc.), the action toward that point ('aim', 'purpose', etc.), and the result of reaching the point ('attainment', 'fulfillment', etc.).[158]

2.   This variety of meanings is a warning against a hasty or simplistic translation. Several connotations are possible in some occurrences of such a polysemous word. At the same time, the possibility of different meanings according to different contexts is also a warning against the fallacy of taking τέλος as a concept, and not what it really is: just a word with multiple semantic associations, for which the main common denominator is—if the expression would not be a pleonasm—their 'teleological' character.

3.   Because of the extensive incidence of τέλος in Greek literature, a full survey of occurrences was beyond the scope of this study. Since all the basic significations of the term remained in usage during the time of the translation of the LXX and the production of the NT, a full survey was unnecessary. Attention, however, had to be paid to the special usages of τέλος which became particularly fashionable in the Hellenistic period, as 'the decisive factor' and 'the *summmum bonnum*'. These are not irrelevant for the interpretation of Paul's use of τέλος if it is accepted that he was aware of the cultural (religious and philosophical) trends of his time.

4.   More important still are the conclusions obtained on the common meaning of τέλος when constructed with a noun in genitive and, particularly, on the general meaning of the phrase τέλος νόμου and related expressions.

Though all these considerations are worthy of being kept in mind as controlling factors for the translation of Rom 10.4, they are still insufficient for determining the sense of τέλος νόμου in the famous Pauline passage. Because of the particular connotations that some words took in biblical usage, the present research needs to be completed with a more comprehensive survey on the meaning and use of τέλος and τέλος νόμου in Jewish Hellenistic and biblical literature.

The Use of τέλος in the Septuagint

The words of the τέλος group are fairly common in the LXX.[159] The most frequently used is τέλος itself, with 160 occurrences.[160] However, the Hebrew language does not have any word corresponding exactly to τέλος.[161] The Greek word is used in the LXX to translate an extremely wide range of Hebrew terms and expressions. In general, τέλος is used in the LXX in a way which does not significantly depart from that of Greek literature. There are, however, some small—but significant—differences which need to be noticed here because of their probable influence on the use of τέλος in the NT, and which make the study of the use of τέλος in the LXX worthy as a background for the study of τέλος in the NT.

Τέλος *in prepositional phrases*

Of the 160 τέλος passages in the LXX 100 are constructed with the formula εἰς (ἕως) (τὸ) τέλος, and in 55 of these 100 instances this adverbial construction indicates degree of intensity, meaning 'completely' or similar expressions. Very often the idea of totality, entirety, and related notions simply enhances the meaning of the original Hebrew which τέλος translates:

1.   In Ps 37(38).7(6), ἕως τέλους, 'utterly', translates the Hebrew expression for the superlative עד מאד.

2.   In some instances (only in the Hexateuch), adverbial expressions with τέλος are used to translate the root תמם ('be complete') and derivates. So ἕως εἰς τέλος is used for עד־תמם, with the meaning of 'wholly', 'entirely' in Deut 31.24, 30; Josh 8.24 (A), and 10.20. The non-adverbial form εἰς τέλος is used for תמים in Josh 10.13, in the phrase εἰς τέλος ἡμέρας μίας, with the meaning of 'for about a *whole* day'.[162]

3.   Εἰς τέλος is used with the sense of 'totally' for the characteristic emphatic Hebrew construction of infinitive absolute in connection with the finite verb of the same stem.[163] The phrase לא השמיר אשמיר is translated οὐκ εἰς τέλος ἐξαρῶ in Amos 9.8 ('I will not *utterly* destroy'). And the phrase ואנכי אעלך גם־עלה of Gen 46.4 is translated

καὶ ἐγὼ ἀναβιβάσω σε εἰς τέλος: 'I will also *surely* bring you up again' (NASB).

4. Adverbial expressions with τέλος also translate in the LXX forms of כלה.[164] Thus, εἰς τέλος is used for כלה, 'totally' (Ezek 20.40; 36.10; cf. 22.30, without Hebrew correspondence), for כלה, 'altogether' (Ps 73.11), and for לכלה, 'completely' (2 Chr 12.12; 13.1; cf. Sir 10.3). The expression τοῦ ἐπὶ τέλος ἀγαγεῖν is used in 1 Chr 29.19 for עשות הכל for the fulfillment or execution of an obligation in a way which could have been expressed perfectly by the verb τελέω.[165] In occurrences without correspondence with the Hebrew text τέλος is also used in adverbial combinations with the basic meaning of 'fully', 'perfectly', 'wholly', 'utterly', 'completely', 'at all', etc.[166]

In a few instances τέλος is used in ἀρχή–τέλος totality sayings. Thus, in Eccl 3.11, 'the ways of God are *completely* hidden from man (ἀπ' ἀρχῆς καὶ μέχρι τέλους)'. In Wis 7.18 it is found in an even more detailed formula of totality: 'God has the power of making known *the totality* of His times and mysteries (εἰδέναι . . . ἀρχὴν καὶ τέλος καὶ μεσότητα χρόνων)'. In 2 Macc 5.5 τέλος is used alone, without any preposition, with the evident meaning of totality.

In the superscription of fifty-five Psalms[167] the phrase εἰς τὸ τέλος is used to translate the Hebrew למנצח, as a *terminus technicus* whose intelligibility is much discussed. Even the first Greek translators disagreed on the meaning of these enigmatic headings.[168] From the time of the early Fathers the interpretation of εἰς τὸ τέλος as a title of psalms has been debated. Some give to the phrase 'for the end' an eschatological sense, as referring to the final victory of the Messiah.[169] Others link this usage with the 'authority' connotation of τέλος, and they translate εἰς τὸ τέλος by 'for the choirmaster', 'for the one in charge, the overseer'.[170] Others, finally, paying more attention to the impersonal character of the infinitive original and the neuter Greek form take τέλος here in its well-attested meaning of 'act' in divine worship (in the sense of 'rite' and 'ceremony'), and translate εἰς τὸ τέλος simply 'for the cultus', understanding by that that the psalms titled thus were composed for the explicit purpose of liturgical performance.[171]

Τέλος *in expressions of time*

In temporal contexts τέλος is used in construction with a preposition for indicating the completion of a period of time. This generally translates the Hebrew קץ or one of its cognates. The attested forms are: ἀπὸ τέλους (2 Kgs 15.17) μέτα (τὸ) τέλος,[172] ἐν τέλει (Judg 11.39), διὰ τέλους (2 Chr 18.2), ἕως τέλους (Dan 9.26 [Θ]), and εἰς (τὸ) τέλος.[173] This use is a particular feature of biblical literature. The fact that τέλος is used in the LXX in temporal expressions, while this use is so rare in Greek literature, is explained by Du Plessis by the fact that in the Hebrew notion of time 'the idea of turning is present' (p. 57). Flückiger explains better this anomaly by referring to the Hebrew concept of time, which he sees as eminently teleological.[174] Each period of time has been appointed by God for a purpose. So the end of a fixed lapse of time corresponds to the completion or fulfillment of its appointed end. Even Delling concedes that the adverbial expressions with τέλος have such a particular breadth of meaning that 'it is hard to say whether the reference is to *time* or to *extent*', for in them 'τέλος becomes a term of completeness'.[175]

Two times the phrase ἕως τέλους is used to translate the Hebrew סוף with the meaning of 'to the end'. In Dan 6.26 Θ it certainly means 'for ever'. In Dan 7.26 it could also mean 'utterly', 'completely', although the Hebrew meaning of סוף is predominantly temporal.

The phrase εἰς τέλος is used eighteen times for translating the Hebrew לנצח[176] which is usually rendered by 'for ever' or other similar expressions, three times for translating נצח,[177] and two times for translating לעד,[178] with approximately the same signification. Though the meaning of these expressions is, without any doubt, predominantly temporal, it seems to be less due to τέλος than to the context, τέλος carrying primarily the notion of 'completion'. So εἰς τέλος is better translated in Job 20.7 by 'utterly' and in Ps 9.32 (10.11), by 'at all' or other similar expressions. The point is even clearer in the case of Job 23.7 and Hab 1.4, where the expressions ἐξαγάγοι δὲ εἰς τέλος τὸ κρίμα μου and οὐ διεξάγεται εἰς τέλος κρίμα, respectively, show that εἰς τέλος denotes the *action* of carrying out (in this concrete instance 'carrying out judgment') and not the temporal termination of the mentioned action.

In one occasion διὰ τέλους is found for תמיד (Isa 62.6), with the meaning of 'constantly', when usually תמיד is translated by διὰ πάντος.[179] For those who pretend that the notion of termination is basic in τέλος it becomes very difficult to explain how it may mean here 'duration'. Delling feels it necessary to acknowledge that even 'in some temporal statements τέλος indicates totality' and not termination.[180] Most of the temporal passages where εἰς τέλος has

been translated by 'to the end' or 'forever' could be translated by
'completely' or a similar phrase.[181]

Used as an adverb τὸ τέλος means 'finally', 'ultimately', in 2 Macc
13.16, 3 Macc 4.14, and 2 Macc 5.5 (without the article). In Dan
6.26(27) and in 9.27 (Θ) τέλος is used for designating the eschatological
end, or the consummation of the ages. This usage is, obviously, new
in Greek literature, and only possible because of the teleological
understanding of time in biblical theology. The newness of this usage
may be noticed in the reluctance to use, or even the avoidance of,
τέλος by the LXX to express the eschatological end.[182] Thus, the
phrase ἡ κυριεία αὐτοῦ ἕως τέλους of Dan 6.26(27) in the Θ version
is still rendered in the LXX by the phrase ἕως τοῦ αἰῶνος. For the
'end of times' the LXX does not use τέλος but συντελεία, the most
emphatic word for 'completion'.[183] However, in the NT the term
τέλος is used several times for designating the consummation of the
age, probably by influence of its use in the Greek translation of
Daniel.

Substantive use of τέλος

Compared with the use of τέλος in prepositional phrases, the
substantive use is much less frequent, but it is attested in most of the
basic meanings in which this term was used in contemporary Greek
literature. Τέλος means 'tax' or 'tribute' ten times and translates the
Hebrew מכס ('number', 'price', 'tribute') in Num 31.28, 37, 38, 39, 40,
41; מכסה in Lev 27.23[184] and מס in Esth 10.1. It is also used for 'tax'
(without Hebrew parallels) in 1 Macc 10.31 and 11.35.

Τέλος means 'execution' or 'carrying out' in connection with the
verbs ἄγειν and ποιεῖν. So, ἐποιεῖτο τέλος in 3 Macc 1.26 is
translated 'with the view of carrying out his design' (cf. 3.14; 5.19; 1
Chr 29.19).

Τέλος probably means 'goal' in Job 23.3, departing from the
Hebrew in the sentence: 'Oh that I knew where I might find him, and
reach the goal (ἔλθοιμι εἰς τέλος)'.[185] Τέλος is used in the sense of
'the highest point' in 2 Macc 6.15, πρὸς τέλος ἀφικομένων ἡμῶν τῶν
ἁμαρτιῶν ('When our sins have reached their *full height*' or '*extreme
limit*'); cf. 2 Macc 5.49.

Τέλος means 'issue' in 4 Macc 12.3 (τῆς μὲν ἀδελφῶν σου
ἀπονοίας τὸ τέλος ὁρᾷς, 'you see the issue, result of the madness of
your brethren'), 'outcome' in 2 Macc 5.7 (τὸ δὲ τέλος τῆς ἐπιβουλῆς
αἰσχύνην λαβών, 'the final result of his campaign was a complete

disgrace') and probably also in Wis 11.14.[186] In Wis 3.19 it designates the 'final destiny' (γενεᾶς γὰρ ἀδίκου χαλεπὰ τὰ τέλη, 'for horrible is the end of the unrighteous generation').

Τέλος is translated 'end' in a quantitive sense in Bar 3.17 (καὶ οὐκ ἐστὶν τέλος τῆς κτήσεως αὐτῶν, 'there is no end to their greediness'), and in a temporal sense in Wis 14.14 (διὰ τοῦτο σύντομον αὐτῶν τὸ τέλος ἐπενοήθη, 'therefore their speedy end has been planned').[187]

Some special uses of τέλος *in the Septuagint*

The occurrences of τέλος in the book of Ecclesiastes (3.11; 7.3(2); and 12.13) deserve to be treated separately because they preserve, more than anywhere else in the LXX, the Greek 'teleological' character of τέλος.[188] In fact Ecclesiastes reflects better than any other book of the OT the biblical teleological reasoning.[189]

The point of departure of Ecclesiastes is the reflection on man's insurmountable ignorance of the real significance of life and events (cf. 8.7). This incapacity of man to grasp the source and purpose of the whole creation is expressed in 3.11 by translating מראש ועד־סוף, a Hebrew idiom for 'totality', by ἀπ' ἀρχῆς καὶ μέχρι τέλους, an uncommon variant of the common ἀρχὴ καὶ τέλος formula. This is the theme of the whole book behind the ματαιότης *leitmotiv*: man sees 'vanity' in everything when he deduces from his human observations the absence of a τέλος.[190]

First of all, man sees his life as 'vanity' because he is incapable of grasping 'the *whence* and the *whither* (ἀρχὴ καὶ τέλος) of creation'[191] (cf. 3.11). The trouble is that man cannot find by himself the ἀρχὴ καὶ τέλος of God's plan. Man's feeling of meaninglessness comes from his impotence for changing his lot, foreseeing his future, and knowing the ultimate good (6.10-12). Then, the apparent 'end' of man (second occurrence of τέλος) as stated in 7.3(2) is indeed death, an ultimate fate which man apparently shares with all the other creatures of this world. This is not, however, the central message of Ecclesiastes. In a very skillful and imperceptible way, the author leads the reader, little by little, towards a very different conclusion.

Von Rad has noticed that 'in spite of all these depressing observations, Qoheleth is far from holding that events in the world are simply a haphazard jumble. He is aware of something which mysteriously rules and orders every event . . .'[192] Thus, Qoheleth goes on to say that though man cannot know 'the ultimate τέλος' in an absolute sense, life is worthy to be lived, and certain attitudes, certain *prises de position* in favor of 'the good' should be taken.[193] The question of man's lot, the question of meaning, has an ultimate positive answer because God is still in charge.

This means that, in spite of all human, reasonable evidence, death is not man's final 'end'. The essence of existence escapes man when he sees himself just as another mortal being among the other creatures of the world. The last citation of τέλος concludes the book with a hint for facing positively the mystery of existence: The universe, life, man are not ultimately μάταιοι. They have a τέλος, however obscured to our view it may appear. The τέλος λόγου, 'the end of the matter', 'the τέλος of all', is:[194] 'fear God[195] and keep his commandments; for this is the whole (duty) of man.[196] For God will bring every deed into judgment' (12.13). This is the paradoxical conclusion[197] of Ecclesiastes: in spite of the apparent meaninglessness of life and history, *'life has a direction, an irreversible direction'*.[198] God has a purpose and everything, everybody, takes on significance in relationship with the divinely ordained τέλος. While the world and events appear to be completely outside human understanding they are completely within the scope of God's activity.[199]

It is important to notice that with this unexpected reference to the judgment, the question of the meaning of life is shifted by Ecclesiastes to the question of salvation.[200] Human life, in every present moment, is of extreme value because it must be seen against the perspective of eternity. Salvation is the τέλος of life. Human life becomes significant and meaningful only when put in the perspective of God's will, God's end. And the final purpose of God's revelation is to lead man to that end.[201] As Du Plessis has said, 'If one sentence aptly recounts the essence of Israelite religion this one does (12.13). In a minimum of words a minute description is given of the essential purpose or fundamental principle of all existence: the knowledge and communion with God.'[202]

The wisdom writings, where the word τέλος is used nine times, are deeply permeated with teleological thinking.[203] The idea of God's having a plan for nature, man, and history is a central one in Wisdom of Solomon (9.13-18),[204] and much more so in Ben Sira,[205] which ends with a lengthy hymn about the absolute purposefulness of creation (chs. 39–42):[206]

> The works of God are all good [cf. Gen 1.31]
> and they are appropriate for each purpose in his time (39.16).
> Nothing is small and of no account with him,

and nothing is incomprehensible and difficult to him.
No one can say, 'What is this for?',
for everything has been created for its purpose . . .[207]

This emphasis on the purposefulness of God's works is presumably a reaction against the skeptical influence of Greek philosophy.[208] The theme of the purpose of God's works leads to the main point of the wisdom writings, namely, to the idea that God's revealed Wisdom (Torah) has been given to man in order to teach him his purpose in life. The summary of the wisdom books is that 'man's ultimate goal is union with God, which may, however, be achieved only through union with his Wisdom (Wis 8.17; 9.10)'.[209] Ben Sira ends with the words 'let the end of the discourse be "He is the all"' (43.27) (συντελεία λόγων τὸ πᾶν ἐστιν αὐτός). This abstract concept of God as the 'all-embracing-one' (τὸ πᾶν or הכל)[210] is very much in line with the Hellenistic search for the τέλος. The highest *summum bonum* is God himself.

With this background in mind several conclusions on the use of τέλος in the LXX may be briefly summarized:

1.   The terminological data do not allow us to adduce an OT τέλος 'concept', because a 'τέλος-*Begriff*' simply does not exist as such. The very nature of this word requires that its meaning depends considerably on what is connected with it. Like 'end' in English, the Greek τέλος is an ambiguous word. The context has to determine in each instance to which of the stages of the 'telic' action τέλος is pointing, and therefore, whether it means 'aim', 'attainment', or 'result' (or equivalent terms).

2.   The predominant uses of τέλος in the LXX are indicative of fullness, totality and consummation. Τέλος is used in the LXX more often than in classical Greek literature in temporal expressions, frequently for designating the completion of a specific period of time, and in two instances for the consummation of the eschatological end, which is also a novelty.

3.   Though nowhere in the LXX is an explicit teleological system spelled out, the teleological theme is not only present, but has deep roots in LXX thought. Basic to LXX theology is the idea that history, man, the whole creation, not only have their origin in God but also have a purpose given by God, and therefore are teleological. The OT eschatological and Messianic dimension gives to OT religion a 'lure of the future'[211] which is only understandable from a teleological perspective. This essentially teleological view of God's dealing with

man and reality is new to Greek philosophical reasoning and helps us to understand why the LXX could use τέλος so commonly in temporal and eschatological contexts.

The Use of τέλος in the Pseudepigrapha

In the existing Greek passages of the Pseudepigrapha there have been registered thirty-five τέλος occurrences. About half of them (seventeen) belong to the *Testament of the Twelve Patriarchs*.[212] In general, the use of τέλος in these books does not depart from the classical one, and is very comparable to the use found in the LXX.

Τέλος is often used in expressions of totality or intensification. So in Ps Sol 1.1 the sentence 'I cried to the Lord when I was in distress' is modified in the Greek version by the addition of the phrase εἰς τέλος, probably as an expression of totality ('when I was *totally* distressed') or intensification ('when I was in *sore* distress').[213]

Τέλος is the 'issue' or the 'outcome' of an action in TAsh 2.1, 4 (τὸ τέλος τοῦ πράγματος εἰς κακίαν, τὸ δὲ τέλος τῆς πράξεως ἔρχεται εἰς κακόν, 'the issue of the action led unto evil', or 'the outcome of that action was evil').[214] Charles translates TAsh 1.3: 'Two ways hath God given to the sons of men, and two inclinations, and two kinds of action, and two modes, and two *issues* (δύο τέλεα)'. Τέλος here could also mean 'power', a meaning that is attested in classical Greek and was fairly common in the Hellenistic period. But more probably τέλος is used here in its basic, 'teleological', and 'directional' sense. The meaning is that man's behavior—according to the Jewish belief—may follow two opposite 'directions' leading to two different trends of action, and therefore to two different 'goals' and 'outcomes'.

Τέλος means 'final fate' or 'destiny' in several occurrences: τὰ τέλη τῶν ἀνθρώπων δεικνύουσι τὴν δικαιοσύνην αὐτῶν is to be translated by 'the latter ends (final outcome or destiny) of men show their righteousness' (TAsh 6.4). In TBenj 4.1, speaking of the happy outcome of the life of Joseph, Jacob says: Ἴδετε οὖν, τέκνα μου, τοῦ ἀγαθοῦ ἀνδρὸς τὸ τέλος, 'see you, therefore, my children, the end (τέλος) of the good man'. In 1 Enoch 10.2, when Uriel says to the angel: 'Reveal to him [Noah] the end (τέλος) that is approaching', τέλος refers to the flood. Here either translation, 'outcome' or 'end', would fit, but the former would correspond more exactly to the thrust of the context.[215]

Τέλος is also used for designating the 'final consummation' in 1 Enoch 25.4, though for that apolyptic event the common terms in Enoch and the' rest of apolyptic literature are τελείωσις (cf. 2.2; 10.12, 14; 16.1; 18.16) or συντέλεια, generally constructed with the modifiers τῶν αἰώνων (TLevi 10.2), τοῦ αἰῶνος (TBenj 11.3), or in the phrase καιρὸς συντέλειας (TZeb 9.9). In TLevi 14.1 τέλος is used in its plural form in the sentence ἐπὶ τὰ τέλη τῶν αἰώνων ('at the end of the ages').[216] The apolyptic end is seen as a *turning point* rather than as a termination. 4 Ezra calls it 'the parting asunder of the times', for the end of the first age is the beginning of the second.[217] This use of τέλος with the meaning of *turning point* seems to be attested in 1 Enoch 18.14, where the term τέλος has been chosen for depicting an imaginary cosmic point where heaven and earth meet each other, called there 'the end (τέλος) of heaven and earth'. Τέλος is used in Rev Ezra 27.26 without any qualification for designating the eschatological end: τότε γνώσεσθε ὅτι ἐγγύς ἐστιν τὸ τέλος ('and then you will know that the end is near').[218]

On three occasions τέλος may be translated as an adverb, with the sense of 'at last' or 'finally',[219] and twice as a noun in the sense of 'termination'. In Sib Or 3.211, it is said that 'when the first (evils) have reached their end (ἄλλα ὁπόταν τὰ πρῶτα τέλος λάβῃ), straightway then shall be another series upon them'.[220] When the final outcome is destruction it coincides with the definitive end. Thus in TDan 6.5, 'the kingdom of the enemies shall be brought to an end (εἰς τέλος)'. In ApMos 24 it is difficult to state whether the issue is temporal or not. God says to Adam: 'Weary shalt thou be and shalt not rest . . . abundantly shalt thou busy thyself . . . but come to no end (εἰς τέλος μὴ ὑπάρξεις)'. Τέλος may mean as well 'conclusion' as 'outcome'.[221] The apocalyptic character of most of the Pseudepigrapha makes it understandable that τέλος was so often used in eschatological contexts. The teleological Jewish concept of time and history ('God-directed history') allowed perfectly that particular use. This concept is grounded on the basic belief that each of God's actions has a definite, transcendent purpose. The fact that the Hebrew has no defined term for τέλος (much less for *teleology*) does not mean that the Hebrew mind was unable to grasp that concept. In fact, the Hebrew *Weltanschauung* was much more teleologically oriented than the Greek one.[222]

In the Pseudepigrapha there are no references to the 'end' of the law in the sense of termination, or cessation. Moreover, the glorification of the law is one of the main themes of the Book of Jubilees,[223] 4 Ezra, and the letter of Aristeas. On the profound intention, or 'true meaning' of the Law, there is a particularly interesting text in the Zadokite Document (CD 8.12), where severe menaces are decreed against the children of Israel 'unless they observe to do according to *the true meaning* of the law'.

The τέλος *of the Law in Aristeas*

Besides being an apology for the Greek translation of the Hebrew Scriptures, the Letter of Aristeas is a beautiful vindication of the purpose of the Jewish law. It is obvious that 'the section on the Jewish law (128-71) is the outstanding feature of the book'.[224] This section aims to prove that all the Jewish laws, even those which may seem more trivial, have a profound, hidden meaning attached to them, and an important ethical, didactic purpose.[225] This is explicitly said in 168-69.

> My brief account of these matters ought to have convinced you, that all our regulations have been drawn up with a view to righteousness, and that nothing has been enacted in the Scripture thoughtlessly or without a due reason, but its purpose is to enable us throughout our whole life and in all our actions to practice righteousness before all men, being mindful of Almighty God (*APOT*, II, p. 110).

The ethical teaching of the book may be summed up in the words of 195:

> The highest goal in life is to know that God is the Lord of the universe and that in our finest achievements it is not we who attain success but God who by his power brings all things to fulfilment and leads us to the goal (θεὸς δὲ τελειοῖ τὰ πάντων καὶ καθηγεῖται δυναστεύων) (*APOT*, II, p. 88).

The word τέλος occurs three times in the Letter of Aristeas, always in prepositional constructions: μέχρι τέλους (187), with the meaning of 'totally', 'to the end'; ἐπὶ τέλει (196), with the sense of 'finally'; and in the phrase ἐπὶ τέλος ἄγειν (9), signifying 'to carry into execution'.[226] For 'goal' other cognates of τέλος are preferred;[227] for 'purpose' the term πρόθεσις is found; and for 'the highest good of life' or *summum bonum* the phrase κάλλιστον . . . τὸ ζῆν is used (9; 312).[228] However, though the Letter of Aristeas does not offer any direct help for determining the sense of τέλος in Rom 10.4, it still remains a very valuable witness of the Judeo-Hellenistic interest in the questions of the purpose of the law and the search for the highest good.

The Use of τέλος *in Philo*

A survey on the use of τέλος in Philo of Alexandria (c. 30 BC–AD 45) is of the greatest importance here because of the many points of comparison between Philo and Paul. Both were Jews living at about the same time in the same Judeo-Hellenistic world. Both wrote, in Greek, religious apologetic treatises in which they dealt—though from very different viewpoints—with the common problem of the understanding of the Hebrew Scripture and its religious significance for the people of their time. It is obvious that their theological positions would diverge, at least in the distinctive points which distinguish their different religious confessions. But at the same time, and this is the important fact here, it is reasonable to suppose that they shared the same general understanding of the word τέλος, which was common to their vocabulary. It seems logical to assume that the expression τέλος νόμου used in a biblical context might have had for both of them the same basic connotations, independent of the particular theological nuances that they might have given to it in each occurrence.

The first observation that imposes itself on the student is the frequency of the τέλος occurrences in the Philonic corpus. In his *Index Philoneus*, Günter Mayer lists 204 τέλος occurrences distributed throughout practically all the existing Greek works[229] and covering all the basic meanings of τέλος.[230]

This abundant use of the word τέλος may be explained by three main reasons: Philo's teleological conception of the created world,[231] his endeavor to explain in philosophical categories the reason, meaning, and value of the Jewish laws,[232] and his particular interest in the quest of the ethical *summum bonum*, which he shared with the philosophers of his time.

In almost half of the instances Philo uses τέλος in its basic sense of 'attainment' for designating both the movement which leads anything to the attainment of its highest point and the culminating point itself. Accordingly, τέλος is most often to be translated by 'object', 'goal', 'aim', 'purpose', 'climax', or by some other expression of culmination. Thus τέλος is equated with the winning-post of a race,[233] with a target,[234] with the goal or aim of life,[235] and with the object or purpose of an art.[236] In some instances τέλος means 'result' (*Leg. All.* 1.84; *Vit. Mos.* 2.287; *Agr.* 26), 'consequence' (*Virt.* 182), 'outcome' (*Spec. Leg.* 3.98; *Somn.* 2.141), 'issue' (*Ebr.* 204), or 'fulfillment' (*Spec. Leg.* 3.86; *Virt.* 75).

The directional character of τέλος as 'movement towards' a goal would be better rendered in verbal sentences with the verb 'to lead' or similar expressions. So the phrase ὧν ἀθεότης τὸ τέλος (*Praem.* 162) means that 'it *finally led* to atheism', and the phrase ἧς ὁσιότης τὸ τέλος (*Abr.* 172) '[the road] at the end of which is holiness' is better rendered '[the road] *leading* to holiness'. In *Vit. Mos.* 2.181 τέλος is explicitly defined in terms of 'aspiration': τέλος δὲ ὅτι πρὸς αὐτὴν ὁ κατὰ φύσιν βίος σπεύδει ('the τέλος is the aspiration of the life which follows nature'). More often τέλος means 'the consummation', 'the summum', 'the highest stage or degree'.[237] Thus, 'parents find the consummation of happiness (τέλος εὐδαιμονίας) in the high excellence of their children' (*Spec. Leg.* 2.236). Not to honor God is 'the supreme (τέλος) misery' (*Spec. Leg.* 3.29). 'Shamelessness carried to the end (μέχρι τέλους) is the culmination (ὑπερβολή) of wickedness' (*ibid.*, 54). 'The factors which produce consummate excellence (τὸ ἄριστον τέλος) are three in number: learning, nature, practice' (*Jos. 1*). 'The knowledge of God is the τέλος of happiness' (*Spec. Leg.* 1.345). In 1.336 the τέλος is defined as τὸ μέγιστον ἀγαθόν. In *Cher.* 86 it is said of God that 'since his nature is most perfect God is himself the summit (ἄκρα καὶ τέλος καὶ ὅρος) of happiness'.[238] The expression οἱ ἐν τέλει occurs twenty-one times in Philo's writings. This phrase shows that τέλος means the culmination of a progressive (not regressive) series, the highest point, since οἱ ἐν τέλει are not 'the last ones' but on the contrary, those who are *at the top*.[239]

In most of the occurrences Philo uses τέλος as a *terminus technicus* for the ethico-philosophical concept of man's *summum bonum* which was a very pressing issue in his time. Philo knows and uses all the leading τέλος definitions, but when he quotes them for his own purposes he changes their meaning.[240]

Philo seems to share the features of the Stoic definition of τέλος, but, in fact, Philo's concept of the *summum bonum* is highly superior to that of the Stoa. Though in *Quod Omn.* 160 he defines the τέλος of man in the same terms as Zeno as 'a life according to nature (τέλος . . . τὸ ἀκολούθως τῇ φύσει ζῆν)', he takes good care to state precisely that this end 'an oracle higher than Zeno bids us seek' and that 'this end (τέλος) extolled by the best philosophers, to live agreeably to nature' must be understood in the sense of 'walking in the track of right reason and following God' (*Migr.* 128). The Stoic goals of 'moral beauty' (τὸ καλὸν ἀγαθόν) or even the superior goal of 'piety' (εὐσέβεια, *Vit. Ent.* 88) are but the means towards a higher end: God.

In contrast with the multiplicity of τέλη with which the philosophy of his time was confronted, and in contrast with their supreme uncertainty,[241] Philo emphatically states that 'to follow God is ... our τέλος' (*Migr.* 131). This τέλος is worded in many different ways:[242] to seek 'the wisdom of God' (*Heres.* 315), 'to be pleasing to God' (*Abr.* 235), 'to aim at the glory of God (τοῦ θεοῦ τιμή)' (*Spec. Leg.* 1.317), etc. In *Op.* 144 the τέλος of man is most beautifully defined as 'to be fully conformed to God (τὸν θεὸν ἐξομοίωσιν)'.[243] This supreme goal can only be attained by keeping the law of God following the instructions of divine revelation (θεῖα δόγματα).[244] Seeking this right τέλος is what gives meaning to human life (*Sacr.* 21). Man discovers his τέλος because in the law God (through Moses the lawgiver) endeavored to urge man towards the best: 'The Lawgiver who aims at the best must have one end (τέλος) only before him to benefit all whom his work reaches' (*Quod Deus* 61), for 'the lawgiver ... set before himself one task and purpose (ἕν ἔργον καὶ τέλος προέθετο) ... to lead man to love God' (67-69).

The word τέλος appears forty-three times used in connection with ἀρχή in the formula ἀρχὴ καὶ τέλος, in several of its forms as an expression of totality: ἐξ ἀρχῆς ἄχρι τέλους, [245] ἀπ' ἀρχῆς ἄχρι τέλους (*Agr.* 180-81), etc. This phrase should be translated by 'completely' or other adverbial expressions rather than 'from first to last' or similar idioms, which do not fit the real meaning of this expression, since it is very often referred to God[246] or to the philosophical final cause,[247] or used in expressions indicating a metaphorical apex, acme, vortex, or turning point,[248] or in other phrases meaning culmination or fulness.[249]

In about ten instances τέλος occurs in contexts or phrases which seem to denote duration or termination. Half of them are occurrences of prepositional constructions with adverbial import.[250] In most cases the notion of accomplishment may prevail over that of conclusion or cessation. In one instance τέλος seems to be used adverbially in the sense of 'finally' (*Aet.* 36). In *Spec. Leg.* 4.12 there is an occurrence of τέλος used for the 'end of the crops'. The temporal nuance is probably unavoidable. Both the context and other cognate passages dealing with the same topic show that the notion of 'maturity reached' prevails. So in *Leg. All.* 3.249, Philo speaks of the 'standing corn' and compares it with 'gradual advance, since either it is incomplete and is earnestly set on its completeness' (στάχυσι δὲ τὴν προκοπήν, ἐπεὶ καὶ ἑκάτερον ἀτελὲς ἐφιέμενον τοῦ τέλους). That the issue is 'completeness versus incompleteness' and not 'end of a period' is very evident in the opposition ἀτελές–τέλος. In *Vit. Mos.* 1.194 we have a reference to the 'end of a journey' (of the Israelites through the desert), and the question is raised of 'what will be the end (τί τέλος ἔσται) of this long, interminable journey (τῆς ἀνηνύτου καὶ μακρᾶς οὕτως ὁδοῦ)?' But reading the rest of the paragraph one can easily see that the question is not of *time* but of *outcome* or *purpose*.

That for Philo τέλος did not carry any particular terminal connotations is made most evident by his use of the phrase τέλος βίου ('end of life'). This phrase appears many times with the unmistakable meaning of goal, aim, or purpose (*Gig.* 53; *Somn.* 2.107, 142; *Abr.* 230). Only in *Abr.* 230 is τέλος βίου used in connection with death, in the phrase 'the end of everything in life is death' (τέλος τοῦ βίου ἁπάντων . . . τελευτήν). That the reference may also be to 'culmination' seems possible from a parallel passage (*Op.* 103) in which the last of the ten ages of man is described as the age when 'comes the desirable end of life'.[251]

In no reference to 'the τέλος of something' (τέλος plus genitive) does the context allow translation of the phrase in the sense of 'cessation', 'abrogation', 'supercession', etc. On the contrary, most of the τέλος-plus-genitive phrases are expressions of enhancement: thus εὐδαιμονίας τέλος is not the 'cessation' of happiness, but on the contrary 'the supreme happiness',[252] and the τέλος of marriage is not its dissolution, but its object.[253] The same may be said of other similar constructions such as τέλος ἐστιν σοφίας παιδεία where the reference is not to the end or cessation of wisdom, but to 'the height of wisdom' (*Plant.* 168), or τῆς τέχνης ἀφιγμένων τὸ τέλος, where the reference is not to the abrogation of art, but to the attainment of its very summit (*Ebr.* 218). In any case the word τέλος could not have had a basically temporal meaning when it could be equated with 'life' and 'immortality', in phrases like ζωὴν καὶ ἀθανασίαν ἔχουσα τὸ τέλος (*Plant.* 37).

In *Virt.* 15, the 'end' of the instruction (διδασκαλία) and of the given laws (νομοθεσίας) is not their supersession, but their purpose. In the relation of τέλος and law (νόμος) there is a passage in *Migr.* 139 whose wording recalls closely Rom 10.4. After saying that man, 'when he has reached the summit (τὸ τέλος), will render the sum of his tribute (τελειωθείς) to God the consummator (τῷ τελεσφόρῳ θεῷ), Philo, playing on the double meaning of τέλος, says that 'there is a law that the sum is the Lord's' (νόμος γάρ ἐστι τὸ τέλος εἶναι κυρίου).[254] The strong connotations taken by τέλος allowed Philo to identify the τέλος with God's will or purpose, to the point of making a general rule from the phrase that 'the τέλος belongs to God'. In any case, the idea of the cessation of the law, and even less, of its abrogation, is completely alien to Philo.[255] This may be said of other phrases very near to τέλος νόμου. In *Migr.* 143, the phrase τὸ τέλος τῆς ὁδοῦ does not mean at all the 'putting an end' to the way of God, but on the opposite, this is an emphatic way of saying 'the very way'.[256] The phrase τὸ γὰρ τέλος τοῦ λόγου ἀλήθειά ἐστιν[257] cannot be translated in the sense that ἀλήθεια 'ends', 'makes to cease', or 'does away' with λόγος, because, on the contrary, ἀλήθεια is the very essence of the λόγος, as the context makes so clear. It is important to take this use of τέλος into consideration for the interpretation of τέλος νόμου in Rom 10.4, since Paul was Philo's fellow countryman and contemporary.

The Use of τέλος *in Flavius Josephus*

Though our survey of the use of τέλος by Flavius Josephus (AD 37/38-100) is not as thorough as our examination of the usage of Philo and the Pseudepigrapha,[258] the more than forty occurrences that have been analyzed show that there is no significant difference in the usage of τέλος between Josephus and the other Judeo-Hellenistic writers thus far reviewed. It must be said, however, that, in general, Josephus's use is more similar to that of Philo and the Greek Classical authors than to that of the Pseudepigrapha. Josephus seldom uses τέλος in temporal sentences and never in reference to the eschatological end.

Τέλος is used sometimes for 'tax' (*BJ* 2.4), but more commonly for 'the coming to pass',[259] the 'issue' (*Vit.* 154), the 'result' (*Vit.* 196), the 'fulfillment' of a prediction or prophecy,[260] the 'object', aim', or 'goal'.[261] Sometimes prepositional phrases with τέλος are used for the purpose of intensification (*Vit.* 406). The phrase οἱ ἐν τέλει is used for designating 'the influential' or 'those in authority' (*BJ* 1.243; *AJ* 4.171; 14.302), while the comprehensive formula ἀρχὴ καὶ τέλος is used for denoting 'totality,' as for the absolute reality of God (*AJ* 8.280).[262] The construction of τέλος with the verb ἔχειν is used as well for the completion of a work (*AJ* 3.189; 10.58) as for the 'reaching of one's life end' (as a euphemism for 'to die').[263]

As in Philo, and in the Greek language in general, so in Josephus τέλος with genitive has a resultive or purposive meaning (similar to that of a verbal phrase with the verb τελέω), not a terminal one. Thus, in *Vit.* 19 'the end of the war (τοῦ πολέμου τέλος) would be disastrous for us' does not refer to the termination of the hostilities, but to the result or outcome of the conflict. As it has already been said for other occurrences, τέλος with genitive is especially used for indicating the 'fate'. Thus, speaking of the story of Saul, *AJ* 6.47 says that 'the servant who accompanied him told him that there was there a true prophet and counseled that they should go to him, since they would learn from him what had become of the asses (γνώσεσθαι γὰρ παρ' αὐτοῦ τὸ περὶ τῶν ὄνων τέλος'. Here τέλος does not point to the disappearance of the animals or their 'termination' (death), but obviously to their fate. And in *BJ* 5.459 τὸ γὰρ τέλος εἶναι τοῦ θεοῦ has obviously nothing to do with the cessation of God's existence, but with his being able to determine the outcome of any specific situation.[264]

Though there is no specific occurrence in Josephus of the precise phrase τέλος νόμου, there are some instances where νόμος is constructed with the verb τελέω. In all the cases the sentences refer to the 'carrying out' or 'fulfillment' of the law. Thus, in *AJ* 2.193 ὅ τε τοῦ τελεῖν τὴν πέμπτην τῶν καρπῶν νόμος refers to the fulfillment (here the 'payment') of what the law requires (cf. 9.237; 10.72; 11.127; *Ap.* 2.147). In *BJ* 2.495 the verb τελέω is constructed with ἐντολάς, with the evident meaning of 'fulfilling the orders' or 'carrying out the requirements of the law'.[265] When Josephus speaks of 'abrogation' or 'cessation' of laws, he never uses τέλος, τέλειν, or any τέλος cognate.[266] And, of course, all the instances refer to other laws, because Josephus did not contemplate any possibility of the 'cessation' or 'supersession' of the divine Torah.[267] In conclusion, Josephus's use of τέλος with genitive or in phrases similar to τέλος νόμου does not depart from the common one in the Hellenisitc literature of his time. In the same line of thought as Philo and the

Pseudepigrapha, Josephus deals in many instances with the meaning, significance, and purpose of the Jewish laws, a topic about which he often said that he was planning to write a whole book.[268]

The Use of τέλος in the New Testament

The word τέλος appears forty times in the NT.[269] The range of meanings is very similar to those found in the LXX.

To understand the use of τέλος and cognates in the NT it is important to keep in mind the originally dynamic ('teleological') character of this term, especially since—Delling says—'not all the statements can be arranged with lexical certainty. Sometimes where one meaning is more or less sure another may be involved too.'[270] In the non-prepositional use of τέλος (which is the one subject to discussion), the determination of the actual meaning depends on the context.

Τέλος *in prepositional phrases*

Τέλος is used twelve times in prepositional phrases, six of them in the formula εἰς τέλος. Though less frequently than in the LXX, τέλος is also used in the NT in adverbial expressions of totality. In most non-dynamic versions of the Bible, the phrase εἰς τέλος has been literally translated 'to the end' in a quite indiscriminate and unqualified manner, which misleads the reader by its ambiguity. It gives the impression of rendering temporal or eschatological statements, while, in fact, in many instances the point is measure and not time.

In 2 Cor 1.13 the phrase ἕως τέλους ἐπιγνώσεσθε logically refers to a full, complete understanding, rather than to an understanding that goes on up to a certain period of time. Accordingly, it is better translated, as Delling does, by 'wholly and utterly'.[271] In 1 Thess 2.15, ἡ ὀργὴ εἰς τέλος depicts the eschatological wrath of God. In parallelism with the '*full* measure of their sins' (εἰς τὸ ἀναπληρῶσαι αὐτῶν τὰς ἁμαρτίας), the '*full* measure of God's wrath' is the just retribution expected. Τέλος indicates here 'fullness' and could be translated 'to the uttermost'.[272]

In Heb 3.14, the phrase μέχρι τέλους emphasizes the idea of 'absolute and continual confidence'. However, the eschatological import of the context (v. 13) seems to favor the translation of τέλος in v. 14 as referring to the eschatological end. Though this notion may not be alien to τέλος, it is evidently secondary to the key concept of the sentence, which is obviously ὑπόστασις. The 'absolute' confidence will be, of course, a 'confidence which remains until the end'. But again, the point is a certain quality, not time. This notion of fullness or plenitude is also central in the expression ἄχρι τέλους in Heb 6.11 and Rev 2.26.[273] It should be acknowledged, with Delling, that with τέλος in prepositional phrases 'the reference is not linguistically to the apocalyptic end, though materially the still awaited end is or might be in view'.[274]

Since the adverbial construction ἕως τέλους may denote time and degree, in some instances it is difficult to determine which one of the two notions is primarily intended. Thus, in ὃς καὶ βεβαιώσει ὑμᾶς ἕως τέλους ('who will sustain you to the end', 1 Cor 1.8), both notions are possible, and the import of τέλος may be as well a qualification of the verb βεβαιόω[275] as an eschatological indication. In a similar way the phrase ὁ δὲ ὑπομείνας εἰς τέλος ('he who endures to the end') in Matt 10.22, 24.13, and Mark 13.13 may refer as well to the duration of the endurance as to its quality. That the context must decide whether these expressions are to be taken temporarily or qualitatively appears clearly in the two remaining occurrences. In ἵνα μὴ εἰς τέλος ἐρχομένη ὑπωπιάζῃ με (Luke 18.5) τέλος denotes the *continual* plaguing attitude of the oppressed widow[276] rather than the judge's fear of a final act of violence from her. The context calls forth the notion of duration, because the very point of the parable is perseverance, i.e. steadfast (πάντοτε) prayer and enduring (μὴ ἐνκακεῖν) courage (v. 1).

In the phrase εἰς τέλος ἠγάπησεν αὐτούς (John 13.1) which describes the love of Christ for his disciples (in the context of his washing of their feet), τέλος is certainly not temporal. It indicates degree, not time. The text then should be better translated 'he loved them to the uttermost', or 'in full, supreme measure', rather than 'he loved them to the end'.[277] The stress is on the utmost degree of love, not on its duration.

Two times (Rev 21.6 and 22.13)[278] τέλος occurs in the phrase ἡ ἀρχὴ καὶ τὸ τέλος as part of a self-designation of God. The phrase may denote either God's eternity, his absolute majesty, or his being the supreme source (ἀρχή) and final goal (τέλος) of all.[279] The very fact of this expression being used in reference to God rules out any connotations of 'termination'.[280] It must be, therefore, understood as an expression of totality and fullness.

Τέλος is used adverbially in 1 Pet 3.8. For completing a list of admonishments with a 'last and crowning consideration',[281] τέλος is used 'with an element of crescendo'[282] in the adverbial accusative construction τὸ δὲ τέλος, meaning 'finally'[283] or 'to sum up' (NASB). Some scholars include also 1 Cor 15.24 in the adverbial uses of τέλος. But the case is not clear and the question is still debated.[284]

Nominal use of τέλος
The nominal use of τέλος is far more frequent in the NT than in the LXX. Besides three uses for 'tax',[285] τέλος is always used for abstract concepts. Τέλος as *nomen actionis* is especially well attested in Luke 22.37: 'For I tell you that this scripture must be fulfilled (δεῖ τελεσθῆναι) in me, "And he was reckoned with transgressors" [Isa 53.12], for what is written about me has its fulfillment (καὶ γὰρ τὸ περὶ ἐμοῦ τέλος ἔχει)'.[286] That τέλος means here 'fulfillment' is clearly made evident by the context.[287] The expressions δεῖ τελεσθῆναι and τέλος ἔχει are correlative: the OT prophetic prediction (τὸ γεγραμμένον) has come true in present reality (τέλος ἔχει) and the Messiah is being misjudged and treated as a criminal.

In Matt 26.58 the phrase ἰδεῖν τὸ τέλος (without synoptic parallels) points to the 'outcome' or 'issue' of the trial of Jesus. It is not the 'end of Jesus' life' (i.e. his death) which Peter wants to see, but rather 'how things would turn out'.[288] There seems to be general consensus on this meaning. More debated is the meaning of the phrase τέλος κυρίου in Jas 5.11. It has often been incorrectly interpreted as 'the Lord's death'.[289] Recently the discussion turns around two main positions: τέλος as 'outcome' or as 'aim', 'purpose'.[290] For Du Plessis, the point of the text is 'the object or purpose of God's dealing with Job' (pp. 126-28). Dibelius hesitates between 'purpose' and 'outcome'.[291] The context of Rom 6.21-22 makes clear that the meaning of τέλος here is 'fate' or 'result'.[292]

There are other passages where τέλος is given its teleological meaning of 'aim', 'goal', or 'purpose'. So, in 1 Tim 1.5 the apodictic statement τὸ τέλος τῆς παραγγελίας ἐστιν ἀγάπη means that love is the 'end, goal, aim, object, purpose, etc.' of the Christian instruction. The teleological meaning of τέλος is required and emphasized by 1.3 (ἵνα παραγγείλῃς). A similar statement, but with the word τέλος substituted by the often synonymous πλήρωμα, is found in Rom 13.8: πλήρωμα οὖν νόμου ἡ ἀγάπη ('love is the fulfillment of the law').[293]

The phrase εἰς οὓς τὰ τέλη τῶν αἰώνων in 1 Cor 10.11 has been much discussed. Paul warns the Corinthians against immorality using as an example and reason for his warning the history of the experiences of Israel, a history written especially for their instruction, πρὸς νουθεσίαν ἡμῶν εἰς οὓς τὰ τέλη τῶν αἰώνων κατήντηκεν. This enigmatic phrase has been commonly interpreted as referring to 'the eschatological end'.[294] The problem with this interpretation is that 1 Cor 10.11 would be the only occurrence of the plural τέλη with this meaning. Moreover, the context is not eschatological and the parallel passages have ἐπ' ἐσχάτου (Heb 1.2) and ἐπὶ συντελείᾳ (Heb 9.26), not τέλη. Others translate τέλη as 'inheritance', 'the revenues of the ages'. Du Plessis rendered this verse as follows: 'Now they suffered these misfortunes by way of warning, but we benefit from their history, because we are heir of the wealth of the ages' (p. 123). M.M. Bogle, building his argumentation on the sacramental character of the context, translated τέλος by 'mystery' and proposed the rendering: 'to whom the eternal mysteries have come down' or 'who are the heirs of the Mysteries of the Ages'.[295] Delling rejected Bogle's interpretation, arguing that τέλος, in spite of its plural form, retains its essential meaning and that, therefore, the phrase needs to be understood as 'the aims of the times', because the prominent times of Israel's exodus (vv. 1-10) find their fulfillment in the Christ event,[296] giving thus to τέλος a certain typological or prospective import. Delling included also 1 Pet 1.9 in this group. In the light of its context, τὸ τέλος τῆς πίστεως σωτηρίαν ψυχῶν makes, indeed, better sense if τέλος is translated 'object' than if it is translated 'outcome'.[297]

In six instances τέλος is used for designating the notions of 'destiny' or 'fate' in the sense of the final result or outcome of human decision. In 1 Pet 4.17 there is an unanswered question concerning the τέλος 'of those who do not obey the gospel of God'. In 2 Cor 11.15 it is said that τὸ τέλος ἔσται κατὰ τὰ ἔργα αὐτῶν ('the end [of Satan's servants] will be according to their deeds'). In Heb 6.8, as a metaphor of the final destruction of the wicked, it is said that the final fate (τέλος) of the land which 'bears thorns and thistles' is 'to be burned'. In Phil 3.19 'the τέλος of the enemies of the cross of Christ' is described as 'destruction' (ἀπώλεια).[298] In Rom 6.21-22 the eschatological result of man's decision, or man's final destiny, is also designated by τέλος. So, two different kinds of τέλη are described: for some it will be 'death' (τέλος ἐκείνων θάνατος, v. 21), while for others it will be 'eternal life' (τὸ δὲ τέλος ζωὴν αἰώνιον, v. 22).

In the apocalyptic discourse τέλος is used three times for designating the eschatological end, in the phrases ἀλλ' οὔπω [ἐστὶν] τὸ τέλος ('but the end is not yet', Matt 24.6 and Mark 13.7) and καὶ τότε ἥξει τὸ τέλος ('and then the end will come', Matt 24.14). In 1 Pet 4.7 τέλος is also used for the *eschaton* in the phrase πάντων δὲ τὸ τέλος ἤγγικεν ('the end of all things is at hand').[299] Notice that τέλος is used here in a way similar to the analogous expression συντέλεια τοῦ αἰῶνος.[300] Because of its dynamic, goal-directed character τέλος could be chosen for designating the final consummation, the definitive completion, and realization of God's purpose. The eschatological τέλος is not understood simply as a temporal cessation, but, as Schippers says, 'it is the consummating conclusion of a dynamic process' (p. 65).

In 2 Cor 3.13 τέλος is most probably used in a sense very near to that of 'summit', 'culmination', 'climax', etc., which was so common in the Hellenistic literature contemporary with Paul. The text is generally translated in the sense that Moses 'put a veil over his face so that the Israelites might not see the end of the fading splendor'. Although this temporal interpretation of τὸ τέλος τοῦ καταργουμένου is supported by the majority of commentators,[301] it is very problematic. It not only works on the assumption that καταργουμένου refers to δόξα, which is grammatically questionable,[302] but it seems to imply that the purpose of the veil was to prevent the Israelites from discovering the temporary nature of the Mosaic economy, which is quite the opposite of what Paul says in the context, where his main charge against the Jews is precisely that they misunderstood the nature of τοῦ καταργουμένου, regarding as ultimate and permanent what was preparatory and provisional.[303] Jean Héring gives to τέλος the meaning of 'goal',[304] which would imply that Moses was pictured by Paul as trying to conceal the true object of τοῦ καταργουμένου. The translation proposed by the *Knox Bible* ('the *features* of the old order') does not seem to resolve the problems of the passage either. A better solution would be to give to the verb ἀτενίζω its proper meaning, which is not merely 'to see' but 'to keep the eyes fixed',[305] and to translate τέλος in its most common meaning in Hellenistic Greek. Then, the object of the veil, according to 2 Cor 3, would be that the Israelites 'should not strain their eyes on *the crown* of a passing glory',[306] or even better, that they did not keep on contemplating as *the supreme reality* something which was destined to be superseded.

In spite of all, some have contended that the basic feature of the use of τέλος in the NT is its character of termination. Thus Abbott-Smith speaks of the 'termination or limit . . . of a period of time',[307] and Robinson of the 'end, completion, termination generally of time and condition' (p. 715). However, the texts adduced for proving that τέλος means 'termination' are Luke 1.33; Mark 3.26; Heb 7.3; 1 Cor 10.11; 2 Cor 3.13; 1 Pet 4.7; and Rom 10.4.[308] Of these seven references, three have already been discussed here (1 Cor 10.11; 2 Cor 3.13; and 1 Pet 4.7) and found not to have a terminal import. Omitting Rom 10.4, which is the object of the present study, only three references remain which are definitely temporal. The strange construction τῆς βασιλείας αὐτοῦ οὐκ ἐστιν τέλος in Luke 1.33 ('of his kingdom there is no end') is used for expressing eternity.[309] Christ's future kingdom will exist forever. The idea of everlasting duration is emphasized by the two parallel statements: καὶ βασιλεύσει ἐπὶ τὸν οἶκον Ἰακὼβ εἰς τοὺς αἰῶνας and καὶ τῆς βασιλείας αὐτοῦ οὐκ ἔσται τέλος. This saying has its counterpart in Mark 3.26, where it is said that 'if Satan has risen up against himself and is divided, he cannot stand, but is coming to an end' (τέλος ἔχει). Although the phrase τέλος ἔχειν usually means 'to be fulfilled', it seems evident that it is used here denoting 'cessation' or 'termination'. Heb 7.3 offers another clear use of temporal τέλος. Melchizedek is described μήτε ἀρχὴν ἡμερῶν μήτε ζωῆς τέλος ἔχων, i.e. as having 'neither beginning of days nor end of life'. Whatever may be the exact significance of this double statement,[310] it obviously refers by analogy to Christ's eternal priesthood,[311] and it must therefore be concluded that the negation of τέλος is used for expressing the notion of eternity.[312] These passages show that there is an unquestionable use of τέλος in the NT as 'termination', but compared with other uses it is far from being the prevailing one.

Cognates of τέλος

The words of the τέλος group occur in the NT about 160 times.[313] Excluding τέλος (forty occurrences), the term most frequently used is the verb τελέω (twenty-eight times). Its meaning is essentially the same as the one found outside the Bible. As Du Plessis says, 'The idea embodied in the verb is dynamic activity in accordance with a τέλος' (p. 130). The intrinsic character of the verb is particularly evident in the phrase τὸν δρόμον τετέλεκα (2 Tim 4.7), 'I have finished the race'. Thus, τελέω is used for 'to achieve one's object', as well for 'to gratify the desires of the flesh' (Gal 5.16), as for 'to make perfect' the power of Christ in the weakness of the apostle (2 Cor 12.9).[314] Accordingly τελέω is used for 'to carry out' or 'perform' religious obligations (Luke 2.39), or legal indictments, hence 'to pay' (Matt 17.24; Rom 13.6). More often τελέω means 'to put into effect, to accomplish, to fulfill [divine] designs'.[315] In the gospel of Matthew it is used five times for 'to conclude' (7.28; 11.1; 13.53; 19.1; 26.1)[316] and once for 'to finish' (10.23).[317] In Rev 15.1 it means 'to fill up' (the wrath of God).

The nouns συντέλεια and τελείωσις overlap some of the basic meanings of τέλος. The first appears only seven times in the N1, always in eschatological sayings, namely, in the phrase συντέλεια [τοῦ] αἰῶνος[318] (or τῶν αἰόνων in Heb 9.26), which seems to be the favorite expression in Matthew for 'the close of the age', 'the end of the age' (NASB) or 'the end of the world' (JB).[319] Τελείωσις is used only twice in the NT. In Luke 1.45, it refers to the 'fulfillment' ('execution' or 'actualization') of the words of the angel in the experience of Mary. In Heb 7.11 it refers to the 'perfection' or 'qualification for the cultus'[320] required of the Levitical priests. The NT uses several other terms belonging to the semantic field of τέλος, but their survey would be irrelevant to the object of the present study.

More relevant seems to be the fact that the phrase τελεῖν τὸν νόμον in its only two occurrences in the NT means 'to keep the law' or 'to carry out the demands of the law'.[321] Thus, Rom 2.27 reads: 'Then those who are physically uncircumcised, but keep the law (τὸν νόμον τελοῦσα) will condemn you who have the written code and circumcision but break the law'. The meaning of τὸν νόμον τελοῦσα is unmistakably related to 'keeping' the law, since it is used in parallel with τὸν νόμον φυλάσσῃ ('if he keeps the precepts of the law', v. 26). The same use is evident in Jas 2.8, where it is said that 'if you really fulfill the royal law (εἰ μέντοι νόμον τελεῖτε βασιλικόν), according to the Scripture, "You shall love your neighbour as yourself", you do well'. If τέλος and τελέω have the same basic semantic import, the meaning of τέλος νόμου in a nominal phrase would not be essentially different from that of τελεῖν νόμον in a similar verbal phrase.

Τέλος *with genitive*

Of forty occurrences in the NT, thirteen times τέλος is constructed with a noun in genitive.[322] As has already been shown, in most of the instances this construction is used to indicate the final lot, the ultimate fate of someone or something.[323] In four other instances the construction is grammatically identical to that of Rom 10.4. The word order is the following:

	Predicate formed by τέλος + a noun in genitive	Verb εἰμι (or ellipsis)	Subject (a noun in nominative)
Rom. 10.4	τέλος γὰρ νόμου		Χριστὸς
Rom. 6.21	τὸ γάρ τέλος ἐκείνων		θάνατος
Rom. 6.22	τὸ δὲ τέλος		ζωὴν αἰώνιον
1 Tim.1.5	τὸ δὲ τέλος τῆς παραγγελίας ἐστιν		ἀγάπη
1 Pet 1.9	τὸ τέλος τῆς πίστεως		σωτηρίαν

It is generally agreed that in Rom 6.21, 22, 1 Tim 1.5, and 1 Pet 1.9 τέλος has a teleological, directional, or consecutive meaning. Thus, Rom 6.21, 22 is translated 'the outcome of those things is death . . . / eternal life' (NASB, in the sense that those things lead to death/eternal life); 1 Tim 1.5 is translated 'the aim of our charge is love' (in the sense that our instruction leads to love);[324] and 1 Pet 1.9 is translated 'the outcome of your faith is salvation' (in the sense that our faith leads to salvation). However, this meaning is refused to Rom 10.4. It would seem reasonable that—unless there is sufficient evidence to the contrary—the normal meaning of this type of construction should be kept in the translation of Rom 10.4 also.

The Use of τέλος in Paul

It has been argued that Paul's use of τέλος varies from normal Greek usage in that for him τέλος consistently means *end* in the temporal sense of 'termination'.[325] But a closer investigation of the Pauline usages shows that the most vigorous proponents of this thesis have been considerably selective in their use of the Pauline evidence. For example, Luz makes his case by citing only three (1 Cor 10.11; 15.25; Phil 3.19) of the thirteen uses of τέλος in the Pauline writings.[326] And J. Murray cites seven, but takes good care to omit precisely the five uses that challenge his theory.[327]

A review of the thirteen uses of τέλος in the Pauline writings shows the following picture: (1) Twice (in Rom 13.7) τέλος means 'tax' or 'custom'; (2) two more times it is used in an adverbial phrase meaning 'fully', 'completely' (2 Cor 11.13; 1 Thess 2.16); (3) three times (1 Cor 1.8; 10.11; 15.24) τέλος seems to refer to the eschatological end; (4) two times τέλος means 'final destiny' (2 Cor 11.15; Phil

3.19); and (5) five times τέλος seems to have a teleological meaning (Rom 6.21, 22; 10.4; 2 Cor 3.13; 1 Tim 1.5),[328] although Rom 10.4 and 2 Cor 3.13 are still much discussed. It is remarkable, and perhaps not without significance, that three of these five 'teleological' references occur in Romans, and that Rom 10.4 presents—as it has been shown—almost the same grammatical construction as 1 Tim 1.5, an occurrence unanimously interpreted in a teleological way. This indicates that the alleged Pauline 'consistent definition of τέλος as temporal end' turns out to represent just three to five instances out of thirteen of Paul's total usages, with the particularity that all the 'temporal' instances appear in eschatological contexts.

In view of these facts it seems safer to conclude that these 'terminal' cases occurring in eschatological contexts, represent 'the Pauline exception to normal Greek use rather than the normative Pauline use which legitimizes a consistent break with conventional use'.[329] Consequently, the evidence on the Pauline use of τέλος seems to shift the burden of proof from the teleological interpretation—which stands in consistency with Hellenistic Greek—to the temporal-terminal interpretation—which stands in discontinuity with normal use. So, unless the context of Rom 10.4 clearly requires a non-teleological understanding of τέλος it would seem more logical to assume a normal Greek meaning.

Summary

The results of the present survey on the meanings and uses of τέλος support the following conclusions:

1.   Τέλος is a dynamic, polysemic word whose precise semantic import in the phrase depends on the concrete context, but whose basic connotations are primarily directive, purposive, and completive, not temporal.

2.   Τέλος with genitive is generally used in expressions indicating result, purpose, outcome, and fate, not termination.

3.   Τέλος νόμου and related expressions are indicative of the purpose, fulfillment, or object of the law, not of its abrogation.

4.   The use of τέλος in the LXX and the NT does not depart essentially from the secular use. However, τέλος is used sometimes in eschatological contexts.

5.   Though τέλος is sometimes used in biblical literature in temporal and eschatological expressions, the particular view of time,

history, and divine revelation in biblical theology favors an understanding of τέλος in which the prevailing connotations are more teleological than terminal.

6. Around the NT era, the teleological questions were very much alive in the Hellenistic world, and τέλος was especially used for designating the sum, the final cause, the goal, the purpose, the decisive factor, or the *summum bonum*.

7. Jewish Hellenistic literature witnesses to the existence of an important interest in the question of the purpose and object of the Torah law, of which Paul was probably aware.

8. The teleological use of τέλος is well attested in the NT in general and in the Pauline writings in particular.

9. In all the NT occurrences of phrases having the same grammatical structure as Rom 10.4, τέλος is unanimously translated in a teleological way.

In conclusion, the use of τέλος in biblical and cognate literature should be considered as a controlling criterion for understanding the phrase τέλος νόμου. Semantics, grammar, and literature strongly favor a teleological interpretation of this phrase. Yet, the very meaning of τέλος in Rom 10.4 has to be ascertained from the study of its context. This is the task of Chapter 3.

Chapter 3

AN EXEGETICAL APPROACH
TO THE MEANING OF ROMANS 10.4

The exegesis of Rom 10.4 is a highly problematic task. The context of
this passage (namely, Rom 9–11, and more specifically, 9.30–10.21)
has been customarily treated (or avoided) as one of the most difficult
and obscure sections in Romans.[1] It is not surprising, then, to find
that the interpretation of this section has tended to be determined—
as has been shown in Chapter 1—more by theological convictions
than by objective criteria, or, in the words of W.S. Campbell, 'more
by the understanding of Pauline theology that one brings to it than
by what the text actually says'.[2] It seems as if the concern to keep the
interpretation of Rom 10.4 in harmony with Paul's law theology, as it
appears elsewhere in his writings, has prevailed over the duty of
interpreting the text as it stands.

The present exegetical approach begins with the hypothesis that
Rom 10.4 and its immediate context is better understood within its
larger context in Romans than through Paul's law statements in
other epistles (especially Galatians). References to other Pauline
passages are made whenever necessary but without using them *prima
facie* to decide the meaning of Rom 10.4 and its context. Since the
purpose of the present undertaking is to determine the fundamental
notion which Paul intended to express by τέλος in the phrase τέλος
νόμου Χριστός to describe the relationship between Christ and the
law, the meaning of νόμος is dealt with especially.[3] The other
theological themes of the passage are contemplated only insofar as
they shed light on the relation between τέλος, νόμος, and Χριστός.

Contextual Setting: Romans 9–11

Although Rom 10.4 sounds like a dictum, it is not an isolated saying.
Besides the logical connections of thought, this text is so closely tied

to its context that even its syntactical construction compels us to look at the context for clarification.[4]

There is a certain disagreement in contemporary scholarship concerning the basic structure of Romans.[5] The opinions vary between two,[6] three,[7] and four main divisions. But it is unanimously agreed that chs. 9–11 form a literary unit within the epistle. Since Rom 9–11 is a literary unit with its own introduction (9.1-5) and conclusion (11.33-36), clearly separated from what precedes and follows,[9] the meaning of 10.4 has to be found within the context of this main section.

So much has been said on the occasion of Romans that such a debated question need not be dealt with here.[10] Even the task of reconstructing the *Sitz im Leben* of Rom 9–11 goes beyond the scope of the present study.[11] Examination of the formal and thematic aspects of this section shows, however, that its argument might be related to the occasion of Romans, and therefore it is hermeneutically more appropriate to approach it as a part of a situational document rather than as a timeless theological treatise.[12] At the same time, it seems also methodologically preferable to attribute the difficulties of Rom 9–11 more to our ignorance of its background than to the inconsistencies of Paul's thought.[13] In any case, some knowledge of Paul's particular concerns in writing this section and the issues at stake is needed for a proper understanding of the passage.

It has been argued that Paul wrote Rom 9–11 against his 'Jewish opponents',[14] or against 'his enemies the Jewish Christians',[15] but a careful reading shows that 'the thrust of Paul's argument is most certainly in the opposite direction'.[16] Not only are the intended recipients not Jews, but Paul explicitly says that he is addressing *Gentile* Christians (11.13, 17-28; cf. 1.5-6, 13-16; 6.19; 14.4, 10; 15.15-18). However, it is evident that the argument of Rom 9–11 (and even the whole epistle) is presented somehow in dialogue with the Jews.[17]

The analysis of these two facts seems to favor the hypothesis that Romans is addressed to a mixed congregation formed by a majority of Gentile Christians (1.5-6) and a minority of Christian Jews[18] confronted with an unspecified 'Jewish problem'. This particular composition and situation of the Roman church would help to explain why Rom 9–11, being a section addressed to a predominantly Gentile Christian community, deals with the question of Israel, and why can it at the same time exalt the success of the Gentile mission against Israel's failure while reaffirming the priority and election of Israel in a manner which salvages Israel's role in salvation history.[19]

Among the circumstances which contributed to Paul's writing of Romans he mentions the preparation of his visit to Rome in his projected mission to Spain (15.16-29) and his asking for support in his imminent trip to Jerusalem with the collection (15.25-28). The situation and problems of the Roman church might also have something to do with the object of the epistle.[20] It would be hard to prove the relevance of the first factor for our understanding of Rom 9–11.[21] The remaining two, however, deserve serious consideration. Some passages in Rom 9–11 give the impression of having been written to check a trend of anti-Jewish sentiments within the church. Paul's severe rebukes against the Gentile believers vis-à-vis the Jews—the Gentiles are proud (11.20); the latecomers (11.24), the undeserving branches (11.17-18), etc.—and his repeated expressions in favor of the salvation of the Jews (9.1-5; 10.1-2; 11.1-2, 11, 24-28) seem to point to a concrete 'Jewish concern' in the background.[22] Even if that concern did not imply the existence of a strong anti-Jewish polemic in the Roman church, the very existence of a mixed community formed by a majority of Gentile Christians would necessarily have raised some problems in Paul's time. The issues treated in Rom 9–11, such as, Why has Israel rejected the Messiah? (9.30-33; 10.11-21); Have God's promises to Israel failed? (9.6); Has God changed his designs vis-à-vis Israel? (11.25-29); Does Israel's rejection of Christ imply God's rejection of Israel? (11.1-2), etc., were essential to 'the Jewish question' in the early church.[23] Rom 11 hints at the existence of tensions produced by Gentile Christians treating the Jews with despite and disdain as if they had been rejected by God (vv. 1-14), and as if the Gentile Christians had taken their place as the people of God (vv. 13, 17-25; cf. 14.15; 15.1).

Another factor which Paul implicitly relates with the occasion of Romans is his concern 'that the offering of the Gentiles may be acceptable' (15.16) to the church of Jerusalem. The relation between Paul's writing of Romans and the question of the collection is still not clear. How much the Roman church could do to help Paul get a favorable reception in Jerusalem is difficult to know. The fact is that Paul tries to involve the recipients of Romans as much as possible with the Jerusalem enterprise (15.30-31). If the collection was a symbol of the unity of Jewish and Gentile Christians within a single people of God, Rom 9–11 played an important role in the argument

prepared by Paul in advance of his final visit to Jerusalem and strikes
the reader as a significant example of what N.A. Dahl calls 'missionary
theology'.[27] Several details in this section betray Paul's missionary
concern. The apostle develops his theological exposition on the fate
of Israel in an ongoing dialogue with—as it seems—the Gentile
members of the church, reminding them of their own specific place
within the divine economy, of what God has granted and promised to
them (9.24-26, 30), and therefore, of what he can also expect from
them (11.11-15). Paul warns them against misunderstandings of their
actual position and role in the church of Christ (11.17-24), and
against anything that might threaten the unity which must reign
between the members of the new people of God (10.21; 11.1-2, 25-
32). Out of all the doctrinal body of the epistle, here is the place
where Paul most clearly presents himself both as apostle to the
Gentiles and intercessor for Israel.[28] Nowhere else is the paraenesis
found so organically related to the theological argument of the
epistle.[29] In this section Paul sets the theological perspective for
solving the question of the relationship between the mixed Christian
community and Israel. Paul deals with this question, trying to bring
unity and love where he sees a threat of division and discord. And he
does it not as a 'Jew', as Michel argued,[30] but, as Osterreicher put it,
'as an apostle whose love is not bounded, whose love encompasses
the Church *and* Israel'.[31] Therefore, Rom 9–11 should be approached,
as G. Eichholz suggests 'nicht als primär israelkritisch sondern als
primär kirchenkritisch',[32] keeping in mind its profound missionary
concern.

The theme of Romans 9–11

The determination of the concrete issue at stake in Rom 9–11 has
been subject of much discussion.[33] This section has traditionally
been approached either as a perplexing theodicy on the doctrine of
predestination[34] somehow unrelated with the rest of the epistle, or
by comparison with Rom 1–8 as a section of secondary interest, a
mere appendix to a famous tractate on the doctrie of justification,[35]
or even as an anti-Jewish treatise.[36]

Only neglect of the formal composition and contextual setting of
Rom 9–11 has allowed such issues to dominate the discussion of this
section, and obscured the identity of its proper theme.

In recent times, however, Rom 9–11 has attracted renewed attention,
and valuable efforts have been made to interpret this section in its

own right.[37] There is today a growing agreement on the importance of Rom 9–11 for the proper understanding of Romans as a whole.[38] Moreover, Rom 9–11 is being considered by some as the climax of the letter,[39] 'the keystone of Paul's theology',[40] and even 'the key to the understanding of the New Testament',[41] and used to stress the continuity between the church and Israel,[42] as a bridge to Judaism.

A careful exegesis of Rom 9–11 shows that the question of the nature or constitution of the new people of God is central to this section.[43] The fact that the majority of the Christian converts were Gentiles, and the fact that the majority of the Jews had rejected Christ raised questions in the minds of Christian Jews and Gentiles about the very raison d'être of Israel and about the trustworthiness of God's word.[44] Two main questions dominate the thought of Rom 9–11: (1) How can the Torah be true since it states the election of Israel? ('It is not as though the word of God has failed', 9.6); and (2) How can Israel be saved since it has rejected Christ? ('Has God rejected his people?', 11.1).[45] In both questions the issue at stake is the faithfulness of God.[46]

This issue is related in Rom 9–11 to the question of 'election' (ἐκλογή). However, this is not the election of individuals to eternal salvation, but the election of communities to be God's people on earth, that is, the election 'of a chosen body to especial conditions of knowledge and responsibility'.[48] As God *once* chose Israel to bless through it all nations, *now* he has chosen the Church, formed mainly by Gentiles to bless through it all nations, including Israel. Election is, then, presented by Paul as a free and creative act of God's wisdom and power (9.16-24; 11.25-36) so that not only is the unbelief of the Jews being used by God for a wider belief of the Gentiles (11.11-14), but even more, the belief of the Gentiles will finally work for the ultimate return of Israel (11.11). This apparent reversal of roles is presented as just a phase of God's mysterious plan of salvation (11.29-36), for God always achieves his purposes (9.6; 11.29) and his final aim is salvation for all (11.25-26).[49] In Rom 9–11 Paul explains to a mainly Gentile church that Israel's rejection of Christ does not affect God's righteousness or God's election of Israel.[50] On the contrary, it makes more evident that God is faithful to his promises. For, on the one hand, the righteousness of God is creating the new people of God in which there is no distinction between Jews and Gentiles (10.8-12; cf. 1.16-17; 3.21-22), as intended in the Scripture (9.24-26; 10.19-20); and on the other hand the fidelity of God to his election plan is being manifested in the remnant (9.27-29; 11.5-7). The doctrine of justification as presented by Paul in chs. 1–8 (3.21-31) is also an essential and decisive component of Paul's theological argument in chs. 9–11: While election is a responsibility which only depends on God's choice (9.26-33), acceptance within the people of God is available to all, Jews and Gentiles, on the sole basis of faith in Christ (10.8-13).[51] This concept of righteousness is the basis for Paul's theology of mission. By approaching the question of the 'righteousness of God' in Rom 9–11 not as something which affects only the individual but as something which also has corporate and social relevance,[52] Paul emphasizes the universal scope of the gospel, showing that acceptance of Christ is not only the solution to the 'Israel question' but also Israel's only hope for salvation. For it belongs to the heart of the gospel that God shows no partiality (10.11-13). He has a single aim for all, and this is salvation (11.25-32), and a single way, and this is Jesus Christ (10.9-13). Therefore— and here comes the practical application of Paul's doctrine—the Gentile Christians, who call themselves God's people, should not create an ethnic separation which God rejects. With regard to this concept of equality before God,[53] Paul elaborates his answer both to the question of 'the rejection of Israel' and the question of the faithfulness of God's word.[54] If Jews and Gentiles are equal before God (10.12), God cannot reject the Jews (11.1) and accept the Gentiles (9.30) but shows mercy to all (11.30-32). So, although Israel has rejected Christ, the last and greatest gift of God to his people (9.4-5), God remains faithful to his word. Election is not reversed by human decision making (11.28-29). The same mercy of God, who once called Israel (9.5-6) and now has also called the Gentiles (9.25, 26, 30; 10.19-20) to be his people, will not cease to call Israel to conversion (10.21; 11.1-2, 11-12) 'until the πλήρωμα of Gentiles come in' (11.25) and 'πᾶς Israel will be saved' (11.26), 'for the gifts and the κλῆσις of God are irrevocable' (11.29). Hereby Paul urges the Roman church to share God's and Paul's concern (9.2-3; 10.1; 11.1-2, 13-14) and work for the conversion of the Jews as well as for the conversion of the Gentiles.

Closely related to the issue of God's faithfulness to Israel in Rom 9–11 is the issue of God's faithfulness to his word. By means of numerous references to the Scriptures Paul endeavors to show that acceptance of Christ is neither betrayal of Judaism nor rejection of Torah but rather faithfulness to God's word (10.8-12).[55] For the gospel does not mean the failure of God's promises to Israel but rather their fulfillment (10.9-13; 11.25-26). In spite of a perplexing and apparently discontinuous salvation history, there is a design in God's salvific plan (11.25-29). God has not failed but has been faithful to his word (9.6). The failure is Israel's and, in spite of its gravity, it is not an obstacle to God's purpose of salvation (11.11-12).

The way Paul treats Scripture and the law in Romans seems to indicate that he wanted, at least *en passant*, to correct certain impressions that the Torah had a purely negative place in salvation history, and that the coming of Christ had definitively done away with it (3.31; 7.7; 9.32–10.13). Paul seems to address in Romans a twofold problem: (1) anti-Judaism—hence his insistence on his concern for the salvation of Israel: he has not turned his back on his people (9.1-5; 10.1; 11.1), on the contrary, salvation for Israel is the ultimate goal toward which he is working even as an apostle of the Gentiles (11.11-26); and (2) antinomianism—hence his efforts to oppose 'Marcionite' ideas (3.31; 7.7-14), to refute the pretexts for Christians continuing to sin (chs. 6–7), and to exalt the holiness of the law and its relation to the gospel (10.6-13).[56] Only if Paul could present his gospel as the outcome and fulfillment of the hopes and Torah of Israel could he adequately refute the charges of the Jewish Christians (of Jerusalem?) and the arguments of Gentile Christians, which seemed to contain an incipient 'Marcionism', and prove that he was neither an antimonian nor an apostate from Judaism.[57]

If this brief analysis is correct and the issues mentioned are really the thrust of the passage it follows that Rom 9–11 is not intended to solve the 'law-gospel' question, but a problem (both of Paul's audience and of Paul himself) having to do more with ecclesiology and mission than with anything else—a problem which is not at all peripheral to Romans but central to the epistle,[58] in which Paul has been able to integrate the universality of the gospel and the peculiarity of Israel.

Sequence of thought and literary features
One must confess that at first reading Paul's sequence of thought in Rom 9–11 is not easy to follow. Paul seems to jump easily from one idea to another by means of verbal and conceptual connections established according to patterns of relationship which are not always immediately discernible.[59] The exegete's task would be much easier if one could enter into the 'mental atmosphere' of Paul, into his

very categories of thought. But perhaps an examination of the particular features of Paul's style will help to disclose the underlying structure of this section and the particular patterns of thought which has produced it.

It has been said that the antithesis is the principal rhetorical device employed by Paul.[60] The apostle shows, in fact, a clear predilection for expressing his ideas by pairs, putting against each other two antithetical concepts, as if his natural thought always centered around two poles, and as if it could only express itself in antithetical form.[61] This dialectical tension is particularly perceived in Rom 9–11. Paul opposes 'the children of the flesh' to 'the children of the promise' (9.8), 'Esau' to 'Jacob' (9.10-13), 'those who were not my people' to 'my people' (9.25). Every step in the argumentation is expounded through a new contrast, such as 'faith'/'works' (9.32), 'God's righteousness'/'their own (righteousness)' (10.3); 'enemies'/'beloved' (11.28) πότε/νῦν (11.30), etc. By means of a series of paradoxical statements, Paul attempts to unfold the mysteriousness of God's saving design through the troublesome polarity of Jewish existence: thus, 'not all who are descended from Israel belong to Israel' (9.6), and 'not all are children of Abraham because they are his descendants' (9.7); 'Gentiles who did not pursue righteousness attained righteousness' (9.30) while 'Israel pursuing the Law did not reach the Law' (9.31), 'Israel has stumbled (9.32) and yet has not fallen' (11.11), etc. These literary features warn the exegete against interpreting any 'extreme' statement in isolation from its context, as an absolute and exclusive 'truth', and against considering as antithetical realities what might merely be contrasting rhetorical devices.[62]

Although the basic pattern of Pauline thought has been sometimes reduced to 'antithesis'[63] and sometimes to 'parallelism',[64] a careful study of Rom 9–11 shows that it is more complex than just one or the other: parallelism would imply simple repetition and antithesis would suggest contradiction. Oscillation seems better to define Paul's procedure, which, according to Collins, consists in 'moving between two poles . . . back and forth and back again'.[65] Since in Rom 9–11 Paul's argument advances in successive 'waves' or restatements,[66] in order to have the whole picture of what Paul says on one point, one needs to look constantly back and forth. When his thought has to be summarized or systematized, one cannot proceed by simply grouping 'verses' or 'passages' but by grasping whole 'themes' from the whole context.[67] Precisely because Paul does not lose sight of his goal, the programmatic statements at the beginning of his exposition must always be kept in mind (9.6; cf. 1.16-17; 3.21-31). Each particular stage in the argument 'looks before and after', and thus it finds its meaning only with reference to the whole. The result, as appears in chs. 9–11, is never systematic, but neither is it fragmentary. Paul's successive insights and flashes are deeply interwoven by an underlying thread. To isolate any of the particular statements would mean to take the risk of seriously misinterpreting it.[68]

Paul's synthetic and holistic approach, which seems to have in mind from the beginning the whole argument to be exposed, and Paul's habit of always coming back to the point of departure are clearly discerned in his predilection for building his most elaborate constructions according to chiastic structures (cf. 10.9-10).[69] Since the central idea comes at the vortex of the chiasmus, the determination of the structure of Rom 9–11 may prove extremely revealing for the understanding of Paul's intention.[70] It should not be overlooked that in a unit elaborated in the form of a chiasm its message is easily distorted when one section is isolated from the rest.

Probably the most evident feature of Paul's rhetoric is his dialectical argumentation.[71] In Rom 9–11—as almost anywhere else—Paul expresses this thought by means of contrasting two opposite conceptions, and resolving then the tension either by an *argumentum a fortiori*,[72] a proof from Scripture, or a simple statement of fact. His way of developing an argument follows a generally consistent pattern. Starting from a concrete question (9.6a), Paul immediately gives the general principles governing the entire discussion (9.6b-7). Then he presents the conflicting views. Once he has shed light on the subject by referring to Scripture (9.7b, 9, 12, etc.), he descends again to the level of facts, exposes their implications, and again returns to his point of departure[73] (9.8, 14, 16, etc.). This dialectical procedure is what gives such a crushing force to his logic, but at the same time, this is what makes interpreting Paul such a risky enterprise: one might take as the final product of his reasoning that which is still a simple step (or a partial aspect) of the whole argument. It is then very important to determine the literary boundaries of the context concerned and always to interpret any verse in the light of the whole context.

The epistolary character of Romans is more evident in chs. 9–11 than in the whole section from 1.17 to 8.39.[74] Paul addresses his audience with interjections and personal expressions emotionally involved: in 9.1-3 Paul tells the Romans his feelings of sorrow for Israel; in 10.1 he calls them 'brethren' and confesses his intercessory prayers on behalf of his people; in 11.13 he addresses only one part (probably the majority) of his audience: 'Now I am speaking to you, Gentiles'. More often than elsewhere in Paul's writings, in Rom 9–11 he ascribes to an imaginary interlocutor (9.20; 10.1; 11.13, 25) a series of objections and false conclusions (9.14, 19; 10.18-20; 11.1-2, 4, 7, 11, 19-24) in a way which has many points in common with the Hellenistic diatribe, as it has already been noted.[75] By means of a series of questions and answers (9.14, 30; 10.14, 15, 18, 19; 11.1, 2, 4, 7, 15),[76] Paul treats some of the issues which perplexed his audience.

The argument looks more complicated than it is, because Paul, at various points, leaves his topic in order to refute objections (9.14, 18, 19-24; 10.14-15, 16-19; 11.1), clarify presuppositions (9.6-8), or take up special problems (9.30; 10.1; 11.11) directly related to the main theme by breaking for a while his flow of thought. However, when one looks Paul's structuring of the material and takes into consideration Paul's features of style in this section—namely, his taste for antithesis and paradoxes, his oscillating pattern of thought, his dialectical manner of argumentation, his use of chiasmus, and the epistolary character of the passage—Paul's argumentation appears to be more cohesive than some authors have allowed it to be.[77]

The use of the Old Testament in Romans 9–11
One fact which has been generally overlooked, but which needs to be noticed when exegeting Rom 9–11,[78] is that nowhere else in his writings does Paul quote the OT so frequently as in Romans, and nowhere else in Romans does Paul quote the OT so frequently as in chs. 9–11. Of the seventy-five OT quotations found in this epistle forty-five belong to chs 9–11.[79] This record is so remarkable that we cannot but suspect the existence of very special reasons for it.[80]

The order of the citations is also impressive (see table 3).[81] The texts of the Pentateuch are quoted first, as the basic theses. They give concrete examples of how God intended to carry out his plan in the history of his people. Then, these Torah texts are commented on by texts from the Prophets and Ketubim,[82] which support and confirm the arguments which Paul draws from the Torah texts. The passages are quoted almost in a 'canonical' sequence, following the order of the history of Israel from Isaac to Elijah, in an arrangement which may hardly be taken as accidental or irrelevant. It seems as if Paul wanted to prove from all the Scriptures the total agreement of the revealed word on the point he wished to make.[83]

TABLE 1

DISTRIBUTION OF OT QUOTATIONS IN ROM 9-11

Romans	Pentateuch	Samuel/Kings	Prophets	Ketubim
9. 7	Gen. 21.12			
9	Gen. 18.10			
	Gen. 18.14			
12	Gen. 25.23			
13			Mal. 1.2-3	
15	Exod. 33.19			
17	Exod. 9.16			
20			Isa. 29.16	
			Isa. 45.9	
21				
22			Jer. 27.25(LXX)	
23			Hos. 2.25	
26			Hos. 2.1 (1.10)	
27			Isa. 20.22	
28			Isa. 10.23	
29			Isa. 1.9	
33			Isa. 28.16	
			Isa. 8.14	
10. 5	Lev. 18.5			
6	Deut. 9.4			
	Deut. 30.12			
7	Deut. 30.13			
8	Deut. 30.14			
11			Isa. 28.16	
13			Joel 2.32	
15			Isa. 52.7	
16			Isa. 53.1	
18				Ps 19.4
19	Deut. 32.21			
20			Isa. 65.1	
21			Isa. 65.2	
11. 2		1 Sam. 12.22		
				Ps 94.14
			Amos 3.2	

Romans	Pentateuch	Samuel/Kings	Prophets	Ketubim
11.3		1 Kgs 19.10		
		1 Kgs 19.14		
4		1 Kgs 19.18		
8	Deut. 29.3		Isa. 29.10	
			Isa. 6.10	
9				Ps 69.23
10				Ps 69.24
26			Isa. 59.20	
27			Isa. 59.21	
			Isa. 27.9	
(33)				(Job 5.9)
34			Isa. 40.13	
35				Job 41.3

A detailed study of these quotations cannot be given here. A few general remarks will suffice at the moment:

1. Paul quotes generally according to the LXX, but he knows the MT and follows it when its wording serves his purpose better (9.33).[84]

2. About half of the the quotations are introduced with a concrete and specific reference to their author.[85] It seems as if Paul intended to show the general agreement of the different authors on the important matter with which he was dealing[86] (9.25, 27, 29; 10.5, 16, 19, 20, etc.).

3. Paul generally simplifies the OT text, or draws from it its main idea. He seems more concerned with the idea than with the words, although sometimes his arguments are based upon the words (10.15-18). But it is evident that he looked more for the 'spirit' than for the 'letter' (9.33; 10.5-8, 13, 21).

4. Paul interprets the OT in the light of the Christ event[87] (10.6-9, 10-13).

This exceptional accumulation and arrangement of Scriptural quotations is hardly understood if Paul's argumentation in Rom 9–11 was not at least partially intended to persuade his audience of the continuity between the teaching of the Torah and the Christian message. This possibility needs to be taken into consideration for the interpretation of Rom 10.4.

Summary outline of Romans 9–11

The general theme of the epistle to the Romans is presented in a way which shows that God's plan of salvation through faith in Christ has been carried out according to the Scriptures (1.2; 3.21; 16.25-26). Its three main parts deal with three specific aspects of God's plan:[88]

1. How God's plan applies to the salvation of all mankind, Jews and Gentiles (chs. 1–8).

2. How God's plan squares with his word to Israel and Israel's unfaithfulness to God (chs. 9–11).

3. How the plan affects community life of the Christians (chs. 12–15).

In chs. 1–8 Paul shows that the absolute prevailing condition of sin among men (Jews and Gentiles) has not been an obstacle to the realization of God's design of salvation. In chs. 9–11 Paul shows that the apparently insurmountable obstacle of Israel's rejection of the Messiah will not prevent the full realization of God's purpose. The divine plan will be carried out, and God's promises to Israel will be fulfilled as announced in the Scriptures.

Rom 9–11 deals with the problem of how God's salvific designs—finally fulfilled in the Christ event—relate to the destiny of Israel.[89] The question that Paul wants to answer is explicitly stated in 9.6: 'Has the word of God failed?', i.e. 'How can the fact of Israel's rejection of Christ coordinate with the immutability of God's promises of salvation for Israel?' and 'How can these promises be true when Israel as a nation has jeopardized its election as God's people on earth?'[90]

We cannot emphasize enough the importance of these questions in the apostolic church, which was formed by many Judeo-Christians and founded on the basis of an originally Jewish body, namely, the Twelve Apostles and the first disciples. The issue was how to explain that the people of the old covenant, who had been blessed by God with the greatest of privileges (9.4-5), were now separated from the community of the new covenant, which, as a matter of fact, was nothing other than the extension of Israel. The problem is all the more distressing for the apostle since he himself is a Jew, ready to sacrifice himself for the sake of his 'kinsmen according to the flesh' (9.3).

Paul has organized his answer to these questions in three points, which correspond to the three main divisions of Rom 9–11:

1. God's dealing with his people, when seen from the perspective of God, has always been consistent. God's election has never been based on human merits, but on God's sovereignty and mercy.

Therefore, the inclusion of Gentiles following Israel's misstep is not contrary to the divine promises nor unjust. It rather implies the confirmation and fulfillment of God's promises and the triumph of God's plan over man's failure, as contemplated in the Scriptures (9.6-29).

2. Israel's rejection of Christ, when seen from the viewpoint of human responsibility, comes from a guilty misunderstanding of God's purposes as revealed in the Scriptures and manifested in the Christ event (9.30–10.21).

3. The failure of Israel, seen again from the perspective of God, is only partial and temporary. Contemplated in God's plan—it had in fact already been predicted in the Scriptures—and used by God for the inclusion of the Gentiles, Israel's misstep still serves the purpose of God for the definitive and final salvation of the 'whole Israel'. God has not changed his first intention (11.1-36).

The outline of Rom 9–11 (see table 2) shows that Paul has organized his exposition according to an almost chiastic structure, probably the clearest example of ABA' development in Paul's letters.[91]

This scheme may be summarized in the following three points:

A   God has not revoked his promises to Israel (9.6-29)
B   Israel has rejected God's plan (9.30–10.21)
A'   God has not rejected Israel (11.1-32)

The points A and A' state God's sovereignty with respect to Israel, and point B states Israel's responsibility before God.

TABLE 2

*Structure and Outline of Romans 9–11 on the
Theme 'Has God's Design Failed?'*

Text

9.1-5   *Introductory Doxology*: Lament over Israel's failure: God's plan for Israel seems to have failed.

9.6-29   A.   God's design has not failed. In spite of Israel's failure God's purpose is being fulfilled, as announced in the Scriptures.

6-13   Israel's election was not exclusive nor meritorious.*

14-18		Israel cannot claim election as a right. God chooses according to his plan on the basis of his grace.*
19-29		God's plan is fulfilled in the remnant of Israel and the Gentile believers.*
9.30–10.21	B.	The failure is on the side of Israel: it failed to recognize Christ—both in the Torah and in the gospel— as the only way of salvation established by God for both Jews and Gentiles.
9.30–10.3		Some Gentiles, by accepting Christ, obtained God's righteousness while most Jews, by rejecting Christ, have stumbled.*
10.4-13		The Scriptures teach that God's only way of righteousness is by Christ's grace, through faith.*
10.14-21		The gospel has been preached to all Jews and Gentiles— by the Scriptures and by the Christian kerygma—but Israel has not yet accepted the gospel and Gentiles have.*
11.1-32	A'.	God's design is being fulfilled. God is using the failure of Israel to carry out the fullness of his salvific purposes, as promised in the Scripture.
1-10		God's plan vis-à-vis Israel is being fulfilled in a faithful remnant.*
11-27		As the Jew's failure has been used by God for the conversion of the Gentiles, the Gentiles' faithfulness is being used by God for the final return of Isrel.*
28-32		God's way of salvation goes from man's disobedience to God's mercy for all.
11.33-36		*Closing Doxology.* Praise of God's wisdom: God's ways are unsearchable.

*Statements supported with proof from the Scriptures.

If the whole section is taken as an answer to the question: 'Has the word of God failed?', or, How can God carry out his purpose as announced in the Torah when the elected Israel has rejected the Messiah? (9.1-6), the final answer is: God carries out his purpose in surprising ways, both faithfully to his Torah promises and unsearchably to human minds (11.33-36).[92]

Concerning the question of election, this section shows:

Rom. 9.1-29	*Rom. 9.30–10.21*	*Rom. 11.1-32*
The election of Israel did not imply:	The new situation depends on faith response to the gospel:	The acceptance of Gentiles does not imply:
immovable status of the once elected Israel (9.6-13, 27-29)	believing in Christ Gentiles are included (9.30-33; 10.19-20)	immovable status of the once accepted Gentiles (11.11-24)
exclusion of Gentiles (9.25-26)	rejecting Christ Israel excludes intself (9.31-33; 10.1-3, 21)	exclusion of Israel (11.1-10)
For	For	For
the election of Israel was intended to work for the salvation of both Israel and Gentiles (9.23-24)	the gospel of Christ is intended to work for the salvation of both Israel and Gentiles (10.4, 9-13)	the acceptance of Gentiles was intended to work for the salvation of both Gentiles and Israel (11.25-32)

Summarizing, in spite of Israel's failure God's word has not failed (9.1–10.21), and in spite of Israel's failure, God has not rejected Israel (11.1-36). From analogy with other ABA' patterns in Paul (cf. 1 Cor 8, and 12–14), it may be deduced that the middle passage (9.30–10.21) is intended to contain the heart of the message of the whole section (chs. 9–11).[93] To the question 'Has God's word failed?' (9.6), this passage answers: No, God's word is being fulfilled in the Christ event, in the remnant and in the Christian church. To the question 'Has God rejected Israel?' (11.1), this passage answers: No, it is not God who has rejected Israel but rather Israel which has rejected God in the person of his Messiah. Therefore, the acceptance of Christ is the answer to both questions: God's promises are fulfilled in those who believe in Christ, both Jews and Gentiles, for in God's new people 'there is no distinction' (10.12-13). Rom 9.30–10.21, then, has to be seen not dialectically but as a corollary to 9.1-29 and as an anticipation of 11.1-36. Although in 9.30–10.21 Paul presents the inclusion of the Gentiles as taking place in contradistinction to the failure of Israel, the issue is not 'rejection of Israel / inclusion of the Gentiles' but response to the Gospel as the only basis for inclusion of both Israel and the Gentiles in the new people of God.[94]

Immediate Context: Romans 9.30–10.21

Rom 10.4 belongs, therefore, to the central section of Rom 9–11, namely to the division formed by 9.30–10.21. This division is generally accepted as a natural unit within chs 9–11.[95] There is only a slight disagreement on the delimitation of its internal subdivisions and, consequently, on the immediate boundaries of 10.4. Some authors hold it as the conclusion of 9.30–10.4;[96] a few as the beginning of 10.4–13.21,[97] others as the central statement of 10.1-21.[98] Since 9.30–10.21 is a rather short section, and it is not easy to establish its internal divisions, it should be taken as the immediate context of Rom 10.4.

The theme of 9.30–10.21 is a continuation of 9.1-29. Paul does not forget that he is answering the implied question of 9.6. God's word has not failed (9.6) because God is free and does not make the gift of δικαιοσύνη dependent on human works. The cause of the reverse historical situation of a people of God formed mainly by Gentiles rather than by Jews (9.30–10.3) is not God's unfaithfulness to his work vis-à-vis Israel, but rather Israel's unfaithfulness to God's word as proclaimed both by the law (10.4-8) and by the gospel (10.8-21). Therefore, the fault is not God's but Israel's. It did not submit to God's plan (10.3), but stumbled against the rock of scandal (9.33) which is Christ (10.13), and neither listened to the word of the law (10.4-8) nor obeyed the word of the gospel (10.8-13). Israel may then be rightly accused of being a 'disobedient and contrary people' (10.21). However, despite accusing Israel of inescapable guilt, Paul's emphasis is not exactly on Israel's guilt. Paul's charge against Israel is not motivated by anti-Jewish feelings but rather by his missionary concern for the salvation of his people (10.1). Paul's emphasis is that the gospel message has been announced in the Torah and in the Christian kerygma, so that rejection of this message is not due to the failure of God but to human hardening. God has always stretched out his arms trying to save his people (10.21).

The argument of this section is presented according to the following disposition:

A. Israel has rejected God's way of salvation (9.30–10.3)

    Israel's situation (9.30-33)

1. Gentiles who did not seek God's righteousness found it by faith in Christ
2. Israel failed because it relied on its own ways

| Announced by the prophets (9.32b-33) | a. Isa 8.14 'God would lay in Zion a Stumbling Stone'
b. Isa 28.16 'He who believes in him will not be disappointed' |
| Paul's explanation (10.1-3) | 1. Israel rejected God's way (the gospel)
2. Israel sought to establish its own way |

B. The Torah announced the Gospel: Christ brings δικαιοσύνη to whoever believes (10.4)

| Taught by the Torah (10.5-8a) | b. Lev 18.5 'Whoever follows God's way will live in it' (cf. 1)
a. Deut 30.12-14 'God's way is the work of God, not of human performance' (cf. 2) |
| Paul's *midrash-pesher* (10.6-8b) | 2. Man cannot obtain it by himself alone (cf. a)
1. Christ has obtained it for us (cf. b) |

The Gospel confirms the Torah: 'That is the word of faith that we preach' (10.8b)

| Paul's kerygma (10.9-10) | 1. If you confess Jesus as Lord you shall be accepted
2. If you believe in him as the risen Messiah you shall be saved |
| Confirmed by the prophets (10.11-13) | b. Isa 28.16 'Whoever believes in him will not be disappointed' (cf. 2)
a. Joel 2.32 'Whoever will call upon the name of the Lord will be saved' (cf. 1) |

A'. Israel is still rejecting God's way of salvation (10.14-21)

| Paul's charge (10.14-15) | 1. The gospel has been preached to Israel
2. Israel has heard but refused to accept it |
| Foretold in the prophets and psalms (10.16-18) | a. Isa 53.1 'Who has believed our report?' |

	b. Ps 19.4 Their voice has gone out into all the earth'
Paul's statement of Israel's situation vis-à-vis the Gentiles	1. Gentiles who did not seek God found Him (Deut. 32.21; Isa. 65.1).
(19.19-21) supported by the law and the prophets	2. Israel, sought by God, refuses to come (Isa 65.2)

If this retracing of the structure of Rom 9.30–10.21 is correct, the following is true: (1) According to the chiastic pattern of arrangement the central statements are intended to be 10.4 and 10.8, which, in fact, seem to resume the thrust of the context: the word of God has not failed. The failure is Israel's. For the same 'word' announced by the Torah is the 'word' preached by the gospel, namely, Christ. (2) According to the literary technique of the *inclusio*, the guilt of Israel is stressed by the parallel statements describing the situation of the Gentiles (who did not seek but found acceptance within the people of God) and Israel (who was sought by God but refused to answer) at the beginning and at the end of the section (cf. 9.30-33 and 10.20-21).

Summary of the argument in Romans 9.1-29

Although ch. 9 obviously introduces a new topic, it is not unrelated to chs. 1–8.[99] Rom 9.1-5 is both introductory and transitional.[100] Paul's agonizing confession of sorrow[101] in 9.1-3 comes just after his statement that nothing can separate the elect from the love of God (8.39) and sets the tone of apostolic concern for the salvation of Israel which permeates the whole section (cf. 10.1; 11.1, 26). Paul makes clear that his main concern is to bring Israel to Christ. The incomparable privileges conceded by God to Israel make the situation even more painful for Paul. For besides ἡ υἱοθεσία καὶ ἡ λατρεία καὶ αἱ ἐπαγγελίαι, and οἱ πατέρες, gifts often praised in Judaism,[102] Paul has to add ὁ Χριστός (9.4), the last and supreme gift of God to Israel, precisely the gift which Israel has rejected.

As 9.6 seems to indicate, the present separation of Israel from Christ was interpreted by some as implying that God has not been faithful to his word in his promises to Israel. The whole section from 9.6 to 9.29 is an elaboration of this theme and is preparatory for the final answer, which comes only in 9.30–10.21, and which emphatically states that God has been faithful to his word and that it is rather Israel who has not been faithful to God's word (ὁ λόγος τοῦ θεοῦ).[103] First of all Paul endeavors to correct a wrong concept of election.[104] By making a distinction between τὰ τέκνα τῆς σαρκός and τὰ τέκνα τῆς ἐπαγγελίας (9.7), Paul brings his argument on the faithfulness of God's word to a logical end. From a series of scriptural references carefully selected, Paul shows that 'God's purpose of election' (ἡ κατ' ἐκλογὴν πρόθεσις τοῦ θεοῦ, 9.11) does not depend on Israel's merits of ancestry, but on God's free will.[105] Paul's insistence that what matters is not 'the one who wills or runs' (9.16) but 'God who shows mercy' (τοῦ ἐλεῶντος θεοῦ), seems to be intended to refute the rumor that God has been unfaithful to his promises to Israel.[106] Paul reinterprets completely the meaning of election, arguing that election is an *undeserved gift* of God and not an *inherited right* (9.8, 11-12; cf. 3.2). This allows Paul, in the middle of the discussion, to answer questions about the apparent injustice and arbitrariness of God by categorical refutations (9.14-18 and 19-21).[107]

Related to the concept that the word of God cannot fail but always fulfills God's purposes is the idea that God's purposes are always grounded on God's will of salvation. Since election has salvation as its purpose, it follows that the ultimate determining factor in the achieving of God's plan of salvation is not human performance but God's mercy (ἔλεος, 9.16).[108] If the very purpose of God's plan is salvation and mercy for all (cf. 9.11, 16, 24), God cannot reject Israel despite Israel's rejection of Christ. Therefore, God's patience with Israel is not a sign that the word of God has failed, but a sign of God's faithfulness to his salvific design. Neither Pharaoh (9.17), 'the vessels of wrath' (9.19-24), nor the disobedience of Israel are obstacles to God's mercy.[109] Moreover, the remnant proves both that Israel has not been rejected (11.5) and that God's word has not failed. For that 'only a remnant has proved faithful and believing is entirely consonant with the entire history of Israel from the days of Abraham'.[110] It is the remnant, formed by Jews and Gentiles, that inherits God's promises and carries out the divine purpose (9.7-13; cf. 27-29; 11.1-6).

Thus in carrying out his plan of salvation partially 'outside' Israel God has not been unfaithful to his word. He has not acted according to human expectations or human norms, but by his free choice and mercy (9.6-13). In the realization of his objectives God cannot be judged to have acted unjustly. He must be acknowledged to have acted creatively in order to fulfill, in spite of human failure, his designs of salvation (9.14-26).[111] God has fulfilled his promises faithfully, to the highest good of those for the sake of whom they had been promised, and in full accord with his word in Scripture (9.25-30). Paul carries this argumentation further in 9.30–10.21, a section which constitutes the immediate context of Rom 10.4 and consequently needs to be interpreted in greater detail.

Exegesis of Romans 9.30–10.21

Romans 9.30-33

This first section has a decisive thematic importance for a proper understanding of the whole passage and particularly of 10.4.[112] The question, Τί οὖν ἐποῦμεν,[113] introduces the explanation of Israel's misstep and the contrasting situation hinted at in 9.1-29 of Israel and Gentiles vis-à-vis the new community which God is establishing on earth through Christ's gospel.

The contrast ἔθνη—Ἰσραήλ

In this community it happens that *some* of those who were not God's people are becoming God's people (9.24-26)—ἔθνη obviously refers to the Gentiles who have believed the Gospel; while *most* of those who were God's people—only a remnant of Israel has responded to the Gospel (9.19-29)—are excluding themselves from the new people of God. The frequent and consistent use in this section of the collective term Ἰσραήλ[114] (instead of the more common expression οἱ Ἰουδαῖοι) and ἔθνη indicates an emphasis on the concept of 'peoplehood' in its corporate sense.[115] The issue here is not individual salvation but inclusion into and exclusion from God's eschatological people.

To explain the historical paradox presented in the preceding verses Paul uses, in a combined way, two main literary resources: a series of images from the vocabulary of the foot-race and a series of antitheses.

The athletic imagery includes the following terms:[116] διώκων (for denoting the earnest pursuit of a goal),[117] κατέλαβεν (for describing the attaining of the goal),[118] οὐκ ἔφθασεν (for the stumbling over an obstacle),[120] καταισχύνω (for the disappointment and shame of the defeat),[121] and τέλος (for the goal, winning post, or finishing line itself).[122] The role, import, and significance of these images are shown throughout the exegetical process.

The series of antitheses begins with the following ironic and contrasted situations:

	(9.30)	9.31	
Gentiles	(ἔθνη)	Israel	(Ἰσραήλ)
Not pursuing	(μὴ διώκοντα δικαιοσύνην)	Pursuing	(διώκων νόμον δικαιοσύνης)
Reached	(δικαιοσύνην κατέλαβεν)	Did not reach	(νόμον οὐκ ἔφθασεν)

The irony, which lies in the unforeseen reversal of normal expectations, is formulated by Paul from the perspective of Israel rather than from that of the Gentiles. So, Paul states that Gentiles who never were in the race after δικαιοσύνη obtained δικαιοσύνην τὴν ἐκ πίστεως, while Israel, the people of the law,[123] described as διώκων νόμον δικαιοσύνης, did not reach the goal of its race. Paul does not give any explanation for this paradoxical reversal until 9.32-33 and 10.2-4.

Although the interpretation of δικαιοσύνη has been debated,[124] today it is generally agreed that the Greek δικαιοσύνη must be understood through the Hebrew concept of צדק, which it translates.[125] Our modern renderings of 'justification', 'righteousness', or 'rectification'[126] hardly evoke all the theological connotations that צדק-δικαιοσύνη had in Jewish milieus at the time of Paul. It described primarily a relationship and was particularly used for denoting God's saving activity. Though it could also be used in a moral sense, it conveyed predominantly 'legal' connotations and pointed rather toward God's mercy than toward man's virtue.[127]

It is important to notice that each time Paul deals with the theme of God's δικαιοσύνη in Romans, it is in connection with the inclusion of the Gentiles (1.16-17; 3.21-31; 9.30–10.21). The emphasis is always on God's impartiality, to the point that God's δικαιοσύνη seems to describe the absolute fairness with which God is willing to save sinners, the Gentile as well as the Jew.[128] This particular meaning of δικαιοσύνη is consequential for the understanding of the whole section. The ἐκ πίστεως qualifying δικαιοσύνη seems to underline the idea that by faith the Gentiles have obtained the same 'election status' as Israel.[129]

It must be noted that the goal ascribed by Paul to Israel is not the one reached by Gentiles. Unlike indifferent Gentiles, Israel has been running hard and for a long time (διώκων) towards νόμον δικαιοσύνης. Except for a few authors[130] most scholars understand νόμος here as meaning 'Torah' or the OT law.[131] As happens with other Hebrew terms, the basic nuances of signification of תורה (namely *haggada* or 'story' and *halaka* or 'stipulation')[132] have been transferred to the Greek νόμος in the NT. Paul uses νόμος sometimes in one sense and sometimes in another, either in a positive way or in a negative way. But νόμος in this context seems to keep its basic connotations of 'divine revelation in its wide sense'.[134] Paul has listed in 9.4-5 the giving of the law (ἡ νομοθεσία) among the greatest privileges of Israel, side by side with the covenants (αἱ διαθῆκαι), the promises (αἱ ἐπαγγελίαι), and the Messiah himself (ὁ Χριστός). Since 9.31 is the first reference to νόμος after 9.4, it seems likely that Paul uses νόμος with the sense of תורה 'as the story of divine election and redemption, on the eschatological conviction that God's recent work in Christ had made that election and that redemption available to all mankind'.[135] Only this understanding of νόμος allows a coherent and consistent interpretation of the passage and of (1) εἰς νόμον οὐκ ἔφθασεν in 9.31, (2) τέλος νόμου of 10.4, and (3) Paul's exegesis of the Torah quotations in 10.5-8.

If the meaning of νόμος in 9.31 is still debated, it is only in relation to the interpretation of the genitive construction νόμον δικαιοσύνης, a *hapax legomenon* in the NT.[136] This phrase has been interpreted as 'the law whose aim is righteousness',[137] 'the righteous law',[138] 'the law which requires righteousness',[139] or even 'the law falsely understood as a way of righteousness'.[140] Reading Rom 9.31 through the idea of the incompatibility between 'law' and 'righteousness by faith', it has been translated: 'but that Israel who pursued the righteousness which is based on law did not succeed in fulfilling that law' (RSV), assuming that when Paul says νόμον δικαιοσύνης he really means δικαιοσύνην νόμου, and therefore he refers to 'righteousness by works'. This translation has to be corrected because it disregards the text and imposes upon it unwarranted presuppositions. Though it is true that the shift from νόμον δικαιοσύνης to δικαιοσύνην νόμον might theoretically be explained by a hypallage, nothing proves that it really occurred here. Therefore, it seems more objective to take the text as it is, than to correct it in order to make it fit one's theology. If Paul has νόμον δικαιοσύνης in 9.30 while he has τὴν δικαιοσύνην τὴν ἐκ νόμου in 10.5, the most probable reason is that he meant νόμον δικαιοσύνης in 9.30 and τὴν δικαιοσύνην τὴν ἐκ νόμου in 10.5.

Starting with 9.4, where the cognate term νομοθεσία is used, a positive evaluation of νόμος is always at the background of the discussion in chs. 9–11. The thrust of the passage then favors interpreting νόμον δικαιοσύνης as the Torah viewed from the perspective of the δικαιοσύνη it promises, aims at, or bears witness to (cf. 3.21).[141] It is noteworthy that in all the four insances of νόμος in the whole section, this word is used in construction with δικαιοσύνη, not in opposition to it:

9.31 Ἰσραὴλ δὲ διώκων νόμον δικαιοσύνης εἰς νόμον οὐκ ἔφθασεν
10.4 τέλος γὰρ νόμου Χριστὸς εἰς δικαιοσύνην
10.5 τὴν δικαιοσύνην τὴν ἐκ [τοῦ] νόμου

It is important to notice that the unattained goal Paul ascribes to Israel is not δικαιοσύνην but νόμον.[142] Consistently with the athletic imagery of the passage, Paul describes Israel's failure to reach its expected goal of νόμος in contrast with the Gentiles, attaining of their unexpected goal of δικαιοσύνην. The paradox is in the fact that this νόμος rendered by God to Israel as a special privilege (9.4), this νόμος whose pursuit distinguished Israel from the Gentiles (9.31), is precisely what became the unattained goal, the destination not reached.[143] The choice of the verb φθάνω to describe the particular character of Israel's failure is very significant. Paul depicts it as a defeat in a race, for φθάνω means 'to arrive *first*', 'to *precede* someone',[144] 'to win through'.[145] What Paul says, then, is that in spite of Israel being first 'in the race', the Gentiles, the latecomers, have reached the goal while most Jews have not. Keeping in mind the thrust of his argumentation, Paul takes good care in saying (by his use of φθάνω) that Israel has not been disqualified, but merely overtaken. Israel has taken the wrong course (νόμον . . . ὡς ἐξ ἔργων) and, therefore, has missed the true winning-post (τέλος). It has not reached the right goal *yet*, but it will (11.11-26).

The fact that Israel's 'not attaining yet the goal of Torah' is put in parallel with the Gentiles' 'attaining of δικαιοσύνη ἐκ πίστεως' seems to indicate that for Paul both realities (namely 'attaining the goal of Torah' and 'attaining righteousness ἐκ πιστεως') are closely related. Since the 'attaining δικαιοσύνη' by the Gentiles is obviously identified with their acceptance of Christ, the 'not attaining yet the goal of Torah' by Israel has to indicate Israel's failure to accept Christ. If this is so, the δικαιοσύνη ἐκ πίστεως attained by Gentiles (9.30) and the δικαιοσύνη—promised, witnessed, made known or aimed at by the Law—are implicitly related to Christ himself.[116] If this interpretation of 9.30-31 is correct, then Paul not only does not disparage νόμος in this passage but, on the contrary, puts it on the side of δικαιοσύνη ἐκ πίστεως (cf. 3.21-22, 27; 3.31–4.25; 10.2-10).

The question δια τί asks for the reason why Israel εἰς νόμον οὐκ ἔφθασεν. The answer is worded in a somewhat veiled form in 9.32-33 by means of an elliptical statement and a conflated reference to the Scriptures. The phrase ὅτι οὐκ ἐκ πίστεως ἀλλ᾽ ὡς ἐξ ἔργων is so elliptical that something has to be supplied. Although other insertions have been proposed,[147] it seems most natural that the verb διώκω governing the preceding sentence is to be understood also here.[148] Paul states the nature and reason of Israel's failure in 9.32 by means of the antithesis ἐκ πίστεως / ἐξ ἔργων which contrasts again the attitude of Israel with that of the believing Gentiles (9.30).

It is important, however, not to dislocate the polarity from the place where Paul put it. For the text does not indicate that what Paul complains about is either Israel's pursuit of the law[149] or Israel's inability to comply with its demands,[150] but rather the way Israel pursued it.[151] Although the expression ἐξ ἔργων is used in other contexts in contrast with ἐκ πίστεως in the sense of 'works' versus 'faith', in 9.32 it seems to be used with a slightly different emphasis.[152] In all the instances of ἐξ ἔργων in this section (9.11, 32; 11.6-7), it is used in relation to election and put in contrast with God's initiative. The polarity is between total reliance on God (ἐκ πίστεως) and reliance on ancestry or merits (ἐξ ἔργων). There is an interesting difference between the Gentiles' 'receiving' (κατέλαβεν) and Israel's not 'arriving' (οὐκ ἔφθασεν). As 9.16 explicitly says: 'So it does not depend on the man who wills (θέλοντος) or the man who runs (τρέχοντος) but on God who has mercy (ἐλεῶντος θεοῦ)' (NASB).[153] Israel relied so much on ethnic belonging to the people of God and on its own merits that it overlooked that the basic relation of man to God can only be based on faith (ἐκ πίστεως). The wrong character of Israel's perception is underlined by the ὡς which Paul put before ἐξ ἔργων.[154] Paul's main reproach seems to be addressed against Israel's predominant way of looking at Torah, namely, as a legal code instead of as the record of God's salvific dealings with his people.[155]

The question of the 'stone of stumbling'

Rom 9.32 presents a problem of punctuation. The question is to determine whether a comma or a period is to be placed after ἔργων, and whether the form of the verb διώκω to be supplied is διώκοντες or ἐδιώξαν.[156] Whatever punctuation is preferred,[157] the context seems to indicate that ὅτι οὐκ ἐκ πίστεως ἀλλ᾽ ὡς ἐξ ἔργων and προσέκοψαν τῷ λίθῳ τοῦ προσκόμματος go together, and therefore, that Paul saw as the cause of Israel's failure in 'not yet arriving at the goal of the Law' both (1) its looking at it 'not from a perspective of faith but as it were from a perspective of human accomplishment' and (2) its 'stumbling over the stumbling stone'. The choice of the phrase λίθῳ τοῦ προσκόμματος is probably due to consistency with the imagery of the foot-race and to the rich symbolism of this word. For the 'stumbling block' is both a 'stone against which the runner dashes his foot or over which he stumbles',[158] and a symbol of salvation.[159]

The statement about the stone is formed by a conflation of two prophetic utterances of Isaiah which have in common the term λίθος (Isa 8.14 and 28.16). Although this reference to the OT is presented under a form which stands closer to an allusion than to a real quotation, the intention of appealing to Scripture is unmistakable.[160] The identity of λίθος is not immediately evident. In Isa 8.14 אבן refers to God himself, but here λίθος seems to point to the Messiah. The fact that the same two quotations are combined in 1 Pet 2.6-8 in a way which agrees better with the Pauline quotations than with either the MT or the LXX might indicate that these texts had already been associated together in the early church with a Messianic import.[161]

However, recently a few scholars, like Toews and Meyer, have suggested that 'the stone of stumbling in this passage is the law which was not accepted in faith rather than Jesus Christ'.[162] But although they have invoked some interesting arguments in support of the identification λίθος = νόμος,[163] it cannot be denied that in this context Paul explicitly applied Isa 28.16 to Christ (10.13).[164] Even accepting with K. Barth that the stone of Isa 28.16 is 'God's free mercy',[165] there is no major difficulty in understanding why Paul applies to the Christ event an OT text speaking of God's mercy and will of salvation. For what Paul wants to make clear is that if Israel had recognized in Christ the salvific mercy of God promised by the Scriptures, it would already have reached the goal of the law (9.31), and would not have been 'put to shame' by Gentiles (9.30).[166] Even if λίθος referred to the law itself (or to God), Paul still would say that Israel stumbled over the law's true meaning. Isa 8.14 would have been intended by Paul in the sense that if Israel had put its trust in God (ἐπ᾽ αὐτῷ[167] as the giver of Torah who is always faithful to his word, Israel would have recognized in the Christ event the fulfillment of Torah.

But if the stone is an allusion to Christ, as it seems to be, then this text becomes an additional indication that Paul viewed the OT in a teleological relation to Christ. For 'the stone encounter', as it is presented by Paul, is not a mere accident. It comes from God's deliberate intent. God has put it in the way of humankind (both for Israel and for the Gentiles), although it is particularly announced that the Stone would be put 'in Zion' (Isa 28.16). Therefore, the Stone was intended as an 'unavoidable obstruction' leading to an 'avoidable encounter'.[168] The issue is none other than acceptance/rejection of Christ. Taking the 'following of the law' as an end in itslf Israel did not realize that the goal of the law was to call the whole of mankind to salvation. And when Christ came, Israel did not see that in him God had manifested his faithfulness to his promises.

In 9.33b comes another image related to the 'contest theme' of the passage. Explicating the οὐκ ἔφθασεν of 9.31, Isa 28.16 is quoted: 'He who believes in him will not be put to shame'. Paul suffered the 'shame' of being overtaken by Gentiles. Paul refers again to Israel's defeat in terms which do not imply anything definitive. He simply compares it to the public shame of the humiliation of the overtaken contester.[169] Paul hopes that the momentary victory of the Gentiles will make Israel jealous (11.11) and will stimulate it to turn also to the winning-post.

Summarizing the argument of this passage one may say that Paul presents the failure of Israel in the fact that it did not recognize from Scriptures (εἰς νόμον οὐκ ἔφθασεν) Jesus Christ as the promised Messiah, 'the goal and substance and meaning of the Law'.[170] Looking at Torah from the human perspective—as a code primarily interested in human performance—Israel overlooked the importance of looking at it from the perspective of God's saving acts and mercy. Having failed to take their own law seriously in that particular respect, they did not see that God's promises had been fulfilled in Jesus of Nazareth. In other words, Israel's misunderstanding of Torah is presented by Paul as blindness to the law's witness to Christ (cf. 9.31-33 with 10.4-13 and 3.21), which was epitomized in Israel's rejection of Jesus as the Messiah.[171]

The intimate connection of νόμος and Christ—which Toews disregards by overlooking the explicit identification of the λίθος with Christ in 10.11[172]—appears to be precisely one of the most revealing features of the passage. It is explicitly stated in 10.4-8. By means of the 'Stone' quotations of 9.32b-33, Paul showed that the failure of

Israel is, in the first instance, a matter of relationship to Christ, and secondly, a matter of relationship to Torah (cf. 9.31). If this interpretation of Rom 9.30-33 is justified, then this passage must be recognized as much more important for a proper understanding of Paul's attitude toward the law than is generally accepted. And it must be concluded that it argues strongly in favor of a teleological interpretation of Rom 10.4.

Romans 10.1-3

Rom 10 does not introduce a new subject.[173] It just continues in more detail the explanation of Israel's failure begun in 9.31-33. The interposition of 10.1, which evidently cuts the flow of thought for a moment, does not break, however, the logical development of the argument. After it there is a return to the same verbal form (aorist third person plural, referring to the 'Jews') as in 9.31-33, and the same sequence of events is in view.[174]

Paul's prayer of intercession in favor of his kinsmen in 10.1 (ἡ εὐδοκία τῆς ἐμῆς καρδίας καὶ ἡ δέησις πρὸς τὸν θεὸν ὑπὲρ αὐτῶν εἰς σωτηρίαν) shows that Paul's main concern is 'how Israel may in the end be brought to make the necessary faith-response'.[175] It points back to 9.1-3 and forward to 11.25-26. It is important to notice that, for the first time, the word σωτηρία is used.[176] Paul's concern has shifted from 'election' to 'salvation'. What worries Paul the most is not that Israel has lost its role as people of God, but that many Israelites, in their religious attitude, are risking their very salvation.

The introductory heading, Ἀδελφοί, is significant. It means that this prayer is more than a personal expression of Paul's wish for Israel. It is also a call of attention to the Romans ('I am speaking to you who are Gentiles', 11.13) who have an arrogant attitude of contempt towards the 'unbelieving Jew' (cf. 11.17-24). Paul wants them to share his concern for the salvation of Israel. The μέν *solitarium* at the beginning of 10.1 probably has a restrictive signification.[177] Paul likely means that 'even though the fall of Israel has happened in accordance with what God himself has declared, even though it was the Lord who laid the stone of stumbling in the path of his people, it remains my desire and my prayer that they may yet attain salvation'.[178] For Paul Israel has stumbled but it has not yet fallen (11.11).

Israel's ζῆλος *without* ἐπίγνωσις

In 10.2 Paul states in favor of Israel 'that they have a zeal for God' (ὅτι ζῆλον θεοῦ ἔχουσιν). This phrase commonly designated the proverbial piety of Jews,[179] particularly expressed in their 'zeal for the law' (cf. Gal 1.14).[180] After saying this Paul resumes the theme left over in 9.33 and gives another reason for Israel's failure, or even better, states the same basic reason with a different wording: Israel's zeal for God is οὐ κατ' ἐπίγνωσιν. Note that the term chosen here is not γνῶσις but ἐπίγνωσις. The Jews did not lack knowledge. They lacked something else. Concerning the word ἐπίγνωσις, there is no agreement on the function of the prefix ἐπί. Most take it as intensive[181] or directive.[182] What Paul wants to say is that Israel's zeal was not based on a true apprehension of God's will.[183] It lacked discernment, 'an ability to go to the true nature of a thing'.[184] In fact, Israel's misapprehension was not merely cognitive but also—and primarily—volitional.

The nature of Israel's misunderstanding is unfolded in v. 3: 'Ἀγνοοῦντες God's righteousness and attempting to set up their own they did not submit (ὑπετάγησαν) to the righteousness of God'. This ἀγνοοῦντες explains the οὐκ κατ' ἐπίγνωσιν of v. 2. The conjunctive γάρ indicates that v. 3 is intended to explain v. 2.[185] It is evident that Israel's ἀγνοεῖν does not refer to a lack of information but to practical disobedience. As 'to know' God means to accept him and obediently to submit one's will to God's, 'to ignore' God means to reject submitting oneself to him.[186] This meaning is made obvious by the parallelism of ἀγνοεῖν with οὐχ ὑπετάγησαν.[189]

God's δικαιοσύνη *versus Israel's*

What Israel ignored or refused to know is called τὴν τοῦ θεοῦ δικαιοσύνην, a phrase whose meaning is still a debated question.[188] Two leading views predominate: (1) for some τὴν τοῦ θεοῦ δικαιοσύνην refers primarily to a 'right relation' (forensic and/or otherwise) with God;[189] (2) for a growing number of interpreters, this phrase designates God's own saving power or activity.[190] Without entering that debate, it seems problematic to separate both concepts.[191] Due to the difficulty of determining the sense of this phrase, Paul's concept of δικαιοσύνη θεοῦ needs to be understood in light of the OT notion of צדק יהוה, which is closely related to the concept of God's faithfulness to his (covenant) word.[192] In interpreting δικαιοσύνη θεοῦ it is important to notice that: (1) the starting point of the epistle is the declaration that the δικαιοσύνη θεοῦ is announced in the Gospel (1.16-17); (2) that each time Paul deals with the expression δικαιοσύνη θεοῦ he takes good care to repeat that it had already been announced by the Torah and the prophets (1.16-17; 3.5-6, 19-31; and 10.3-13); and (3) that each section treating of God's righteousness has at its center the proclamation of the Christ event (cf. especially vv. 24-26 in 3.21-31; and v. 12 in 10.1-13). So, by saying that the 'zealous' Jews were 'ignorant of the δικαιοσύνη of God and sought to establish their own' (10.3) 'Paul has in mind a particular point in the history of salvation; the categories are not timeless'.[193]

One should note that the contrast here is between the Jews' attempt to set up (ζητοῦντες στῆσαι) their own δικαιοσύνη and a willingness to *subject* (ὑπετάγησαν) themselves to God's δικαιοσύνη. The point that Paul wants to make clear—here and in the whole epistle to the Romans—is that God's righteousness has been manifested in Christ. In fact, 'God's righteousness' is even explicitly identified with Christ (1.17; 10.3-5; 3.5, 25-26; 1 Cor 1.30; 2 Cor 5.21).[194] Israel's 'refusal of subjection' (οὐχ ὑπετάγησαν is very close in meaning to the refusal of faith in 9.31-33, which 10.3 seems to explain and expound. When compared with the Gentiles' 'attainment' in 9.30, Israel's 'not submitting themselves to the righteousness of God' cannot mean anything but Israel's rejection of Christ.[195] That Israel did not submit to God's righteousness means that it did not recognize (when he came) the One who is the embodiment of God's righteousness.[196] Thus, Rom 10.3 seems to equate Christ with the personified righteousness promised in the law.[197] 'Only an attitude of submission to the Word of the divine promise—an attitude of which Abraham had furnished the pattern—could lead to righteousness, that is, to grace.'[198]

Instead of submission, Israel went on in its own search (ζητοῦντες), in its own ignoring (ἀγνοοῦντες) God's righteousness manifested in the Christ event. The use of these present participles seems to emphasize a continuing attitude.[199] By rejecting God's righteousness Israel kept on seeking its own. The issue here is not Israel's misunderstanding of the role of 'law' and 'faith' in salvation but its misunderstanding of the role of Christ in salvation. 'Israel's relation to Christ is the decisive problem.'[200] That Israel could not grasp in Scripture the nature and scope of God's rigteousness nor see its fulfillment in Jesus Christ was, at the same time, a matter of blindness to the righteousness which God was making available to all in Christ as a free gift, and 'a failure to recognize Christ as the true innermost substance of the Law'.[201]

If the righteousness of God refers to God's faithfulness to his promises to Israel (Gen 15.1-6; Isa 51.1-8; cf. Rom 1.1-2; 4.1-12; 15.8), it results that among the notions which define God's righteousness are its impartiality and its universality, and Howard is probably correct when he argues that 'to establish their own righteousness' involved on the part of Israel a collective self-'righteousness' which excluded the Gentiles.[202] If this is so, it follows that God's righteousness here is 'that absolute fairness with which God is willing to save'.[203] Since God cannot be partial (2.4-11), in the gospel he has given to all (Jews and Gentiles) the same chance of salvation (1.16). The righteousness announced by the law (10.4) is made accessible to all in Christ (3.24-26), who is God's 'wisdom, righteousness, holiness, and salvation' (1 Cor 1.30), that is to say, the perfect revelation of God's righteousness understood as 'power to save' (1.16; 4.21). As the missionary to the Gentiles Paul was eager to point out that the same impartiality which God has shown he wants to see among his people. By faith in Christ they are all equal, and therefore the Jews can obtain the same righteousness now obtained by Gentiles.

In this section, motivated by several different concerns, Paul wishes above all to demonstrate that the gospel he preaches is in full accord with the divine plan as it was manifested in the Scriptures, or even more exactly, as Williams says, 'he wants to show that his gospel agrees with who God *is*—Lord of all peoples and forever true to his own nature and purpose'.[204] In the gathering of the remnant in the Christian church God is bringing to completion what he promised to Abraham, 'the father of us all' (4.16). Therefore, the word of God 'has not failed' (9.6).

Summarizing this passage (9.30–10.3) one may say that Paul concludes the first part of his defense of the efficacy of God's word by pointing out that its apparent failure is really the failure of Israel to grasp it.[205] If Paul's argument is not followed by many here, it is largely because they have lost sight of its relation to the whole context, and particularly to the theme of the section stated in 9.6, to which the whole passage constantly refers. Paul demonstrates by the Scriptures and by the events of history that in the actual situation of Israel there is no failure of God's word and deed. The failure is

Israel's: failure to grasp what God has said (in the Scriptures) and done (in the Christ event). Therefore Israel's problem was not the law, nor their striving after it. Their 'non-attainment of law' (9.32) is to be accounted as a lack of proper perspective. They thought that the basic factor in the law was what it required as human accomplishments. They did not see that 'the righteousness of God' has been disclosed in a 'superlative realization',[206] namely, the coming of the promised Messiah in Jesus of Nazareth. The Jews looked at the Torah in order to see what man could do, and they did not see what God, beyond the measure of their human expectations, had already done.[207] This is why they missed the central fact of the law: Christ, as Paul says in 10.4.

Romans 10.4

The phrase τέλος γὰρ νόμου Χριστός

Our first observation concerns the presence of the conjunction γάρ at the beginning of four consecutive verses.[208] This particle may introduce an explanation of cause, inference, or simple continuation.[209] Whatever the relation intended by γάρ actually is, it implies that vv. 1-5 contain a continuous explanation within the development of Paul's flow of thought[210] and it is an important hint for the understanding of this passage. It compels us to interpret 10.4 in close connection with its context because at least vv. 1-5 have to be read together and most likely they explain each other.

Rom 10.4 is a nominal sentence presented in the form of a statement of fact. The phrase τέλος νόμου Χριστός reads like a classical aphorism. The verb ἐστιν—generally omitted when acting as a copula in this kind of proverbial assertion[211]—must be suplied.

Although Χριστός could be the subject of the sentence, it is clear that the phrase τέλος νόμου, put at the beginning of the sentence in position of emphasis, is the part of the statement which Paul wants to underline.[212] The structure of the phrase makes it a statement about τέλος νόμος (defined in reference to Χριστός), rather than a statement about Χριστός (defined in reference to the τέλος νόμου). Since in the immediately preceding verses the issue was the Torah and how Israel had misunderstood it, it seems likely that 10.4 is primarily a statement about the law rather than about Christ,[213] who is explicitly mentioned here for the first time in the whole section (chs. 9–11).[214] It should not be overlooked that Χριστός is the designation for the *Messiah* as such. As 10.9 shows clearly, the identification of Χριστός with Jesus as the Messiah is implied.[215] But it is significant—and this is certainly due to the fact that the passage deals with 'the Jews'—that Χριστός (i.e. the 'Messiah') is the term which has been chosen. An emphasis upon Messiahship is certainly in the background of Paul's thought (cf. 9.5; 10.6, 7, 17, 21).

If Rom 10.4 is a statement about νόμος, the determination of its meaning is decisive for the interpretation of this text. Νόμος, as is well known, may carry in the NT several different nuances of meaning. Some scholars have tried to establish the meaning of νόμος on a grammatical basis. Taking as criterion the absence or presence of the article, they have assumed that νόμος with article meant 'the law of Moses', or 'the law of God', while in its anarthrous form it meant 'law in general', 'law as a principle', 'the law as a means of justification', or 'legalism', and consequently, they also needed to interpret τέλος as '*terminus*'.[216] Without entering into a discussion of the theological validity of the positions mentioned it must be said at this juncture that the criterion of the absence of article before νόμος cannot be accepted for determining the signification of this term in Rom 10.4, for the following three reasons:

1. The syntactical form of the phrase τέλος νόμου Χριστός does not allow us to infer any special signification from the anarthrous use of νόμος because in this apodictic statement all the elements are anarthrous. The article being dropped before τέλος, it is also natually dropped before νόμος, for syntactical reasons.[217] Χριστός is usually used without the article in Romans.[218]

2. There is no evidence of such a distinction of meaning based on the use of the article. As has been sufficiently proved,[219] there is clear evidence of νόμος used indifferently with article and anarthrously referring to the same reality.[220] Moreover, the anarthrous use of νόμος meaning 'Torah' is very well attested in Paul's contemporary Judaism.[221]

3. The immediately preceding occurrences of νόμος in the context (and the only ones in this section), namely, the two mentions of νόμος in 9.31, are both anarthrous and unanimously accepted as referring to Torah. There is no indication in the passage, nor any logical reason to prove that Paul meant something else in 10.4.[222]

Νόμος in the sense of Torah (not as mere legal code, but as the revelation of God's will) has been at the centre of Paul's discussion since 9.6, and particularly since 9.31, where it was described as νόμος δικαιοσύνης, or as 'the Law which holds forth the promise of righteousness'.[223] Unless τέλος is to be interpreted as 'termination' there is nothing in the context suggesting that νόμος and Χριστός and even less νόμος and δικαιοσύνη[224] are intended to stand in a conflicting relationship or antithesis. In 9.32-33 Paul had clearly declared that if Israel had believed in Christ (the 'stone') it would have certainly ἔφθασεν the law which offers, aims, or promises righteousness.[225] It would be against Paul's main argument here to state—in order to prove that the word of God's Torah has not failed (9.6)—that Christ has abolished it! Therefore, it is much more consistent with the context to take νόμος here as the Torah which bears witness to Christ rather than the law which Christ has abrogated. This would not only be an inexplicable disruption of Paul's trend of thought, but in fact would work against his main argument.

Concerning the interpretation of the phrase τέλος νόμου it has already been shown in the second chapter that the Hellenistic, biblical and cognate parallels favor a teleological or purposive interpretation. If Paul had intended a terminal or temporal understanding of this construction, it would stand, in the literature of his time, as a remarkable exception. And in that case, one would wonder whether Paul's readers in Rome would have been able to understand τέλος νόμου in a terminal or temporal way when they were used to understanding that expression and its cognates teleologically. Only the context would solve the possible ambiguity (if there was any). But thus far there is no serious indication that τέλος νόμου was to be understood in a way different from the one which was current for a phrase like this. The real problem is, then, not only that the construction of the sentence τέλος νόμου Χριστός could hardly mean 'Christ has abolished the law', but that one does not see how such a statement would fit into this context.[226]

Since it has already been done in Chapter 2 it is not necessary to insist here on the meaning of τέλος and the importance of the τέλος question in the Hellenistic world at the time of Paul.[227] In view of the teleological character of several Pauline passages[228] it is difficult to prove that the τέλος question had not influenced Paul's choice of the term τέλος in Rom 10.4. However, since the teleological use of τέλος by Paul has already been surveyed it is not necessary to insist on it here. Suffice it to give due attention to the role of τέλος in the context of Rom 10.4. Consistency with the athletic metaphors used in the immediately preceding paragraph (9.30-33) would require that τέλος be understood as 'goal' or 'destination', for τέλος was precisely one of the terms used for the winning-post, the mark set to bound a race, or the finish line.[229] If Rom 10.4 is not an isolated saying and looks back to 9.30-33, 'the expressly goal-oriented nature of the language'[230] suggests that τέλος relates νόμος and Χριστός in a teleological-eschatological way. If by accepting Christ Gentiles reached the winning-post of δικαιοσύνη and, thereby, acceptance within the new people of God (9.30), and by rejecting Christ Israel did not reach the goal of the law and thereby admission into God's new people, the logical conclusion is what Rom 10.4 says: that the goal of the law and the winning-post of δικαιοσύνη and entrance into God's eschatological people are to be found nowhere else than in Christ. Precisely because the Jews did not see Christ as the final destination, fulfillment, and object of their scriptural search, but rather as an obstacle in their way, they stumbled over him and kept on running—in the wrong direction.

The sense of εἰς δικαιοσύνην παντὶ τῷ πιστεύοντι
The phrase τέλος νόμου Χριστός, which is obviously the main clause of the sentence,[231] has a modifier, εἰς δικαιοσύνην παντὶ τῷ πιστεύοντι, which is often overlooked.[232] This modifier is formed by a prepositional phrase in the accusative (εἰς δικαιοσύνην) and a participial phrase in the dative (παντὶ τῷ πιστεύοντι),[233] whose function in the sentence needs to be determined. The meaning of the whole sentence depends very much on whether one construes εἰς δικαιοσύνην with Χριστός, with νόμος, or with the whole main clause:

    1. If εἰς δικαιοσύνην is construed with Χριστός, Χριστός becomes the subject of both phrases: (a) τέλος νόμου Χριστός, and (b) Χριστὸς εἰς δικαιοσύνην παντὶ τῷ πιστεύοντι. Since this second phrase does not have any logical meaning something needs to be supplied in order to give sense to the sentence. So the supporters of this interpretation have cut the verse into two clauses and have related them to each other by inserting a connecting καί. Thus they translate this verse: 'Christ ends the law *and brings* righteousness for everyone who has faith'.[234]

    2. If εἰς δικαιοσύνην is construed with νόμος, then νόμος εἰς δικαιοσύνην forms a unit of meaning, something like 'Christ is the end of *the-law-as-a-way-of-righteousness* for everyone who has

faith'.[235] This construction makes better sense, but it is grammatically very unlikely in view of the existing order of the sentence. If εἰς δικαιοσύνην were really intended to modify νόμου it would be next to νόμου and not after the whole main clause.[236]

3. If εἰς δικαιοσύνην is construed with the whole main clause, it becomes an explanation of the first statement. Since the basic meaning of εἰς is directional and purposive,[237] it should likely be translated 'for' (NASB); but since it may also be consecutive[238] and referential it has been also translated 'so that' (NEB, JB) and 'so far as', 'with respect to'.[239] The difficulty of translating this nominal phrase has been resolved in some modern translations by transforming it into a verbal sentence, for example, 'that everyone who has faith may be justified' (RSV). The verb πιστεύω, in its absolute use, is characteristic of Paul for speaking of faith in Christ (cf. Rom 1.16; 3.22; 10.4).[240] The role of παντί seems to be to stress the universality of God's way of salvation in Christ: this way applies *also* to the Jews.

If τέλος νόμου Χριστός is interpreted in a temporal sense, the interpretation of εἰς δικαιοσύνην παντί τῷ πιστεύοντι becomes problematic. It seems improbable that Paul would have said in Rom 10.4 that 'Christ has put an end to *the-law-as-a-way-of-righteousness*' in the sense that prior to Christ righteousness was obtained by the works or the law, since in ch. 4 he has emphasized the fact that the way of righteousness has always been by faith.[241] It seems still more improbable that Paul would have said here that 'Christ has put an end to the law *in order that* righteousness based on faith alone may be available to all men',[242] because this would imply that the existence of the law was the insurmountable obstacle to the existence (or the exercise) of 'righteousness by faith', since Paul explicitly says that the law not only was not opposed to God's righteousness but was a witness to God's righteousness (cf. 9.31 and 3.21, 31). The temporal interpretation would only be possible: (1) if νόμου stood for ἔργα νόμου, 'legalism', or a related concept (which is evident in other contexts, but not here); (2) if τέλος meant 'termination' (which would be an exception and would have to be proved); and (3) if the context would require this antinomian interpretation (which it does not).

Romans 10.4 and the thrust of the passage
In view of the difficulties of the temporal interpretations, it seems more appropriate: (1) to translate νόμος as 'Torah' in consistency

with the other νόμος references in the context; (2) to translate τέλος as 'object', 'purpose', or 'goal', in consistency with the Pauline, biblical, and cognate extra-biblical use of this and similar phrases; and (3) to relate Χριστός and νόμος in a positive, teleological way, in consistency with the thrust of the passage. It is the contention of the present study that a teleological interpretation of Rom 10.4 is the only proper way to understand this verse, not only in harmony with its context, but as contributing to the explanation of such important elements in the context as 'the word of God has not failed' (9.6), the 'attainment of righteousness' by the Gentiles (9.30), Israel's 'not attaining' to the law (9.31), its 'ignoring God's righteousness' (10.2-3) and its 'stumbling over the stone' (9.33). Rom 10.4 fits in better with these main themes of the context if it is understood in the sense that the Torah, in its promise of righteousness to whoever believes pointed to Christ[243] rather than in the sense that 'Christ has superseded the law bringing justification to anyone who will believe'[244] or 'Christ means the end of the struggle for righteousness-by-the-law for everyone who believes in Him',[245] notwithstanding how much more 'Pauline' the latter interpretation might seem.

One wonders what statements such as 'Christ has abolished the law (the whole of it or only in part)' or 'Christ has fulfilled the law (in our stead)' would be doing in the context of Rom 9–11.[246] These interpretations not only do not naturally arise out of the context nor fit the argument of the passage: they interrupt the flow of the argument and work against it. They say something which may be true, but which is irrelevant for the main purpose of the passage. But if the interpretation proposed here is correct, then this verse becomes the key statement and the logical conclusion of the whole passage. It means that this righteousness that Christ has brought for all is the object and goal to which all along the law has been directed, its true intention and meaning.[247] If Israel had misunderstood the Torah and God's righteousness, it is because it failed to recognize in Christ the Messiah who fulfilled the Torah's main purpose—to lead *all* men to salvation.

Rom 10.4 in this passage would say then that the Christ event has revealed in history that the righteousness which the law promised was nothing other than the righteousness manifested to all by Christ.[248] Israel, biased by its wrong understanding of the law in its relation to righteousness, did not recognize in the Christ event the manifestation of 'the righteousness of God' to whom the law pointed.

It did not see, therefore, that 'Christ is the goal, the aim, the intention, the real meaning and substance of the Law—apart from him it cannot be properly understood at all'.[249]

If this interpretation is correct, then Rom 10.4 becomes the logical continuation of the reasoning initiated in 9.30-33 and followed in 10.2-3, and not the beginning of a new digression about 'Christ's abrogation of the Law'. Paul clearly states in Rom 10.4 what he had only hinted in the previous verses, namely that Christ embodies that righteousness which the law promised, that righteousness which some Gentiles obtained through faith and which Israel rejected. Zealous Israel, faced with the Christ event, thought that it was to choose between the law and Christ and decided to pursue the law and to reject Christ. Paul shows that that was a wrong choice, for the law led to Christ and Christ was the true τέλος of the law. So, Paul summarizes all his preceding argumentation by stating that the end which the law intended to accomplish—the justification of all— Christ has accomplished. The suggestion of the present exegetical approach to Rom 10.4 is, then, that τέλος should be interpreted in a teleological way rather than in a temporal, terminal or even completive way. For what Paul wants to say is that the law pointed, promised intended, etc., Christ, in order to bring righteousness to whoever believes. This Paul proves from the Scriptures and explains in further detail in the following verses.

Romans 10.5-8

In order to prove the truth of what he has said in 10.4, namely, that the law already pointed to the Messiah for bringing righteousness to all who believe, and to indicate that the Jews should have known this, Paul quotes Lev 18.5 and Deut 30.11-14.

Romans 10.5 and the quotation of Leviticus 18.5

This quotation presents two main textual problems: (1) the position of ὅτι, affecting the construction of δικαιοσύνη, and (2) certain variations involving the pronouns αὐτά and αὐτοῖς, which affect the object of ποιήσας. The reading which has more witnesses[250] has ὅτι immediately before ὁ ποιήσας and reads: Μωϋσῆς γὰρ γράφει τὴν δικαιοσύνην τὴν ἐκ [τοῦ] νόμου ὅτι ὁ ποιήσας αὐτὰ ἄνθρωπος ζήσεται ἐν αὐτοῖς. This rendering is very close to the LXX text (ἃ ποιήσας αὐτὰ ἄνθρωπος ζήσεται ἐν αὐτοῖς), but has a syntactical problem: the pronouns αὐτά and αὐτοῖς have no antecedent and, therefore, the quotation does not fit syntactically within its context. At the same time, although τὴν δικαιοσύνην may be understood as an accusative of specification,[251] the construction of ὅτι after it is somehow irregular.[252] The alternative reading has ὅτι following immediately after γράφει, which is the natural construction, thus extending the quotation and making δικαιοσύνην the object of ποιήσας. Since now δικαιοσύνην is the antecedent of the pronoun αὐτῇ (substituted for αὐτοῖς), and having omitted αὐτά,[253] the sentence is now syntactically correct, and reads: ὁ ποιήσας ἄνθρωπος ζήσεται ἐν αὐτῇ ('the man who does [the righteousness of the law] shall live by it'). In spite of departing more from the LXX, this reading has better witnesses than the former, and, therefore, should be preferred.[254]

Assuming that Lev 18.5 teaches salvation by works, most commentators interpret Rom 10.5 in opposition to Rom 10.6-8, on the assumption that Lev 18.5 is quoted here by Paul to state his condemnation of righteousness 'by works of the Law'. It is argued that the verb ποιέω is here connected with νόμος in a sense close to the phrase ἔργα νόμου.[255] This assumption, however, is questionable in this context.[256] This interpretation has been traditionally supported by the way Paul quotes Lev 18.5 in Gal 3.12. However, the use of this text in Galatians cannot determine its meaning in Romans.[257] Paul not only can quote the same passage with different emphases and for different purposes in different contexts,[258] but the various ways he renders Lev 18.5 in each instance proves that in each case he had a different intention in mind. Quoting Lev 18.5 in Rom 10.5 Paul introduces τὴν δικαιοσύνην τὴν ἐκ νόμου as the object of ποιήσας and retains the original subject ἄνθρωπος, while in Gal 3.12 Paul drops ἄνθρωπος and keeps the object αὐτά because he wants to retain the reference to the practices and ordinances of the OT text.[259] If Paul changed the αὐτοῖς of Lev 18.5 for the αὐτῇ of Rom 10.5, it was certainly because he wanted to refer that passage not to the ordinances of the law but to the δικαιοσύνη to which the law pointed, according to Rom 10.4.

The common interpretation of this passage assumes that Paul is stressing the contrast between two ways of righteousness: righteousness by works of the law (described in 10.5, quoting Lev 18.5) and righteousness by faith (described in 10.6-8, quoting Deut 30.12-14). The former would represent the Jewish way of righteousness and the latter would represent the way of righteousness preached by Paul. However, since this interpretation sets scripture against scripture, it appears to some authors as rather problematic.[260]

Trying to resolve the hermeneutical problem which this interpretation involves, Bandstra has proposed to interpret Rom 10.5 in the light of Phil 2.7-10, referring ὁ ποιήσας not to the believer, but to Christ. Christ is *the man* (ἄνθρωπος) who 'did' the righteousness of the Law, and therefore, 'he lives'. Consequently, Rom 10.4-5 would not deal with what men cannot do, but with what Christ has done (and he gives as a parallel statement Rom 5.18).[261] In a line of thought more consistent with the context, Bring has tried to explain this passage by stating that the 'righteousness of the Law' in Rom 10.5 is not the opposite of 'the righteousness of faith' in 10.6-8, as is assumed, but an explanation of it.[262] Since righteousness is possible only through faith—argues Bring—ὁ ποιήσας ἄνθρωπος has to be the man who seeks righteousness by faith, and ποιεῖν τὸν νόμον has to refer to fulfilling the law through faith in Christ. Therefore, Bring concludes, Paul is interpreting Lev 18.5 by means of a Christian reading of Torah: 'In the light of the Gospel he sees deeper meaning in the OT text, a reference to the coming of righteousness through Christ'.[263] Although Bring's interpretation is an important attempt to solve the problems of the passage, it does not seem to fully fit within the thrust of the passage. For the point is not 'fulfilling' the law but finding which is God's way of righteousness according to Scripture (τὴν δικαιοσύνην ἐν αὐτῇ).[264] It must be always remembered that what Paul wants to show is that the Jews have failed because they did not submit themselves (οὐχ ὑπετάγησαν) to τῇ δικαιοσύνῃ τοῦ θεοῦ (10.3), which is equated in 10.4 with Christ.

In the way Paul uses Lev 18.5 he seems to give to τὴν δικαιοσύνην νόμου a Christological sense (cf. vv. 6-10), which departs from the interpretation held by contemporary Judaism,[265] but which is less alien to the OT text than it would seem at first reading. It is interesting to notice that Lev 18.5 is one of the most often quoted passages of the Pentateuch,[266] and apart from Gal 3.12 it is hardly used in any legalistic context.[267] Lev 18.5 is quoted in Ezek 20.11, 13, 21 to describe the law as God's great gift of life to Israel.[268] In Neh 9.29 it is quoted as a reference to the covenant relationship of Yahweh with his people, and the promise of life which he gives to his children.[269] Even in the rabbinic writings Lev 18.5 is used frequently to illustrate the principle that 'the laws were given that men should live by them, not die by them'.[270] It is also used to emphasize how easy it is to do the law, and how much reward awaits the followers of the law.[271] Moreover, the phrase 'the man who' in Lev 18.5 was understood in rabbinic Judaism in a universal way. Rabbi Meir (c. AD 150) quotes Lev 18.5 to prove that a Gentile who lives according to the law is to be regarded as highly as a high priest, and will also share in the promises of the Torah, for the text says 'a man'.[272] The retention of ἄνθρωπος in Rom 10.5 might be intended by Paul to emphasize the universality of God's way of salvation, a prominent theme in chs. 9–11.[273]

Although it cannot be ascertained that Paul understood Lev 18.5 in continuity with the OT texts (and some Jewish traditional interpretations), the way he quotes this text in Rom 10.5 puts the burden of proof upon those who pretend he understood it in opposition to them. Moreover, they would have to explain a supplementary difficulty, namely, why Paul would have used Lev 18.5 in a way which weakens his argument in the context. For by quoting Moses in Lev 18.5 as teaching righteousness by works, Paul would be—in a certain sense—excusing Israel's 'pursuit of law righteousness ἐξ ἔργων' (9.31-32). If this was the way of righteousness taught by Moses, the Jews could not be accused of 'establishing their own way of righteousness' (10.3). They were, vis-à-vis Moses, theologically right! They were doing what the law commanded, and their understanding of the law would be correct! But this is the contrary to what Paul says. One of Paul's charges against Israel is precisely their wrong understanding of Scripture.

The relation between Romans 10.5 and 10.6-8
The principal problem in the quotation of Lev 18.5 in Rom 10.5 is, then, not the quotation itself but its relation to the quotation of Deut 30.12-14 in Rom 10.6-8. In fact, the major objection presented against the teleological interpretation of Rom 10.4 is this double citation in 10.5-8. Very few scholars have attempted (and even less succeeded) to explain these two quotations as complementary, as related in a positive way.[274] Most (namely, those who interpret τέλος as 'termination') take the two quotations as presenting two conflicting 'ways of righteousness': v. 5 (quoting Lev 18.5) describing 'righteousness by works' (τὴν δικαιοσύνην τὴν ἐκ τοῦ νόμου) and vv. 6-8 (quoting Deut 30.11-14) describing righteousness by faith (ἡ δὲ ἐκ πίστεως δικαιοσύνη), assuming with Munck that these verses

present 'an account of the Jews' self-appointed way to salvation, and of the Christian way to salvation . . . The two ways to salvation are so diametrically opposed that they exclude one another.'[275]

The arguments invoked in support of this generalized interpretation are the following:

1. The quotation of Lev 18.5 (Rom 10.5) is separated from the quotation of Deut 30.11-14 (Rom 10.6-8) by the particle δέ; therefore they stand in antithesis against each other.

2. Verse 5 presents the teaching of Moses (justification by works) while vv. 6-8 presents the teaching of Paul (justification by faith). The quotation from Lev 18.5 emphasizes the idea of *doing* while the quotation from Deut 30.11-14 emphasizes the idea of *faith*, the passage showing then that there is discontinuity between the OT and the NT doctrine of justification.

3. Since v. 5 says 'Moses *writes*' and v. 6 says 'righteousness of faith *speaks*', this second instance is not a quotation proper, but an accommodation. Paul is putting his thought into OT language.[276]

4. Since Paul quotes Lev 18.5 in Gal 3.12, the meaning of this reference needs to be seen in the light of Galatians.

Käsemann represents well the position which sees a contrast between v. 5 and vv. 6-8. For him Paul sets up the personified righteousness by faith over against the lawgiver Moses.[277] Moses requires achievement of the law; faith demands reception of the word. Although Paul knows that Lev 18.5 and Deut 30.11-14 belong to the same Torah, 'he is not afraid to apply to Scripture too the distinguishing of spirits demanded of the prophets in 1 Cor 12.10; 14.29ff.'. And Paul does so because of his 'dialectical understanding of Scripture' according to which something is 'letter' when it raises a demand for achievement and something is 'spirit' when it is oriented eschatologically to the righteousness of faith.[278] Käsemann sees in this distinction the key for Paul's hermeneutic of Torah.[279] This antithesis, concludes Käsemann, 'secures the meaning "end of the law" in v. 4'.[280] In spite of its apparent logic and consistency with Paul's law theology elsewhere, this interpretation is still problematic, both on syntactical and contextual grounds.

The interpretation of Rom 10.5 and 6-8 as two opposite statements is not required by the syntax of the phrase. The introductory γάρ is a connecting particle which probably indicates that v. 5 explicates v. 4 (as in v. 4 it indicated that v. 4 explicated v. 3). It seems to suggest that v. 5 is in harmony with v. 4, and not in contrast with it. Even

Käsemann, who ends up exegeting v. 5 as a contrast to v. 4, states that this verse is presented as a scriptural proof of the thesis put forward in 10.4.[281]

The traditional interpretation supports the antithesis between v. 5 and vv. 6-8 by emphasizing the adversative meaning of δέ: 'Moses writes . . . *but* the righteousness of faith says . . . ' However, δέ is a basically connective particle, which only sometimes means 'but'. It may be conjunctive and mean 'and'.[282] In fact, in this context Paul does not use this set of particles in an adversative way (with the meaning of 'for . . . *but*') but in a connective way with the meaning of 'for . . . *and*' (cf. 10.10 where Paul uses γάρ . . . δέ in the phrase 'for with the heart . . . *and* with the mouth'; cf. the same use in 11.15 and 7.8).

The context does not compel us either to interpret these two quotations as antithetical, opposing Scripture against Scripture.[283] By jeopardizing the unity of Scripture and by discarding a part of it as 'wrong' in its teachings, Paul not only would have been very unconvincing in his argument with the Jews and Jewish Christians to whom, at least indirectly, this passage was addressed (cf. 9.1-4 and 10.1), but he would have worked against his main argument. Instead of proving that the new situation brought by the gospel does not imply that the divine word had failed (9.6), which was the thesis that Paul wanted to prove in this section, Paul would have ended by stating that something in Scripture had failed and had been superseded because it was wrong and deceiving![284]

Just as difficult to accept is the idea that Paul did not intend both quotations to be attributed to Moses, or to assume, with Käsemann, that Paul was identifying 'Moses' with 'the letter', as something superseded by the gospel.[285] If he had considered some scriptural passages as superseded, he would not have built all his argument on scriptural proofs, as he did in such a prolific way. It seems, therefore, more consistent with Paul's usage of the OT—and with the Jewish usage in general—to see in the two quotations of Rom 10.5-8 the biblical 'two witnesses'[286] invoked to confirm the veracity of an affirmation (cf. Rom 9.25-26, 27-28, 30; 10.11-13, 20-21; 11.8-9, 26-27; etc.). For the two quotations are not antithetical in the Pentateuch (nor in any Jewish writings).[287] On the contrary, taken in their original contexts, both quotations deal with similar matters. Deut 30.16 is almost a repetition of the main idea of Lev 18.5. Besides that, never in Paul (nor in the whole of the NT) is Moses set against Moses or against any other biblical statement.[288] If Paul quoted Deut 30.11-14 after Lev 18.5 it is not necessarily because he thought that Deuteronomy teaches righteousness by faith while Leviticus teaches righteousness by works. It may also be because he thought that both texts in their contexts were complementary.[289]

It may appear surprising, though, that Paul applies to δικαιοσύνη ('of the law' in Lev 18.5, and 'of faith' in Deut 30.11-14) two passages which deal originally with 'commandments'. This apparent inconsistency in Paul's argumentation may be explained by two factors:

1. The words used for 'commandments' (κρίματα, προστάγματα, ἐντολάς) do not refer only to the legal indictments of the Torah but, as Zorn has rightly argued, to 'the whole doctrine of God which already comprehended the Gospel bound up with it'.[290] So, when Paul changes 'commandment' in Deut 30.11-14 to 'righteousness by faith', he is not doing it against the thrust of Moses' teaching, for *commandment* in its broader sense includes the whole revelation of God for man's salvation as summarized in the gospel, but already present in the larger context of the law and the prophets. What Paul is doing, from his Christian perspective, is trying to show that justification by faith is found already in the OT.

2. Paul's way of quoting the OT does not seem intended to provide mere 'proof-texts' in support of his thesis. As may be demonstrated, his quotations are references to whole contexts.[291] It is interesting to notice that, in the context of Deut 30, the themes of God's promise to circumcise the hearts of his people in order that they may learn to love him (30.6), and the theme of the gathering and restoration of Israel from all nations (30.3) are related; and that the immediate context of Lev 18.5 deals with the theme of the 'blood' which God has given to his people to make atonement for their souls and to give them life (17.11), three themes, in fact, extremely relevant to the doctrine of 'righteousness by faith'.

Summarizing Paul's interpretation of Lev 18.5 in Rom 10.5, it appears that the syntax and wording of this verse does not require to interpret it in opposition to vv. 6-8. Although it can be argued that, by quoting Moses, Paul might refer to a legalistic Jewish interpretation of this passage, the wording of the verse and the thrust of the passage do not allow us to ascertain it. It seems more fitting to the context to interpret Rom 10.5 as an explanation (by means of Scripture) of Paul's statement in Rom 10.4, that 'the τέλος of the law for righteousness is Christ', in the sense that 'whoever follows the way of righteousness taught by the law will live by it', as an introductory statement to the next quotation (Deut 30.12-14), where the way of righteousness is identified as 'righteousness by faith' in 'the word which is near'. By putting these two references together Paul equated 'the righteousness taught by the law' with 'righteousness by faith' in a clearly new way, meaning thereby that doing the righteousness taught by the law is coming to Christ for salvation, and thus, receiving life. Paul could apply Lev 18.5 in this Christological way not only because he was conscious of his own role as authoritative exegete of the OT and because he saw Christ as the hermeneutical key of Scripture (cf. 2 Cor 3)[292] but also because the thrust of the OT texts allowed him to do so.

Romans 10.6-8 and the quotation of Deuteronomy 30.12-14

The interpretation of this citation is at least as controversial as that of Lev 18.5 in Rom 10.5. The problems turn around two main issues: (1) Paul's use of Deut 30.12-14,[293] and (2) the meaning of this passage for the argument of Rom 9.30–10.13.

The way Paul used the OT here presents several problems to the interpreter: (1) the citation of Deut 30.12-14 is not attributed to Moses, or to the Scripture, but to ἡ ἐκ πίστεως δικαιοσύνη; (2) the text in Romans departs considerably from that of Deuteronomy: (a) the introductory formula of Deut 30.12, ἐστιν λέγων, has been replaced by a citation of the introductory formula of Deut 8.17 and 9.4: μὴ εἴπῃς ἐν τῇ καρδίᾳ σου; (b) the pronoun ἡμῖν is omitted from the phrase τίς ἀναβήσεται ἡμῖν εἰς τὸν οὐρανόν of Deut 30.12; (c) the whole phrase τίς διαπεράσει ἡμῖν εἰς τὸ πέραν τῆς θαλάσσης of 30.13 is changed to τίς καταβήσεται εἰς τὴν ἄβυσσον; (d) the word ἐγγύς is moved into the emphatic position and the term σφόδρα has been dropped so that the phrase becomes sharper; (3) Paul deletes all the expressions of Deut 30.12-14 which refer directly to the observance of the law: καὶ ἀκούσαντες αὐτὴν ποιήσομεν (v. 12), καὶ ἀκουστὴν ἡμῖν ποιήσει αὐτὴν καὶ ποιήσομεν (v. 13), and καὶ ἐν ταῖς χερσίν σου αὐτὸ ποιεῖν (v. 14); (4) Paul inserts two phrases into the OT quotation in order to relate what the passage says with Christ's 'descending' and 'ascending': τοῦτ' ἔστιν Χριστὸν καταγεῖν (at the end of v. 6) and τοῦτ' ἔστιν Χριστὸν ἐκ νεκρῶν ἀναγαγεῖν (at the end of v. 7); (5) Paul applies the whole passage to the Christian proclamation, adding at the end of the quotation the following words: τοῦτ' ἔστιν τὸ ῥῆμα τῆς πίστεως ὃ κηρύσσομεν (v. 8).

This way of treating the OT has been qualified by some as 'supremely arbitrary' and 'outrageous',[294] and by others as 'a remarkable example of skillful and correct exegesis'.[295] Most commentators avoid such extremes by admitting that this passage is somehow 'disconcerting'.[296]

This perplexing quotation has been explained in very different ways:

1. Most commonly, it is assumed that Paul is not interpreting Deut 30.12-14 but simply using its language for expressing his own ideas.[297] Paul is inserting into the OT his personal conception of 'righteousness by faith' and showing—by opposing this doctrine to the 'righteousness of the law' as stated in Lev 18.5 (Rom 10.5)—that 'righteousness by faith' has become the hermeneutical criterion for the understanding of Scripture.[298]

2. Other scholars argue that Rom 10.6-8 is not a quotation, but just a rhetorical application of a proverbial saying intended to depict superhuman efforts to realize the impossible. Paul did not have the OT proper in mind, but only the idea that all has been done by Jesus for our salvation. Therefore, human response can only be that of 'righteousness by faith' as opposed to 'works'.[299]

3. Others claim that Paul uses Deut 30.12-14 in an allegorical way, following an exegetical procedure not interested in the literal meaning, but in the deeper, spiritual meaning of the OT text.[300]

4. Finally, some authors see here a true OT quotation explained by Paul in a midrash/pesher manner.[301] This position is preferable, for the following reasons: (a) The similarities between Rom 10.6-8 and Deut 30.12-14 are too many to accept them as merely coincidental or allusive. (b) The phrase τοῦτ' ἔστιν, which appears three times in this quotation, was an important *terminus technicus* in rabbinic exegesis for introducing scriptural interpretation.[302] (c) The formula τί λέγει is also an introductory expression used in rabbinic exegetical terminology as an abbreviation of the citation formula τί λέγει ἡ γραφή.[303] This is confirmed by the efforts of the scribal emendation supplying ἡ γραφή (D, G, and others) as the subject of λέγει (cf. Rom 4.3; 11.2, 4; Gal 4.30). (d) Finally, this reference comes in a context (Rom 9.30–10.21) which contains eleven OT quotations, none of them allusive or allegorical. Nothing suggests that this one is not intended to be considered also as a real quotation.[304]

But here comes the problem. Paul generally uses his Scripture citations as proofs confirming the force of his argumentation. Here we have a 'quotation' which seems to depart considerably (in the way Paul uses it) from the OT original, and, as Hanson has rightly observed, 'proof texts that have been arbitrarily tampered with are ineffective as proofs'.[305] The question is how Paul could have discredited his argument by an arbitrary use of Scripture. The occasion and purpose of Romans makes it all the more difficult to understand that Paul would lay himself open to the charge of arbitrary or inept use of Scripture. But this is in fact what some authors claim that he has done.[306]

Some scholars, however, trying to find a better explanation to this problem have compared the way Paul quotes the OT here with other Pauline OT quotations and have found that Paul often cites and interprets Scripture from an existing and accepted tradition. On the basis of this fact, efforts have been made to find Jewish parallels which might shed light on Paul's use and interpretation of Deut 30.12-14.[307] There are those who suggest that Paul might have built his interpretation of Deut 30.12-14 by drawing some material from *Wisdom traditions*, as may be discerned in the interpretation of that passage in 1 Baruch 3.29-30.[308] Some of the most relevant elements of the Wisdom tradition were the personification, the identification of Wisdom with the Torah, and the idea of the inaccessibility of Wisdom to men expressed by the symbols of 'heaven' and 'sea'. It seems that in Rom 10.6-8 Paul is extending the traditional equation Wisdom = Torah to the equation Wisdom = Torah = Christ.[309] It is important to notice that the sermon of Baruch where Deut 30.12-14 is interpreted in terms of Torah (Baruch 3.9–4.4) speaks of 'the gospel of the Torah', of God's gracious election of Israel, and of his gift of the Torah, to the point that it may be said that 'Baruch affirms of the Torah what Paul affirms of Christ; that by their instrument "the word is near you"'.[310] On the basis of these parallels it has been argued that, by identifying Christ with Wisdom-Torah in Deut 30.12-14, Paul was simply appropriating 'a tradition of interpretation to resolve a continuing tension within his churches over the relation of the gospel to the law'.[311] This interpretation, however, is not without certain difficulties. The key phrase both in Romans and in Deuteronomy, namely, 'the Word is near', is lacking in Baruch.[312]

Other scholars have suggested that Paul's interpretation of Deut 30.12-14 depends on the interpretation of that passage in *Targum Neofiti I*,[313] which uses this text to stress that the law was given to Moses once for all.[314] These scholars base their arguments on the assumption that Targum Neofiti I contains pre-Christian traditions. So, for S. Lyonnet, Paul rereads Deut 30.12-14 through the perspective of Targum Neofiti because in the early church the figures of Moses and Jonah were viewed as types of Christ (Moses as mediator of a new covenant, and Jonah as type of the death and resurrection of Christ), and permitted Paul to relate 'the word which is near' to the incarnated and resurrected Christ.[315] McNamara sees in Eph 4.8-11 an additional support for this view.[316] However, this view has been seriously challenged by J.A. Fitzmyer on the basis of the problematic dating of the Palestinian Targums.[317] Notwithstanding, this position is still very suggestive and has strongly influenced the interpretation of Rom 10.6-8 in recent scholarship.[318] Deut 30.12-14 is alluded to in the OT and in Jewish Hellenistic literature in several different ways.[319] In rabbinic literature it has been used to emphasize that the Torah contains the full revelation of God, and 'nothing has been left in heaven' for further revelation.[320] Targum Onqelos, which translates Deut 30.11-12 literally, paraphrases v. 14 as follows: 'The word is near you in your houses of learning; open your mouths in order to study, and clean your hearts in order that you may do it'.[321] In general, the rabbinic interpretations take this passage as an affirmation of the nearness of the Word-Torah, its fulfillability, and the accessibility of God's will to man's knowledge: God has revealed his will (in the Torah) in a form which is accessible, understandable, fulfillable, and definitive.[322]

The Old Testament Context
Some features of the interpretations mentioned above might in fact have been known by Paul and even be part of his frame of reference in his exegesis of Deut 30.12-14. But since it is practically impossible to determine the exact influence and extent of these sources on Paul's exegesis here, it seems preferable to consider Paul's references to the OT in Rom 10.6-8 as being primarily a real and personal exposition of Deut 20.12-14.[323] The point is to see why Paul chose this passage to support his argument here and how this OT reference fits in its immediate context and sheds light on the understanding of Rom 10.4.

The first surprising factor in this quotation is that it is referred not to Moses, as in v. 5, but to ἡ ἐκ πίστεως δικαιοσύνη. This personification of 'the righteousness based on faith' is seen by many scholars as a 'rhetorical device',[324] common in Hellenistic philosophy where abstract entities such as virtues or vices are sometimes presented as speaking.³²⁵ This seems to be a genitive of source describing the 'righteousness based on faith' or 'obtained through faith' (cf. 9.31-32). D.O. Via, in his interesting attempt to interpret Paul by the categories of structuralism, shows that the personification of 'righteousness by faith' as speaking in the Deuteronomic text is more that a simple 'stylistic flourish' as some scholars have suggested.³²⁶ For Via this personification indicates that Paul saw righteousness by faith as a basic structure in the OT. What Paul wished to prove was that the theological perspective brought by Christ and his message (righteousness available to all through faith) is what the OT text already taught. Thus, when Paul declares that 'the righteousness by faith says' he means that this motif is speaking in the OT, and, therefore, Paul is giving us a basic hint about his understanding of the OT.³²⁷ The question of why Paul alternates τὴν δικαιοσύνην τὴν ἐκ [τοῦ] νόμου (v. 5) and ἡ δὲ ἐκ πίστεως δικαιοσύνη is, indeed, intriguing and not finally solved. The difference between the expression Μωϋσῆς γράφει (v. 5) and δικαιοσύνη οὕτως λέγει (v. 6), which has customarily been understood as a contrast, may also be understood as an explanation. As Giblin has noted, what 'righteousness of faith' says may signify 'how the text reads' (from the perspective of righteousness by faith) in the sense of 'what the text means' (p. 285). By referring to the subject of the citation not as 'Moses' but as ἡ ἐκ πίστεως δικαιοσύνη, Paul seems to indicate that 'it is not the human speaker but the divine theme or gift that is really in question' (p. 286).

A careful analysis of the context of Deut 30.12-14 shows that Paul's use of the OT is less arbitrary and irrelevant than has been assumed.³²⁸ One could even say that for understanding Paul's exegesis here it is more important to know the OT itself than knowing the possible extrabiblical parallels which he might have used.³²⁹ Pau's exegetical procedure departs significantly from contemporary rabbinic exegesis. In the light of the Christ event, Paul draws his argument from the very thrust of the context in order to prove his thesis that the righteousness of God manifested in Christ for all who believe has already been announced by the law and the prophets (Rom 3.21). It is important to observe that the words introducing the quotation, 'do not say in you heart', are taken from two Deuteronomy passages (8.17 and 9.4–6) which warn against the human tendency to forget the absolute initiative of the divine mercy.³³⁰ At the same time, these passages warn against the human attitude of saying 'because of *my* righteousness' (in the LXX, διὰ τὰς δικαιοσύνας μου), a phrase which very much recalls Rom 10.3 and points again to the mistake of Israel—Paul's major concern in the context—of ignoring 'the righteousness of God' and trying to establish *their own*.[331] The fact that Paul sees as a characteristic of the new dispensation the circumcision of the heart (Rom 2.29), and that this is precisely stated in Deut 30.6, 16, makes it easier to understand why has he chosen this chapter as anticipatory of righteousness by faith. The fact that the promised 'circumcision of the heart' was understood as a messianic prophecy (Jer 31.33; 32.39-40; Ezek 11.19-20; 36.26-27) explains that Paul could use this passage as one of those most clearly pointing towards the NT.[332]

It seems that what Paul wishes to show is that already from the very first moments when the Torah was being promulgated, God indicated that his real will for Israel was to pursue, as the way of life, the way of faith.[333] This helps to explain why Paul deleted the expressions referring directly to 'doing' and emphasized the expressions referring to 'believing', a manoeuvre that may only be properly understood when the context of the OT passages is kept in mind rather than disregarded. The law (Deut 30.11) is already identified with the *word* in the same context (30.14) and summarized in 30.6 with the basic precept of 'love God with all your heart, etc.'. But this love of God, by which Israel will live is, according to the context, not the work of man but rather the work of God himself, the result of God's circumcising his people's heart (30.6). So, although Paul may seem to pass beyond the conscious intentions of the OT text, it cannot be said that he gives an entirely new meaning to the OT quotation. In a comprehensive and creative way, he is just developing a theme suggested by the text itself.[334] Since the original passage was already dealing with the accessibility of God's word of grace to his people,[335] it cannot be said that Paul was misapplying a 'law-righteousness' text to a 'faith-righteousness' purpose. He could see his concept of 'righteousness by faith in Christ' with 'the word which is near' (Deut 30.14) because the basic idea underlying both concepts is the same: God bringing life by grace.[336] If the real will of God for his people was the way of faith, as the Targum Neofiti worded it, 'listening to the voice of His Word and cleaving to Him' (the word is personified!),[337] applying this to Christ, Paul remained faithful to the Deuteronomy text.[338]

Paul's Christological interpretation

The phrases τίς ἀναβήσεται εἰς τὸν οὐρανόν and τίς καταβήσεται εἰς τὴν ἄβυσσον in Deut 30.13 refer obviously to the 'commandment': 'For this commandment which I command you this day is not too hard for you; neither is it far off' (Deut 30.11). Whatever may be the tradition which Paul had in mind, it is evident that these expressions indicate inaccessibility.[339] God does not require the impossible, or even better, God has done everything to put his word 'very near to you'. The change of the term 'abyss' for the OT 'Great Sea' is less a deviant variation than it seems at first view if one takes into consideration other parallels in contemporary Judaism where the space dimensions were often changed from horizontal to vertical categories. For example, 'the other side' was changed to "the deep", and "the other side of the sea" was changed to 'under the sea'.[340] Therefore, 'crossing the sea' might be replaced by a descent into the depth without any perception of a real change of meaning.[341] The point Paul wishes to make clear (perhaps not unrelated with the athletic imagery of 9.31-33)[342] is that what God desires from man is not *doing* a superhuman effort ('ascent'/'descent') but *accepting* what God has done. In the concrete case of Israel, what God desires is faith response to the 'Word' of the gospel which God has made 'near' in the Christ event and the apostolic proclamation.

Many scholars have centered their attention on the strange imagery and the Christology involved in the phrases τοῦτ' ἔστιν Χριστὸν καταγαγεῖν and τοῦτ' ἔστιν Χριστὸν ἐκ νεκρῶν ἀναγαγεῖν. But a careful reading of the text in context shows that the point is not here, but in the 'nearness of the Word': the term ἐγγύς is in position of emphasis. If Paul interprets Deut 30.11-14 christologically, it is only to show that the law already pointed towards the manifestation of God's righteousness in Christ, that is to say, that what God said in the OT he has done in the Christ event preached by the Apostle. If Paul seems to feel free to modify the form of the text by inserting his exposition, it is because of the light of the revelation of God in Christ.[343] Paul may at the same time allude to the Jewish belief of his time that if enough people in Israel perfectly and completely obeyed the law, then God would send the Messiah.[344] Paul would have argued that God has already sent the Messiah down and exalted him again in the person of Jesus of Nazareth. Christ, therefore, has already done for us what was not possible for men to do: he has descended to the realm of the dead and ascended to the heights of heaven in order to bring God's salvation 'near' (or even 'nearer') to all.[345] The 'ascent/descent' language in Deut 30.12-14 favored the christological application which Paul made in Rom 10.6-8. This is true more because of Paul's theological view of the relationship between Torah and Christ than because of the existence of pre-Pauline exegetical traditions. It was Paul's perspective on the relation of Christ to the Torah which allowed him to insert these christological phrases without fundamentally changing the original meaning of the text or departing in any way from the thrust of his argument in the context of Rom 10.

The Deut 30.14 statement on the nearness of the Word permitted Paul to see a further link between the divine grace made accessible by God in the Torah with the divine grace made accessible by God in Christ the Word.[346] To claim to read in this passage a radical opposition between Christ and the law is simply nonsensical in the light of Paul's commentary on Deut 30.14 (Rom 10.8-9). It would mean trying to find antithesis where Paul intended continuity. Only because Paul understood Christ as the substance and innermost content of both the Torah and the gospel could he identify the *word* (ῥῆμα of Torah in Deut 30.14 with the *word* of the gospel in the Christian proclamation (τοῦτ' ἔστιν τὸ ῥῆμα τῆς πίστεως ὃ κηρύσσομεν).[347] In the same way as δικαιοσύνη was present (ἐγγύς) in the ῥῆμα of Torah upheld by Israel, so also Christ, the τέλος of Torah, is present in the Word preached by the Christian church, even though he is not present in the flesh. In the same way as God brought the Word of life near to his people in his proclamation of Torah through Moses, so God has brought the Word of salvation near his people in his proclamation of Christ through the church. By means of the categories of δικαιοσύνη and ῥῆμα Paul shows that Christ is the perfect expression of God's will of salvation.

This ῥῆμα τῆς πίστεως, in the light of the context and of 3.27, is to be understood as 'the word which calls for (a response of) faith'.[348] This word is the gospel, the proclaimed message of God's faithfulness.[349] This clear identification of Christ with the Word of Torah and the Word of the gospel shows that the δικαιοσύνην τὴν ἐκ νόμου of Rom 10.5 and the ἐκ πίστεως δικαιοσύνη of Rom 10.6-8 are not two incompatible realities, but one and the same thing.[350] Therefore, Lev 18.5 and Deut 30.11-14 are not intended to be antithetical but to explain each other. The δικαιοσύνη now revealed in Christ is that which the Torah promised. Life by God's mercy made available through faith was the focal point of both passages. The Word who was near in the Torah is the same Word which is now near in the gospel, namely, Christ.[351] It seems, then, that both quotations are intended to explicate Rom 10.4. Understood against the thrust of the passage, they make perfect sense in their context: God's δικαιοσύνη as announced in the OT has been made accessible to all through faith in God's Messiah. And this, says Paul, Israel should have known.[352] Therefore, it may be concluded that Paul has probably quoted the OT *ad sensum*. For his apparent 're-interpretation' of the OT texts is nothing but the result of the teleological, deeply organic relationship which he saw between the Torah's promises and message and their fulfillment in Christ. For this kind of relationship Paul found a perfect formulation: τέλος νόμου Χριστός.

Romans 10.9-21

It is not necessary for the present purpose to interpret the rest of the chapter in detail. There are, however, several points in these remaining verses which are worth noticing. 'The Word which is near' is the basis for the following development. By means of a true *catena* of rhetorical questions and Scriptural proof-texts, Paul stresses the concept that salvation has been made accessible to all in Jesus Christ. The emphasis is both on the universal scope of the divine initiative and on the absolute responsiblility of human response. The whole passage looks very much like a *pesher*,[353] in which every statement is sustained by (and explains) one or more Scriptural citations,[354] carefully constructed and closely linked by a most intricate series of conjunctions.[355] It seems as if vv. 5-8 were the explanation of Rom 10.4a ('Christ is the τέλος of the law'), and vv. 9-13 were the explanation of Rom 10.4b ('for righteousness to everyone who believes'). This new section explains the practical way in which salvation has been made accessible to all, with an emphasis on Israel's guilty rejection of the gospel.[356]

In v. 9 the content of τὸ ῥῆμα τῆς πίστεως is equated by Paul with the Christian κήρυγμα (ὃ κηρύσσομεν): ἐὰν ὁμολογήσῃς ἐν τῷ στόματί σου κύριον Ἰησοῦν, καὶ πιστεύσῃς ἐν τῇ καρδίᾳ σου ὅτι ὁ θεὸς αὐτόν ἤγειρεν ἐκ νεκρῶν, σωθήσῃ.[357] Some scholars see in this verse a pre-Pauline formula of confession[358] coming from a baptismal setting[359] or at least as a summary of baptismal instruction.[360] In any case, the recitative aspect makes this sentence appear like a formula of Christian confession. Ὁμολογεῖν is a juridical term which usually refers to 'public declaration'.[361] Here it probably means 'to confess' or 'to proclaim' in the sense of having the courage to stand for the Christian message, which is, indeed, what Paul desires for his kinsmen (cf. 10.1; 9.1-3). The phrase κύριον Ἰησοῦν proves that for Paul Israel's failure was nothing but the rejection of Jesus as Messiah. The point in the confession is precisely the specific Christian belief that God raised Jesus from the dead and that now he is Lord.

Verse 10 is almost a repetition of v. 9, in a chiastic way. This shows that the two sentences καρδία γὰρ πιστεύεται εἰς δικαιοσύνην and στόματι δὲ ὁμολογεῖται εἰς σωτηρίαν[362] are parallel, and no substantial distinction is intended here between δικαιοσύνη and σωτηρία, both referring to God's saving acts.[363] The constructions εἰς δικαιοσύνην and εἰς σωτηρίαν help us to understand the phrase εἰς δικαιοσύνην in Rom 10.4 and the meaning of δικαιοσύνη in this context.

Verse 11 quotes Isa 28.16b for the second time (cf. 9.33). That ἐν αὐτῷ is intended to refer to Christ is clear, and confirms that Christ was also the object of ἐπ’ αὐτῷ in 9.33.[364] The addition of πᾶς (in the sense of 'anyone', 'whoever') to this citation betrays Paul's concern for universality.[365] If the universal scope of salvation is highly emphasized throughout chs. 9–11, in the immediate context of Rom 10.4 it is particularly stressed by the frequent use of the word πᾶς (repeated in 10.4, 5, 11, 12, 13, and 16) and in the explicit declaration of v. 12: 'There is *no distinction* (οὐ γάρ ἐστιν διαστολή) between Jew and Greek; the same Lord is Lord of *all*, and bestows his riches upon *all* who call upon him'. God's grace is not only ἐγγύς but available to πᾶς. This abolition of the distinction between Jew and Greek in salvation history is an essential concept which needs to be taken into consideration for the understanding of this passage, since it is its very issue. According to Käsemann, 'problems arise if one emphasizes that individual faith is at issue'.[366] The accent of the passage is on the ecclesiological aspect, on the coming together of a community where Jews and Gentiles are included on the same basis before God. As ch. 11 confirms, Paul's emphasis on οὐ διαστολή, 'no difference', between Jews and Gentiles, presupposes the existence of a (Gentile) tendency to exclusiveness which Paul wishes to correct on the theological basis that 'to the universality of guilt and doom there now corresponds that of grace'.[367]

Verses 12 and 13 insist on the theme of universality and recall 3.21-22 (cf. Eph 2.14): 'But now the righteousness of God has been manifested apart from the law, although the law and the prophets bear witness of it, the righteousness of God through faith in Jesus Christ for all who believe. For there is no distinction . . . ' In 3.23 the 'no distinction' is referred to the fact that since all are sinners, Gentiles and Jews alike can only be justified by God's mercy, through faith. In 10.11-13 this 'no distinction' is referred to the fact that the promises of acceptance through faith apply equally to Jews and Gentiles.[368] In both passages (3.21-22 and 9.30–10.13) Paul emphasizes the point that this δικαιοσύνη, which is the same for all in Christ, was the inner teaching of the Torah. What the Jews need to learn, according to Paul in this passage, is that righteousness is not theirs by right of descent or merits (ἐξ ἔργων). All mankind (Jews as well as Gentiles) stand under the promise of Scripture that they may reach righteousness by grace, for Christ (not explicitly stated, but obviously implied) 'is Lord of all (ὁ γὰρ αὐτὸς Κύριος πάντων) and is rich in mercy'. Insisting on the theme of universality, Paul quotes Joel 2.32 in v. 13 (3.5 LXX): Πᾶς [γὰρ] ὃς ἂν ἐπικαλέσηται τὸ ὄνομα κυρίου σωθήσεται. Again Paul applies to Christ what the OT said about God.[369] But here, the 'calling upon the name of the Lord' (ἐπικαλεῖ τὸ ὄνομα κυρίου), which is, indeed, a worship expression,[370] since 'the Lord' is identified with Jesus Christ, may imply an invitation to join the fellowship of the Christian communities.[371]

When 10.4 is compared with the quotations in 10.11 (Isa 28.16) and 10.13 (Joel 2.32), it appears that Paul has not departed at all from his topic and that 10.4 seems to be echoed as the *leitmotiv* of the passage:

10.4	*10.11*	*10.13 (and 9.33)*
τέλος νόμου	λέγει ἡ γραφὴ	λέγει ἡ γραφὴ
παντὶ	πᾶς	πᾶς ὃς ἂν
τῷ πιστεύοντι	ὁ πιστεύων	ἐπικαλέσηται
Χριστὸς	ἐπὶ αὐτῷ	τὸ ὄνομα κυρίου
εἰς δικαιοσύνην	οὐ καταισχυνθήσεται	σωθήσεται

Verses 14-18 answer possible objections against Paul's argument that the Word of the gospel was sufficiently made known to Israel. Paul concludes that there is no excuse for 'ignoring' Christ and, therefore, for unbelief (cf. 10.2-3): the Christian message (ῥήματος Χριστοῦ) has been preached to Israel (v. 17). Paul supports his argument (10.18) with a surprising reference to Ps 19.4. Since for Paul there is only one gospel (Gal 1.6-9) and Christ is both the τέλος (sum, apex, climax, etc.) of the Torah and the center of the gospel, the gospel was heard wherever the Torah was heard, and, therefore, it should have been known all through Israel's history.[372] What Paul seems to imply is that to know the Torah means to know the real meaning of God's δικαιοσύνη. If Israel had looked at the Torah from the standpoint of God's design of salvation, Israel would have found that Christ is the messianic manifestation of God's δικαιοσύνη and would have believed in Jesus Christ and confessed him as Lord (or κύριος).[373]

Verses 19-21 are also better understood in terms of the basic principle stated by Paul in 10.4, that Christ is the τέλος of the Torah. Since all Scriptures are intended to reach their ultimate fulfillment in Christ (the Word of God 'which never falls off' [9.6] ultimately also refers to Christ), the application to the Christ event of the words of Moses (v. 19, quoting Deut 32.21) and of Isaiah (v. 20, quoting Isa 65.1) is not for Paul an 'actualization' or 're-reading' of the OT words, but a verification of their fulfillment. If in Christ the plan of God has been fulfilled, to believe in Christ, for Paul, is simply to believe that the Word of God has come true. If Christ is as much present in the Torah as in the ῥῆμα τῆς πίστεως which Paul is preaching, then in Christ is speaking the same God who spoke in Deut 32.21 and in Isa 65.1. Therefore, to reject his word—by rejecting the gospel—is nothing but actualizing the rejection already experienced in the time of Moses and in the time of Isaiah.

In vv. 19-21 Paul sheds light on his understanding of election and God's faithfulness to his people. Even the election of the Gentiles has an essentially salvific purpose: 'I will make you jealous of those who are not a nation; with a foolish nation I will make you angry' (v. 19; cf. 11.11, 'through their trespass salvation has come to the Gentiles, so as to make Israel jealous'). The final aim of God is salvation for all (11.32; cf. 11.25-26, 'the fullness of the Gentiles' and 'all Israel').[374]

The last verse of this section (v. 21) summarizes a basic fact: 'Israel has, at least for the present, fallen from the destiny appointed for the people of God'.[375] Israel has rejected the person and message of Jesus and the gospel preached by Paul. Israel's traditional disobedience and obstinance (v. 21)[376] has culminated now in its rejection of Jesus. Israel has known but has rejected God's grace manifested in Christ. Yet Paul's emphasis is not on Israel's unfaithfulness but on

God's faithfulness: 'All the day long I have held out my arms to a disobedient and contrary people' (v. 21). For, as may be clearly seen in ch. 11, 'God has not abandoned them for what they are, because his mercy is greater than their guilt and than all human guilt'.[377]

Thus, vv. 14-21 conclude this section (9.30–10.21) in stating clearly that 'the word of God has not failed': the failure is Israel's. 'God's word continues to be valid because God is free and does not make the gift of justification dependent on human works.'[378] The phrase ἐκ πίστεως (10.9) removes all distinctions and special privileges. The obedience to the gospel remains Israel's only hope for salvation. This is why God has done (and will do) everything to bring Israel to faith in Christ. The practical point that Paul wishes to make for his Roman readers is clearly that the Church's mission to Israel has not ended: If God 'has not rejected his people' (11.1-2), and if in spite of their disobedience he is still 'all the day stretching his arms' to them (10.21),[379] the implication, which Paul develops later in the epistle,[380] is that the Church is supposed to do the same.[381]

Romans 10.4 within the General Context of Romans

The present exegetical approach has shown, on the one hand, that a temporal/terminal interpretation of τέλος in Rom 10.4 makes this passage strangely unrelated to the flow of thought of Rom 9–11. On the other hand, it has also shown how intimately related 10.4 is to the structure and theme of chs. 9–11 (and especially 9.30–10.21) if νόμος means Torah and if τέλος is understood teleologically. But there is more. If this interpretation is correct, then 10.4 not only concurs with the particular argument of chs. 9–11 but also serves the main message of Romans.

Examination of the *Sitz im Leben* and the occasion of Romans shows how closely related is the argument of Rom 9–11 with Paul's concern for the unity in the church.[382] The Israel problem had affected the relationship of members within the church. In chs. 9–11 Paul sets the theological basis for the solution of the problem. In chs. 12–16 he addresses to the church a moving call to unity: 'I bid everyone among you not to think of himself more highly than he ought to think' (12.3), 'for as in one body we have many members . . . so we, though many, are one body in Christ' (12.4-5); 'love one another, for love is the πλήρωμα of the law' (13.8-10). 'Welcome one another, therefore as Christ has welcomed you, for . . . Christ became a servant to the circumcised to show God's truthfulness, in order to confirm the promises given to the partiarchs, and in order that the Gentiles might glorify God for his mercy' (15.7-8). With this background, Paul expresses in 15.14-33 his concern for the problems related to the offering and his going to Jerusalem. In Rom 10.4 and context Paul shows that in Christ *all* the believers, Jews and Gentiles, are united in the same 'righteousness' of God, through their common faith. The theme that this new situation was, in fact, the fulfillment of Scripture is emphatically expressed in Rom 16.25-26:

16.25-26	*10.4*
According to the revelation of the mystery . . .	
and by the Scriptures of the prophets,	τέλος νόμου
according to the commandment	Χριστός
of the eternal God,	
has been known	
—according to my Gospel	
and the preaching of Jesus Christ -	
to all nations,	εἰς δικαιοσύνην
leading to obedience of faith.	παντὶ τῷ πιστεύοντι

Thus, Paul concludes by summarizing in this recapitulative sentence the basic theme of the epistle, stated in 1.16-17 and 3.21-31, and formulated in a brief but striking way in 10.4.

Though the relation between 10.4 and chs. 5–8 is less evident, it nevertheless exists. The main theme of chs. 5–8 is the result of living within 'God's righteousness'. In chs. 9–11 Paul deals with the concept of 'God's righteousness' and its particular implications at a corporate level, showing how it affects the concepts of 'election' and the sense of mission of the church, especially in relation to Israel. Some specific themes also relate these two section of the epistle. The motif that the law was intended to 'give life' in 10.5 is already announced in 7.10 (cf. 7.12-14). And Paul's concern for the salvation of his kinsmen the Jews, with the assurance that God has not rejected them, is somehow hinted at or anticipated in 8.28-38, with the question, 'Who shall bring any charge against God's elect?' (8.33), and the subsequent development.

The relationship between Rom 10.4 and the content of chs. 1–4 is much more evident. Chapters 1–4 and 9–11 are linked both thematically (Jews and Gentiles vis-à-vis the gospel) and formally (by the common diatribe style). Some questions of ch. 3 are answered only in chs. 9–11. The material and formal relation of chs. 1–4 and 9–11 is so completely self-consistent, and it shows such a continuous development of thought and use of Scripture when compared with chs. 5–8 that some have suggested that chs. 1–4 and 9–11 are part of the same document, while chs. 5–8 constitutes a unity in itself, independent of the rest of the letter.[383] Though this view is not convincing, it is evident that there is an extremely close relationship between the argument of Rom 1–4 and 9–11, which can be perceived in several internal links:

1. Chapters 9–11 are the final unfolding of the theme stated in 1.16: 'I am not ashamed of the gospel: it is a power of God for salvation to everyone who has faith, to the Jew first and also to the Greek'. Only in chs. 9–11 does Paul explain at length what he meant by 'to the Jew first and also to the Greek'.[384]

2. In Rom 9.30–10.21 Paul answers some of the questions he asked but did not answer in 3.1-5. Thus, the question, 'What advantage has the Jew?' (3.1) Paul partially answered in 3.2: 'Much in every way. To begin with, the Jews are entrusted with the oracles of God (τὰ λόγια τοῦ θεοῦ).' But only in chs. 9–11 does Paul show how these privileges make the situation of Israel particularly perplexing: Israel's privileges (enumerated in 9.4-5), including 'the giving of the law' and 'the promises', should have allowed Israel to be the first to recognize Jesus as the Messiah. But the facts turned out a different way, and some Gentiles—who did not have the law nor any desire to be accepted into God's people—were accepted by their faith in Christ (9.30). However, Israel, who had the Torah, did not get its message (9.31-32), and, rejecting Christ, did not understand that the Torah pointed to Christ as God's way of righteousness (10.2-4).

3. The affirmation that the 'righteousness of God' announced in the Scripture pointed to Christ is not a new idea introduced for the first time in 10.2-4. From the very beginning of Romans Paul states that 'the gospel of God . . . he promised beforehand through his prophets in the holy scriptures . . . concerning his Son . . . Jesus Christ our Lord . . . to bring about the obedience of faith among all the nations' (1.1-5). The main themes of the epistle are linked to this statement: 'In it [the gospel] the righteousness of God is revealed through faith for faith; as it is written, 'He who through faith is righteous shall live' (1.16-17). From the programmatic affirmation in 3.21-22 that 'the righteousness of God has been manifested apart from the law, although the law and the prophets bear witness to

it . . . for all who believe', there is a logical movement in the reasoning of Paul whose final purpose is to show that the 'righteousness of God' is to be found in Christ, *and* that this was the ultimate teaching of Scripture. Paul states that 'we do not overthrow the law by this faith', 'on the contrary, we uphold the law' (3.31) precisely because the teachings of the law (as Paul sees it in ch. 4 with the examples of Abraham and David) is that man is justified by faith in God's promises (which ultimately all pointed to Christ). Thus 9.30–10.13 is in a certain sense just an extension of the thematic and scriptural development started in ch. 4.

4. Similarly, the issue of the consistency and reliability of God's word, started in 9.6 and developed in 9.7–11.35, is not a new issue in Romans. It appears as the scriptural proof for the statement made in 3.21. ὁ λόγος τοῦ θεοῦ probably refers to the oracles which promised to Israel the Messianic salvation. It is, indeed, a programmatic statement for the argument in chs. 9–11.[385] It certainly refers to a series of OT statements on the efficacy, immutability, and irrevocability of the divine word.[386] Now, in the light of the Christ event, Paul sees that what God said he has fulfilled in Christ, the true Λόγος θεοῦ. From this perspective, Paul sees the answer to the paradox of how Israel, 'the people of the promises' (9.1-6), by rejecting the gospel has rejected the very righteousness of God announced by the law and the prophets (3.21), while Gentiles, by accepting Christ, have become heirs of the divine promises (9.8, 25-26, 31). The basic idea that Paul wants to make clear in this passage is that what God promised he has really done. What we find in Christ is what God promised in his word.

5. In the same way, the question of 3.3-5, 'Does their faithlessness nullify the faithfulness of God?', is answered in the epistle only in chs. 9–11. That 'God is righteous' (cf. 3.26) means that he keeps his promises. And since God's promises to the patriarchs included the blessing of all nations, the theme of the righteousness of God encompasses both concepts: (a) that he is self-consistent and (b) that he rectifies the ungodly, both aspects treated together in chs. 1–4 and in 9–11.

6. If the consensus that Rom 3.21-26 is a programmatic summary of Paul's theology in Romans is accepted,[387] then the relation of Rom 10.4 to the argument of the epistle becomes even more evident. In Rom 3—and throughout the letter—Paul endeavors to demonstrate that the gospel which he preaches, which Gentiles believe, is none

other than the good news of the fulfillment of God's promises. The Christ event proclaimed by the gospel is the definitive revelation and culmination of the divine purpose for which God first entered into covenant with Israel. In the gospel the righteousness of God has been revealed as a power which, through faith in Christ, leads to salvation (cf. 1.16). The gospel is to Jews first but also to the Gentiles. This 'theological center' seems to be the basis for Paul's argument in Rom 9–11.[388] One could say that, to some extent, Rom 3.21–4.25 is a presupposition for 9.30–10.21,[389] and that in a certain sense chs. 9–11 are the criterion by which one may judge whether 3.21-22 (and hence, the message of Romans) has been rightly understood.[390]

7. Perhaps the most interesting link between Rom 10.4 (within the context of 9.30–10.21) and the programmatic passages of the beginning of the epistle, particularly 3.21 (within the context of 3.21–4.25) is the positive relationship which they state between 'faith', 'righteousness', 'the law', and 'Christ'. Nowhere in the Pauline writings do we find two more positive statements of this kind. As Rhyne has rightly observed, though Paul could also present some aspects of this relationship in negative terms, as he did in several other places, it is undeniable that in these two instances he wanted to take a positive viewpoint.[391] Only because Paul regarded the law as teleologically oriented to Christ concerning righteousness for whoever believes (10.4) could he say that 'faith establishes the Law' (3.21).

8. Finally, the close relation of Rom 10.4 to the theme of the epistle may be most clearly seen when 10.4 is placed in parallel with the programmatic statements in 1.1-5, 1.16, and 3.21-22, as the following chart shows:

Rom. 1.1-5	*Rom. 1.16*	*Rom. 3.21-22*	*Rom. 10.4*
εὐαγγέλιον θεοῦ περὶ Ἰησοῦ Χριστοῦ	τὸ εὐαγγέλιον δύναμις θεοῦ ἐστιν	διὰ πίστεως Ἰησοῦ Χριστοῦ	Χριστός
προεπηγγείλατο		μαρτυρουμένη ὑπὸ τοῦ νόμου	τέλος νόμου
διὰ τῶν προφητῶν αὐτοῦ ἐν γραφαῖς ἁγίαις		καὶ τῶν προφητῶν	

Rom. 1.1-5	Rom. 1.16	Rom. 3.21-22	Rom. 10.4
εἰς	εἰς		εἰς
ὑπακοὴν	σωτηρίαν	δικαιοσύνη θεοῦ	δικαιοσύνην
πίστεως		πεφανέρωται	
ἐν πᾶσιν	παντὶ	εἰς πάντας	παντὶ
	τῷ πιστεύοντι	τοὺς πιστεύοντας	τῷ πιστεύοντι
	Ἰουδαίῳ τε	οὐ γάρ ἐστιν	
	πρῶτον		
τοῖς ἔθνεσιν	καὶ Ἕλληνι	διαστολή	

The basic content of these passages may thus be summarized: the all-embracing scope of the gospel, extending God's righteousnesss to whoever believes in Christ—Jews as well as Gentiles—is nothing but the fulfillment of Scripture. So, it may be concluded that Rom 10.4 is not only fully related to the general argument of Romans, but it contains, as in a nutshell, the main themes of the epistle.

Summary

The results of the present exegetical approach to Rom 10.4 and its context may be summarized in the following conclusions:

1. Rom 10.4 belongs to 9.30–10.21, the central part of the literary and theological unit formed by chs. 9–11. At the background of this large section is the problem of the Jewish question and its consequences for Jewish-Gentile relations within the church and its mission. The issues addressed in chs. 9–11 are related to Israel's rejection of Christ, and how this rejection affects: (a) the faithfulness of God's word ('Have God's promises to Israel failed since most of Israel is "outside" the new people of God?', 9.6), and (b) the status of Israel vis-à-vis God ('Has God rejected Israel?', 11.1).

2. The theme of how the self-exclusion of Israel is determined by its rejection of Christ dominates Rom 9.30–10.21. Basing his argument on the consistency of God's word and action, Paul shows that righteousness and salvation in the Messianic era—like election in the patriarchal era—do not depend on merits or works, but only on God's grace, and, therefore, can only be obtained through faith in Jesus the Messiah.

3. In order to prove the point of God's consistency, Paul endeavors to show, by means of abundant recourse to Scripture, that the new situation was foretold in the law and the prophets. Therefore, the

gospel is not contrary to God's promises but rather is the fulfillment of those promises.

4. Christ is, then, the λίθος προσκόμματος (9.33): Israel stumbled over him because it did not follow the law from the perspective of faith but from a perspective of works (9.31-32), and did not submit to God's δικαιοσύνη (by acceptance of Christ, 10.2-4). Gentiles, however, believed in Christ and received δικαιοσύνη (9.30).

5. When the term δικαιοσύνη is used in this section, it seems that the emphasis is on its corporate implications, to the point that sometimes 'righteousness' refers to status within the new people of God, or even acceptance within God's people (9.30).

6. The use of the term νόμος in this context (9.31; 10.4, 5) suggests that it refers to the general concept of 'Torah' as it was understood in Paul's contemporary Judaism, and designates the OT, perhaps mainly in its revelatory aspects.

7. The thrust of the passage does not favor the interpretation of Rom 10.4 in the sense that Christ has abrogated, or terminated, the law (in whatever sense it may be understood). Christ is not presented in the context as antithetical to νόμος; therefore, τέλος makes better sense if it is understood teleologically rather than temporally. The meaning of Rom 10.4, then, would be that the way contemplated in the law for receiving God's righteousness is through Christ, by faith, and that this way applies to all (including the Jews).

8. Rom 10.5 and 10.6-8 do not need, then, to be interpreted in contrast, as though δικαιοσύνη ἐκ νόμου and πίστεως δικαιοσύνη stand in opposition to each other as two antithetical realities, or as two successive, or parallel ways of 'righteousness'. Paul does not oppose Lev 18.5 to Deut 30.11-14 nor 'law' to 'faith' in order to demonstrate the unfulfillability of the law or to show that righteousness by works was superseded as a way of salvation by Christ. The issue of fulfillability of the law is completely absent from Paul's argument here, and Paul never accepts the possibility (after or prior to Christ) of salvation by works. Both quotations seem intended to be taken as complementary, to explicate the meaning of Rom 10.4: that God's way of righteousness was 'by faith' already in the writings of Moses. The quotation of Lev 18.5 (Rom 10.5) is probably intended to prove that 'life' for the believer comes through the way of righteousness indicated by God in Scripture.

9. Paul's so-called *pesher* in Rom 10.6-8 is better understood in the light of Deut 30.11-14 and its context than in the light of its Jewish

parallels. The point which Paul wants to make by referring to the 'ascent/descent' motif is 'the nearness of the word': God has made everything in order to bring salvation near to his people. What was inaccessible for man, God made accessible through Christ. He is the word which is near, both in the Torah and in the gospel.

10. Thus, it may be concluded that the relation between Christ and the OT is described by Paul in teleological categories. The OT is presented as teleologically oriented toward Christ, and Christ is presented as the fulfillment and realization of God's design as expressed in Scripture. Therefore, when Paul interprets and applies the OT christologically, he cannot be charged with doing it in an arbitrary way. His vision of Christ allowed him to extend to Jesus Christ what the OT text said about God or about God's action. Perhaps it could be said that Paul's use of the OT in this section of Romans is not so much for proof as it is for proclamation.

If this contextual interpretation is correct, Rom 10.4 appears to contribute to the theological argument which Paul develops in Rom 9–11: (1) It supports the statement that 'the word of God has not failed', for the OT already pointed to Christ for righteousness; (2) it implies that Israel has not been rejected by God, since in Christ righteousness is available to whoever believes; and (3) it appeals to unity and mutual concern among Gentiles and Jews within the Christian community, since in Christ all the believers are united in the eschatological people of God.

SUMMARY AND CONCLUSION

The historical survey of Chapter 1 has shown that the interpretation of Rom 10.4 suffered a considerable shift in the course of time. The early, Greek-speaking church saw in Rom 10.4 a statement of the fulfillment (τέλος) of the OT (νόμου) in Christ in its prophecies and/or in its purposes. As the church grew and developed beyond its original Jewish environment, it gradually lost sight of the problems of its origins and it became more and more unable to understand Paul's situational concerns in Rom 9–11. At the same time, as the language evolved, the polysemy of τέλος allowed this word to be translated in various ways, and Rom 10.4 was given several new interpretations. During the Middle Ages, all these interpretations were preserved as containing facets of the multifold biblical truth. The Reformers, however, with their emphasis on literal and contextual exegesis, reacted against the multiple-meaning tradition and returned to a single meaning for τέλος, generally teleological (Luther), but also perfective (Calvin). In the post-Reformation era, the old Pauline arguments between Judaism and Christianity were read through the new theological controversies between Protestantism and Catholicism, and the conflict between works and faith was transferred—sometimes indiscriminately—to the relationship between law and gospel. A systematic depreciation of the 'law statements' followed, and mis-understanding of the thrust of Rom 9–11 resulted, favoring an antinomian interpretation of Rom 10.4. The nineteenth-century understanding of the progressive character of religious history con-tributed, among other factors, to the widespread temporal, terminal, and antinomian interpretations of this verse. Because of its concise and axiomatic form, the phrase 'Christ is the end of the law' became a common theological dictum, summarizing in a short and easy formula a whole conception of Paul's doctrine of the law which may be true of a certain understanding of Paul's law theology, but which has not proved to be true to its original intent and context.

Recent scholarship has largely supported the temporal interpret-ations by means of eschatological or existential developments. How-ever, some authors have come back to teleological interpretations on the basis of theological and philological arguments, while a growing number of scholars have felt the necessity of adding some teleological explanations to their temporal/terminal interpretations. Most of their attempts, however, have failed to fully grasp the nature of the problem of Rom 10.4 and have thus been unable to provide a satisfactory solution. The contemporary debate on the interpretation of Rom 10.4 appears to be governed by two dominant factors: the inevitable weight of a generalized tradition of interpretation and the customary habit of interpreting this passage from the starting point of Paul's law theology elsewhere. The thrust of the context and the semantic analysis of its vocabulary have been largely neglected. The attention has concentrated on νόμος and the question of legalism, while the meaning of τέλος has generally been assumed from the understanding of νόμος without any semantic substantiation.

The study of Chapter 2 has shown that the semantic import of τέλος is primarily 'teleological' (directive, purposive, completive), not temporal or terminal. Τέλος with genitive is specifically used to indicate result, purpose, outcome, but not termination. The phrase τέλος νόμου, in all the instances that have been found in the present research, denotes either the object/purpose of the law or its fulfillment, never its abrogation. Therefore, the current translation of Rom 10.4 as 'end of the law' in the sense of termination/cessation/abrogation would be, linguistically speaking, exceptional and hardly—if at all—correct. Although it is true that biblical terminology has to be understood primarily in its biblical context, it is methodologically problematic 'to separate the biblical language from other language as belonging to a different kind'.[392] The recourse to extra-biblical controls was particularly necessary in the present case because τέλος is not a theologoumenon and because the expression τέλος νόμου is a biblical hapax legomenon. Since the biblical use of τέλος with the genitive in expressions similar to τέλος νόμου Χριστός does not differ grammatically from that of Paul's contemporaries, the soundest working hypothesis has been to assume that τέλος νόμου in Rom 10.4 has the same syntactical meaning as elsewhere in Hellenistic literature. Moreover, it has seemed methodologically preferable to work on the assumption that τέλος retains its common teleological meaning until the context determines whether the term in Rom 10.4 has received a 'new content'.[393]

A related question is to find, within the teleological spectrum of meanings of τέλος, the precise nuance intended by Paul in the concrete instance. The word τέλος might have had some overtones which led Paul to choose it instead of another, and which might have been discernible to his readers but is not immediately apparent to us. This is why a survey of the use of the word in biblical and cognate literature, especially in Hellenistic Jewish writings contemporary to Paul is deemed necessary. As D.F. Payne has shown, the choice of a word, in the case of a biblical writer, 'is an expression of the depth of his understanding. To subject his utterances too rigidly to the formal rules, and to limit his meaning to one straight equivalent, may be to miss the subtle pictures which he evokes by the use of this word rather than that, this image rather than the other'.[394] Paul's definition of the relationship between Christ and the law in Rom 10.4 by the use of the word τέλος, one of the most fashionable terms in contemporary Hellenistic philosophy, is hardly accidental. The fact that this term was used as a *terminus technicus* for designating the supreme goal, the highest purpose, the *summum bonum*, can be hardly overlooked. Consequently, an effort to be sensitive to Paul's semantic reasons in his choice of this philosophically significant term has governed the cautious attitude of the present study vis-à-vis the determination of the specific meaning of τέλος in Rom 10.4. It has seemed more accurate—though apparently less precise—to delimit a whole cluster of meanings and speak of 'teleological' categories of signification rather than to isolate, between the different possible renderings, only one, such as 'fulfillment', 'climax', or 'goal'. Also, since some of the shades of meaning within the teleological range are hardly differentiable, it is problematic to decide which is *the one* intended by Paul. By the same token, some of these notions are so divergent that it is equally problematic to settle for the view that all are intended.

It is extremely difficult to ascertain from contextual evidence whether Paul intended more than one meaning. It seems more reasonable, therefore, to stay within the margin of latitude allowed by the context and the philological research on parallels. A dynamic translation like 'the law points to (or intends) Christ . . . ' is faithful and broad enough to accommodate the semantically essential content of τέλος without discarding the related nuances of 'purpose', 'goal', 'climax', or 'fulfillment', and without going beyond what the text allows in the delimitation of its precise shade of meaning. However, to claim that τέλος means both 'goal/fulfillment' and 'termination/ abrogation' in Rom 10.4 is another matter. To ascertain such a possibility would require, besides a convincing semantic substantiation and a contextual evidence of such a *double entendre*, a satisfactory solution to the problem of Paul's recourse to ambiguity vis-à-vis his audience.

The exegetical undertaking in Chapter 3 has shown that a teleological understanding of τέλος in Rom 10.4 is substantiated also on contextual grounds. In fact, the teleological understanding of the text is more true to its context and more sensitive to the *Geist* of the passage and its latent dynamics than the temporal/terminal interpret- ations. It is largely agreed that Rom 9–11 revolves around the idea of purpose.[395] Paul's concern in this section is to prove that God's plan (as expressed in Scripture) has not failed (9.6), and that in spite of Israel's rejection of the Messiah God has remained true to his commitment. By continuous and systematic reference to the Scriptures Paul shows that God has been unquestionably faithful to his word and to his people.

In an unmistakably teleological view of *Heilsgeschichte*, Paul contrasts Israel's infidelity to God, manifested in its rejection of Christ, and God's fidelity to Israel, manifested in his sending of

Christ. Paul shows that God's sovereignty and wisdom in the carrying out of his salvific designs are so unsearchable that human resistance to them cannot hinder them (11.25-36). Thus, Israel's rejection of the gospel, instead of being an obstacle to the realization of God's plan, contributes to the expansion of the gospel and results in the conversion of the Gentiles (11.11). Moreover, even the inclusion of the Gentiles is working toward the conversion of Israel, so that God's ultimate goal will be attained and Israel will finally be brought back (11.25-26). In this teleological presentation of salvation history, Paul discusses Israel solely in its relation to Christ.[396] What Paul wishes to prove is that the Christ event is not a disruption of God's plan, but on the contrary, is its very τέλος, as foretold in Scripture (10.4); it is the culminating point to which God's πρόθεσις pointed (9.11) and the key for the understanding of God's salvific μυστήριον (11.25). So Paul shows that God's promises have been fulfilled in an unexpected way (11.33-36), yet faithfully to God's word, in 'Christ and the remnant.

Since the fulfillment of God's word to Israel could be apprehended as such only in the light of the ancient promises and the entire course of Israel's history, Paul proceeds to quote Scripture in a way intended to prove that the Christ event is the *aboutissement* of the whole Torah. The thrust of the passage suggests, then, that Paul uses νόμος in the sense of Torah as it stands for Scripture: the OT, not as something 'old' which has been abrogated by Christ but rather as the living word of God (Paul's only Bible!), ever true to itself (9.6) and, therefore, ever valid and new.[397] This understanding of νόμος is consistently maintained throughout the passage. It allows Paul to describe the relationship between Χριστός and νόμος in Rom 10.4 in a teleological perspective.

It now appears that Rom 10.4 is less ambiguous than it seemed at the beginning. On philological and contextual grounds, it appears that it should be understood teleologically: that Christ brings to the believer the righteousness promised in Scripture. It seems, then, hardly defensible to hold with Mussner and van Dülmen[398] that 'anyone who understands Rom 10.4 in the sense that Christ is the goal of the law had either totally misunderstood Paul's theology or is completely at odds with his conception of *Heilgeschichte*'.

The present exegetical approach has shown that in Rom 9.30–10.13 the law is presented as the witness of righteousness by faith. Paul insists that submission to the righteousness of God (identified with Christ) is, in fact, obedience to the law (10.3-8). This concept is not new, since in Rom 4 Paul quotes Gen 15.6 and Ps 32.1-4 in order to prove that righteousness by grace through faith was the teaching of Scripture. Paul, then, does not see the law invalidated by faith (3.31); on the contrary, in Christ the true content of the law (for Paul, the gospel) is fully revealed (3.21-26). In Rom 9.30–10.21 Paul seems to say that faith in Christ is at the same time true faith in the Torah. For, since the revelation of God is found in the Torah, right understanding of the law leads to faith in Jesus Christ. Therefore Paul can say that since the Jews did not understand the aim of the law and persisted in their wrong search for righteousness, they could not understand Jesus Christ and rejected him. And since they rejected him they could not understand God's righteousness, because it was supremely manifested in the Christ event (9.31–10.4). If this interpretation is correct, it follows that it is not necessary to interpret νόμος in Rom 9.30–10.21 as 'Jewish legalistic understanding of the law'. There is nothing requiring *ex hypothesi* the interpretation of νόμος here as being in opposition to Judaism. In this context Paul is not directly engaged in a polemic against the Jews. Therefore, an interpretation of this passage based on a misrepresentation of Judaism needs to be carefully reconsidered. As has been said, traditional apologetics have been sometimes easy and dangerous. But it cannot be seriously believed any more that it is necessary to identify Judaism and legalism in order to interpret Paul's view of the law in this passage, or denigrate the law in order to make the gospel triumph.[399]

It could be debated whether in Rom 9–11 Paul interprets history through Scripture or the other way around. But it is undeniable that Paul's hermeneutical starting point is his belief in Jesus as the Messiah who has come. If Paul sees the OT as witnessing to Christ, it is because he has first seen Christ. So, in the light of the Christ event Scripture takes on a new perspective for Paul. Since Christ is the fulfillment and climax of God's revelation to mankind, it follows that he is the key to the understanding of Scripture. Paul's hermeneutic is different from that of his contemporaries since it is based upon a new fact that traditional Judaism and the OT itself did not know: the Christ event. Paul's conversion meant, then, also a 'hermeneutical conversion': now he can read the Torah in the light of Christ, its τέλος, from an external point of reference (χωρὶς νόμου, 3.21), yet its very object and goal (μαρτυρουμένη ὑπὸ τοῦ νόμου . . .) and, therefore, the very key that gives full meaning to its promises, prophecies, types, and prefigurations.[400] This new perspective reveals to Paul that the Scriptures could be rightly understood only when seen 'in terms of their goal'.[401] God had so acted in Christ that the focal point of history, which gave meaning to the whole process, no longer lies in its remote ἀρχή but in its fulfilled τέλος. Therefore, Paul could no longer view his Torah as a legal code but as the history of God's salvific dealings with his people (cf. 9.31-33). He could therefore claim that in it the gospel was already promised, testified, and proclaimed (1.1-5, 16-17; 3.21-31; 10.4-21; 16.25-26). This is why Paul relates the Jews' wrong interpretation of Torah (9.31–10.8) to their not listening to the gospel (10.8-21). Only their acceptance of the gospel would allow them to see what the Torah is really about. For Paul the issue of hermeneutic is closely related to faith.

When examined from this perspective, Paul's treatment of the OT in Rom 9.30–10.21 cannot be called arbitrary or out of context.[402] It aimed to render the new situation brought about by the Christ event intelligible in the light of Scripture, to show that the Word of God not only 'has not failed', but is coherent with God's intervention in history. From the perspective of the 'Word of God which has been made near in Christ' (10.8-9), the OT message becomes meaningful even if the new realities differ from the traditional interpretations of the Scriptures and Israel's expectancies. The expressions of the OT may seem hidden and obscure—God's word is always a mystery (11.25)—but they hint at the full truth and look forward to it. For Paul the eternal gospel of God is the true meaning of every passage of the Torah. This is why he could explain his axiomatic declaration in Rom 10.4 by means of Lev 18.5 and Deut 30.12-14. For Christ is the hermeneutical key which makes intelligible what was always the law's true meaning and purpose (10.4-8). From such a perspective, Paul saw that the law always required a response of faith.

In the light of such an encompassing understanding of the Torah-Christ relation, it is not difficult to see why the simple fulfillment of historical predictions seems to be less important to Paul than to other NT writers. Even the broader fulfillment of types seems to him of secondary importance. For Paul the relation of the OT to Christ is much deeper and more consistent than that. Its structure cannot be reduced to the categories of prediction–fulfillment or typology.[403] Paul expresses it in a category more basic and comprehensive than these, namely, in the teleological category of purpose and realization. Since Paul saw Christ as the end toward which the law was directed, it may be deduced that Christ took the place of the centrality of the law in Paul's life, but that Paul's respect for the law remained the same (3.31; 7.12, 14). However, Paul's veneration for the law was surpassed by his veneration for Christ. This surpassing of Torah by Christ is what Paul wished to teach Israel and this is what Israel did not accept. As a corollary to Paul's understanding of the law in the light of Christ, it follows that he could not view the law any more as an end in itself but as a means. Precisely what Paul reproached the Jews for was their looking at the law as a goal in itself (9.31-32); they did not see that it pointed and led to Christ (10.4).[404]

Paul appears in Rom 9–11 as 'a rabbi who became a Christian evangelist'[405] or, even better, as an apostle charged with a mission.[406] The originality of Paul, his capacity to assimilate and transform the elements of the thought of his world (Jewish and Hellenistic) and incorporate them in a biblical perspective, and his genius of creativity are better understood in the light of the mission he claims to have received through divine relevation (Rom 1.1-5; cf. Gal 1.11-12). His way of explaining the inspired writings and the meaning of the facts of salvation history is similar to that of the OT prophets. Paul, called and guided by the Spirit, needs to be understood, first of all, in light of revelation (Rom 1.1). He stands as an authoritative interpreter who uses the OT for proclamation more than for proof. His way of dealing with the sacred writings, then, it is not 'archeological', i.e. interested mainly in what the text *meant* but 'teleological', i.e. interested primarily in what the text intended to mean, and, therefore, *means*.

In order to test the validity of the thesis that Paul dealt with the OT 'teleologically', the results of the present interpretation should be brought to bear on other related passages in Paul and the rest of the NT. The observations presented here may contribute constructively to the solution of the extremely complex problem of continuity and discontinuity between the OT and the NT. Teleology, perhaps, is the category that bridges and reconciles the conflicting issues of continuity and discontinuity. The present research attempts to serve as an introductory study to investigate an aspect of Paul's thought that has not been sufficiently explored. This approach seems to offer a rich and rewarding field for further research.

Notes to Introduction

1. See, for example, G.S. Sloyan, *Is Christ the End of the Law?* (Philadelphia: Westminster, 1978), a book in which Rom 10.4—the text which apparently motivated the title—is not only not examined, but is mentioned only once (p. 181).

2. See Günther Bornkamm, *Das Ende des Gesetzes* (Munich: Kaiser, 1961), a book in which, despite the title, Rom 10.4 is not only not dealt with, but never quoted.

3. Even a Pauline scholar of the category of Ernest Käsemann not only denies the possibility of understanding Rom 10.4 differently, but despises any other attempt at interpretation of τέλος, arguing that 'the message of the NT soon would no longer be recognizable if exegesis were allowed to exploit every linguistic possibility' (*Commentary on Romans*, trans. G.W. Bromiley [Grand Rapids: Eerdmans, 1980], p. 282).

4. So J.A. Fischer, 'Dissent within a Religious Community: Rom 9–11', *BTB* 10 (1980), p. 107, who argues, 'Paul's purpose in Rom 9–11 is to make the Jews understand that Christ is the end of the law', but does not explain how.

5. C.F.D. Moule, 'Obligation in the Ethics of Paul', in *Christian History and Interpretation: Studies Presented to John Knox*, ed. W.R. Farmer, C.F.D. Moule, and R.R. Niebuhr (Cambridge: University Press, 1967), p. 406.

6. For discussion of the question of Paul's view of νόμος in recent scholarship, see C.E.B. Cranfield, 'St. Paul and the Law', *SJT* 17 (1964), pp. 43-68; P. Démann, 'Moïse et la loi dans la pensée de Saint Paul', in *Moïse, l'homme de l'alliance*, ed. H. Cazelles et al. (Paris: Desclée de Brouwer, 1955), pp. 189-242; Lloyd Gaston, 'Paul and the Torah', in *Antisemitism and the Foundations of Christianity*, ed. A. Davies (New York: Paulist Press, 1979), pp. 48-71; W. Gutbrod, 'Νόμος', *TDNT*, IV, pp. 1036-91; F. Hahn, 'Das Gestzesverständnis im Römer- und Galaterbrief', *ZNW* 67 (1976), pp. 29-63; H. Hübner, *Das Gesetz bei Paulus: Ein Beitrag zum Werden der paulinischen Theologie* (FRLANT, 119; Göttingen: Vandenhoeck & Ruprecht, 1978), pp. 44-80; E. Käsemann, 'Sentences of Holy Law in the New Testament', in *New Testament Questions of Today* (London: SCM, 1969), pp. 66-81; O. Kuss, 'Νόμος bei Paulus', *MTZ* 17 (1966), pp. 173-227; G.E. Ladd, 'Paul and the Law', in *Soli Deo Gloria: New Testament Studies in Honor of W.C. Robinson*, ed. J.M. Richards (Richmond: J. Knox, 1968), pp. 50-67; P. von der Osten-Sacken, 'Das paulinische Verständnis des

Gesetzes im Spannungfeld von Eschatologie und Geschichte', *EvT* 37
(1977), pp. 549-87; A. Sand, 'Gesetz und Freiheit. Vom Sinn des Paulus-
wortes: Christus des Gesetzes Ende', *TGl* 61 (1971), pp. 1-14; J.A. Sanders,
'Torah and Paul', in *God's Christ and His People: Studies in Honor of Nils
Alstrup Dahl*, ed. J. Jervell and W.A. Meeks (Oslo: Universitetsforlaget,
1977), pp. 132-40; Peter Stuhlmacher, 'Das Gesetz als Thema biblischer
Theologie', *ZTK* 75 (1978), pp. 251-80; G. Wallis, 'Torah und Nomos: Zur
Frage nach Gesetz und Heil', *TLZ* 105 (1980), pp. 321-32; U. Wilckens, 'Zur
Entwicklung des paulinischen Gesetzesverständnis', *NTS* 28 (1982), pp. 154-
90; R. McL. Wilson, 'Nomos: The Biblical Significance of Law', *SJT* 5
(1952), pp. 36-48.

7. According to Cranfield, it is 'vital for the understanding of both 9.30–
10.2 and also of 10.5-13' (*A Critical and Exegetical Commentary on the
Epistle to the Romans* [ICC; Edinburgh: T. & T. Clark, 1979], II, p. 515).

8. *Commentary on Romans* (Andover: Gould & Newman, 1832), p. 455.

9. Käsemann, *Romans* (1980), p. 282.

10. The first, by Mary Ann Getty, 'Christ Is the End of the Law: Rom 10.4
in its Context' (Th.D. dissertation, Katholieke Universiteit Leuven, 1975), is
intended to challenge the Bultmannian interpretation of Rom 10.4 as it has
been recently defended by U. Luz. It approaches the passage from a
salvation-historical perspective and interprets 10.4 in the sense that the
Christ event has put an end to the era of the law (pp. 411-26). Thus far
unpublished, Sister Getty's study has been consulted for the present
research by special courtesy of its author. The second, by J.E. Toews, 'The
Law in Paul's Letter to the Romans: A Study of Rom 9.30–10.13' (Ph.D.
dissertation, Northwestern University, 1977), deals at length with the
immediate context of Rom 10.4 (especially 9.30-33), but does not take into
consideration the larger context of chs. 9–11. It interprets τέλος as 'goal' on
'philosophical and contextual grounds' (p. 335), although the only rationale
given for that interpretation is theological. Toews's dissertation ends by
arguing that the debated passage teaches a double and parallel way of
salvation: via faith in Christ and via the fulfillment of the law (p. 106). The
third, C.T. Rhyne, *Faith Establishes the Law: A Study on the Continuity
between Judaism and Christianity, Romans 3.31* (SBL Dissertation Series,
55; Missoula: Scholars Press, 1981), dedicates one chapter to Rom 10.4
(pp. 95-116). It interprets τέλος as 'goal' on the basis of Rom 3.31 and
concludes that Rom 10.4 teaches the end of salvation by works (pp. 112-16).
Surprisingly enough none of these studies deals at all with the problem of
τέλος nor dedicates a single paragraph to discuss criteria other than
theological for the interpretation of τέλος in Rom 10.4.

11. H. Räisänen, 'Paul's Theological Difficulty with the Law', in *Studia
Biblica 1978. Papers on Paul and Other New Testament Authors. Sixth
International Congress on Biblical Studies*, ed. E.A. Livingstone (Sheffield:
JSOT Press, 1980), III, p. 306.

12. C.K. Barrett, 'Rom 9.30–10.21: Fall and Responsibility in Israel', in *Die Israelfrage nach Röm 9–11*, ed. L. de Lorenzi (Rome: Abbazia S. Paolo Extramuri, 1977), p. 115. W.S. Campbell, 'Christ the End of the Law: Rom 10.4', in *Studia Biblica 1978*, III, p. 73.

13. H.G. Liddell, R. Scott, and H.S. Jones, *A Greek-English Lexicon* (Oxford: Clarendon Press, 1968), pp. 1772-74, lists the meanings of τέλος in the following order: 'Coming to pass, performance, consummation, fulfilment, execution, power of decision, magistracy, decision, task, duty (offered to the gods or exacted by the state), completion, attainment, end, cessation, achievement, goal, winning-post, highest point, purpose'. W. Bauer, W.F. Arndt, F.W. Gingrich, and F. Danker, *A Greek-English Lexicon of the New Testament and Other Early Christian Literature* (Chicago: University of Chicago Press, 1979), pp. 811-12, lists the following NT meanings: 'End in the sense of termination, cessation; the last part, close, conclusion; end or goal toward which a movement is being directed, outcome; finally (in adverbial expression); rest, reminder; and tax, custom duties'. Cf. G. Delling, 'Τέλος', *TDNT*, VIII, pp. 49-57; and R. Schippers, 'Goal', *NIDNTT*, II, pp. 61-65.

14. So W. Sanday and H.C. Headlam, *A Critical and Exegetical Commentary on the Epistle to the Romans* (ICC; 5th edn, Edinburgh: T. & T. Clark, 1958), p. 285.

15. So A. Nygren, *Commentary on Romans* (5th edn; Philadelphia: Fortress, 1980), p. 380.

16. So K.S. Wuest, *Word Studies in the Greek New Testament: Romans* (Grand Rapids: Eerdmans, 1955), p. 173.

17. So Delling, p. 56.

18. M.J. Lagrange, *Saint Paul: Epître aux Romains* (Paris: Lecoffre, 1950), p. 164.

19. So H.J. Schoeps, *Paul. The Theology of the Apostle in the Light of Jewish History* (trans. H. Knight; Philadelphia: Westminster, 1961), p. 171.

20. H.A. Meyer, *Critical and Exegetical Hand-Book to the Epistle to the Romans* (New York: Funk & Wagnalls, 1889), p. 405.

21. *The New Testament of the Holy Bible. Confraternity Version* (New York: Guild Press, 1966), p. 541.

22. D.P. Fuller, *Gospel and Law, Contrast or Continuum? The Hermeneutics of Dispensationalism and Covenant Theology* (Grand Rapids: Eerdmans, 1980), p. 84.

23. J.A. Ziesler, *The Meaning of Righteousness in Paul. A Linguistic and Theological Inquiry* (Cambridge: University Press, 1972), p. 207.

24. So R. Bring, 'Paul and the Old Testament. A Study of the Ideas of Election, Faith and Law in Paul, with Special Reference to Rom 9.30–10.13', *ST* 25 (1971), p. 47.

25. So F. Michels, *Paul and the Law of Love* (Milwaukee: Bruce, 1967), p. 25.

26. So G.E. Howard, 'Christ the End of the Law: The Meaning of Rom 10.4ff', *JBL* 88 (1969), p. 337.

27. So Cranfield, *Romans*, II, p. 519.

28. So W. Barclay, 'Law in the New Testament', *ExpTim* 86 (1974-75), p. 100.

29. So Henry Alford, *The Greek New Testament* (with revision by E.F. Harrison; Chicago: Moody Press, 1958), II, p. 417.

30. So P.W. Meyer, 'Rom 10.4 and the End of the Law', in *The Divine Helmsman: Studies on God's Control of Human Events, Presented to Lou H. Silberman*, ed. James L. Crenshaw and Samuel Sandmel (New York: Ktav, 1980), p. 68.

31. So H.C.G. Moule, *The Epistle of St. Paul to the Romans* (The Expositor's Bible; New York: Hodder & Stoughton, 1893), p. 268.

32. So K. Barth, *The Epistle to the Romans* (Oxford: University Press, 1933), p. 375.

33. So V. Strigel and S. Le Moyne, quoted in F.A. Philippi, *Commentary on St. Paul's Epistle to the Romans* (trans. J.S. Banks; Edinburgh: T. & T. Clark, 1879), II, p. 146. The whole quotation says: 'For Christ is the *Toll* of the Law, xiii, 7, i.e., He paid to the law, as the toll-taker at the gate of heaven, the toll of absolute righteousness due on our account, and thus made possible to us entrance to heaven toll-free'.

34. J.B. Phillips, *The New Testament in Modern English* (New York: Macmillan, 1958), p. 336.

35. G.E. Ladd, *A Theology of the New Testament* (Grand Rapids: Eerdmans, 1974), p. 503.

36. E.K. Lee, *A Study in Romans* (London: SPCK, 1962), p. 97.

37. Delling, 'Τέλος', p. 56.

38. J. Knox and G.R. Crag, *Romans*, vol. 9 of *The Interpreter's Bible* (New York: Abingdon, 1954), p. 554.

39. M. Black, *Romans* (New Century Bible; London: Oliphants, 1973), p. 138.

40. *Modern Language Bible, The New Berkeley Version*, ed. G. Verkuyl (Grand Rapids: Zondervan, 1969), *ad loc.*

41. D. Guthrie, *New Testament Theology* (Downers Grove, Ill.: Inter-Varsity Press, 1981), p. 694.

42. *The Modern Speech New Testament*, ed. E. Hampden-Cook (Boston: Pilgrim Press, 1909), alternate reading, in note on Rom 10.4.

43. C.E.B. Cranfield, 'Saint Paul and the Law', *SJT* 17 (1964), p. 48.

44. *The Translator's New Testament* (London: BFBS, 1981), p. 694.

45. In many cases the differences between the completive/perfective and the temporal/terminal interpretations are irrelevant for the ultimate understanding of Rom 10.4. Whether the law has historically ceased at the cross, or has been definitely fulfilled in our stead, or has been existentially terminated at one's conversion, the result is somehow the same: Rom 10.4 is perceived as a statement of the supersession of the law by Christ.

46. On the validity and theological consequences of the application of this widespread hermeneutical principle, see H. Hummel, 'Are Law and Gospel a Valid Hermeneutical Principle?', *CTQ* 46 (1982), pp. 181-208.

47. Rhyne, p. 8.

48. For survey and discussion of the different trends, see below, chap. I, pp. 35-36.

49. It is impossible to list here all the supporters of this trend. The following names are given as representative examples: P. Althaus, *Der Brief an die Römer* (Das Neue Testament Deutsch, 6; Aufl. 11; Göttingen: Vandenhoeck & Ruprecht, 1970), p. 108; G. Bornkamm, *Paul* (trans. D.M.G. Stalker; New York: Harper & Row, 1969), p. 134; R. Bultmann, 'Christ and the End of the Law', in *Essays, Philosophical and Theological* (trans. J.C.G. Greig; London: SCM, 1955), p. 54; Hans Conzelmann, *An Outline of the Theology of the New Testament* (trans. J. Bowden; New York: Harper & Row, 1969), pp. 223-24; C.H. Dodd, *The Epistle of Paul to the Romans* (Moffatt NT Commentary; London: Hodder & Stoughton, 1954), p. 165; G. Ebeling, 'Reflections on the Doctrine of the Law', in *Word and Faith* (trans. J.W. Leitch; Philadelphia: Fortress Press, 1963), pp. 270-71; F. Godet, *Commentary on St. Paul's Epistle to the Romans* (trans. A. Cusin; Grand Rapids: Zondervan, 1956), p. 376; W. Gutbrod, 'Νόμος', *TDNT*, IV, p. 1075; Käsemann, p. 282; J. Knox, *Romans*, p. 554; G.E. Ladd, 'Paul and the Law', pp. 57-58; Lagrange, pp. 253-54; H. Lietzmann, *Die Briefe des Apostels Paulus: Einführung in die Textgeschichte der Paulusbriefe an die Römer* (Tübingen: J.C.B. Mohr, 1919), p. 96; U. Luz, *Das Geschichtsverständnis des Paulus* (BEvT, 49; Munich: Chr. Kaiser Verlag, 1968), pp. 139-41; Meyer, *Romans*, p. 405; O. Michel, *Der Brief an die Römer* (KExKNT, 4; Aufl. 10; Göttingen: Vandenhoeck & Ruprecht, 1955), pp. 223-24; J. Munck, *Christ and Israel: An Interpretation of Romans 9–11* (trans. I. Nixon; Philadelphia: Fortress, 1967), pp. 83-84; F. Mussner, '"Christus (ist) des Gesetzes Ende zur Gerechtigkeit für jeden, der glaubt" (Rom 10,4)', in *Paulus—Apostat oder Apostel? Jüdische und christliche Antworten*, ed. M. Barth et al. (Regensburg: Verlag Friedrich Pustet, 1977), pp. 31-44; Nygren, pp. 379-80; H. Ridderbos, *Paul: An Outline of His Theology* (trans. J.R. de Witt; Grand Rapids: Eerdmans, 1975), pp. 137, 155-56; C.C. Ryrie, 'The End of the Law (Rom 10.4)', *BSac* 124 (1967), pp. 239-47; Sanday and Headlam, pp. 379-80; Schoeps, p. 171; P. Stuhlmacher, *Gerechtigkeit Gottes bei Paulus* (FRLANT, 87; Göttingen: Vandenhoeck & Ruprecht, 1965), p. 93; '"Das Ende des Gesetzes": Über Ursprung und Ansatz der paulinischen Theologie', *ZTK* 67 (1970); J.F. Walvoord, 'Law in the Epistle to the Romans', *BSac* 94 (1937), p. 286; Ziesler, p. 20.

50. So A.J. Bandstra, *The Law and the Elements of the World. An Exegetical Study in Aspects of Paul's Teaching* (Kampen: J.H. Kok, 1964), pp. 102-105; W. Barclay, 'Law in the New Testament', p. 100; Barth,

Romans, p. 375; idem, *Church Dogmatics* (trans. G.W. Bromiley and T.F. Torrance; Edinburgh: T. & T. Clark, 1957), pp. 240-47; M. Barth, 'Die Stellung des Paulus zu Gesetz und Ordnung', *EvT* 33 (1973), pp. 496-526; 'St. Paul—A Good Jew', *HBT* 1 (1980), pp. 7-45; P. Bläser, *Das Gesetz bei Paulus* (Neutestamentliche Abhandlungen, 19; Munich: Aschendorffsche Verlagsbuchhandlung, 1941); R. Bring, 'Die Gerechtigkeit Gottes und das alttestamentliche Gesetz: Eine Untersuchung von Röm. 10.4', in *Christus und das Gesetz. Die Bedeutung des Gesetzes des Altes Testaments nach Paulus und sein Glauben an Christus* (Leiden: Brill, 1969), pp. 35-72; idem, 'Paul and the Old Testament', p. 47; C.E.B. Cranfield, 'Rom. 9.30–10.4', *Int* 34 (1980), pp. 70-74; 'St. Paul and the Law', pp. 48-50; *Romans*, II, p. 519; Démann, p. 235; F. Flückiger, 'Christus das Gesetzes τέλος', *TZ* 11 (1955), pp. 153-57; Fuller, p. 84; S. Grzybek, '"Finis Legis Christus" (Rom 10.4)', *RBL* 14 (1961), pp. 181-82; Howard, pp. 331-37; Meyer, p. 68; Rhyne, pp. 114-16; J.A. Sanders, 'Torah and Paul', in *God's Christ and His People: Studies in Honor of Nils Alstrup Dahl*, ed. J. Jervell and W.A. Meeks (Oslo: Universitetsforlaget, 1977), pp. 132-40; E.G. Selwyn, *The First Epistle of St. Peter: The Greek Text with Introduction, Notes, and Essays* (London: Macmillan, 1946), pp. 132-33; Toews, p. 335; A. Viard, *Saint Paul, Epître aux Romains* (Paris: Gabalda, 1975), p. 224; J.S.-J. Wang, 'The Pauline Doctrine of Law' (Ph.D. dissertation, Emory University, 1970), pp. 149-51; U. Wilckens, *Der Brief an die Römer* (Benziger: Neukirchener Verlag, 1980), p. 220 (he held a different position in 'Die Bekehrung des Paulus als religionsgeschichtliches Problem', in *Rechfertigung als Freiheit: Paulusstudien* [Neukirchen-Vluyn: Neukirchener Verlag, 1974], pp. 14-15).

    51. So C.K. Barrett, *A Commentary on the Epistle to the Romans* (London: A. & C. Black, 1957), pp. 197-98; *Reading Through Romans* (Philadelphia: Fortress, 1977), p. 53; 'Rom 9.30–10.21', pp. 115, 121; Bauer–Arndt–Gingrich, p. 811; R. Baules, *Commentaire de l'Epître aux Romains* (Paris: Editions du Cerf, 1968), pp. 236-37; J.C. Beker, *Paul the Apostle: The Triumph of God in Life and Thought* (Philadelphia: Fortress, 1980), pp. 91, 106, 121, 184-87; P. Benoit, 'La loi et la croix d'après Saint Paul', *RB* 47 (1938), pp. 481-509; *Exégèse et Théologie* (Paris: Editions du Cerf, 1961), II, p. 32; J.M. Bover, *Teologia de San Pablo* (Madrid: B.A.C., 1967), p. 351; F.F. Bruce, *The Epistle of Paul to the Romans* (Grand Rapids: Eerdmans, 1963), pp. 56, 203; *An Expanded Paraphrase of the Epistles of Paul* (Exeter: Paternoster, 1965), p. 217; 'Paul and the Law of Moses', *BJRL* 57 (1975), p. 262; J. Cambier, 'La justice de Dieu. Rom 10.3-13', in *L'Evangile de Dieu selon l'épître aux Romains: Exégèse et Théologie Biblique* (Louvain: Desclée de Brouwer, 1967), I, pp. 184-93; Campbell, pp. 76-77; L. Cerfaux, *Christ in the Theology of St. Paul* (New York: Herder & Herder, 1958), pp. 219-29, 496; *The Christian in the Theology of St. Paul* (London: G. Chapman, 1967), pp. 431-33; P.J. Du Plessis, *Teleios: The Idea of Perfection in the New Testament*

(Kampen: J.H. Kok, 1959), pp. 141-42; A. Feuillet, 'Le plan salvifique de Dieu d'après l'épître aux Romains', *RB* 57 (1950), pp. 498; *Le Christ, Sagesse de Dieu* (Paris: Gabalda, 1966), p. 117; J.A. Fitzmyer, 'Romans', in *The Jerome Biblical Commentary*, ed. R.E. Brown, J.A. Fitzmyer, and R.E. Murphy (London: Prentice Hall, 1968), II, p. 321; 'Paul and the Law', in *A Companion to Paul*, ed. M.J. Taylor (New York: Alba House, 1975), pp. 73-87; V.P. Furnish, *Theology and Ethics in Paul* (New York: Abingdon, 1968), pp. 161-62; J. Goldstain, *Les valeurs de la loi. La Torah lumière sur la route* (Théologie Historique, 56; Paris: Beauchesne, 1980), p. 8; P. Grelot, *Sens chrétien de l'Ancien Testament* (Paris, Tournai: Desclée, 1962), p. 21; A. Günther, 'Endziel des Gesetzes ist Christus (Röm. 10.4) zur heutigen innerkirchlichen Gesetzeskrise', *ErbAuf* 43 (1967), pp. 192-205; H. Hellbardt, 'Christus, das *Telos* des Gestzes', *EvT* 3 (1936), pp. 345-46; J. Huby, *Saint Paul: Epître aux Romains* (Verbum Salutis, 10; Paris: Beauchesne, 1957), p. 364; Kirk, p. 224; O. Kuss, '*Nomos* bei Paulus', p. 227; Ladd, 'Paul and the Law', pp. 50-67; C. Larcher, *L'actualité chrétienne de l'Ancien Testament d'après le Nouveau Testament* (Lectio Divina, 34; Paris: Cerf, 1962), p. 262; F.J. Leenhardt, *L'Epître de Saint Paul aux Romains* (Neuchâtel, Paris: Delachaux & Niestlé, 1957), p. 266; R.N. Longenecker, *Paul, Apostle of Liberty* (New York: Harper & Row, 1964), p. 186; S. Lyonnet, *Les Epîtres de Saint Paul aux Galates et Romains* (Paris: Editions du Cerf, 1959), p. 111; *Quaestiones in Epistulam ad Romanos* (Rome: Pontificio Istituto Biblico, 1962), II, p. 89; F. Marín, 'Matices del término "ley" en las cartas de san Pablo', *Est Ecl* 49 (1974), p. 46; C.F.D. Moule, p. 403; E.E. Schneider, '"Finis legis Christus" Rom 10.4', *TZ* 20 (1964), pp. 410-22; C. Spicq, *Théologie morale du Nouveau Testament* (Paris: Gabalda; 1965), I, p. 27; II, p. 635; G. Torti, *La Lettera ai Romani* (Studi Biblici, 41; Brescia: Paideia, 1977), p. 207.

52. *Paul: Libertine or Legalist? A Study in the Theology of the Major Pauline Epistles* (London: SPCK, 1975), p. 133.

53. Cranfield, *Romans*, II, p. 515.

54. Getty, 'Christ Is the End of the Law', p. 1.

55. 'Torah and Christ', *Int* 29 (1976), p. 328.

56. Kirk, p. 224.

57. 'Rom 10.4', p. 72. Meyer attributes this biased attitude to 'our Protestant habit of reading Paul through the eyes of Luther' (pp. 72-73).

Notes to Chapter 1

1. B. Hall, 'Biblical Scholarship: Editions and Commentaries', in *The Cambridge History of the Bible*, ed. P.R. Ackroyd and C.F. Evans (Cambridge: University Press, 1970), III, p. 76.

2. For general surveys on the interpretation of Paul, see M.F. Wiles, *The Divine Apostle. The Interpretation of St. Paul's Epistles in the Early Church* (Cambridge: University Press, 1967); J.S.-J. Wang, 'Pauline Doctrine of Law' (Ph.D. dissertation, Emory University, 1970), pp. 11-61; J.E. Toews, 'The Law in Paul's Letter to the Romans', pp. 10-104. For a brief survey on the interpretation of Romans see J.D. Godsey, 'The Interpretation of Romans in the History of the Christian Faith', *Int* 34 (1980), pp. 3-16; cf. Cranfield, *Romans*, I, pp. 30-44; and for a cursory survey on the interpretation of Rom 10.4, see ibid., II, pp. 516-19.

3. Particularly helpful for this part of the research have been the *Biblia Patristica* (edited by the Centre d'analyse et de documentation patristiques, Paris: Editions du C.N.R.S., t. I. *Des origines à Clément d'Alexandrie et Tertullien*, 1975; t. II. *Le troisième siècle*, 1977; t. III. *Origène*, 1981); E.J. Goodspeed, *Index Patristicus sive Clavis Patrum Apostolicorum* (Leipzig: Hinrichs, 1907), *Index Apologeticus sive Clavis Justini Martyris operum aliorumque apologetarum pristinorum* (Leipzig: Hinrichs, 1912); K.H. Schelkle, *Paulus Lehre der Väter. Die altkirchliche Auslegung von Römer 1–11* (2nd edn; Düsseldorf: Patmos Verlag, 1959), pp. 364-72; K. Staab, *Pauluskommentare aus der griechischen Kirche aus Katenenhandschriften gesammelt und herausgegeben* (Münster: Aschendorff, 1933). Also of some help are G. Bardy, 'Commentaires patristiques de la Bible', in *Supplément au Dictionnaire de la Bible*, ed. L. Pirot (Paris: Letouzey et Ané, 1934), II, pp. 73-103; F.J. Fesperman, 'Freedom from the Law: Paul's Doctrine and Its Role in Early Church' (Ph.D. dissertation, Vanderbilt University, 1968); B. de Margerie, *Introduction à l'histoire de l'exégèse. I. Les Pères grecs et orientaux* (Paris: Editions du Cerf, 1980); C.H. Turner, 'Patristic Commentaries on the Pauline Epistles', in *A Dictionary of the Bible*, ed. J. Hastings, Extra vol. (New York: C. Scribner's Sons, 1912), pp. 484-513; P.G. Verweijs, *Evangelium und Neues Gesetz in der ältesten Christenheit bis auf Marcion* (Utrecht: V.H. Kemink en Zoon, 1960).

4. Barn. 10.8, 11; 6.8-9; 7.11; 8.8; 2 Clem. 14.1-5; Melito, *Pass.*; Justin, *Dial.* 52.1-2; 53.1-6; 54.1-2; 86.1-6; 91.1-4; 119.8; 138.2; *1 Apol.* 32.1-13; etc. See further J.N.S. Alexander, 'The Interpretation of Scripture in the Ante-Nicene Period', *Int* 12 (1958), pp. 272-80; G. Bardy, 'Commentaires Patristiques', *DBSup*, II (1934), pp. 75; C.A. Bugge, 'L'Ancien Testament, Bible de la primitive église', *RHPR* 4 (1924), pp. 449-55; A. Camelot, 'L'exégèse de l'Ancien Testament par les Pères', in *Rencontres*, 36; ed. P. Auvray, Paris: Cerf, 1951), pp. 149-67. According to D.L. Baker, the crucial question in the exegesis of the early Church was: 'How far was the Old Testament to be considered valid and relevant after the completion of the New Testament, and in what way is the Old Testament related to the New?' (*Two Testaments, One Bible* [Downers Grove: InterVarsity Press, 1976], p. 43).

5. According to Jaroslav Pelikan, the two main purposes of the early Church exegesis were (1) 'to show that Judaism, with its laws, had had its days'; and (2) to prove that 'he who had been foretold has come in accordance with the OT Scriptures' (*The Christian Tradition. A History of the Development of Doctrine* [Chicago: University Press, 1971], I, p. 18).

6. The earliest commentary, according to Hanson (*op. cit.*, p. 419) is the commentary on the Gospel of John, by Heracleon, a Valentinian heretic, only partially preserved in Origen's own commentary. According to Eusebius (*H.E.* 3.39), Papias of Hierapolis wrote five books entitled λογίων κυριακῶν ἐξήγησις. But the few fragments preserved by Irenaeus (*Haer.* 5.33.3) do not allow us to make any judgment about the nature or scope of those writings. Eusebius makes other references to 'commentaries' in *H.E.* 5.8.8. So do Irenaeus (*Haer.* 4.27.1), and Clement (*Ecl.* 50); Jerome (*De vir. ill.* 36) identifies one of these first 'commentators' with Pantene, but we do not have anything left other than his testimony. Origen also refers to previous interpreters and commentators, but he never gives their names (*Hom. 5 in Ex 5*; *Hom. 8 in Lev. 6*; *Hom. 9 in Num. 5*; *Hom. 16 in Jud. 4*). For a complete list of Origen's references to an exegetical tradition prior to him, see A. von Harnack, *Der kirchengeschichtliche Ertrag der exegetischen Arbeiten des Origenes* (Texte und Untersuchungen zur Geschichte des altchristlichen Literatur, XLII, 3-4 [Leipzig: Hinrichs, 1918–1920], VIII, pp. 22-30; II, pp. 10-34.

7. See A. von Harnack, *Marcion, Das Evangelium vom Fremden Gott* (repr.: Darmstadt: Wissenschaftliche Buchgesellschaft, 1960).

8. For a description, see Tertullian, *Adv. Marc.* 4.1 (ed. Kroymann, pp. 422-23).

9. See Turner, 'Patristic Commentaries', p. 484.

10. The most common was to declare that the moral demands of the Law still applied to Christians, while the ceremonial laws did not apply in their literal sense, and consequently, should be allegorized. The earliest explicit formulations of this view are found in *Ep. ad Floram* (PG 7.1281-88); *Did.*; and Cyprian, *Fr.* 2.1.

11. See Harnack, *Marcion*, pp. 30-34.

12. The preserved fragments are contained in the works of Tertullian, Origen, Epiphanius, and others. Our reconstructions remain hypothetical. See John Knox, *Marcion and the New Testament* (Chicago: University Press, 1942), pp. 19-38.

13. According to Harnack, Marcion's text of Romans did not contain 1.17b; 1.19-2.1; 3.31-4.25; 8.19-22; 9.1-33; 10.5–11.32, and the whole 15th and 16th chapters (*Marcion*, pp. 49-50).

14. E.C. Blackman, *Marcion and His Influence* (London: SPCK, 1948), p. 45.

15. According to Harnack (*Marcion*, p. 108) Marcion cut the text after

Rom 10.4 and continued it at 11.33 because the reading of the text in this mutilated way fitted his purpose ('Der Spruch XI,33 passte im Sinne Marcions treffich zu X,4').

16. According to F.C. Burkitt, 'the real battle of the second century centres around the Old Testament' (*Church and Gnosis, A Study of Christian Thought and Speculation in the Second Century* [Cambridge: University Press, 1932], p. 129). For C. Bigg, the debated question was whether Christianity was to be regarded as rooted in philosophy and mythology—so the Gnostics—or in history—i.e. in the Old Testament and the Christ event (*Christian Platonists of Alexandria* [Oxford: Clarendon Press, 1886]).

17. See Blackman, p. 120.

18. See discussion in W.A. Jurgens, *The Faith of the Early Fathers* (Collegeville: The Liturgical Press, 1970), pp. 94-96. Three different positions may be discerned among the Fathers of that time: (1) The Old and the New Testaments have to be seen at the same level (Theophilus Ant., *Autol.* 3.12; Irenaeus, *Haer.* 4.12.3); (2) The NT is superior (Ignatius, *Magn.* 8.1); and (3) The OT is abrogated by the revelation of the NT (Justin, *Dial.* 11, quoting Isa 51.4-5). This last passage is worth quoting because it contains the argumentation that became the most common: 'For the law promulgated on Horeb is now old . . . Now, a law placed against another abrogated that which is before it, and a covenant which comes after in like manner has put an end to the previous one; and an eternal and final law—namely Christ— has been given to us . . . (ANF, 1.99-200, trans. Roberts–Donaldson).

19. *Adv. Marc.* 5.14.12,20 (CCSL, 1.706). In *De Pud* 4.1 he states that 'statu legis Christus non dissolvit, sed implevit'. Even in *Adv. Jud.* 3.10, where Tertullian says that the Old Law has ceased and is now substituted by the *nova lex Christi*, only the ceremonial aspects of the OT are considered superseded, but Rom 10.4 is not quoted. See further S. Means, *St. Paul and the Ante-Nicene Church* (London: A. & C. Black, 1903), pp. 334-35; Van der Geest, *Le Christ et l'Ancien Testament chez Tertullien: Une Recherche terminologique* (Nijm: Dekker & Van de Vegt, 1972), pp. 99-131; T.P. O'Malley, *Tertullian and the Bible: Language, Imagery, Exegesis* (Utrecht: Dekker & Van de Vegt, 1967); and R.P.C. Hanson, 'Notes on Tertullian's Interpretation of Scripture', *JTS* 12 (1961), pp. 273-79.

20. See Elaine H. Pagels, *The Gnostic Paul: Gnostic Exegesis of the Pauline Letters* (Philadelphia: Fortress Press, 1975), pp. 1-2.

21. See W. Schmithals, *Paul and the Gnostics* (Nashville: Abingdon, 1972), p. 236.

22. Hippolytus, *Haer.* 4.7.14 (GCS, 26.1916); Irenaeus, *Adv. Haer.* 1.8.2-3; Clement, *Strom.* 7.17.

23. See J.M. Robinson, 'Jesus: From Easter to Valentinus (or the Apostles' Creed)', *JBL* 101 (1982), pp. 5-37.

24. Pagels, pp. 38-39.

25. Origen, *Comm. in Jo.* (on John 4.22) 13.17-19, 107-08 (trans. C. Blanc, SC, 22.87-89).

26. On the Gnostic view of law and Scripture, see further Bertil Gärtner, *The Theology of the Gospel According to Thomas* (trans. E.J. Sharpe; New York: Harper & Brothers, 1961), pp. 77-81.

27. *Haer.* 4.12.4 (*PG* 1.1006f.). 'And how is Christ the end of the law, if He be not also the final cause of it?' (trans. Roberts–Donaldson, ANF, 1.476). See R.A. Markus, 'Pleroma and Fulfillment. The Significance of History in St. Irenaeus' Opposition to Gnosticism', *VC* 8 (1954), pp. 193-224. See further on this passage W. Sanday and C.H. Turner (eds.), *Novum Testamentum Sancti Irenaei Episcopi Lugdunensis* (Oxford: Clarendon, 1923), p. 125. B. de Margerie calls this feature of Irenaeus' exegesis 'recapitulation christocentrique' (pp. 71-74).

28. *Haer.* 4.13.1 (trans. Roberts–Donaldson, ANF, 1.467). The text goes on to say: 'Only the Jewish additions to the Divine Law have been eliminated' (*Haer.* 4.16 [ANF, 1.482]).

29. οὐ γὰρ τὸ βούλημα τοῦ νόμου ἔγνωσάν τε καὶ ἐποίησαν, ἀλλ' ὃ ὑπέλαβον αὐτοί, τοῦτο καὶ βούλεσθαι τὸν νόμον ᾠήθησαν οὐδ' ὡς προφητεύοντι τῷ νόμῳ ἐπίστευσαν, λόγῳ δὲ ψιλῷ καὶ φόβῳ, ἀλλ' οὐ διαθέσει καὶ πίστει ἠκολούθησαν· τέλος γὰρ νόμου Χριστὸς εἰς δικαιοσύνην, ὁ ὑπὸ νόμου προφητευθείς, ἀντὶ τῷ πιστεύοντι ὅθεν εἴρηται τούτοις παρὰ Μωυσέως (PG 8.978). 'For they did not know and do what the law willed (τὸ βούλημα τοῦ νόμου), but they thought that the law willed (βούλεσθαι) what they supposed. Nor did they believe the law as prophesying, but only the bare word (λόγῳ δὲ ψιλῷ); and they followed out of fear, and not out of disposition of faith. For Christ is the end (τέλος) of the law unto righteousness, who was prophesied by the law to every one that believeth' (trans. Roberts–Donaldson, ANF, 2.357).

30. PG 8.1340-41.

31. *Paed.* 1.6 (PG 8.292 A): ἡ δὲ ἐν Χριστῷ νηπιότης τελείωσις ἐστιν, ὡς πρὸς τὸν νόμον; *Strom.* 4.21 (PG 8.1340 C): νομικοῦ μὲν τελείωσις γνωστικὴ εὐαγγελίου πρόσληψις ἵνα γένηται ὁ κατὰ νόμον τέλειος. (Cf. 2.9 and 6.9, where Christ is also called 'the goal' or 'the fulfillment' of the law.)

32. In *Strom.* 2.21.127-36 Clement lists 30 definitions of τέλος (in the sense of the *summum bonum*) according to various philosophers. After discussing these current opinions on the chief good, Clement concludes that the τέλος *par excellence* is nothing else and nobody else than Christ. For the Platonic influence in Clement, see Salvatore R.C. Lilla, *Clement of Alexandria: A Study in Christian Platonism and Gnosticism* (Oxford: University Press, 1971), pp. 227-34.

33. "'Επαιδαγώγει' γὰρ καὶ αὐτὴ τὸ Ἑλληνικὲν, ὡς 'ὁ νόμος' τοὺς

Ἑβραίους, 'εἰς Χριστὸν' Προπαρασκενάζει τοίνυν ἡ φιλοσοφία, προσδοποιοῦσα τὸν ὑπὸ Χριστοῦ τελειούμενον (PG 8.719). Cf. *Qui div. salv.* 9.2. See further P.T. Camelot, 'Clément d'Alexandrie et l'Ecriture', *RB* 53 (1946), pp. 242-48.

34. Τοῦ τελέσαι ὀραματισμὸν και προφήτην ὅ συνᾴδει τῷ ' Οὐκ ἦλθον καταλῦσαι τὸν νόμον ἢ τοὺς προφήτας, ἀλλὰ πληρῶσαι, πρὸς αὐτοῦ τοῦ Σωτῆρος εἰρημένῳ. Τέλος γὰρ νόμου Χριστός, και πᾶσαί γε αἱ περὶ αὐτοῦ προφητεῖαι ἀπλήρωτοι, καὶ ἀτελεῖς ἔμενον, εἰσόταὐτος ἐπιστὰς ἐπιτέθεικεν ἅπασι τέλος τοῖς περὶ αὐτοῦ προαναπεφωνημένοις (*D.E.* 8.2.33; PG 22.605-06): 'This agrees with the saying of the Savior, "I came not to destroy the law or the prophets, but to fulfil them" [Mt. 5.17]. For Christ is the end of the law and all the prophecies about Him remained unfulfilled and unaccomplished (ἀπλήρωτοι καὶ ἀτελεῖς), until He Himself came and added fulfilment (ἐπιτέθεικεν . . . τέλος) to all the things foretold concerning him' (trans. Cranfield, *Romans*, II, p. 516, n. 2).

35. Πληρωτής εἰμι νόμου, οὐδὲν βούλομαι ἐλλιπὲς καταλεῖψαι εἰς πᾶν τὸ πλήρωμα ἵνα μετ' ἐμὲ βοήσῃ ὁ Παῦλος· Πληρωμα νόμου ὁ Χριστὸς εἰς δικαιοσύνην παντὶ τῷ πιστεύοντι (*Theoph.* 5; PG 10.855-56). 'I am the fulfiller of the Law; I seek to leave nothing to its whole fulfillment, that so after me Paul may exclaim, "Christ is the fulfilment of the law for righteousness to everyone that believeth"' (trans. Roberts–Donaldson, ANF, 5.236).

36. Origen wrote on all the epistles (the complete list is found in Jerome, *Ep.* 33) and produced a commentary on Romans in 15 volumes. See for details J.A. Cramer, 'The Commentary of Origen on the Epistle to the Romans', *JTS* 13 (1912), pp. 209-24, 353-68; 14 (1913), pp. 10-22.

37. See PG 14.831-1294. According to Turner (pp. 490-92), more than a third of the Greek text of Origen's *Comm. in Rom.* has been omitted in Rufinus's translation. The few remaining Greek fragments, collected in the *catenae*, were grouped together by A. Ramsbotham (see Cramer, p. 209). For further information on the extant text, see Heinrich Joseph Vogels, *Untersuchungen zum Text paulinischer Briefe bei Rufin und Ambrosiaster* (Bonner Biblische Beiträge, 9; Bonn: Peter Hanstein Verlag, 1955).

38. 'Finis enim legis Christus: hic est, perfectio legis et iustitia legis Christus est' (PG 14.1160 B).

39. Trans. Roberts–Donaldson, ANF, 4.375. Cf. *Comm. in Jo.* 10.42. *Hom. 9 in Num.* 9.4.23 reads: 'I do not call the Law the Old Testament if I understand it spiritually. The Law is only made the Old Testament to those who understand it carnally . . . but to us who understand it and expound it spiritually and with its gospel meaning, it is always new; both are New Testament to us, not in terms of temporal sequence but of newness of understanding' (trans. M.F. Wiles, 'Origen as Biblical Scholar', *CHB*, I, p. 483).

40. For a detailed study on this point, see J. Daniélou, 'L'unité des deux Testaments dans l'oeuvre d'Origène', *RSR* 22 (1948), pp. 27-56; and *Gospel Message and Hellenistic Culture. A History of Early Christian Doctrine* (trans. J.A. Baker; Philadelphia: Westminster, 1977), II, pp. 273-80.

41. This renewal of literal exegesis seems to be due to the influence of the Arians, for they based their arguments on the literal sense of the Scriptures as they read them (cf. Hanson, p. 443).

42. In *Ep. fest.* 14.4 (on Easter 342), Athanasius says: 'Non ut legem destruat, absit! sed ut lex statuatur atque ut culmen legi imponatur. "Finis enim legis Christus est ad iustitiam omni credenti" (Rom 10.4) ut beatus Paulus ait: "Num legem fide destruimus? Absit! sed legem statuimus" (Rom 3.31)... Olim vero quotiescum propheta aut legisperiti Sacras Scripturas legerunt, cavebant prorsus ne quid ad se traherent, sed potius ad alios referendum curabant, quod legebant' (PG 26.1421). So also does Gregory of Nazianzus (pp. 329-389), explaining τέλος by the 'pedagogic' relation of the Law to Christ: τοῦτο ἡμῖν ὁ παιδαγωγὸς βούλεται νόμος. τοῦτο οἱ μέσοι Χριστοῦ καὶ νόμος προφῆται· τοῦτο ὁ τοῦ πνευματικοῦ νόμου τελεωτῆς καὶ τὸ τέλος Χριστός (*Or.* 2.12.13; PG 35.431-32).

43. See PG 66.845-46. The ancient Latin version, together with the Greek fragments, has been published by H.B. Swete, *Theodori Episcopi Mopsuesteni in Epistolas B. Pauli Commentarii* (Cambridge: University Press, 1880). See also D. de Bruyne, 'Le commentaire de Théodore de Mopsueste aux épîtres de Saint Paul', *RBén* 33 (1921), pp. 53-54.

44. PG 60.565-66; cf. *Hom. in Eph.* 5.3 (PG 62.39-40): ἔδωκεν ἡμῖν νόμον, ἵνα φυλάττωμεν, ἐπεὶ δὲ οὐκ ἐφυλάξαμεν, δέον κολασθῆναι, ὁ δὲ καὶ τὸν νόμον κατέλυσεν. 'He gave us a law that we should keep it, and when we kept it not, and ought to have been punished, He even abrogated the law itself' (NPNF, 2.12.72).

45. The simile of the medicine is more clearly used to stress the idea of 'fulfillment' and 'purpose' in *Hom. 2 in 1 Tim. 1.1* (PG 62.509): τὸ δὲ τέλος τῆς παραγγελίας ἐστιν ἀγάπη [1 Tim 1.5-7]. ὥσπερ οὖν ὅταν λέγῃ, Τέλος νόμου Χριστός, τουτέστι συμπλήρωμα, καὶ τοῦτο ἐκείνων ἔχεται. οὕτως ἡ παραγγελία αὕτη ἐνέχεται τῇ ἀγάπῃ τέλος ἰατρείας ὑγεία...

46. (PG 62.263-64). The repetition καὶ πλήρωμα νόμου Χριστός, καὶ τέλος νόμου Χριστός is probably intended to underline the double function of Christ, both as end and goal of the law.

47. Trans. Schaff-Ware, NPNF, 2.13.412-14.

48. Ibid., p. 414. Cf. *Hom. 33 in Jo. 4.22*, where the law is called the ὑπόθεσις, the 'root' or the 'groundwork' of the Gospel (trans. Schaff-Ware, NPNF, 2.14.116).

49. PG 57.241-42 (NPNF, 2.10.105).

50. On the notion of σκοπός in the exegesis of Cyril, see Alexander Kerrigan, *St. Cyril of Alexandria Interpreter of the Old Testament* (Rome: Pontificio Istituto Biblico, 1952), pp. 87-110, and Margerie, pp. 270-303. On

the purpose of Scripture in Gregory of Nyssa (330–c. 395), see *Hex.* (PG 44.69D), and *Nom. opif.* (PG 44.128 A-B). Cf. Margerie, pp. 240-69.

51. Though the fragment corresponding to Rom 10.4 is lacking from the extant commentary of Cyril on Romans (see PG 74.842), other references to Rom 10.4 show how this passage was understood by Cyril. See *Glaph. Gen.* 5.150 (PG 69.241B); *Glaph. Ex.* 2.284 (PG 69.448B); *Adv. Jul.* 9 (PG 76.992A-B); *Glaph. Gen.* 1.2 (PG 69.16A); *Is.* 1.5 (PG 70.220C).

52. εἰς αὐτὸν οἶμαι ποῦ παντὸς ὁρῶντος καὶ τετραμμένου προφητικοῦ τε καὶ νομικοῦ θεσπίσματος (PG 68.140B-C). In this passage Cyril relates Gal 3.24 to Rom 10.4 and John 5.45-46: 'Accordingly if he says he has come not to destroy the law, but rather to perfect it, do not think that a complete overthrow of the ancient oracles has been accomplished but rather a transformation or, if I may say so, a moulding of what were types into the truth' (trans. Kerrigan, p. 137 n. 3).

53. 'For Christ is the τέλος of the law and the prophets, who is not to be thought of as lying when he said: "I came not to destroy the law, but to fulfil it".' Then, Cyril illustrates what he means, saying that the addition of colours to an artist's preliminary drawing does not destroy the drawing, μεθίστησι δὲ μᾶλλον εἰς ὄψιν ἐναργεστέραν (trans. Cranfield, *Romans*, p. 417).

54. According to Bardy, 'Théodoret marque le début d'une période nouvelle, celle des compilateurs qui se contentent trop souvent de rechercher ce qu'ont dit leurs devanciers' (p. 102).

55. PG 82.163-64.

56. 'Some men by a study of the law may be enlightened to gain faith in Christ, who is the end of the law and the prophets (Rom 10.4), and shines forth prefigured and prophesied in all their books' (*Ep.* 13.4 [ACW, 30.121]).

57. 'Quid ergo, Iudaee, adhuc *umbram futurorum* et lege sectaris, cum iam *finis legis Christus* advenerit, in quo non umbra sed veritas, non figura, sed *plenitudo* religionis est reddita? Tunc etenim omnia in imagine quasi per inigmate [aenigmata] querebantur, nunc veritas inlustrata successit . . . ' (Tract. Origen. 8.28 [CCSL, 69.69-70]).

58. *Iob et Dan.* 4.4.18 reads: 'For the law was only half-filled and thus it was necessary that someone should come to fulfill it. "For Christ is the end of the law, not to destroy it . . . "' (trans. M.P. McHugh, FC, 65.402-403. Cf. *Luc.* 5.21 (on Lk 5.32): 'Hoc est: abiecit iustitiam et gloriam legis; iustitia enim legis sine Christo vacua est, quia plenitudo legis Christus est'; 5.94 (on Lk 7.19): 'plenitudo legis est Christus'; cf. 7.21 (CCSL, 14.66, 142, 166, 222).

59. *Tract.* 1.3.9, 17 (CCSL, 22.28).

60. 'Finis enim legis Christus ad iustitiam omni credenti, hoc dicit, quia perfectionem legis habet, qui credit in Christum. Cum enim nullus iustificaretur ex lege, quia nemo implebat legem, nisi qui speraret in Christo promisso, fides posita est, quae crederet perfectionem legis, ut omnibus

praetermissis fides satisfaceret pro tota lege et profetis' (CSEL, 81.344-45). Cf. Alexander Souter, *The Earliest Latin Commentaries on the Epistles of St. Paul. A Study* (Oxford: Clarendon Press, 1927), pp. 39-95.

61. See R.F. Evans, *Pelagius. Inquiries and Reappraisals* (New York: Seabury Press, 1968), pp. 31, 66-68.

62. 'Finis enim legis Christus (est) ad iustitiam omni credenti. Talis est qui Christo cre(di)dit die qua credit quasi qui universam legem implev(er)it' (Alexander Souter, *Pelagius' Exposition on Thirteen Epistles of St. Paul* [Texts and Studies, 9; ed. J. Armitage Robinson; Cambridge: University Press, 1922–1931]), II, pp. 81-82.

63. *Exp.* 248. pp. 14-15: 'Ita et lex non intellegitur usque in finem eius, id est (usque dum) Christo credatur'.

64. For Pelagius, since Christ is both the Savior and the new Lawgiver, grace and law are not opposite (*Exp.* 339.5). Grace is law (*Exp.* 179.2-3). The NT as a whole is law, and the Gospels are *supplementum legis* (*Exp.* 3.1). See further Evans, pp. 96-98.

65. See C.H. Turner, 'Pelagius' Commentary on the Pauline Epistles and Its History', *JTS* 4 (1902-1903), pp. 132-41; A. Souter, 'The Character and History of Pelagius' Commentary on the Epistles of St. Paul', *Proceedings of the British Academy* 7 (1915-1916), pp. 269-96; on Pelagius's interpretation compared with Ambrosiaster's see Souter, *Pelagius' Exposition*, pp. 51-59. For an interpreted text attributed to Jerome, see PL 30.693.

66. On the importance of Jerome in the history of Biblical interpretation, see H.F.D. Sparks, 'Jerome as Biblical Scholar', *CHB*, I, pp. 510-41.

67. 'Tempus, inquit, requirendi Dominum est, cum venerit, Christus atque Salvator, qui docebit vos iustitiam; quam nunc sperantis in lege: Finis enim legis Christum est ad iustitiam omni operanti bonum . . . ' (In *Os.* 3.10.12; CSL, 76.116). Codex Namurcensis reads *et ad* instead of *est ad* (ibid., n. 416). Observe that *operanti bonum* has here taken the place of *credenti*, which is Jerome's translation of πιστεύοντι, treating thus 'faith' and 'works' not as antithetical, but as synonymous! In *Hom.* 35.1 (on Ps 108/109), Jerome gives an eschatological interpretation of *ad finem* referred to Christ as 'end of the law'; cf. *Hom.* 2,1 (on Ps 5); 4,1 (on Ps 9); 8,1 (on Ps 74/75) (FC, 48.15, 35, 60).

68. Gerald Bonner, 'Augustine as Biblical Scholar', *CHB*, I, p. 550.

69. 'Omnia que dicta sunt antiquo populo Israel in multiplici scripturae sanctae legis, quae agerent, sive in sacrificiis, sive in sacerdotibus, sive in diebus festis, et omnino in quibuslibet rebus quibus Deum colebant, quaecumque illi dicta est praecepta sunt; umbrae fuerunt futurorum. Quorum futurorum? Que impletur in Christo. Unde dicit apostolus: [quotes 2 Cor 1.20, 1 Cor 10.11, and Rom 10.4] "Finis legis Christus est"' (*In Evang. Johan.* 28.9 [CCSL, 36.282]).

70. Commenting on the phrase 'in finem' in the title of several psalms, after quoting Rom 10.4 Augustine says: 'We know the meaning of *unto the*

end if we know Christ; as the apostle says: For the end of the law is Christ ... an end which does not destroy but perfects ... Unto the end, therefore, denotes unto Christ' (*En. in Psalm.* 2.9, trans. Hebgin-Corrigan, ACW, 29.9). Similar interpretations are found in *En. in Psalm.* 12.111; 13.1.2; 38.14; 54.1.3-17; 55.1.12; 59.2.1; 60.1.8; 64.6.72; 65.1.4; 67.23.2; 78.4.8; 78.6.7; in a slightly different form see also 79.1.12; 87.7.5-6; 96.2.10; 118.22.2 and 11. In 84.2.2 the end is described as the Christian's personal goal or purpose in life: 'In finem, direxit cor nostrum in Christum'. Cf. 139.3.2; 37.14.6. Only in 78.6 Augustine departs from his teleological interpretation of Rom 10.4 and says that 'the beginning is the Old Testament, the end (*finis*) is the New' (trans. Schaff, NPNF, 1.8.368). Cf. *In Evang. Johan.* 55.2.6; *Serm.* 16.1; *Pat.* 19; *Sp. et lit.* 50.51 (on Rom 9.30–10.13); *Nat. et grat.* 1.1; 36; 47; *Bap. c. donat.* 5.9.11.

71. *En. in Psalm.* 56.2.2; 67.1.5; cf. 30.1.1; 4.1.1.

72. 'Ita eis iam lex subintrabat, ut abundaret delictum [quote of Rom 5.20-21] et postea superabundaret gratia per Dominum Christum, qui *finis est legis ad iustitiam omni credenti*' (*Qu. in Hept.* 7.28.699 [CCSL, 33.331]).

73. Augustine, of course, put Christ on a higher level than the OT law, but he did not see him in opposition to it. In *Qu. in Ex.* 73 he expressed his view of that relationship in words that have become classical: 'quanquam et in Vetere Novum latet, et in Novo Vetus patet'. Cf. Baker, pp. 47-48.

74. Thus, Leo Magnus (c. 400–461) in *Tract.* 53 following Augustine in *En. in Psalm.* 73.2, says: 'Et ipse [Christus] est *finis legis*, non evacuando significationes ipsius, sed implendo. Qui licet idem sit auctor veterum qui novarum ...' (CCSL, 88.385); *Ep.* 16.7; *Serm.* 67.5; Quodvultdeus of Cartagus (c. 427–438?), *Liber Promissionum*, 1.7.12 (pp. 94-95) (CCSL, 60.22); *De Virt.* 11.1.3-4 (CCSL, 60.374); Prosper Aquitanus (c. 390–463), *Exp. in Ps.* 118.97-98; 139.3 (CCSL, 68A.107, 173); Cassiodorus, *Exp. in Ps.* 4.1.6; *Praef.* 3.11.12; *Exp. in Ps.* 65.1.7-8; 84.1.3; 139.1.5. 'Quid significet *in finem*, ... qui est ... finis sine fine et bonorum omnium completive perfectio'; Gregory the Great (540–604), *Hom.* 2.4.12-14 (In Hiezechihelem Prophetam): 'Scriptum namque est: *Finis legis Christus ad iustitiam omni credenti*. Finis videlicet, non qui consumit, sed qui perficit. Tunc etenim legem perfecit, cum, sicut lex praedixerat, incarnatus apparuit ... cum ea quae de se promisit Dominus impleverit' (CCSL, 142.269); cf. Dionysius Exiguus (d. 525–544), *Ex. Sanct. Pat.* 88.908 (CCSL, 85.124).

75. So Caesarius of Arles (470–453), *Serm.* 137 (on Ps 118.96): 'What is the end? asks Paul: "Now the *purpose* of this charge is charity ... " (1 Tim 1.5), and in another place: "Love is the *fulfillment* of the law" (Rom 13.10) ... Therefore whatever you do do it for the love of Christ, and let the *intention* or *end* of all your actions look to Him ... When the Psalm is read and you hear: "Unto the end, a psalm of David" (Ps 4.1), do not understand it except as Christ, for the apostle says: "*Christ is the consummation of the*

law unto justice" (Rom 10.4). If you come to anything else, pass beyond it
until you reach the end. What is the end? "But for me, to be near God is *my
good*" (Ps 72.28). Have you adhered to God? you have finished your
journey . . . seek the end . . . ' (trans. Mueller, FC, 47.270, emphasis his); cf.
Fulgentius of Ruspe (468–533), *Ad Trasamundum*, 2.5.3; *De veritate prae-
destinationis et gratiae*, 2.4 (85-88).

76. So Vergundus, bishop of Junca (d. 552), *Comm. s. cant. eccl.* 10.7-8
(Canticum Azariae Prophetae): 'Et ne tradas nos in finem propter nomen
tuum . . . Tropologice *in finem* se tradi propheta metuit, hoc est in Christo,
quia in eo traduntur qui in illo scandalum patiuntur. Propheta precatur ne in
finem traduntur. *Finis vero Christus est ad justitiam omni credenti*. Vel certe
in finem: intellege: usque ad consummationem mundi vel vitae nostrae'
(CCSL, 92.92). Cf. *Canticum Deuteronomii*, 37.51 (on Deut 32.36) (CCSL,
92.56). The law was seen so little in antagonism with the gospel that in *Ps.
Cypr. Abus.* 12 (TU, 34.59) 'Christ is the end of the Law' is interpreted as
meaning that 'those who are without the Law come to be without Christ'!
(trans. Pelikan, *The Christian Tradition*, III, p. 25). See K. Hermann
Schelkle, *Paulus, Lehrer der Väter*, p. 368.

77. C. Spicq, *Esquisse d'une histoire de l'exégèse latine au Moyen Age*
(Paris: Librairie Philosophique J. Vrin, 1944), pp. 10-11. Cf. Henri de
Lubac, *Exégèse Médiévale. Les Quatre sens de l'Ecriture* (Paris: Aubier,
1959), I, pp. 23-36. B. Smalley says that 'Bible study meant the study of the
sacred text together with the Fathers. The two kinds of authority were
inseparable' (*The Study of the Bible in the Middle Ages* [Oxford: Basil
Blackwell, 1952], p. 37).

78. See PG 95.439-1034. The first *catena* on the epistles of Paul that was
printed is the one ascribed to Oecumenius (563–614), published in Verona in
1532. The greatest compilers were Theophylact, archbishop of Bulgaria (c.
1075), Euthymius Zigabenus (c. 1100), and Nicetas of Serrae, deacon of St
Sophia, contemporary of both. Cf. Turner, p. 485.

79. We follow the editions of John Anthony Cramer, *Catena in Sancti
Pauli Epistolam ad Romanos*; *Catenae Graecorum Patrum in Novum Testamentum*, IV (Hildesheim: Georg Olms, 1967); Karl Staab, *Die Pauluskatenen
nach den handschriftlichen Quellen untersucht* (Rome: Scripta Pontificii
Instituti Biblici, 1926), and *Pauluskommentare aus der griechischen Kirche
aus Katenenhandschriften gesammelt und herausgegeben* (Neutestamentliche
Abhandlungen, 15; ed. M. Meinertz; Münster: Aschendorff, 1933).

80. The authors most quoted are: Chrysostom, Theodore of Mopsuestia,
Theodoret, Cyril of Alexandria, Gennadius, Severian, Apollinaris, Diodorus,
and Photius. See further Turner, p. 487, and Cramer, *Catena in Romanos*,
pp. 368-71.

81. So Chrysostom Euthymius, who renders Rom 10.4: τέλος καὶ βούλημα
νόμου ὁ Χριστός (Cramer, p. 118).

82. Thus, νόμου σκοπὸν ὁ Χριστός (Cramer, p. 370, lines 3, 16); Theodore

of Mopsuestia: ὥστε ὁ νόμος πληροῦται σκοπὸν ἐν ἡμῖν (Staab, p. 150); Gennadius of Constantinople: τοῦ νόμου σκοπὸς Χριστός (Staab, p. 395). Cf. Cramer, p. 369, lines 32-33.

83. Thus, πλήρωμα νόμου καὶ προφητῶν τὸν Χριστόν (Cramer, p. 370, line 35); Apollinaris of Laodicea: τέλος νόμου Χριστός, καὶ εἰς Χριστὸν ὁ νόμος παρεσκεύαζεν, δεικνὺς τοῦτον ὄντα πλήρωμα μὲν ἑαυτοῦ, σωτηρίαν δὲ ἀνθρώπων (Staab, p. 69); Diodorus of Tarsus: ὁ τὸν νόμον πληρώσας (Staab, p. 101).

84. Thus, τέλος γὰρ νόμου καὶ προφητῶν ὁ Χριστός (Cramer, p. 371, line 10; cf. p. 370, line 35).

85. See Cramer, p. 371, lines 10-12: Τέλος γὰρ νόμου καὶ προφητῶν ὁ Χριστός, ὃς οὐκ ἂν διαψεύσατο λέγων, οὐκ ἦλθον καταλῦσαι τὸν νόμον, ἀλλὰ πληρῶσαι. Cf. Braulius of Saragossa (619–631), *Ep.* 22 (FC, 63.59).

86. Διὰ δύο οὖν τέλος νόμου, ὅτι τε ἐχρήσατο αὐτῷ καὶ ὅτι ἔπαυσεν αὐτόν (Staab, p. 222). Cf. p. 523.

87. See *In I Samuhelem* 4.433 (on 23.26-28); 4.772 (24.21-23); 4.2306 (30.26-31) (CCSL, 119.222, 230, 266).

88. *Homelia* 2.19.166; *Homelia* 1.23.216. *In Lucam* 3.2280 (on 10.35) contains an allegoric explanation of the unity of the testaments: 'Duo denarii sunt duo testamenta, in quibus aeternis regis nomen et imago continetur. *Finis enim legis Christus.* Qui altera die prolati dantur stabulario quia *tunc aperuit illis sensum ut intelligent Scripturas*' (CCSL, 120.224).

89. *In Lucam* 6.904-907 (on 22.41): 'Ad ipsum perducerent *intentionem legis* quae scripta erant in lapide. Usque ad illum enim potest pervenire ille lapis quoniam *finis legis est Christus ad iustitiam omni credenti . . .*' (CCSL, 120.385).

90. *Expositiones in Apocalypsin*, 1.1.8 (CCCM, 27.55-56; cf. 3.5.1 (CCCM, 27.252); 9.21.6 (CCCM, 27.785); 10.22.13 (CCCM, 27.860).

91. 'Quia omnia quae Lex et prophetae verbis et mysteriis de ipso praedixerant, per semetipsum complevit. Unde pendens in cruce, ait: Consummatum est (Joan. XXI) . . . ' (*In divi Pauli epistolas expositio. In epistolam ad Romanos* [PL 117.449]).

92. *Enarrationes in Epistolas Beati Pauli. Expositio in epistolam ad Romanos* (PL 111.1507).

93. *Expositio in epistolas beati Pauli ex operibus sancti Augustini collecta. Expositio in epistolam ad Romanos* (PL 119.307).

94. 'Finis legis Christus, non consumptionis, sed consummationis, quoniam non legem consumit, sed perficit, juxta quod Evangelio loquitur: Non veni solvere legem, sed implere (Mt v. 17). Finis est Christus . . . perfectio autem nostra Christus est . . . ' (*Expositio in epistolas Pauli. In epistolam ad Romanos* [PL 134.229-30]).

95. '*Christus ad implementum legis est. Finis enim legis . . .* Et est sensus: Intentio legis, ut justitiam habeat homo, est; id est fides Christi. AMBROS. *Finis legis.* Quoniam perfectionem legis habet qui credit in Christo' (*In*

omnes Pauli epistolas commentarii cum glossula interjecta. Ad Romanos [PL 150.139-40, emphasis theirs]).

96. See H. de Lubac, *Exégèse médiévale: Les quatre sens de l'Ecriture*, I, pp. 110-69.

97. Usually, when the notion of *terminatio* is mentioned, it applies to the end of the Jewish observances. See Bruno the Carthusian (c. 1030–1101), *Expositio in epistolas Pauli. Epistola ad Romanos* (PL 153.88).

98. The term *glossa* comes from the Latin verb *glossare*, 'to open, to uncover, explain, interpret' (Spicq, p. 68). Cf. Smalley, *The Study of the Bible in the Middle Ages*, pp. 31-33, 156-60.

99. For Farrar the *glossae* are 'a promiscuous mass of literal, moral, and mystic fragments intermingled with grammatical remarks of the most elementary character' (p. 251), showing an 'absolute lack of exegetical insight' (p. 272), while for Leclercq, 'this blending of the most authentic elements of the past with a new ardour and freshness proved highly creative in the sphere of exegesis' ('From Gregory the Great to Saint Bernard', *CHB*, II, p. 193).

100. On the *Glossa Media*, composed by Gilbert de la Porrée, see M. Simon, 'La Glosse de l'Epître aux Romains de Gilbert de la Porrée', *RHE* 52 (1957), pp. 51-80. On the *Glossa Magna* attributed to Anselm of Laon, see *ibid.*, p. 32.

101. '*Finis*, Non consumens sed perficiens: perficit ergo justitiam per fidem sine operibus legis. *Christus*: Ex Christo est justitia; quia si per legem scriptam vel naturalem esset, et non fide Christi, ergo Christus gratis moreretur. *Ad justitiam*. Non humanam, sed divinam. Est enim humana et divina: de humana ibi, *Moyses*: de divina ibi: *quae autem ex . . .* ' (*Ad Romanos* 10.4 [PL 114.504]).

102. Most of these works have only partly come down to us in excerpts from lost lecture courses which have been reworked into collections. A. Landgraf, 'Quelques collections de "Quaestiones" de la seconde moitié du XIIe siècle', *RTAM* 7 (1935), pp. 122-26.

103. The increasing tendency to stress the literal meaning seemed influenced by contemporary Jewish scholarship, e.g. Rashi. See Wood, *The Interpretation of the Bible*, p. 74; Smalley, p. 185; Spicq, pp. 87-89.

104. See A.M. Landgraf, 'Untersuchungen zu den Paulinenkommentaren des 12. Jahrhunderts', *RTAM* 8 (1936), pp. 253-81, 345-68.

105. Spicq says that the *ratio* began to take an important place besides the *auctoritas* of the Fathers in biblical exegesis (p. 69). Cf. Leclercq, p. 198.

106. See, for example, the definition of *finis* by Alain of Lille (d. 1202), *Liber in distinctionibus dictionum theologicalium* (PL 210.836): '*Finis . . .* Christus etiam dicitur finis consummationis, quia Christus consummavit quae de eo prophetae praedixerunt, ut hic secundum alia expositionem: Titulus psalmi dirigens nos in finem, id est in Christum'.

107. See A.M. Landgraf, 'Familienbildung bei Paulinenkommentaren des

12. Jahrhunderts', *Biblica* 13 (1932), pp. 61-72, 169-93.

108. *Quaestiones in Epistolam Pauli ad Romanos* (PL 175.495): 'Quaeritur quomodo Christus sit finis legis et consummatio, cum legis justitia sit sine gratia adjuvante, nec habebant apud Deum meritum. *Solutio.* Christus non dicitur finis, vel consummatio legis secundum hoc, quod a Judaeis servabatur, sed quia spiritualiter eam in se, et in suis adimplet'.

109. The text of Hugh is so similar to the text of Robert of Melun that it is generally accepted that Hugh copied from Robert's. Cf. *Questiones de Epistolis Pauli. De Epistola ad Romanos* (ed. R.M. Martin, *Oeuvres de Robert de Melun* [Louvain: Specilegium Sacrum Lovaniense, 1938], II, p. 136 [on Rom 10.4]).

110. '*Finis enim*. Vere ignorantes Dei justitiam, quia fidem Christi non habent qua unusquisque fidelis iustificatur. Quod vere ex fide Christi quisque iustificetur et non ex sua justitia, legalium scilicet operum, sic dicit quia *omni credenti*, id est unicuique fideli, *Christus*, id est fides Christi, *ad iustitiam*, hoc est legalium operum, quia quamdiu in illis operibus spes salutis constituunt, Christus eis non proderit. Unde et ad Galatas dicit: *Si circumcidamini, Christus vobis nihil proderit*, et per semetipsum Christus ait: *Usque ad Johannem lex et prophetae*' (*Commentarius super S. Pauli epistolam ad Romanos* [CCCM, 11.249]).

111. However, in this same book Abelard resolved the relation between faith and law in a positive and continuous way (*Ad Romanos* 3.279-71 [CCCM 11.195]). On Abelard's view on the law, see Ralf Peppermüller, *Abälards Auslegung des Römerbriefes* (Beiträge zur Geschichte der Philosophie und Theologie des Mittelalters, NF 10; Münster: Aschendorff, 1972), pp. 147-70.

112. See A.M. Landgraf, *Commentarius Cantabrigensis in Epistolas Pauli et Scholia Petri Abaelardi*, vol. I, *In Epistolam ad Romanos* (South Bend, Ind.: Notre Dame University, 1937), p. 145.

113. 'Vere ignorabant justitiam Dei nam *Christus* quem caeci respuebant, est *finis*, id est *consummatio legis*, quia in eo lex consummatur et perficitur. *Finis*, id est *perfectio* legis, est Christus *ad justitiam* complendam omni in se *credenti*, quia omnis qui in Christum credit, habet ipsum Christum consummationem legis, ut per eum faciat justitiam. Sunt enim opera quae videntur bona sine fide Christi, et non sunt bona, quia non referentur ad eum finem ex quo sunt bona . . . Finis enim dicitur ipse Christus quia quidquid agimus, ad illum referimus; et cum ad eum pervenimus, non habebimus ultra quod quaeramus, sed ibi permanebimus. In eum namque dirigitur nostra *intentio*. Ad quem cum pervenerimus, non erit ultra quo tendamus, qui ibi est omnium honorum *plenitudo*' (Hervaeus Burgidolensis, *Commentaria in Epistolam Pauli. Ad Romanos* [PL 181.740-41]).

114. '*Christus finis* est *legis*, id est qui adimplet in se et in nobis quod lex praedixit. Qui etiam valet *ad justitiam omni credenti*, id est qui est dator justitiae omni credenti. Ex Christo ergo non ex lege est justitia, quia si per

legem scriptam vel naturalem esset justitia sine fide Christi, ergo Christus gratis moreretur. Si autem non gratis mortuus est, ergo in illo solo justificatur impius, cui credenti in eum deputatur fides ad justitiam. Omni ergo humana natura et justificari et redimi ab ira, id est a vindicta nullo modo potest, nisi per fidem, et sacramentum sanguinis Christi. *Finis enim Christus*, in quo lex justitia non consumitur, sed impletur. Omnis enim perfectio in ipso est, ultra quem non est quo spes se extendat. *Finis* etiam fidelium Christus est. Ad quam cum pervenerit currentis intentio, non habet amplius quod posset invenire, sed habet in quo debeat permanere. *Finis* ergo dicitur, non quia consumit, sed quia perficit. Perficit ergo justitiam per fidem sine operibus legis, et sunt opera quae videtur bona sine fide Christi; et non sunt tamen vera bona, quia non referuntur ad eum finem ex quo sunt bona, id est Christum, qui est finis legis ad justitiam non utique humanam, sed divinam' (*Collectanea in Epistolam Pauli ad Romanos* [PL 191.1473]).

115. According to Roger Bacon, *Opus Minus*, p. 324 (ed. Brewer), during the following centuries the *Glossa Magna* and the *Sentences* of Peter Lombard and the *Summa Theologica* of Thomas Aquinas were studied and expounded far more than the Scriptures; cf. Farrar, p. 262.

116. Smalley, 'The Bible in the Medieval Schools', *CHB*, II, p. 206. According to Farrar (p. 258), the pattern of approach of Scholasticism to the Biblical text may be summarized in the words of Bernard of Clairvaux (1090–1153): '*Disce primus quid tenendum sit*': 'first learn what you are to believe, and then go to Scripture to find it there' (cf. p. 265).

117. The 13th century produced such an impressive series of tools and aids for Biblical study (*Correctoria, concordantiae, vocabularia, exempla*, etc.) that Spicq called it 'le grand siècle scriptuaire du Moyen Age' (p. 143; cf. pp. 166-77).

118. See A. Landgraf, 'Les preuves scriptuaires et patristiques dans l'argumentation théologique', *RSPT* 15 (1931), pp. 287-92.

119. 'Deinde cum dicit *Finis legis Christus*, etc., manifestat quod dixerat, scilicet eos Dei iustitiam ignorare et quod ei subiici nolunt, cum tamen iustitiam legalem statuere velint. Circa quod considerandum est, quod sicut etiam philosophi dicunt, intentio cuiuslibet legislatoris est facere homines justos: unde multo magis lex vetus hominibus divinitus data ordinabatur ad faciendum homines iustos. Hanc tamen iustitiam lex per semetipsam facere non poterat, quia neminem *ad perfectum adduxit lex*, ut dicitur Hebr. vii,14, sed ordinat homines in Christum quem promittebat, et praefigurabat. Gal. iii,24: *Lex paedagogus noster fuit in Christo, ut ex fide justificemur*. Et hoc est quod dicit *Christus enim est finis legis* ad quem scilicet tota lex ordinatur. Ps. cxviii,96: *Omnis consummationis vidi finem*. Finis, inquam, ad iustitiam, ut scilicet homines per Christum iustitiam consequantur, quam lex intendebat' (*Super Epistolas S. Pauli. Lectura ad Romanos* [8th rev. edn; Raphaelo Cai, 1.819]).

120. *Summ.*, 30.245 (ed. Bourke). Cf. 1.23.5; 3.28.4 (ed. Blackfriars, 51.52). In *Lib. Sent.* 1.43.1, Thomas Aquinas gives the following definition of finis: 'Finis quantum ad essentiam'. In *Lib. de somn.* 4.2, he defines *finis* as 'quod est optimum in unoquoque est finis ejus'. Cf. *C. gent.* 3.22. For the current understanding of *finis* and *causa finalis* in Scholasticism, see Richard of St Victor, *Alleg. in NT* 6 C; 893 A; see further Albert Blaise, *Dictionnaire Latin-Franc;ais des auteurs du Moyen Age. Lexicon Latinitatis Medii Aevi, praesertim ad res ecclesiasticas investigandas pertinens* (CCM; Turnholt: Brepols, 1975), p. 385: '*finis*: achèvement, perfection, fin, but, terme'; p. 386: '*causa finalis*: cause finale, ce qui explique un fait en le faisant connaître comme moyen d'une fin'.

121. D. Bourke and A. Littledale explain the importance of this final understanding of the law in the theology of Aquinas in the following terms: 'It is important to notice how the philosophical part of St. Thomas's argument, which is based on the Aristotelian metaphysics of final causality, "dovetails" into the theological part, which is based on St. Paul's evaluation of the Old Law as set forth primarily in *Romans*. The key "point of intersection" between the two is St. Paul's statement that "Christ is the end (telos) of the Law" (Rom 10.4). This may be taken as axiomatic for the treatise as a whole' (*Summa* 1.2.98, ed. Blackfriars, 29.2-3, n.a.). 'The Aristotelian metaphysic of final casuality may be summed up in the axiom that that which is last in the order of execution is first in the order of conception and intention. Between the "first" and the 'last' are interposed a number of subordinate means by which the initial concept is duly put into execution. The very *raison d'être* of such a subordinate means is determined by the ultimate end which is conceived of prior to it, and to the ultimate execution of which it is ordained. Applying this to the Old Law, it is a subordinate means ordained to salvation for God through Christ. As has been said, Christ is the end (telos) of the law (Rom 10.4), and since in his role as Savior he has been ordained as such by God, the Law, as the subordinate means to that end, has come from God also' (*ibid.*, 29.8-9, n.a).

122. See Francisco Canals Vidal, 'La justificación por la fe sin las obras de la ley: el evangelio de San Pablo en la exégesis de Santo Tomas de Aquino', in *Problemi di Teologia* (ed. S. Lyonne; Rome: Pontifical Biblical Institute, 1974), pp. 113-21; cf. Carlos López-Hernández, 'Ley y Evangelio. Notas para un diálogo entre Santo Tomás, Francisco de Vitoria y Martín Lutero', *DiálEcum* 25 (1980), pp. 3-33.

123. For Thomas Aquinas the OT law was provisional and had the function of bringing man to accept the gospel. The OT was, therefore, imperfect, and the NT was perfect 'like a seed compared with a tree' (Baker, p. 49). But both are God's and esentially related, for the OT was oriented towards the gospel and could only find in it its end and fulfillment. See further, D. Bourke, *Thomas Aquinas and the Old Law* (New York: McGraw-Hill, 1969), pp. 8-9, 245; P. Griboment, 'Le lien des deux Testaments selon

la théologie de saint Thomas', *ETL* 22 (1946), pp. 70-89. For Aquinas's exegesis of Romans, see M. Arias Reyero, *Thomas von Aquin als Exeget* (Einsiedeln: Johannes Verlag, 1971), passim.

124. Smalley, p. 363.

125. Grant, p. 127.

126. *Postilla in epistolas omnes d. Pauli. In Romanos* (ed. Venetia, 1703), *in loc.*

127. Walter C. Kaiser, Jr, attributes Lyra's emphasis on the letter to his Jewish background (*Toward an Exegetical Theology* [Grand Rapids: Baker, 1981], p. 60); W. Affeld, 'Verzeichnis der Römerbrief-Kommentare der lateinischen Kirche bis zu Nikolas von Lyra', *Traditio* 13 (1957), pp. 369-406; Spicq, pp. 318-30.

128. *Biblia Latina*, vol. 4, *Ad Romanos* (Strasburg: J.R. Gruninger, 1492) *in loc.*

129. On the medieval understanding of the relationship between the OT and the NT, see H. de Lubac, *Exégèse médiévale*, I, pp. 305-63. The NT was generally considered superior to the OT, but continuous to it. Most interpreters preferred to keep the difficult tension between the Old and the New Scriptures rather than to break the *unitas Scripturarum*.

130. Basil Hall says that 'the history of Biblical exegesis in both Catholicism and Protestantism would provide profounder insights for the understanding of the age of the Reformation than the more usual study of the polemic of attack and counterattack which was largely peripheral to the religious needs and aspirations of the writers of the time' ('Annotations and Commentaries on the Bible', *CHB*, III, p. 76).

131. For a list of the most important (mainly Protestant) commentaries on Romans from the end of the sixteenth century to the nineteenth century, see R. Corney, *Commentarius in S. Pauli Apostoli Epistolas* (Paris: Beauchesne, 1896), I, pp. 25-26. Cf. H.A. Meyer, *Critical and Exegetical Hand-Book to the Epistle to the Romans* (New York: Funk and Wagnalls, 1889), pp. xv-xxiii.

132. See Bernard Roussel, 'La découverte de sens nouveaux de l'épître aux Romains par quelques exégètes français du milieu du XVIe siècle', in *Histoire de l'exégèse au XVIe siècle*, pp. 331-50.

133. *Enarratio in Epistolam S. Pauli ad Romanos*, trans. and ed. J.H. Lupton (London: Gregg Press, 1873), p. 52. Colet's lectures on Romans were delivered in Oxford about the year 1497 (*ibid.*, p. v). One may find some of the elements of this interpretation in the commentaries of Lefèvre d'Etaples (d. 1537): *Sancti Pauli epistolae xiv ex Vulgata editione adiecta intelligentia ex graeco, cum commentariis* (Paris: J.F. Stapulensis, 1512).

134. According to Louis Bouyer, 'Erasmus represents the first flowering of New Testament exegesis based on criticism and philology, through which the Renaissance—while restoring the link with the patristic tradition, and especially with the Alexandrians—was to prepare the way for modern

exegesis' ('Erasmus in Relation to the Medieval Biblical Tradition', *CHB*, II, p. 493). For Bouyer the contribution of Erasmus is as well in the rediscovery of the Greek Fathers as in that of the Greek New Testament text (p. 492).

135. Erasmus's critical edition of the New Testament, revised five times by the author in its five editions, from the *Novum Instrumentum* (Basle: Hieronymus Frosten, 1511) to the *Editio Regia* of 1550, became the *textus receptus* until the end of the 19th century. Cf. R.H. Bainton, 'The Bible in the Reformation', *CHB*, III, pp. 1-37.

136. Lorenzo Valla, *Collatione Novi Testamenti*, ed. Alessandro Perosi (Studi e testi, 1; Firenze: Istituto Nazionale di Studi sul Rinascimento, 1970; see Albert Rabil, *Erasmus and the New Testament* (San Antonio: Trinity University Press, 1972), pp. 58-61.

137. *Opera Omnia*, vols. 6 and 7 (facsimile reproduction of the 1703–1706 Lugduni Batavorum edition; Hildesheim: Georg Olms, 1961–1962), hereafter cited as *LB*. On the influence of Luther on Erasmus's interpretation of Romans, see J.B. Payne, 'The Significance of Lutheranizing Changes in Erasmus' Interpretation of Paul's Letters to the Romans and the Galatians in His Annotationes (1527) and Paraphrases (1532)', *CHB*, III, pp. 312-30. In the 5th edition of the *Novum Testamentum*, Romans is the book with most annotations (574 for 543 verses) and quotations (Origen, 139 times, Augustine, 67) (*ibid.*, p. 17). Cf. A. Godin, 'Fonction d'Origène dans la pratique exégétique d'Erasme: Les Annotations sur l'Epître aux Romains', in *Histoire de l'exégèse au XVIe siècle* (Etudes de Philologie et d'Histoire, 34; Geneva: Droz, 1978), pp. 17-44.

138. *Adnotationes ad Romanos*, 10.4: '*Finis enim legis Christus*. Τέλος hoc loco *consummationem* ac *perfectionem* sonat, non *intentum*: quod indicavit S. Augustinus explanans Psalmum quintum. Rursus adversus Priscillianistas & Origenistas capite septimo. Nam Graeci quod absolutum & omnibus, quae solent requiri, perfectum est, τέλος appellant. Summa igitur legis est Christus. Et in Psalmis, quorum titulus habet *In finem*, existimant aliquid reconditius & secretius esse vestigandum. Quod hic dixit τέλος, alias vocat πλήρωμα' (*LB* 6.617 E-618 A).

139. 'Through the Gospel, the Law of Moses has not been totally repealed; instead, the mystery which was formerly hidden for many ages is now revealed according to the oracles of the ancient prophets and made known by the radiant Gospel' (*LB*7.832 B). Cf. *LB* 7.793 C, 785 C-D, 800 F–801 A.

140. *Luther's Works*, 2.279 (Weimar edition), hereafter cited as *WA*. Cf. R.W. Doermann, 'Luther's Principles of Biblical Interpretation', in *Interpreting Luther's Legacy*, ed. F.W. Meuser and S.D. Schneider (Minneapolis: Augsburg Press, 1969), pp. 14-25.

141. *LW*, 6.411-12; 1.2.391-92; 2.282; 2.309, 34. Cf. Zwingli, *Sämtliche Werke*, 1.479-569; 1.319; 1.293-94; Calvin, *Inst.* 1.7.1-2.

142. Hilton C. Oswald, *Lectures on Romans. Glosses and Scholia* (*LW*, 25; St Louis: Concordia Publishing House, 1972), p. xi. Oswald notes further that 'a prophetic preview as it were of the whole series of lectures on Romans is sounded in the marginal gloss to *de filio suo* in Rom 1.3: "Here the door is thrown open wide for the understanding of the Holy Scripture, that is, that everything must be understood in relation to Christ"' (*ibid.*)

143. *Martin Luther's Commentary on the Epistle to the Romans*, trans. J.T. Mueller (Grand Rapids: Zondervan, 1954), p. 131; cf. *WA*, 56.99. In *WA*, 57.89 (commenting on Rom 10.4) we read: '*Finis*, i.e. plenitudo et consummatio, impletio *enim legis Christus*: non opera q. d. lex fine Christo nihil est, quia non se, sed illum ipsa querit et intendit ut finem suum ad iustitiam omni credenti, sive Iudaeo sive Graeco'.

144. Luther wrote: 'Christ is the point in the circle from which the whole circle is drawn' (*WA*, 47.338, trans. Grant, p. 131). On Luther's Christological interpretation of the OT see Bainton, p. 16; H. Bornkamm, *Luther and the Old Testament* (Philadelphia: Fortress Press, 1969), pp. 135-49; On Luther's conviction that the whole Bible is Christocentric, and on Luther's hermeneutical principle of 'was Christum treibet' see *WA*, 63.157. For Luther the Christological sense of the OT was the literal sense. Through typology, prophecy, and prefigurations, in the OT 'God was operating with the constituents of a great *intent* anticipated prior to its perfect realization in Christ' (*WA*, 42.189, trans. Bainton, p. 16). According to John Goldingay, even when Luther gives to the OT law a negative function, he still understands it teleologically: 'The fact that Moses himself looks forward to Christ—in Luther's view—indicates that he did not even see his own Law as the last word. Moses' best pupils are those who see his demands clearly and are driven to Christ by the impossibility of fulfilling them . . . Luther finds a stray thread of continuity between the Testaments' ('Luther and the Bible', *SJT* 35 [1982], pp. 49-50). Cf. Bornkamm, *Luther and the OT*, p. 266; J.S. Preuss, *From Shadow to Promise: Old Testament Interpretation from Augustine to the Young Luther* (Cambridge and Harvard: University Press, 1969), p. 200.

145. The sharpest division between law and gospel made by Luther is to be found in his lectures on Galatians (delivered in 1531). See Markus Barth, 'Paulus und das Gesetz', in *Die Israelfrage nach Röm 9–11* (ed. L. De Lorenzi; Rome: St Paul's Abbey, 1977), pp. 252-53. In the lectures on Romans (delivered between 1515 and 1516) are found, nevertheless, all the ideas that were later regarded as the most characteristic of Luther. Cf. Wilhelm Pauck, 'Introduction' to *Lectures on Romans* (LCC, 15; ed. J. Baillie, J.T. McNeill, and H.P. Dusen; Philadelphia: Westminster, 1961), p. lxv. For Luther on the 'abrogation of the law' and on a certain opposition of 'law' and 'Christ' see pp. 132, 134, 114, 117, 199, etc. Luther explained the opposition law–gospel in these terms: 'Gesetz und Evangelium sind zwei ganz widerwärtige Dinge die sich mit oder neben einander nicht leiden oder

vertragen können' (*WA*, 22.654). On Luther on the 'end of the law' see *WA*, 39.1, pp. 349-50 (see p. 66). See further Paul Althaus, *The Theology of Martin Luther*, trans. R.C. Shultz (Philadelphia: Fortress, 1966), pp. 218-38; and especially Bornkamm, *Luther and the OT*, pp. 81-87, 135-49.

146. On the theological consequences of Luther's translation of τέλος by 'Ende' in Rom 10.4, see Bring, 'Paul and the OT', pp. 47, 51.

147. Farrar, p. 341.

148. 'Iudaei quaerunt iustitiam ex lege, nec intelligunt Christum esse finem legis, hoc est, promissum esse, ut ipse tolleret peccatum et mortem, quae lex tantum revelat . . . Christus est finis legis, id est impletio seu consummatio, donat id, quo lex postulat, id est, est iustus imputatione, et liberatur a peccato et morte' (*Scripta exegetica. Ad Romanos 10.4* [CR 15.688]).

149. 'Haec interpretatio aliena est disputatione Pauli' (*ibid.*).

150. See *The Latin Works and the Correspondence of Hulderich Zwingli* (ed. S.M. Jackson; Philadelphia: Fortress, 1922), 1.213; 2.48; 3.178.

151. 'Dann wie Christus das End des Gesetzes ist, und alle Schrifften, Rom x(4), also zeügen sie auch alle von im. (Johan v[39], Lu xxiii[26, 46])' (*Martin Bucers Deutsche Schriften. Opera Omnia*, ed. Robert Stupperich [Gütersloh: Gerd Mohn, 1978], V, p. 63).

152. Bullinger translated *finis* in Rom 10.4 by 'consummatio, perfectio, summa' (*In Sanctissimam Pauli ad Romanos Epistolam Heinrychi Bullengeri Commentarius* [Zurich, 1533]); *The Decades* (ed. Thomas Harding for the Parker Society; Cambridge: University Press, 1849, III, p. 237). Susi Hausammann, *Römerbriefauslegung zwischen Humanismus und Reformation. Eine Studie zu Heinrich Bullingers Römerbriefvorlesung von 1525* (Studien zur Dogmengeschichte und systematischen Theologie, 27; Zürich, 1970), pp. 281-84.

153. *In Epistolam B. Pauli Apostoli ad Romanos Adnotationes a Ioanne Oecolampadio Basileae praelectae et denuo recognitae* (Basel, 1525), *in loc.*

154. 'For that which here says "the end" the Greek word (telos) signifies consummation or perfection, and in such case St. Paul would wish to say, that he who has the righteousness of Christ fulfils the Law, or that the Law aimed at leading men to Christ, that this was its end, its design' (*Commentary on the Epistle to the Romans* [trans. J.T. Betts; London: Trubner & Co., 1883], pp. 179-80).

155. Farrar, p. 342.

156. '*Finis enim legis Christus*: Mihi non male videtur hoc loco verbum *complementi* [sicut etiam Erasmus *perfectionem* vertit], sed quia altera lectio omnium fere consensu recepta est, et ipsa quoque non male convenit [liberum per nuerit lectoriem retinere]' (*Ioannis Calvini Commentarii in Epistolam Pauli ad Romanos* [Strasbourg, 1540], OC 49.1960. Passages in brackets added in 1556. Cf. *Commentaire de M. Jean Calvin sur l'Epître aux Romains* (Geneva, 1550), *in loc.*).

157. J. Owen translates this passage in the following terms: 'The word *completion* (*complementum*) seems not to me unsuitable in this place, and Erasmus has rendered it *perfection*: but as the other reading is almost universally approved, and is not inappropriate (*end*) readers, for my part, may retain it' (John Calvin, *Commentaries on the Epistle of Paul to the Romans* [Grand Rapids: Eerdmans, 1947], pp. 383-84). See also J. Calvin, *The Epistle of Paul the Apostle to the Romans and to the Thessalonians* (trans. R. Mackenzie), in *Calvin's Commentaries*, ed. D.W. Torrance and T.F. Torrance (Grand Rapids: Eerdmans, 1961), VIII, pp. 221-22; cf. *Institutes of the Christian Religion* (trans. F.L. Battles, ed. J.T. McNeill; Philadelphia: Westminster, 1960), LCC, 20.347; 21.1163. The sense in which 'Christ is the end of the law' appears clearly in *Institutes*, 1.6.2: 'With this intent the law was published, and the prophets afterwards added as its interpreters. For even though the use of the law was manifold, as it will be seen more clearly in its place, it was especially committed to Moses and all the prophets to teach the way of reconciliation between God and men, whence also Paul calls Christ the end of the law' (trans. Battles, LCC, 20.71-72). Cf. 4.8.13; 2.8.7; 2.11.1. On the idea that 'the law in all its parts has a reference to Christ', see 2.6.4; 3.2.6. For a full discussion on Calvin's view of the relation between Christ and the law, see Benoit Girardin, *Rhétorique et Théologie. Calvin: le commentaire de l'épître aux Romains* (Paris: Beauchesne, 1979), pp. 310-55. Calvin weaves closely together the pedagogical use of the law with the typological system of the Old Testament, so that 'the gospel points out with the finger what the law foreshadowed under types' (*Institutes*, 2.7.2).

158. '*Finis*, τέλος. Id est τὸ οὗ ἕνεκα, quod Latini tum finem, tum extremum, tum etiam scopum translatitie vocant. Finis autem Legis est illos iustificare qui eam observant; quem finem quominus assequamur, impedit non ipsius Legis ulla qualitas, sed carnis nostra vitiositas; cui demum ita medetur Christus ut in ea uno, gratis per fidem nobis imputato, finem Legis consequamur, per illum iustificati qui pro nobis legem implevit, factus nobis iustitia, sanctificatio, etc. Quamobrem etiam Apostolus dixit supra, 3,31, se per fidem non tollere Legem, sed stabilire' (*Novum Testamentum Annotationes* [London: C. Baker, 1582], *in loc.*).

159. Beza's commentary on Rom 10.4 follows this way: 'Erasmus *perfectionem* maluit interpretari, id est τελείωσιν vel πλήρωμα: cuius sententia mihi non placet omni ex parte. Nam τέλος non memini legere in ea significatione, & Paulum opinor non modo Legem a Christo impletam dicere, sed de huius impletionis efficacia differere, nobis videlicet per imputationem iustificandis . . . ' (*Annotatione in Rom* 10.4, lines 20-25).

160. Sadoletus adds to the classical interpretations the concept that righteousness only comes through faith in Christ. 'Etenim finis legis CHRISTUS est, vel ut spectatus ipse & propositus a lege, ad quem lex tota tanquam ad ultimum, summum contenderet, vel ut legis perfectio, qui

addiderit legi, quod ex se lex habere non potuit' (*In Pauli Epistolam ad Romanos Commentariorum libri tres* (Lyons: Sebastianus Gryphius, 1535), *in loc.*

161. The vitality of Catholic exegesis declined after Trent. The council pronounced severe admonitions against those who interpreted Scripture in a different way from 'the sense in which Holy Mother Church has held it' and compelled exegesis to return into orthodox allegories and prolix moralizing; see the *Decree Concerning the Canonical Scriptures* (The Fourth Session of the Council of Trent, 8 April 1546, *CHB*, III, p. 91). We may say that medieval exegesis survived among the counter-reformation interpreters. Cf. R.E. Brown, *The 'Sensus Plenior' of Sacred Scripture* (Baltimore: St Mary's University, 1955), p. 64. Cf. F.C. Crehan, 'The Bible in the Roman Catholic Church', *CHB*, III, pp. 199-205, 236-37.

162. *Epistolae Pauli et Aliorum Apostolorum ad Graecam veritatem castigatae et iuxta sensum litteralem enarratae* (Venice: Apud I. Badium, 1532), *in loc.* Lapide gives these four senses of Rom 10.4: '*Primo.* Christus legis umbras implens eam terminavit et cessare fecit; *Secundo.* perfectio et consummatio legis est Christus, quia quod lex non potuit, scilicet justum facere hominem, hoc fecit Christus; *Tertio.* sine fide Christi lex perfici et impleri non potuit; *Quarto.* et aptissime, scopus legis est Christus, quia tota lex ad Christum, quasi ad finem, terminum et scopum suum, refertur, tendit, ducit et vocat' (*Commentaria in Omnes Sancti Pauli Epistolas*, Tomus I: *In Epistolas ad Romanos et I ad Corinthios* (A. Taurinorum: Typographia Pontificia, Petri Marietti, reprint 1909), pp. 238-39.

163. '*Finem*, Latini fere intelligunt causam finalem: ut Christus dicatur finis legis mosaicae, quia tam lex ceremonialis figurando & praenunciando, quam lex moralis infirmitatem hominis arguendo, Christum, salvatorem ut finem & scopum spectabant. Sic etiam Theodoritus Graecus. At vero caeteri Graeci & inter Latinos Hugo Victorinus atque Hervaeus finem interpretantur impletionem, consummationem, perfectionem, ut vertit Erasmus; & quod Apostolus infra cap. 13 vocat plenitudinem, cum ait: *Plenitudo legis est dilectio.* Quam interpretationem Graeca vox *telos* magis recipit quam latina *finis*: quemadmodum e diverso finis apud Latinos magis *telos* apud Graecos, significationem habet causae cujus gratia quippiam fit. Hoc igitur modo sensus est: Christum esse per quem lex impletur, & vera justitia acquiritur; . . . Porro nihil hic locus facit pro sectariis docentibus solam fidem sufficere ad iustitiam . . . (*Absolutissima in omnes Beati Pauli et septem catholicas apostolorum epistolas commentaria* (Douay, 1614-1616; ed. F. Ricciardi [Paris: 1741], vol. I, *in loc.*).

164. Among the rare commentaries on Romans in a vernacular language, the one in French by A. Godeau (1605–1672) deserves mention: 'S'ils entendoient bien la Loy dont ils parlent tant, ils scauroient que Iesus Christ non seulement en est la fin, comme celuy que toutes les figures regardent, mais qu'il en est l'accomplissement, comme celuy qui justificant tous ceux

qui croient en luy, fait ce qu'elle ne pouvoit exécuter' (*Paraphrase sur l'épître de saint Paul aux Romains* [Paris: Camuset et Le Petit, 1651], *in loc.*). Other commentaries worth mentioning are: A. Salmeron, *Disputationes in epistolam ad Romanos* (Colonia Agrippinae: A. Hierat, 1612-1615, reprint of the Madrid edn, 1597); F. Romolo, Cardinal Bellarmin, *Explanationes triplicis, literalis, moralis et dogmaticae in epistolas S. Pauli apostoli* (*Opera Oratoria Postuma*, VII; Rome: P.U.G., 1612–1613, reprint 1946), p. 340; A. Calmet, *Critici sacri sive doctissimorum virorum in ss. Biblia annotationes et tractatus*, t. 7, *Annotata ad Acta Apostolorum et Epistolas Pauli* (London, s.l., 1660), p. 611; cf. B.A. Piconio, *The Epistle to the Romans* (trans. A.H. Pritchard; London: J. Hodges, 1880, from 1703 edition), p. 128.

165. So Aegidius Hunnius (1550–1603), *Epistolae divi Pauli Apostoli ad Romanos expositio plana & perspicua* (Frankfurt: I. Spies, 1587); Mathias Flacius Illyricus, *Clavis Scripturae Sacrae* (Basel: Per Q. Querum, 1567).

166. Luther had endeavored to overcome the divorce between exegesis and theology, which prevailed in medieval scholasticism. But after Luther, the best contributions of the great reformer were used in a distorted way. The principle of *analogia fidei* or *analogia Scripturae* turned to the practice of doctrine-controlling exegesis, and the principle of *was Christum treibet* led to the theory of 'a canon within the canon', and consequently to the relegation of the OT to an inferior place, and to the interpretation of any passage as a function of the doctrine of righteousness by faith. See Grant, p. 135, and P. Lehmann, 'The Reformers' Use of the Bible', *Theology Today* 3 (1946), pp. 328-44. The old ecclesiastical authority, which Luther and the reformers had so decidedly rejected, was brought back. The paradoxical result was that while Lutherans were erecting Luther into a sort of pope they were diverging most widely from the spirit of his writings.

167. According to Farrar, the Protestant churches had produced 'nothing of first rate importance in exegesis since the death of Flacius in 1575' (p. 380 n. 3). Cf. Wilhelm Pauck, *The Heritage of the Reformation* (The Free Press of Glencoe, 1961), pp. 328-29.

168. Forde, p. 184; cf. p. 176. Lauri Haikola finds that the major difference between Luther and later orthodoxy lies precisely in the understanding of the Law (*Studien zu Luther und zum Luthertum* [Uppsala: Universitats Årsskrift, 2, 1958], pp. 9-12, 106-107).

169. Hunnius interpreted Rom 10.4 as a statement of Christ's having fulfilled the law in our stead: 'Nam perfectio legis Christus, id est, cum nos non possemus implere legem, Christus in nostrum succedens locum, eam perfecte adimplevit' (*Loci Communes*, p. 160). Hunnius explains how this substitionary fulfillment was realized by Christ: 'Christus non tantum passiva obedientia, hoc est passione et morte, sed etiam obedientia activa seu impletione legis vitam & iustitiam nobis comparasse'. So, though Christ's fulfilling of the law was not intended to abrogate it ('Christus non venisse ut tollat legem sed ut eam impleat') it resulted in its fulfillment in our stead: 'At

qui constat non venisse Christum pro se legi Dei satisfaceret . . . ut pro nobis legem adimpleret. Qua perfectio vel impletio legis servit nobis' (*ibid.*, p. 164).

170. It is very difficult to ascertain with precision the first 'terminal-temporal-antinomian' interpretations of Rom 10.4. The earliest works mentioned as supporting this kind of interpretation are: Jonasz Schlichting (1592–1661), *Commentaria posthuma in plerosque Novi Testamenti Libros* (Irenapoli: S.I. Philalethii, 1656); J. Le Clerc (1657–1736), *A Supplement to Dr. Hammond's Paraphrase and Annotations on the New Testament. In Which His Interpretation of Many Important Passages Is Freely and Impartially Examined* (London: S. Buckley, 1699); Philippus Limborch (1633–1712), *Commentarius in Acta Apostolorum et in Epistolas ad Romanos et ad Hebreos* (Rotterdam: B. Bos, 1711), and even these are said to interpret Rom 10.4 in the sense of 'ending-termination' of the ceremonial law (Moses Stuart, *Commentary on Romans* [Andover: Gould & Newman, 1832], p. 456).

171. Bernhard Rothmann of Münster wrote that 'by all Christians the Old Testament had to be received with greater qualification than the New' (quoted by Bainton, p. 17).

172. So Balthasar Hubmaier and Hans Denck (see further Wood, pp. 99-101).

173. For bibliography see *Gesetz und Evangelium. Beiträge zur gegenwärtigen theologischen Diskussion* (ed. Ernst Kinder and Klaus Haendler; Darmstadt: Wissenschaftliche Buchgesellschaft, 1968), pp. 390-95.

174. 'Lex Mosis via tantum fuit ad Evangelium: τέλος (finis) est viae meta, ut supra 6,21-22; 1 Tim. 1,5. Idem sensus Gal. 3,24 et supra 3,31 & 8,4; Hebre. 7,19. Christus saepe ponitur pro Evangelio, ut supra diximus, 9,32: πλήρωμα νόμου ἀγάπη . . .' (*Opera Omnia Theologica* [Paris, s.1., 1644], III: *Annotationes in Epistolas Pauli, in loc.*). Cf. the interpretation of Jacobus Westein: 'Tantum abest ut lex Mosis a Christo arceat, ut potius ad illum adducat, si recte intelligatur, supra iii,21; Gal iii,24. Τέλος, I Tim 1,5' (*Novum Testamentum Graecum* [Amsterdam: Officina Dommeniana, 1752, reprint Graz: Akademischer Druck, 1962], II, *in loc.*).

175. See Charles S. McCoy, 'The Covenant Theology of Johannes Cocceius' (Ph.D. dissertation, Yale University, 1957), pp. 60-61; Holmes Rolson III, 'Responsible Man in Reformed Theology: Calvin Versus the Westminster Confession', *SJT* 23 (1970), p. 129. For a comprehensive survey of the development of covenant theology, see M.W. Karlberg, 'Reformed Interpretation of the Mosaic Covenant', *WTJ* 43 (1980), pp. 1-57.

176. 'Τέλος, *finis*, justitiam et vitam, quam lex ostendit sed dare nequit, tribuens. Τέλος, *finis*, et πλήρωμα, *complementum*, sunt synonyma. Coll. 1 Tim. 1,5 cum Rom. 13,10. Itaque cf. cum hoc loco Matth. 5,17. Lex hominem urget donec et ad Christum confugit. Tum ipsa dicit: Asylum es nactus, desino te persequi, sapis, salvus es' (*Gnomon Novi Testamenti* [1734; ed. Paul Stendel; Stuttgart: J.F. Steinkopf, 1891], pp. 595-96).

177. 'Bengel', *The Concise Oxford Dictionary of the Christian Church* (1977), p. 59.

178. Baker, p. 55.

179. 'We need not trouble ourselves to inquire in what various senses Christ may be said to be *telos nomou*—'the end', the complement, the perfection, 'of the law'. The apostle sufficiently determineth his intention, in affirming not absolutely that he is the end of the law, but he is so *eis dikaiosunen*, 'for righteousness...' unto every one that believeth. The matter in question is a righteousness which the law requires. God looks for no righteousness from us but what is prescribed in the law... That we should be righteous herewith before God was the first, original end of the law. Its other ends at present, of the conviction of sin, and judging or condemning for it, were accidental unto its primitive constitution.... This righteousness that the law requires... the Jews sought after by their own personal performance of the works and duties of it. But hereby, in the utmost of their endeavours, they could never fulfil this righteousness, nor attain this end of the law... Wherefore, the apostle declares, that all this is done another way; that the righteousness of the law is fulfilled, and its end, as unto a righteousness before God, attained; and that is in and by Christ. For what the law required, that he accomplished; which is accounted unto every one that believes' (*The Works of John Owen*, ed. W.H. Gould [London: Banner of Truth Trust, 1967], V, pp. 342-43.

180. Burgess argued for the possibility of two simultaneous meanings for τέλος, namely: (1) 'that to which a thing naturally inclines itself', and (2) 'that for which a thing is appointed by the one who brings it into being' (*Vindiciae Legis: A Vindication of the Morall Law and the Covenants* [London: James Young, 1646], p. 7). The rest of the passage is also worth quoting as a witness to the debate on the meaning of τέλος in the seventeenth century: 'By reason of the different use of the word *telos*, there are different conjectures; some make it no more than *extremitas*, or *terminus*; because the ceremonial Law ended in Christ; Others make it *finis complementi*, the fulness of the Law is Christ; Others add, *finis intentionis*, or *scopi* to it; so that by these the meaning is, The Law did intend Christ in all its ceremonialls and moralls, that, as there was not the least ceremony, which did not lead to Christ, so not the least iota or apex in the morall law, but it did also aime at him' (see further E.F. Kevan, *The Grace of the Law. A Study of Puritan Theology* [Grand Rapids: Baker, 1965], pp. 137-40).

181. So H. Hammond, *A Paraphrase and Annotations upon All the Books of the New Testament* (1653); *Oxford's Paraphrase of the Epistles* (1675); S. Clarke and T. Pyle, *Paraphrase of the New Testament* (1701–1735); D. Whitby, *A Paraphrase and Commentary on the New Testament in Two Volumes* (1702); J. Guyse, *Paraphrases* (1739–1752); P. Doddridge, *Family Expositor or a Paraphrase and Version of the New Testament* (1739); W. Mace, *New Testament* (1929); A. Purver, *Quaker's Bible* (1964); etc.

182. '*For Christ is the end of the law.* The scope and aim of it. It is the very design of the law to bring men to believe in Christ for justification and salvation. And he alone gives that pardon and life which the law shows the want of, but cannot give' (*Explanatory Notes upon the New Testament* [London: Epworth, 1948, reprint of 1754], p. 229).

183. See Kevan, p. 137.

184. Cf. M.W. Karlberg, 'Reformed Interpretation of the Mosaic Covenant', *WTJ* 43 (1980), pp. 1-57; D.P. Fuller, *Gospel and Law: Contrast or Continuum? The Hermeneutics of Dispensationalism and Covenant Theology* (Grand Rapids: Eerdmans, 1980), pp. 51-58.

185. On the passing from the rejection of the authority of the church to the declaration of the absolute independence of the individual reason, see E. Caird, *The Critical Philosophy of Immanuel Kant*, 2 vols. (Glasgow: J. Maclehofe, 1909), I, p. 71.

186. The skeptical approach to Bible study initiated with the works of Hobbes and Spinoza was carried out—with different degrees of intensity—by C. Wolf (1679–1754), H. Reimarus (1694–1768), Ernesti (d. 1781), Michaelis (1717–1791), and many others. See further Grant, p. 173. Of special importance was the influence of J. Semler, called by some 'the father of modern biblical liberalism,' in his most influential book, *Abhandlung von freier Untersuchung des Canons* (Gütersloh: Mohn, reprint edn, 1967).

187. W. Pauck, *The Heritage of the Reformation* (Free Press of Glencoe, 1961), p. 316. Cf. also pp. 255-68.

188. F. Schleiermacher, *The Christian Faith* (Edinburgh: T. & T. Clark, 1948 [1830]), p. 456.

189. F.C. Baur, *Paul, Apostle of Jesus Christ, His Life and Work, His Epistle and His Doctrine* (tr. A. Nezies; Edinburgh: Williams & Norgate, 1875–76), II, pp. 212-27. In pp. 199-200 Baur says: 'It was God's intention, and the scope of this whole scheme of religious history, that only when Christ has come . . . this pedagogic state . . . came to an end . . . as soon as a new stage of the religious consciousness and life has come . . . '

190. D.F. Strauss, *The Life of Jesus Critically Examined* (tr. Marian Evans; New York: C. Blanchard, 1860, from the 1835 edn), p. 316: 'God had permitted to the early Hebrews, *on account of the hardness of their hearts* (Matt. xix,8f.) many things which, in a more advanced stage of culture, were inadmissible . . . ' (emphasis his). This evolutionistic approach became a basic premise in the *Religionsgeschichtliche Schule*. Strauss goes on to say that 'for the spiritualization of religion, and, according to Stephen's interpretation, the *abolition of the Mosaic Law*, which were to be the results of that event, were undoubtedly identified by Jesus with the commencement of the abolition of the αἰὼν μέλλων of the Messiah' (*ibid.*). This interpretation of the abolition of the law on eschatological grounds came later to the foreground with A. Schweitzer.

191. H.A.W. Meyer was the editor of the famous *Kritisch-exegetischer Kommentar zum Neuen Testament* (Göttingen: Vandenhoeck & Ruprecht, 1832–1852), 16 vols.

192. 'Only this view of *telos* as *end, conclusion* . . . is conformable to what follows, where the essentially different principles of the old and the new *dikaiosune* are stated' (*Romans* [1832], II, pp. 172-73).

193. *Ibid.*, p. 173.

194. Baker calls Harnack's 'the nearest significant approach to Christian rejection of the Old Testament since Marcion' (pp. 56-57). According to Harnack's famous phrase, 'The rejection of the Old Testament in the second century [by Marcion] was a mistake which the great church refused to commit; its retention in the sixteenth century was due to the power of a fateful heritage from which the Reformers were not yet able to withdraw; but its conservation as a canonical book in modern Protestantism is the result of paralysis of religion and of the church' (*Kirchliche Dogmatik* 1.2.82; quoted by W. Pauck, *Harnack and Troeltsch. Two Historical Theologians* [New York: Oxford University Press, 1968], pp. 37-38); cf. E. Renan, *Saint Paul* (Paris: Calman Levy, 1869), p. 560.

195. *History of the Dogma*, 7 vols. (tr. N. Buchanan; London: Williams & Norgate, 1894), I, p. 87. The text goes on to say that 'Jesus the Messiah, having fulfilled the Law once for all, founded a new covenant, either in opposition to the old, or a stage above it'.

196. 'Romans', *The Oxford Dictionary of the Christian Church*, ed. F.L. Cross (London: Oxford University Press, 1974), p. 1197.

197. Sanday and Headlam, *Romans*, p. 284. Cf. in a similar trend of thought, H.P. Liddon, *Explanatory Analysis of St. Paul's Epistle to the Romans* (Grand Rapids: Zondervan, 1961 [1876]), p. 179; and W.L. Blackley and J. Hawes, *The Critical English Testament* (London: Daldy, 1878), II, p. 322.

198. E.H. Gifford, *The Epistle of St. Paul to the Romans with Notes and Introduction* (London: J. Murray, 1886), p. 183. See further G.O. Forde, *The Law-Gospel Debate. An Interpretation of its Historical Development* (Minneapolis: Augsburg, 1969).

199. J.A. Beet, *A Commentary on St. Paul's Epistle to the Romans* (7th edn; New York: T. Whittaker, 1892), p. 301.

200. Meyer, p. 404. However, besides Augustine, Meyer does not mention any other name.

201. F.A.G. Tholuck (1799–1877), *St. Paul's Epistle to the Romans* (Philadelphia: Sorin and Ball, 1827/1844), pp. 351-52, still sees 'end and aim' as the best and general interpretatioin; so does M. Stuart, *Commentary on Romans* (Andover: Gould & Newman, 1832/1835), pp. 455-56. C. Hodge, *Comentary on the Epistle to the Romans* (Grand Rapids: Eerdmans, 1835/1955), p. 335, says that the majority of commentators give a teleological interpretation, though he himself preferred already the sense of 'abrogation' (p. 336).

202. H. Alford, *The Greek New Testament*, 4 vols. (Chicago: Moody Press, reprint edn, 1958), II, p. 417. Alford himself interprets τέλος as 'the object at which the law aimed' (*ibid.*). The supporters of the temporal interpretation whom Alford mentions are, besides Meyer: H. Olshausen (1796–1839), *Die Briefe Pauli an die Römer und Korinther* (Königsberg: A.W. Unzer, 1837); C.F. Fritzsche (1776–1850), *Pauli ad Romanos Epistola*, 3 vols. (Halle: Gebauer, 1836); and W.M.L. De Wette (1780–1849), *Kurze Erklärung des Briefes an die Romer* (Leipzig: Weidmann, 1835).

203. See R.A. Lipsius (1830–1892), *Hand-Commentar zum Neuen Testament. Zweiter Band: Briefe an die Galater, Römer, Philipper* (Freiburg: P. Siebeck, 1892), p. 166.

204. So B. Jowett, *The Epistle of St. Paul to the Thessalonians, Galatians, and Romans. Essays and Dissertations* (London: J. Murray, 1855), I, 289-90; cf. T. Robinson, *A Suggestive Commentary on St. Paul's Epistle to the Romans* (London: R.D. Dickenson, 1871), II, pp. 68-69. 'The idea of *télos* is that of *end* in all senses: fulfilment, terminus, object, etc., that to which it (*nomos*) points, and in which it finds its rest (Mt 5:17, etc.)'; C.J. Vaughan (1816–1897), *St. Paul's Epistle to the Romans* (London: Macmillan, 1859), p. 190. W.G.T. Shedd, *A Critical and Doctrinal Commentary upon the Epistle of St. Paul to the Romans* (New York: Charles Scribner's Sons, 1879), p. 313: 'All of these explanations may be combined. Christ is the τέλος in each and any sense here mentioned.' But he pronounces himself in favor of the completive interpretation: 'If a single explanation is to be adopted, the last (end in the sense of *fulfilment*) is preferable, as agreeing with the tenor of the Epistle'.

205. F. Godet, *Commentary on St. Paul's Epistle to the Romans*, 2 vols., ed. A. Cusin (Edinburgh: T. & T. Clark, 1892 [1881]), II, p. 196: '*End*, no doubt implies the notion of *aim*; for if the law terminates with Christ, it is only because it has reached its aim ... Of two contrary things, when the one appears, the other must take end.'

206. *Exposition on St. Paul's Epistle to the Romans* (Halle, 1842; tr. R. Menzies; Philadelphia: Sorin and Ball, 1844), p. 353.

207. *Lectures on Romans* (Edinburgh, 1842; New York: R. Carter, 1853), pp. 396-97.

208. *Notes Explanatory and Practical on the Epistle to the Romans* (New York: Harper, 1834, reprint Grand Rapids: Baker, 1949), pp. 228-29.

209. *A Commentary on the Epistle to the Romans with a Translation and Various Excursus* (2nd edn; London: W. Tegg, 1853), pp. 456-57.

210. *The Epistle of St. Paul to the Romans* (4th edn; London: Hodder & Stoughton, 1897 [1879]), p. 268.

211. For a representative interpretation, see H. Lietzmann, *Römer* (1910), p. 92: 'Die übliche Bedeutung "Ende" für τέλος ist hier die allein sinnegemässe'.

212. Among the first studies on Pauline law theology, see A. Zahn, *Das Gesetz Gottes nach der Lehre und der Erfahrung des Apostel Paulus* (Halle:

Ebend, 1876); J.B. Glock, *Die Gesetzesfrage im Leben Jesu und in der Lehre des Paulus* (Karlsruhe: Renther, 1885); H. Witt, 'Die Stellung des Apostels Paulus zum mosaischen Gesetz', *Programm des Gymnasiums zu Seehause* 1 (1888–1889), pp. 3-12; E. Kühl, 'Stellung und Bedeutung des alttestamentlichen Gesetzes in Zusammenhang der paulinischen Lehre', *TSK* 67 (1894), pp. 120-46.

213. So Zahn, pp. 47-61.

214. So Kühl, who in *Der Brief des Paulus an die Römer* (Leipzig: Quelle und Meyer, 1913), p. 352, interpreted Rom 10.4 saying: 'Nur das mosaische Gesetz bedeuten. *Telos* heisst *Ende*, Aufhebung dass Christus des Gesetzes, "Zweck und Ziel" gewesen sei, ist trotz Gal 3.24 ein unpaulinischer Gedanke'.

215. So N.P. Williams, who in 'The Epistle to the Romans', in *A New Commentary on Holy Scripture*, ed. C. Gore, H.L. Goudge, and A. Guillaume (London: SPCK, 1928), p. 476, says (paraphrasing Rom 10.4) that 'the appearance of Christ has brought all legal systems as such to an end . . . '

216. So C. Clemen, *Die Chronologie der paulinischen Briefe auf das neue untersucht* (Halle: Niemeyer, 1842), pp. 256-58, who argues that Paul's doctrine of the law developed from a period of acceptance, when he wrote Romans, to a period of rejection, when he wrote Galatians. Clemen's position was challenged by F. Sieffert, 'Die Entwicklungslinie der paulinischen Gesetzlehre nach den vier Hauptbriefen des Apostels', in *Theologische Studien. Festschrift für Bernhard Weiss* (Göttingen: Vandenhoeck und Ruprecht, 1897), pp. 332-57. Cf. H.A. Kennedy, 'St. Paul and the Law', *Expositor* 13 (1917), pp. 338-66.

217. So E.D. Burton, *Notes on New Testament Grammar* (Chicago: University Press, 1904), p. 213; and especially A. Slaten, 'Qualitative Use of *Nomos*', *AJT* 23 (1919), pp. 213-19.

218. First by E. Grafe, *Die paulinische Lehre von Gesetz nach den vier Hauptbriefen* (Freiburg: J.C.B. Mohr, 1884); later by P. Bläser, *Das Gesetz bei Paulus* (Münster: Aschendorff, 1941).

219. For bibliography and discussion, see E.E. Ellis, *Paul and His Recent Interpreters* (Grand Rapids: Eerdmans, 1961), pp. 25-26; O. Kuss, 'Νόμος bei Paulus', *MTZ* 17 (1966), pp. 173-227.

220. For Luther the law only will be empty (*vacua*) in heaven, because it will be finally 'fulfilled' (*WA* 39.1.433): '*impletio legis est mors legis*' (WA 3.463.33-37). See further in Forde, p. 184.

221. So M. Friedländer, 'The "Pauline" Emancipation from the Law, a Product of the Pre-Christian Disapora', *JQR* 14 (1901–1902), pp. 265-301; M. Löwy, 'Paulinische Lehre von Gesetz', *MGWJ* 47 (1903), pp. 322-39, 417-33, 534-44; 48 (1904), pp. 268-76, 321-27, 400-16; O. Pfleiderer, *Paulinism. A Contribution to the History of Primitive Christian Theology*, 2 vols. (tr. E. Peters; London: Williams & Norgate, 1877), I, pp. 20-22, 72-74; II, pp. 22-24; *The Influence of the Apostle Paul in the Development of Christianity* (tr.

J.F. Smith; New York: C. Scribner's Sons, 1885), p. 71; A. Deissmann, *Paulus. Eine Kultur- und religionsgeschichtliche Skizze* (Tübingen: J.C.B. Mohr, 1925); E. von Dobschütz, *Der Apostel Paulus* (Halle: B.W.F.S., 1926–1928), 2 vols.

222. So R. Zehnpfund, 'Das Gesetz in den paulinischen Briefen', *NKZ* 8 (1897), pp. 384-419; C. Bugge, 'Das Gesetz und Christus nach der Ausschauung der ältesten Christengemeinde', *ZNW* 4 (1903), pp. 89-110; William Wrede, *Paul* (tr. E. Lummis; Lexington: American Theological Library Association, 1962, reprint of 1904); O. Holzmann, *Das Neue Testament nach dem Stuttgarter griechischen Text übersetzt und erklärt. Der Römerbrief* (Giessen: Töplemann, 1926), p. 658; W. Grundmann, 'Gesetz, Rechtfertigung und Mystik bei Paulus', *ZNW* 32 (1933), pp. 52-65.

223. For full references see W.D. Davies, *Torah in the Messianic Age/or the Age to Come* (Philadelphia: SBL, 1952), pp. 98-99.

224. 'Just as the old age came to its end and *telos* in the new age, so also the Law has its end in the Gospel' (Fitzmyer, 'Paul and the Law', p. 75; cf. Schoeps, *Paul*, p. 171).

225. A. Schweitzer, *The Mysticism of St. Paul* (tr. W. Montgomery; New York: Seabury, 1968), p. 189. Also in the 'eschatological' line but outside the mainstream trend is Adolf Schlatter, *Gottes Gerechtigkeit: Ein Kommentar zum Römerbrief* (Stuttgart: Calwer, 1935; 4th edn, 1965), p. 311. The first lengthy studies on Paul's law theology along the new trend are C. Maurer, *Die Gesetzeslehre des Paulus nach ihrem Ursprung und ihrer Entfaltung dargelegt* (Zürich: Evangelischer Verlag, 1941); P. Bläser, *Das Gesetz bei Paulus* (1941). Both depended on G.F. Moore, *Judaism in the First Centuries of the Christian Era*, 3 vols. (Cambridge: Harvard University Press, 1927–1930); and H.L. Strack and P. Billerbeck, *Kommentar zum Neuen Testament aus Talmud und Midrasch*, 5 vols. (Munich: Beck, 1922–1956).

226. *Paul and Rabbinic Judaism. Some Rabbinic Elements in Pauline Theology* (London: SPCK, 1955), pp. 71-73.

227. *Ibid.*, p. 84. 'For Paul the person and teachings of Jesus has replaced the Torah as center of his religious life, and has assumed for him, therefore, the character' of a new Torah' (p. 173).

228. See *Torah*, pp. 82-83 n. 42.

229. See especially A. Díez Macho, '¿Cesará la Tora en la Edad Mesiánica?', *Est Bíb* 12 (1953), pp. 115-58; 13 (1954), pp. 5-51; S. Sandmel, *The Genius of Paul* (New York: Farrar, Strauss and Cudahy, 1958), p. 37; W.C. van Unnik, 'La conception paulinienne de la Nouvelle Alliance', in *Littérature et théologie pauliniennes*, ed. A. Descamps *et al.* (Louvain: Desclée, 1960), pp. 109-26.

230. *Paul*, p. 213; cf. pp. 168-218.

231. *Ibid.*, p. 172. According to Schoeps Paul made the mistake of divorcing Torah from covenant and of moralizing the law, making it

incompatible with faith, which it was not. 'Paul did not perceive . . . that in the biblical view the law is integral to the covenant' (p. 180).

232. *Ibid.*, p. 171.

233. See, for example, L. Baeck, 'The Faith of Paul', *JJS* 3 (1952), pp. 106-107; Conzelmann, *Outline*, p. 224; A. van Dülmen, *Die Theologie des Gesetzes bei Paulus* (Stuttgart: Katholisches Bibelwerk, 1968), pp. 123-27; Gutbrod, pp. 1069-75; E. Käsemann, *Perspectives on Paul* (tr. M. Kohl; Philadelphia: Fortress, 1974), p. 156; K. Kertelge, *The Epistle to the Romans* (New York: Herder & Herder, 1972), pp. 114-15; Knox, *Romans*, p. 321; Michel, *Römer*, p. 225; Nygren, *Romans*, p. 272. Departing slightly from current scholarship, P. Stuhlmacher argues that Paul's particular view of the apocalyptic relationship between Christ and the law is heavily indebted to Hellenistic influences (*Das paulinische Evangelium: I. Vorgeschichte* [Göttingen: Vandenhoeck & Ruprecht, 1968], pp. 74-75). For a further development of this trend see J. Munck, *Paul and the Salvation of Mankind* (Richmond: J. Knox, 1959), and *Christ and Israel* (1967). More recently E.P. Sanders has proposed a reinterpretation of Paul's view of the Torah also based on a reappraisal of his Jewish background (*Paul and Palestinian Judaism. A Comparison of Patterns of Religion* [Philadelphia: Fortress Press, 1977]). Sanders argues that Paul's view of righteousness was not formulated in opposition to a Jewish conception of salvation through 'the works of the law'. This—Sanders insists—is the invention of Christian theologians. (Cf. W.S. Campbell, 'Revisiting Romans', *ScrB* 12 [1981], p. 6.)

234. E. Stauffer, 'Ἵνα und das Problem des teleologischen Denkens bei Paulus', *TSK* 102 (1930), pp. 232-57; 'ἵνα', *TDNT*, III, pp. 323-33; *New Testament Theology* (tr. J. Marsh; New York: Macmillan, 1955), pp. 208-10.

235. See Edmund Schlink, 'Zur Begriff des Teleologisches', *ZST* 10 (1933), pp. 94-125; and especially G. Delling, 'Zur paulinischen Teleologie', *TLZ* 75 (1950), cols. 706-10; *TDNT*, VIII, p. 54 n. 38; 'Telos-Aussagen in der greichischen Philosophie', *ZNW* 55 (1964), pp. 26-42.

236. C.F.D. Moule, 'Fulfilment Words in the New Testament: Use and Abuse', *NTS* 14 (1968), pp. 293-320.

237. *Dogmatics*, II, 3/4, p. 245; cf. *Romans*, p. 375. Barth fought against the Lutheran tendency to see discontinuity and opposition between the law and the gospel. For Barth 'a law understood apart from the Gospel leads to a Gospel which merely becomes a crutch for man's attemps at self-justification' (cf. Forde, p. 202). So, he argues that Paul did not reject the law, but a wrong use of it. For, he asks, 'where in all these chapters (or in all the rest of the Pauline theology) do we find the slightest indication that the apostle of the Church regarded the Law of Israel as a gift of God cancelled and invalidated by Christ?' (*Dogmatics*, II, 3/4, p. 244).

238. *Ibid.*, p. 245: 'The *kelal*, the ἀνακεφαλαίωσις of the Law . . . is the Messiah who was promised for the justification of everyone who believes in Him and who has now appeared in fulfillment of the promise'.

239. For an excellent survey and evaluation of recent scholarship on Romans, see Robert Jewett, 'Major Impulses in the Theological Interpretation of Romans since Barth', *Int* 34 (1980), pp. 17-31.

240. See especially Delling, p. 54, 2a and note 37 (cf. p. 56d), where the only rationale given for determining the sense of τέλος in Rom 10.4 and 6.21f. is Delling's understanding of Paul's thought (cf. pp. 54-56).

241. Du Plessis, p. 41.

242. Despite the merits of Du Plessis's survey on τέλος it is still incomplete and partial, since it was intended only to be supportive of his thesis on τέλειος. Though Du Plessis arrived at the conclusion that Rom 10.4 had to be interpreted teleologically, he seemed reluctant to abandon the traditional terminal interpretation of τέλος, and, at the end of his study, in a true *tour de force* tried to demonstrate that both meanings are to be taken together. For Du Plessis, then, Paul used the term τέλος in Rom 10.4 in order to express in a single word the two apparently opposite but, in fact, complementary concepts of continuity and discontinuity: this is only possible by giving to τέλος the basic meaning of 'turning point'. So, says Du Plessis, the end of the law is *'an act of transition'* (p. 142). Du Plessis's study has taken seriously all the philological and literary parallels, but has completely disregarded the context of Rom 10.4.

243. Flückiger, pp. 153-57.

244. *Ibid.*, p. 153.

245. *Ibid.*, p. 154.

246. See W. Lohff, 'Τέλος', *RGG*, VI, pp. 678-81. A fair summary of current understanding of τέλος in biblical literature is given by R. Schippers ('Goal', *NIDNTT*, II, pp. 59-66). Schippers emphasizes the fact that τέλος in Greek means basically 'goal, completion, and perfection'. But, surprisingly enough, he ends by saying that *'telos* means end in the sense of cessation in Rom 10.4', giving as the only rationale for this interpretation the parenthetical explanation that 'in Christ the law has ceased to be the way of salvation' (p. 61). Schippers's inconsistency between his excellent survey on biblical and cognate uses of τέλος (in which τέλος is never found to mean 'cessation') and his interpretation of τέλος in Rom 10.4 is very typical—though even more perplexing—of a certain kind of exegesis built upon an *a priori* theological position against the positive data of semantics and lexicography.

247. *BEvT* 1 (1940), pp. 3-27, quoted here from the English translation 'Christ the End of the Law', in *Essays*, pp. 36-66.

248. Taking the law as a symbol of all human effort to attain God through personal endeavor, Bultmann explained Rom 10.4 as the end of this sinful attitude and the beginning of a new life of faith relationship with God (p. 66). Cf. *Theology of the New Testament* (New York: Scribner, 1951), II, pp. 341-42.

249. Representing the Bultmannian trend, see especially Luz, *Geschichtsverständnis*, pp. 31, 188, 202. For an excellent refutation of Luz and the

Bultmannian interpretation of Rom 10.4, see M.A. Getty, *Christ Is the End of the Law*, pp. 178-92, 222-304.

250. Without being necessarily Bultmannian, some scholars also interpreted Rom 10.4 'existentially' or at least 'subjectively'. So, Gutbrod, 'νόμος', *TDNT*, IV, p. 1075, says that 'only for him who in faith appropriates the righteousness of God in Christ is the Law abolished'; and Nygren, p. 389, argues that 'Christ is the end of the law only for those who through Christ have received righteousness. To those outside the realm of faith the law still rules.' Cf. similar statements by Barrett, *Romans*, pp. 197-98; Lagrange, *Romains*, p. 253; Moule, 'Obligation', pp. 402-403; R.M. Wilson, '*Nomos*: The Biblical Significance of Law', *SJT* 5 (1952), pp. 36-48. Shifting the 'subjectivism' of the end of the law from the believer to Paul himself, some interpret Rom 10.4 as an autobiographical reflection of Paul's own conversion. So A.R.C. Leaney, *Manual of Discipline. The Rule of Qumran and Its Meaning: Introduction, Translation, and Commentary* (Philadelphia: Westminster, 1966), p. 103; W. Grundmann, 'The Teacher of Righteousness of Qumran and the Question of Justification by Faith in the Theology of the Apostle Paul', in *Paul and Qumran*, ed. J. Murphy-O'Connor (London: G. Chapman, 1968), pp. 102-103; cf. Wilckens, 'Die Bekehrung des Paulus', pp. 14-15.

251. Compare, for example, the position of E. Brunner, *The Letter to the Romans. A Commentary* (Philadelphia: Westminster Press, 1959), p. 120; and *Dogmatics* (Philadelphia: Westminster Press, 1952), pp. 214-30, with that of Delling: 'For the believer the law is set aside as a way of salvation by the Christ event' (p. 56). With significantly different positions, but with very similar conclusions, see also E. Best, *The Letter of Paul to the Romans* (Cambridge Bible Commentary on the NEB; Cambridge: University Press, 1967), p. 118; G. Bornkamm, 'The Revelation of Christ to Paul and Paul's Doctrine of Justification and Reconciliation', in *Reconciliation and Hope. New Testament Essays on Atonement and Eschatology*, ed. R. Banks (Exeter: Paternoster, 1974), p. 102; *Paul*, p. 128; M. Dibelius and W.G. Kümmel, *Paulus* (Berlin: Walter de Gruyter, 1951), pp. 108-109; Dodd, *Romans*, p. 165; E.G. Gulin, 'The Positive Meaning of the Law According to Paul', *LQ* 10 (1958), pp. 115-28; Gutbrod, p. 1075; W. Marxsen, *Introduction to the New Testament* (tr. G. Buswell; Philadelphia: Fortress, 1968), p. 106; Mussner, pp. 31-44; Nygren, pp. 379-80; B. Reicke, 'The Law and This World According to Paul', *JBL* 70 (1951), pp. 259-76; Ridderbos, *Paul*, pp. 149-53; J.A.T. Robinson, *Wrestling with Romans* (London: SCM, 1979), pp. 122-23.

252. An exception is Dan O. Via, 'A Structuralist Approach to Paul's Old Testament Hermeneutic (Rom 9:30–10:21)', *Int* 28 (1974), pp. 201-20.

253. Käsemann, *Romans*, p. 282.

254. Though Käsemann concedes that τέλος may have other meanings, he

refuses to take them into consideration, arguing that 'Paul does not leave the least room for attempts of this kind' (p. 282).

255. *Ibid.*, p. 283.

256. See K. Barth, *A Shorter Commentary on Romans* (Richmond: John Knox, 1959), p. 48; H.W. Bartsch, 'Paul's Letter to the Romans' (Unpublished Lectures, Bethany Theological Seminary, 1967), p. 39; 'The Concept of Faith in Paul's Letter to the Romans', *BR* 13 (1968), pp. 41-53; Barrett, *Reading Through Romans*, p. 53; M. Black, *Romans* (New Century Bible; London: Oliphants, 1973), pp. 136-43; R. Bring, 'Das Gesetz und die Gerechtigkeit Gottes. Eine Studie zur Frage nach der Bedeutung des Ausdruckes *télos nómou* in Röm 10:4', *ST* 20 (1966), pp. 1-36; Bruce, *Romans*, p. 56; Davies, *Romans*, p. 137; G.A.F. Knight, *Law and Grace* (London: SCM, 1962), pp. 76-89; Ladd, 'Paul and the Law', pp. 50-67; Longenecker, 'The Obedience of Christ in the Theology of the Early Church', in *Reconciliation and Hope* (Exeter: Paternoster, 1974), pp. 147-48; E. Schillebeeckx, *Christ. The Experience of Jesus as Lord* (New York: Seabury, 1980), pp. 158-59.

257. Ladd, *Theology of the NT*, p. 503.

258. Campbell, pp. 76-77; cf. H.P. Liddon, *Explanatory Analysis of Saint Paul's Epistle to the Romans* (Grand Rapids: Zondervan, 1961), p. 179.

259. J.S. Wang, pp. 179-81; cf. Moule, 'Obligation', p. 394; C.H. Dodd, *Gospel and Law: The Relation of Faith and Ethics in Early Christianity* (New York: Columbia University Press, 1951), p. 99.

260. On the basis of the antithesis γράμμα/πνεῦμα in 2 Cor 3.6, it is assumed that in Rom 10.4 and context 'righteousness by works' and 'law' stand for γράμμα and 'righteousness by faith' stands for πνεῦμα. Therefore this verse says that Christ ends γράμμα and institutes πνεῦμα. This is the interpretation proposed by W. Kamlah, *Christentum und Geschichtichkeit* (Stuttgart: Kohlhammer, 1951), II, p. 49; and E. Käsemann, 'The Spirit and the Letter', pp. 156-57; *Romans*, p. 287.

261. This interpretation has been widely accepted from the time of Irenaeus (*Haer.* 4.12.4) to the nineteenth century. In our days it has taken new formulations, but the underlying principle is the same. So, for Longenecker, the law is to be understood in two parallel aspects: 'law as standard of God' and 'law as contractual obligation'. This second aspect is what Christ ends (*Paul*, pp. 144-45). Israel was under contractual obligation in the covenant of works. With the coming of Jesus we are discharged from the contractual obligation and now 'righteousness is no longer to be associated with works' (p. 145). However, the law as standard of God remains. For somewhat similar positions, see P. Althaus, *The Divine Command: A New Perspective on Law and Gospel* (Facet Books, Social Ethics Series, 9; tr. F. Sherman; Philadelphia: Fortress, 1966), p. 11: 'The law ceases as "law" (*Gesetz*) but continues as "commandment" (*Gebot*)';

R.A. Harrisville, *Romans* (Augsburg Commentary on the NT; Minneapolis: Augsburg, 1980), p. 162; C. von Haufe, 'Die Stellung des Paulus zum Gesetz', *TLZ* 91 (1966), cols. 171-79; cf. H. Schlier, *Der Brief an die Galater* (Göttingen: Vandenhoeck & Ruprecht, 1962), p. 135: 'The law is abolished as "law" (*Gesetz*) but restored as "instruction" (*Weisung*)'; P. Vielhauer, 'Paulus und das Alte Testament', in *Studien zur Geschichte und Theologie der Reformation: Festschrift für Ernst Bizer*, ed. L. Abrahowski and J.F.G. Goeters (Neukirchen: Neukirchener Verlag, 1969), p. 55: 'The law as "halakah" is abrogated, but it remains valid as "*haggadah*"' (paraphrasis and translations ours). For discussion on these positions, see Rhyne, pp. 19-21, and Toews, p. 225. In a very different trend, see Michael Wyschogrod, 'The Law: Jews and Gentiles—A Jewish Perspective', *LQ* 21 (1969), pp. 405-15. For Wyschogrod, Paul's 'end of the law' applied only to the Gentile Christians. They were only obliged to keep the so-called Noachian law, while the Jews were obliged to keep the entire Mosaic law (p. 414).

262. R. Aldrich, 'Has the Mosaic Law Been Abolished?', *BSac* 116 (1959), pp. 322-35; J.F. Walvoord, 'Law in the Epistle to the Romans', *BSac* 94 (1937), pp. 15-30, 281-95. For a thorough survey, discussion and refutation of Dispensationalist law theology and hermeneutics, see Fuller, pp. 1-17, 65-88, 121-98.

263. A most significant example of this trend is M.A. Getty, 'Christ Is the End of the Law'. 'End' is understood in the sense of 'termination' from a salvation-historical perspective: justification through Christ's redemptive work 'ends' the era of the law (pp. 528-32). Cf. Bonsirven, *Théologie du Nouveau Testament* (Paris: Aubier, 1951), p. 288; J.M. Bover, *Teología de San Pablo* (Madrid: B.A.C., 1967), p. 89; Díez Macho, '¿Cesará la Torah?', p. 115; van Dülmenn, pp. 212, 223; Fitzmyer, *Romans*, p. 321; Grelot, p. 21; Kertelge, *Romans*, p. 114; Lagrange, *Romains*, p. 253; etc.

264. A typical example of this trend is given by Goldstain: 'Le Christ nous a liberés de cette tutelle et de cette pédagogie. Il était en effet la "FIN" de la loi, au sens complexe du mot grec TELOS: but, fin, achèvement, perfection' (p. 8). See in the same trend, Benoit, p. 32; J.-M. Bover and F. Cantera, *Sagrada Biblia* (Madrid: B.A.C., 1957), p. 351 n. 4; Cambier, pp. 185-93; Cerfaux, *Christ*, p. 496; *The Christian*, pp. 431-43; Feuillet, 'Le plan salvifique', p. 498; *Le Christ sagesse de Dieu*, p. 117; Grelot, p. 21; Huby, p. 364; Kuss, *Römerbrief*, pp. 748-53; Larcher, p. 268; Lyonnet, *Galates et Romains*, p. 111; *Quaestiones*, II, p. 89; Spicq, *Théologie Morale*, I, p. 27; Torti, p. 207; L. Turrado, *Biblia Comentada de los Profesores de Salamanca* (Madrid: B.A.C., 1965), VI, p. 89.

265. So Démann, p. 235: 'Dans ce texte τέλος νόμου Χριστός signifie que le Christ est la fin vers laquelle tendait la Loi, et non pas simplement que "le Christ met fin à la loi". La construction de la phrase s'accorderait mal avec ce dernier sens, et, surtout, on ne voit pas bien ce que la phrase ainsi

entendue viendrait faire dans ce contexte'. Cf. Viard, p. 224: 'La loi conduit au Christ'.

266. '"Das Ende des Gesetze": Über Ursprung und Ansatz der paulinischen Theologie', *ZTK* 67 (1970), pp. 14-39.

267. This position, traditional in Roman Catholicism, is being accepted by many Protestant scholars also. J.C. Beker's treatment of this passage is characteristic of this *multiplex intelligentia* trend. While stressing the meaning of 'termination' 'in a context where this can only mean "the law is finished"' (p. 106), Beker also accepts the meaning of 'goal' and 'fulfillment'. 'Christ is the end of the law (10:4) both in terms of its goal and its termination' (p. 91); 'although Christ is the end of the law (10.4), he is also the one who fulfills the intent of the law (Rom 8:3-4) . . . He brings the era of the Torah to an end (Rom 10:4)' (p. 107); 'Because Christ has opened up our new access to eternal life Christ is both the end (*la fin*) and expiration of the law, and its fulfillment (*le but*)' (p. 187); 'Christ is the end of the condemnation of the law' (p. 336); pp. 150, 262, 243. Cf. Barrett, *Romans*, pp. 197-98; Bruce, *Romans*, p. 56; Campbell, pp. 73-81; Ladd, 'Paul and the Law', pp. 50-67; Longenecker, *Paul*, p. 186; Moule, 'Obligation', p. 403; etc.

268. Getty, pp. 118-92, 220-304.

269. *Ibid.*, pp. 7-117.

270. *Ibid.*, p. 310.

271. Bring, 'Paul and the Old Testament', p. 47. In 'Das Gesetz und die Gerechtigkeit Gottes', pp. 1-36, Bring notes the negative influence that Luther's translation of τέλος by *Ende* had in Lutheran scholarship. He argues that Luther did not dare to utilize the term 'goal', although it was more in line with his theology, because he feared that the gospel could be interpreted as the new Christian 'law'.

272. 'The goal of the law was righteousness. The Jews did not reach it since they sought it in the wrong way. Christ was the righteousness of God; the law pointed to it, but could not give it itself' ('Paul and the Old Testament', p. 47). Cf. 'Die Erfüllung des Gesetzes durch Christus', *KD* 5 (1959), pp. 1-22.

273. Cranfield, 'Saint Paul and the Law', (1964), p. 50.

274. Idem, *Romans*, II, p. 519.

275. Howard, 'Christ the End of the Law', p. 337.

276. Toews, pp. 219-45.

277. *Ibid.*, p. 335.

278. *Ibid.*, p. 106.

279. Rhyne dedicates a whole chapter (pp. 95-116) to the exegesis of Rom 10.4.

280. *Ibid.*, pp. 114-16.

281. Fuller stresses the culminating, perfective, and teleological aspects of τέλος and interprets Rom 10.4 saying that 'Christ is the *telos* of the law, not in the sense of being its termination, but as climaxing it as the one who is in a

continuum with it' (p. xi); cf. Meyer, p. 68; Sanders, 'Torah and Christ', pp. 372-90; 'Torah and Paul', pp. 132-40; Wilckens, *Römer*, p. 220.

282. Since a complete list of supporters of this position would go beyond the scope of the present study, the following references are intended only to illustrate the widespread support of this temporal interpretation: Althaus, *Römer*, p. 108; Bornkamm, *Paul*, p. 134; Bultmann, 'Christ the End of the Law', p. 54; Conzelmann, *Outline*, pp. 223-24; Delling, 'τέλος', p. 56; Dodd, *Romans*, p. 179; Ebeling, 'Reflection', pp. 270-71; Fitzmyer, 'Paul and the Law', p. 75; Godet, *Romans*, p. 376; Gutbrod, IV, p. 1075; Hahn, 'Gesetzverständnis', pp. 50-55; Käsemann, *Romans*, p. 282; Knox, *Romans*, p. 554; Lagrange, *Romains*, pp. 253-54; Luz, *Geschichtsverständnis*, pp. 139-41; Meyer, *Romans*, p. 405; Michel, *Römer*, pp. 223-34; Munck, *Christ and Israel*, pp. 83-84; Mussner, 'Christus Gesetzes Ende', pp. 31-44; Nygren, *Romans*, pp. 379-80; Ridderbos, *Paul*, pp. 137, 155-56; Ryrie, 'The End of the Law', p. 239; Sanday and Headlam, *Romans*, p. 284; Sanders, *Paul*, p. 311; Schoeps, *Paul*, p. 171; Stuhlmacher, *Gerechtigkeit*, p. 93; Walvoord, 'Law in Romans', p. 286; Ziesler, p. 206.

283. It has been argued that for Paul τέλος always meant 'termination', and that if Paul had meant in Rom 10:4 'purpose' or 'fulfillment' he would have used other words, such as τελείωσις or πλήρωμα. So Sanday and Headlam, *Romans*, p. 285; Murray, *Romans*, II, p. 49; Michel, *Römer*, p. 224; Luz, *Geschichtsverständnis*, p. 140.

284. So Delling, 'τέλος', p. 56; Dodd, *Romans*, p. 176; Käsemann, *Romans*, p. 282; Luz, p. 141; Murray, *Romans*, II, p. 50; Nygren, *Romans*, p. 379; Sanday and Headlam, *Romans*, pp. 284-85; Walvoord, 'Law in Romans', p. 286.

285. Kühl (*Römer*, p. 352) rejects the teleological interpretation of Rom 10.4 simply by stating that a teleological relationship between the law and Christ is an 'unpauline idea'. Cf. Käsemann, *Romans*, pp. 282-83; Luz, pp. 145-56; Mussner, 'Rom 10,4', pp. 33-34.

286. A typical case, where the contradictions of such interpretation may be clearly seen, is offered by Moule, who, in spite of having stated that 'legalism, it is true, never was really valid', still translates Rom 10.4 as 'Christ put an end to legalism' ('Obligation', pp. 403-404).

287. Against a negative understanding of νόμος in Rom 10.4, see Rhyne, pp. 63-121.

288. Black, *Romans*, p. 138; Conzelmann, *Outline*, p. 224; Davies, *Paul*, p. 71; *Torah*, p. 93; Diez Macho, 'Cesará la Tora', pp. 115-58; Van Dülmen, *Gesetze*, pp. 126-28; Gutbrod, pp. 1069-75; Käsemann, *Perspectives*, p. 156; Michel, *Römer*, p. 225; Schoeps, *Paul*, pp. 172-73, 218.

289. Though some rabbinic texts seem to point to a certain cessation of the Torah in the Messianic age, it cannot be proved that they contemplated other modifications than those related to the sacrificial system and other

ritual ordinances. Furthermore, it seems out of the question that they imply that the Torah will be more and better observed in the Messianic era. For references, see Str-B, I, p. 247; III, p. 277; for full survey of sources, see Luz, *Geschichtsverständis*, pp. 144-45, who concludes that '*Christ is the end of the law* is a Christian thesis which cannot be grounded in Jewish theology at any moment' (trans. mine). On this trend of thought, see also P. Schäfer, 'Die Torah der messianischen Zeit', *ZNW* 65 (1974), pp. 27-42; E.E. Urbach, *The Sages* (Jerusalem: Magnes Press, 1975), pp. 297-314. L. Gaston, 'Paul and the Torah', in *Antisemitism and the Foundations of Christianity*, ed. A. Davies (New York: Paulist Press, 1979), p. 54, says that 'even if this concept [of the cessation of the law in the Messianic age] could be presupposed for a first century situation, it would still have to fall under the accusation of being a fundamental misunderstanding of Torah within the context of Israel'. Cf. E. Bammel, 'Νόμος Χριστοῦ', *SE* III (TU, 88 [1964]), pp. 120-28; R. Banks, 'The Eschatological Role of the Law in Pre- and Post-Christian Jewish Thought', in *Reconciliation and Hope*, ed. R. Banks (Grand Rapids, Eerdmans, 1974), pp. 173-79; J. Jervell, 'Die offenbarte und die verborgene Tora', *ST* 25 (1971), pp. 90-180; H.M. Teeple, *The Mosaic Eschatological Prophet* (Philadelphia: SBL, 1957), pp. 14-17.

290. Bultmann, 'Christ the End of the Law', p. 36; Gutbrod, p. 1075; Lagrange, *Romans*, p. 253; Nygren, p. 389; Wilson, p. 45.

291. For full discussion and refutation of the existentialist positions, see Getty, pp. 178-92, 222-304.

292. Beck, 'Altes and Neues Gesetz', p. 135; Van Dülmen, *Gesetzes*, pp. 223-25; Haufe, pp. 171-78; Kuss, 'Nomos bei Paulus', pp. 221-23; Longenecker, *Paul*, pp. 144-45; Schlier, pp. 176-88; Wyschogrod, p. 414.

293. Käsemann, *Romans*, pp. 286-87; Liddon, p. 179; Moule, 'Obligation', p. 394; Kamlah, p. 49; Ziesler, pp. 206-207.

294. See Rhyne, pp. 19-21.

295. Bring, *Christus und das Gesetz*, pp. 11-12; Cranfield, 'St. Paul and the Law', pp. 43-68; Du Plessis, p. 41; Flückiger, pp. 153-57; Fuller, pp. 84-86; Howard, pp. 331-37; Meyer, 'Romans 10:4', p. 68; Rhyne, pp. 95-116; Sanders, 'Torah and Christ', pp. 372-90; 'Torah and Paul', pp. 132-40; Démann, 'Moïse et la Loi', p. 235; Toews, p. 335; Viard, p. 224; Wilckens, *Römer*, p. 220.

296. Barth, *Dogmatics*, II/2, p. 245; Black, *Romans*, p. 138; Flückiger, pp. 153-54; Selwyn, *1 Peter*, pp. 132-33.

297. It has been especially argued that the imagery of the race in 9.30-33 stands also for τέλος in 10.4; cf. Bläser, *Gesetz*, pp. 173-77; Bring, p. 46; Flückiger, p. 154. It has also been argued that the phrase εἰς δικαιοσύνην is a purposive expression, which fits better with τέλος as 'goal' than as 'termination'; cf. Bandstra, pp. 102-105; Barth, II/2, p. 244. Some see that the teleological interpretation explains better the connection between 10.5

and 10.6-8 not as antithetic but as complementary; cf. Cranfield, 'St. Paul and the Law', pp. 49-50; Wang, 'Law', pp. 149-51.

298. This interpretation is said to fit better with other law statements in Romans, namely 3.21-31; 7.12; 8.4; 13.8-10; cf. Bring, 'Gerechtigkeit Gottes', pp. 40-48; Cranfield, 'St. Paul and the Law', p. 49; Flückiger, p. 156.

299. This argument is especially advocated by Barth, *Dogmatics*, II/2, pp. 241-48; and Cranfield, 'St. Paul and the Law', pp. 66-68.

300. Bandstra, p. 102; Barrett, *Reading Through Romans*, p. 53; Barth, *Shorter Commentary on Romans*, p. 48; Baules, *Romains*, pp. 236-37; Bring, 'Das Gesetz', p. 36; Cerfaux, *Christ in the Theology of Paul*, p. 221; Davies, *Romans*, p. 137; Hellbardt, p. 334; Knight, p. 76; Ladd, *Theology of the NT*, p. 503; Longenecker, *Paul*, p. 186; Schillebeeckx, *Christ*, pp. 158-59.

301. See Rom 3.31; cf. 7.12-25. On the still binding character of the law according to Paul in Romans, see Rhyne, pp. 63-93.

302. See Beker, pp. 184-89; Benoit, II, p. 32; Bover, p. 89; Bruce, *Romans*, p. 203; Cambier, I, p. 185; Campbell, pp. 73-81; Cerfaux, *The Christian*, p. 431; Du Plessis, p. 142; Furnish, pp. 161-62; Grelot, *Sens chrétien du NT*, p. 21; Goldstain, p. 8; Hellbardt, pp. 331-46; Huby, *Romains*, p. 364; Kirk, p. 224; Kuss, *Römerbrief*, pp. 748-53; Larcher, p. 268; Longenecker, *Paul*, p. 186; Lyonnet, *Galates et Romains*, p. 111; Schneider, pp. 410-22; Torti, p. 207.

303. Campbell, p. 27.

Notes to Chapter 2

1. Studies on τέλος are not particularly abundant. We have found especially useful for the Greek literature: W. Jaeger, 'Das Ziel des Lebens in die griechische Ethik von der Sophistik bis Aristotel', *NJKA* 16 (1913), pp. 687-705; W. Wiersma, 'Τέλος und καθῆκον in die Alten Stoa', *Mnemosyne* 3,5 (1937), pp. 219-28; M. Pohlenz, 'Paulus und die Stoa', *ZNW* 42 (1949), pp. 60-104; *Die Stoa: Geschichte einer geistigen Bewegung* (Göttingen: Vandenhoeck & Ruprecht, 1948–1959), I, pp. 111-18; II, pp. 64-68; D. Holwerda, 'TELOS', *Mnemosyne* 4,16 (1963), pp. 337-63; Z.P. Ambrose, 'The Homeric and Early Epic *Telos*' (Ph.D. Dissertation, Princeton University, 1963); G. Delling, '*Telos*-Aussagen in der griechischen Philosophie', pp. 26-42; F.M.J. Waanders, '*Telos* in Tragedy. Some Remarks', in *Miscellanea Tragica in Honor of J.C. Kamerbeek*, ed. J.M. Bremer (Amsterdam: Hakkert, 1976), pp. 475-82. For the biblical use of τέλος we are particularly indebted to G. Delling, 'Τέλος', *TDNT*, VIII pp. 49-57; Du Plesis, pp. 36-168; W. Lohff, 'Telos', pp. 678-81; H. Holwein, 'Teleologie', *RGG*, VI, pp. 674-78; R. Schippers, 'Goal', pp. 59-66.

2. LSJ (1973) lists about twenty different categories of signification for

τέλος ranging from 'performance', 'magistracy', 'rite', to 'winning-post', 'ideal', and 'final cause' (pp. 1772-74). Cf. BAG (1979), pp. 811-12.

3. Philemon of Athens, *Lexikon Technologikon*, ed. F. Osann, *Philemonis grammatici quae supersunt vulgatis et emendatiora et auctiora edidit Friedricus Osann* (Berlin: F. Dümmler, 1821), p. 233. The authorship and date of this work are not unanimously accepted. It is considered spurious in C. Wendel, 'Philemon 16'; *RE* XXXVIII, p. 2152. See further Ambrose, p. 6 note 10.

4. *Scol. Gen. ad Il.* 10.56; Πόσα σημαίνει τὸ τέλος; ἕξ; cf. 11.729. Ambrose (p. 6) dates this scholion around the middle of the second century, but thinks it is indebted to earlier sources. K. Lehrs (*De Aristarchi Studiis Homericis* [34th edn; Leipzig: S. Hirzel, 1882], p. 149) assigns this gloss on τέλος (cf. *Il.* 10.470) to Aristarchus of Samothrace (c. 217–147 BC).

5. These earlier reflections treat the various meanings and usages of τέλος as belonging to one rather than to two or more homonyms. Eustathius (12th cent. AD) in *ad Il.* 11.729 gives four meanings to τέλος; and Photius, in *Etymologicum Magnum*, s.v. 'τέλος', gives seven. See Ambrose, p. 5 n. 8.

6. Earlier scholarship derived τέλος from τέλλω, 'to accomplish', but did not offer any particular explanation for its polysemy. See Eustathius, *ad Il.* 11.729; W. Wachsmuth, *Hellenische Altertumskunde* (Halle: Schwetschke, 1826), p. 324; and G. Stephanus, *Thesaurus Graecae Linguae* (Graz: Akademische Druck, 1829; reprint 1954), VIII, p. 1992.

7. Georg Curtius, *Grundzüge der griechischen Etymologie* (5th edn; Leipzig: Teubner, 1879), pp. 236-38.

8. *Ibid.*, p. 221.

9. See full discussion in Ambrose, p. 4.

10. Alois Walde, *Vergleichendes Wörterbuch der indogermanischen Sprachen*, edited and revised by Julius Pokorny (Leipzig: Teubner, 1930), I, pp. 728-32.

11. W. Prellwitz, *Etymologisches Wörterbuch der griechischen Sprache* (Göttingen: Vandenhoeck & Ruprecht, 1892), p. 317; Emile Boisacq, *Dictionnaire étymologique de la langue grecque* (Heidelberg: C. Winter, 1950), pp. 952-53; J. Baptist Hofmann, *Etymologisches Wörterbuch des Griechischen* (Munich: Oldenburg, 1966), p. 357; H. Frisk, *Griechisches Etymologisches Wörterbuch* (Heidelberg: C. Winter, 1970), II, pp. 871-73; cf. Walde, p. 514; Du Plessis, pp. 36-38; Holwerda, p. 338.

12. On the phonetic shift, see R.S.P. Beekes, 'The Development of the Proto-Indoeuropean Laryngals in Greek', *Glotta* 47 (1969), pp. 142-43; cf. Frisk, p. 183.

13. Du Plessis, p. 37.

14. Hofmann, p. 357. For him the basic meaning of τέλος is 'Ende, Ziel, Ergebnis: als Wendepunkt (Ort wo man kehrt macht)'. On τέλσον in relation to τέλος, see p. 358.

15. Du Plessis, p. 37.

16. Holwerda, p. 338: 'τέλος *librae iugum* designat' (emphasis his).

17. *Ibid.*, p. 338. Holwerda's hypothesis explains how τέλος as 'beam of

198   *Christ the End of the Law*

scales' may mean both 'turning point' (*quod verti potest*, p. 337) and 'deciding point', while coming from the same root as πόλος and κύκλος (*ibid.*, p. 338).

18. *Ibid.*, pp. 339, 356, 348, 359.
19. *Ibid.*, p. 444.
20. *Ibid.*, p. 346; In Dutch: 'niet *af*gemaakt, maar *uit*gemaakt'.
21. Frisk, II, p. 873. Τελαμών was a strip or band for bearing or supporting something; ἀνατολή (from the verb ἀνατέλλω, 'to rise', 'lift') meant the 'risen sun' and hence 'the east'. For discussion, cf. Boisacq, p. 953; and Walde, p. 793; L.R. Palmer (*Mycenaeans and Minoans: Aegean Prehistory in the Light of the Linear B Tablets* [New York: Knopf, 1962], p. 96) also sees τέλος as connected with the root *tel, 'to lift', and gives to it the basic meaning of 'what is lifted', hence 'charge, due, obligation', etc. Palmer's thesis is strongly rejected by D.L. Page in *History and the Homeric Iliad* (Berkeley: University of California Press, 1959), pp. 184-86.
22. Boisacq, p. 764; see also E. Schwyzer, *Griechische Grammatik* (Munich: C.H. Beck, 1959), I, p. 512; and J. Pokorny, *Indogermanisches Etymologisches Wörterbuch* (Bern: Francke, 1959), p. 639 for *kwel, and p. 1060 for *tel; cf. A. Walde, I, p. 517; Hofmann, *Etymologisches Wörterbuch des Griechischen*, pp. 357-58; *Lateinisches Etymologisches Wörterbuch* (Heidelberg: C. Winter, 1938), I, p. 246; C.D. Buck, *A Dictionary of Selected Indo-European Synonyms* (Chicago: University of Chicago Press, 1949), p. 869.
23. Ambrose, p. 146.
24. A full list of cognates may be found in the best lexica and dictionaries. The following, indisputable cognates are enumerated as examples for semantic elucidation: among the compounds of τελέω, see: ἐπιτελέω (strengthened form of τελέω; to accomplish, perform); συντελέω (to fulfill, to contribute); ἀποτελέω (to complete, produce, perform); διατελέω (to accomplish, to continue); ἐκτελέω (to accomplish, to fulfill); λυσιτελέω (to pay what is due); τελειόω (to make perfect, to complete); τελεσφορέω (to bring fruit to perfection, to bear perfect children); τέλλω (to accomplish, to perform; Med., to come into being); ἀνατέλλω (to make rise up; hence ἀνατολή, rising, growing, east); ἐντέλλω (to make something to be done, to command; hence ἐντολή, order, command, commandment); τέλσον (headland, i.e. land where the plough turns; probably the archaic, poetic form of τέλος; cf. Du Plessis, p. 37; for Walde, 'τέλος τέλσον zeigen den Begriff der Wendung noch deutlich' [p. 516]; for V. Pisani, however, τέλσον did not represent the headland but the furrow itself. The original relation of τέλσον to the root *kwel 'turn', was as 'a thing turned' ['Sul valore di *telson* ed *olka*', *Athenaeum*, N.S. 18 (1940), pp. 3-10; cf. Ambrose, p. 106]). On the adjectives related etymologically to τέλος, see Ambrose, pp. 141-43. Note especially ἐκτελής (perfect); ἀτελής (imperfect); ἐντελής (complete); παντελής (very expensive); εὐτελής (cheap, not costly); τέλειος (full, complete, perfect,

mature); τελικός (final, in the sense of supreme; pertaining to the supreme end, connected with final causality); cf. the nouns τελειότης (completion); τελειωτής (completer); ἀτέλεια (incompleteness, imperfection); συντέλεια (completion, consummation); τελείωσις (development, completion, perfection, consecration); τέλεσμα (payment); τέλμα (piece of land full of water, water meads); τελετή (performance of a sacred rite); cf. J.F. Harrison, 'The meaning of the word *teleté*', *CR* 28 (1914), pp. 36-38. From the meaning of τελετή which Harrison takes as 'rite of adolescent initiation', he concludes that τέλειος might mean originally 'grown up' (to be used as sacrificial victim), and only later 'perfect'. See further Ambrose, pp. 13 and 107-109. Τελευτή (accomplishment, event, issue, euphemism for death; hence τελευτάω, euphemism for to die); for further details on these cognates, see B. Metzger, *Lexical Aids for the Student of the New Testament* (Princeton: Theological Book Agency, 1975), p. 69; cf. Du Plessis, pp. 118-20, 37-39; see also Carl D. Buck, *A Dictionary of Selected Synonyms in the Principal Indo-European Languages* (Chicago: University of Chicago Press, 1949), pp. 856, 979. Other cognates from the same root, but with a less evident relationship with τέλος, are: πέλομαι (root modified by the Aeol. π 'to be, or to set, in motion; to move'); πόλος (the pivot or axis on which something turns); παλέω ('to turn around' [the Anglo Saxon root *hweol*, 'wheel', is derived from the same root]); πάλιν ('backwards', restorative adverb). For further cognates in this line, see Walde, p. 516, and Frisk, II, pp. 871-72.

25. See Delling, 'Τέλος', pp. 57-87; BAG, p. 810; LSJ, p. 1771.

26. Du Plessis, p. 69. The meanings attested in the papyri are 'to accomplish' and 'to pay'. Cf. J.H. Moulton and G. Milligan, *The Vocabulary of the Greek Testament Illustrated from the Papyri and Other Non-Literary Sources* (London: Hodder & Stoughton, 1952), pp. 630-31.

27. Du Plessis, p. 69.

28. For examples, see Ambrose, pp. 21-22.

29. *Ibid.*, p. 36.

30. See Hes. *Op.* 5.2.4; Jos. *BJ* 2.495; cf. Rom 2.27; Jas 2.8.

31. It is not out of discussion whether or not they preserve the intonation of the preposition. The prepositions seem to have a 'perfectivizing' effect, so that these verbs may be translated by 'to complete absolutely or finally'. For Moulton the prepositional import is more often punctiliar than perfective (J.H. Moulton, *A Grammar of New Testament Greek. Prolegomena* [Edinburgh: T. & T. Clark, 1908], p. 118).

32. Already in Herodotus, of 100 occurrences τελευτή means 'death' in 95, and 'termination' in the remaining 5 (cf. J.E. Powell, *A Lexicon to Herodotus* [Cambridge: University Press, 1938], s.v. τελευτή).

33. See M.A. Bayfield, 'On Some Derivatives of *télos*', *CR* 15 (1901), p. 446.

34. According to Ambrose (p. 53), this distinction cannot be discerned in

Homer and in the early epic, where τελέω and τελευτάω seem to be used with the same basic meaning.

35. See LSJ, p. 1770; BAG, p. 818; Delling, 'τέλος', pp. 84-86; Du Plessis, pp. 118-20.

36. See LSJ, pp. 1725-26; BAG, p. 799; Delling, 'τέλος', pp. 64-66.

37. συντέλεια τοῦ αἰῶνος, Matt 13.39, 40, 49; 24.3; 28.20; cf. Heb 9.27 συντέλεια τῶν αἰώνων.

38. *Hellenische Altertumskunde*, p. 324 (cf. p. 326). For Wachsmuth τέλος conveys the concept 'dass etwas sich verwirkliche, zu dem Stande der Reife und Vollendung komme, sein Ziel erreiche, seinen Zweck erfülle'. For discussion of this position see Ambrose, p. 10.

39. J.H.H. Schmidt, *Synonymik der griechischen Sprache* (Leipzig: Teubner, 1876–1886), IV, p. 193.2: '*Telos* ist die Vollendung, der Abschluss eines Dinges . . . *Teleute* ist der Endpunkt, das Ende, womit das Ding aufhört zu sein . . . *Peras* muss der Endpunkt, der äusserste Punkt sein, über den man nicht hinweg kommen kann . . . *Horos* ist die Grenze, die ein Gebiet abschliesst, indem sie bezeichnet wie es geht' (cf. IV, pp. 193.4 and 193.5).

40. Bayfield, pp. 445-47.

41. Du Plessis, p. 45.

42. *Ibid.*, p. 95. Ambrose admits that referred to an action τέλος may be considered as 'the turning point' and, accordingly, 'the arrival of this point marks the conclusion of an activity', but referred to an object τέλος means 'the final touch in the manufacturing of a handiwork' or 'the fulfillment of a word into deed' (p. 96). The τέλη are generally fulfilled desires, promises, commands, etc.

43. Ambrose says that in the Iliad τέλος is used to express 'motion towards' (p. 57), but that in other writings the punctual sense of τέλος prevails (p. 72).

44. For δρόμου τέλος see Plu. *Moralia* 511 F.

45. Pi. *Od.* 10 (πυγμᾶς τέλος); Hom. *Il.* 2.122; Hdt. 1.155; Pi. *Fr.* 9.118 (τέλος ἄκρον, 'the highest prize').

46. Arist. *EN* 1.1 (πρὸς τέλος ἐλθεῖν, 'to reach the goal').

47. Pl. *Grg.* 499 E (τέλος εἶναι ἁπασῶν τῶν πράξεων τὸ ἀγαθόν, 'all the actions have as their goal the good').

48. On the meanings of σκοπός see E. Fuchs, 'σκοπός', *TDNT*, VII, pp. 413-17. Primarily meaning 'watcher' (from σκοπέω 'to look at'), it came to mean a mark on which to fix the eye. Then it was used metaphorically of a goal or object (cf. Phil 3.14). Very often τέλος is used as synonym of βούλημα (from βουλεύω) in the sense of 'purpose', 'resolution' (cf. Acts 27.43; Rom 9.19; 1 Pet 4.3); πρόνοια (from νοέω) in the sense of 'intention'; πρόθεσις (from προτίθημι) in the sense of 'purpose', 'prospect', 'destination', 'expectation' (cf. Rom 8.28; 9.11); γνώμη (from γινώσκω) in the sense of 'forethought', 'opinion', 'purpose' (cf. Acts 20.3); for purposive sentences the

most common constructions are εἰς αὐτὸ τοῦτο or ἵνα used in a final clause (cf. Rom 9.17). See further W.E. Vine, *Expository Dictionary of New Testament Words* (Los Angeles: Fleming H. Revell, ⁵1952), III, pp. 233-34; II, pp. 26-28, 159.

49. *Hom. Od.* 17.496.

50. For examples, see Du Plessis, p. 40.

51. On πλήρωμα, πληρόω, etc., see Delling, 'πλήρωμα', *TDNT*, VI, pp. 283-311. Τέλος is sometimes used indistinctly for τελείωσις, συντελεία, or even phrases with the verb ἐξαρτίζω. Cf. Vine, pp. 135-36, and R. Schippers, 'Fulfillment', *NIDNTT*, I, pp. 733-41.

52. Ambrose, p. 98.

53. Du Plessis, p. 51.

54. See D. Muller, 'Beginning', *NIDNTT*, I, p. 164, and especially Karl Brugmann, *Die Ausdrücke für den Begriff der Totalität in den indogermanischen Sprachen. Eine semasiologisch-etymologische Untersuchung* (Leipzig: A. Edelmann, 1894), p. 39.

55. See below, pp. 52-55.

56. See F.E. Peters, *Greek Philosophical Terms. A Historical Lexicon* (New York: New York University Press, 1967), pp. 191-92.

57. For Thayer, the temporal use of τέλος is so secondary that he considers it as practically confined to biblical authors: 'In the Grk. writ. always of the end of some act or state, but not of the end of a period of time, which they call τελευτή: in the Scripture also of a temporal end; an end in space is everywhere called πέρας' (*Thayer's Greek-English Lexicon of the New Testament* [New York: American Book, 1886], p. 619).

58. Du Plessis, p. 41.

59. So, in δρόμου τέλος it is obvious that the 'end' of the race may coincide with its 'goal' (Plu. *Mor.* 511 F).

60. Du Plessis, p. 41.

61. Ambrose, p. 78.

62. Du Plessis, pp. 37-38.

63. The originally non-temporal character of τέλος may be seen in the expression θανάτου τέλος. Thus, in A. *Th.* 906, the statement 'their strife came to its end in death' means that it happens to result in death. Cf. Hes. *Op.* 165. Later θανάτου τέλος is used as a tragic expression for 'death'.

64. Arist. *Ph.* 2.194 A (trans. Wicksteed-Cornford, LCL, I, p. 123).

65. The *Scholia Gen. ad Il.* 10.56 lists the following six meanings for τέλος: (1) τὸ τάγμα (ordinance, command, group); (2) τὸ πεπληρουμένον ἔργον (the completion or fulfilment of a work); (3) ἡ ταῖς πόλεσι πρόσοδος (tax); (4) ἡ ἀρχὴ καὶ τὸ ἀξίωμα (the principle and axiom); (5) τὸ δαπάνημα (cost, expenses); and (6) ἡ ἑορτή (ritual, religious celebration). Eustathius (*ad Il.* 11.729) lists four meanings: (1) ἀνάλωμα (expenses); (2) τάξις (order); (3) ἀρχή (principle); and (4) γάμος (marriage), and at the same time

he seems to understand τέλος in a sense near to πέρας and τελευτή. For further discussion, see Ambrose, p. 9.

66. Arist. *Ph.* 4.228 A (cf. LSJ, pp. 699-700).

67. Arist. *Ph.* 2.194 A (cf. LSJ, p. 1771).

68. See Buck, p. 856.

69. Surprisingly enough, Edward Ross Wharton only registers the meaning of 'tax' for τέλος (*Etyma Graeca. Etymological Lexicon of Classical Greek* [Chicago: Ares, 1974, reprint of the 1882 edition], p. 122).

70. τέλος in the sense of 'multitude, host, clan, family', occurs frequently in Homer, Herodotus, and Thucydides, very seldom in other authors, and never in biblical literature.

71. This use, very well attested in classical Greek (A. *Supp.* 121; S. *OC* 1050), was substituted progressively in the Hellenistic period by the use of τελετή and forms of the verb τελέω. This use became predominant for esoteric rites and became the term *par excellence* for 'initiation' (in Baccanalian rites, Eleusian mysteries, etc.). See further Jane Harrison, 'The Meaning of the Word τελετή', *CR* 28 (1914), p. 36.

72. F.W. Blass, A. Debrunner, R.W. Funk, *A Greek Grammar to the New Testament and Other Early Christian Literature* (Chicago: University Press, 1961), p. 90.

73. Ambrose, p. 70.

74. Hom. *Il.* 14.83 (R.J. Cunliffe, *A Lexicon of the Homeric Dialect* [University of Oklahoma Press, 1963], p. 377).

75. See examples in Stob. *Ecl.* 2.54: τέλος γάμου ἡ τεκνοποία; and E. *Fr.* 733.51. Cf. Hesychius, s.v. προτέλεια (ed. H. von Blumenthal, *Hesychiosstudien*, 1930). According to Ambrose, the phrase τέλος γάμου, means 'a state of being which fulfills the characteristics of marriage' and the phrase τέλος γάμοιο describes 'the state of being which fulfills the desire for marriage' (p. 95).

76. See Pl. *Smp.* 192 A; Arist. *GA* 776 A.

77. *Cyr.* 8.7: ἐμοὶ μὲν τοῦ βίου τὸ τέλος ἤδη πάρεστιν (cf. Pl. *Lg.* 717 E; 810 E).

78. See Stephanus, *Thesaurus*, VIII, pp. 1998-99.

79. The parallelism between these two passages has already been observed by H. Martin, Jr, in his commentary to Plutarch's *Amatorius* (*Plutarch's Ethical Writings and Early Christian Literature*, ed. H.D. Betz [Leiden: Brill, 1978], p. 467). For Martin τέλος here as in 1 Tim 1.5 and 1 Pet 1.9 means 'goal', 'purpose', 'outcome', or 'final cause'.

80. On the word order see BDF, p. 248; on the omission of the verb εἶναι, see *ibid.*, p. 70.

81. Helmbold, LCL, IX, p. 317.

82. Werner Jaeger, *Paideia: The Ideals of Greek Culture*, (Oxford: Basil Blackwell, 1947), II, p. 381 n. 179. For some examples, see Pl. *Prt.* 354 A-B; *Grg.* 499 E; Arist. *Metaph.* 994 B.

83. In many instances the genitive is what BDF calls a 'genitive of direction, purpose or result' (p. 92).

84. Pl. *Lg.* 625 D (schol. cited by BAG, p. 811).

85. Arist. *Pol.* 6.8 (1322 B 13): 'Besides all these officers there is another which is supreme over them, and to this is often entrusted both the introduction (εἰσφοράν) and the *ratification* (τὸ τέλος) of measures . . . ' (tr. B. Jowett, *The Works of Aristotle*, X, ed. W.D. Ross [Oxford: Clarendon Press, 1946]). The crucial phrase is translated by Delling *'fulfillment* of a law' ('τέλος', p. 49); by Schippers *'ratification* of a law' (*NIDNTT*, II, p. 59); by H. Rackham *'execution* of business' (*Aristotle: Politics* [LCL], p. 526). In 1322 A, 6, where a similar phrase occurs in a similar context, Rackham translates 'when the verdicts are not *put into execution*' (LCL, p. 522).

86. Cf. Hom. *Il.* 14.44.

87. A. *Pr.* 13. Du Plessis translates 'the order of Zeus has final authority'. H.W. Smyth translates 'the behest of Zeus is now fulfilled' (LCL, I, p. 215).

88. Tr. Hicks, LCL, I, p. 361.

89. Pl. *Lg.* 12.960 B 6; cf. 6.768 C and 6.769 E.

90. *Lg.* 2.824 C 4-6: Νῦν οὖν ἤδη πάντα χρὴ φάναι τέλος ἔχειν τάγε παιδείας περὶ νόμιμα ('Now at last we may say that all our laws about education are completed'). Cf. *Lg.* 2.822 D 1-2.

91. The phrase τελευτῶντος δὲ τοῦ νόμου in Hdt. 1.24 has nothing to do with the 'abolition' of any law. It refers to the finishing of the hymn called ὄρθιος νόμος in honor to Apollo (see T.E. Page, LCL, I, p. 27).

92. On the common terms for 'abolition', see J.I. Packer, 'Abolish, Nullify, Reject', *NIDNTT*, I, pp. 73-74.

93. Cf. Rom 7.2; 6.6. On the meaning and use of this term and cognates, see G. Delling, 'καταργέω', *TNDT*, I, pp. 452-54.

94. J. Dillon, *The Middle Platonists, 80 B.C. to A.D. 220* (Ithaca, N.Y.: Cornell University Press, 1977), pp. 43-44.

95. Werner Jaeger, *The Theology of the Early Greek Philosophers* (Oxford: Clarendon Press, 1948), p. 155. See further, ch. IX, 'The Teleological Thinkers: Anaxagoras and Diogenes', pp. 155-71.

96. Anaxagoras taught that 'a divine mind (νοῦς) has ordered everything from the beginning according to a definite plan (διακόσμησις).

97. According to Xenophon (*Mem.* 1.4; 4.3) Diogenes had deduced, from the order of the cosmos, the working of a purposeful divine mind (νόησις). Cf. *Fr.* 3 (H. Diels, *Die Fragmente der Vorsokratiker*, ed. W. Kranz [Berlin: Weidmann, 1954]).

98. Leucippus taught that 'nothing happens by accident, but ἐκ λόγου τε καὶ ὑπ' ἀνάγκης' (*Fr.* 2 Diels).

99. See the list of quotations in A. Döring, 'Doxographisches zur Lehre vom *telos*', *ZPPK* 101 (1893), pp. 165-203; and Diels, 130.2.4. Many of the definitions of τέλος by older philosophers come from later quotations,

especially of the Doxographers. Probably these just took the essence of the teachings of the great old masters and put them in the form of a τέλος definition. The fact that these philosophers were asked for their τέλος definition shows the importance that the τέλος problem had acquired in Hellenistic philosophy. Cf. Delling, 'Telos-Aussagen in der grieschischen Philosophie', p. 29.

100. *Ibid.*, p. 26. They spoke about εὐαρέστησις ('satisfaction' or 'complacency'), εὐθυμία, εὐεστώ ('well-being'), or εὐδαιμονία ('happiness'). Although Democritus is said to have composed a treatise called Περὶ τέλους, thus far his only existent treatise is called περὶ εὐθυμίης (Diels, 2 c), where the definition of εὐεστώ is given. Cf. Clem. Al. *Strom.* 2.130.4 D.L. 9.45. The τέλος is often called εὐδαιμονία, as by Democritus (*Fr.* 170-71); cf. B. Max Pohlenz, *Der hellenische Mensch* (Göttingen: Vandenhoeck & Ruprecht, 1947), pp. 300-304.

101. Jaeger, *Paideia*, II, pp. 68, 120.

102. *Ibid.*, p. 381 n. 179.

103. *Ibid.*, p. 69. Against Jaeger, it must be said that the quest for the τέλος is put by several Greek authors long before Socrates. Thus, Arist. *NE* 1.10.1 gives the famous saying τέλος ὁρᾶν ('look at the end' or 'look at the goal') as a quotation from Solon (c. 575 BC), and Plu. *Sol.* 28 attributes to Chilon (c. 597 BC) the dictum τέλος σκοπεῖν ('keep the goal before you', famous in Latin in the form *respicie finem*), which seems to be a variant of the old saying, already famous and classical in Herodotus' time (cf. Hdt. 1.30-33).

104. See *Phd.* 97 C–99 C; *Lg.* 10.903 E–904 A; *Ti.* 29 C–30 C, 46 C-E.

105. P. Shorey, *What Plato Said* (Chicago: University of Chicago Press, 1962), pp. 346-47.

106. This teleological view of nature is a critique of the science of his time, and an answer to the profound quest for meaning in nature which Socrates desiderated (*Phd.* 97 C) but could not find either in the philosophy of Anaxagoras or discover for himself (*ibid.*, p. 329). Cf. A.A. Long, *Hellenistic Philosophy. Stoics, Epicureans, Sceptics* (London: Duckworth, 1974), p. 8.

107. On Plato's teleology, see *Phd.* 97-99; *Sph.* 265 E; *Ti.* 48 E, 53B, and *passim* (cf. *Mem.* 1.4.8, 17-18).

108. P.E. More, *The Religion of Plato* (Princeton: University Press, 1921, reprint 1970), pp. 75-77.

109. The supreme τέλος is sometimes called τὸ βέλτιστον (*Phd.* 97 C–98 B). The first definitions of τέλος appear in *Prt.* 354 A-E. Though Delling ('τέλος', p. 50) seems to imply that τέλος is a rare word in Plato I have listed more than 150 τέλος occurrences in Plato's writings.

110. Delling, 'Telos-Aussagen', p. 30.

111. See Clem. Al. *Strom.* 2.135-5; Stob. *Ecl.* 2.7.3-4 (p. 49 9W).

112. H. Merki, '"Ὁμοίωσις θεῷ", Von der platonischen Angleichung an Gott zur Gottähnlichkeit bei Gregor von Nyssa', *Paradosis* 7 (Freiburg, Switzerland, 1952).

113. See Xenophon (c. 428–c. 354), *Mem.* 1.4.6; 4.3.3-10; cf. Arist. *de An.* 2.9.

114. The best defense of Aristotle's teleological thought is found in *Ph.* 2.8. Cf. W. Jaeger, *Aristotle*, 2nd edn, trans. R. Robinson (Oxford: Clarendon Press, 1948), p. 74 n. 2; A. Gotthelf, 'Aristotle's Conception of Final Causality', *RevMet* 30 (1976), pp. 226-54.

115. *Ph.* 2.3.194 B; cf. 195 A (trans. Wicksteed–Cornford, *LCL*, I, pp. 130-31).

116. Therefore 'the τέλος of each being or process constitutes what is essential to it' (*Protr.* 1.25; trans. W. Jaeger, *Aristotle*, p. 66).

117. *EE* 2.11, 1227 B 3 (cf. LCL, p. 305). 'Everything in the world comes into being for the sake of its τέλος and is regulated by its τέλος.' 'Each thing is defined by its end (τέλος)' (*Ph.* 2.8.199 B; trans. Wicksteed–Cornford, LCL, I, p. 177).

118. *Metaph.* 9.8.3, trans. P. Weelwright, *Aristotle* (New York: Odyssey, 1951), pp. 39, 93.

119. For a useful evaluation, see H. Veatch, 'Telos and Teleology in Aristotelian Ethics', in *Studies in Aristotle*, ed. D.J. O'Meara (Washington, D.C.: Catholic University of America Press, 1981), pp. 279-96.

120. *Ibid.*, 1094 A 13-18; cf. *Metaph.* 1072 B, 1074 B.

121. *Ibid.*, 1.5.1097 A 33-34; 1097 B, 20-21.

122. Delling, 'Telos-Aussagen', p. 31. The most distinctive feature of Aristotle's teleology when compared with Plato's is that Aristotle's teleology is immanent in nature. John Hermann Randall, *Aristotle* (New York: Columbia University Press, 1960), pp. 126, 128.

123. *EN* 3.7.1115 B 20-24 'each thing is defined by its end': ὁρίζεται γὰρ ἕκαστον τῷ τέλει. Cf. 4.1139 A 31-1139 B 14.

124. W. Theiler, *Zur Geschichte der teleologischen Naturbetrachtung bis auf Aristoteles* (Berlin: de Gruyter, 1965).

125. Diogenes Laertius mentions, among others, the works of Epicurus (10.27), Cleanthes (7.175), Chrysippus (7.91), Posidonius (7.87), and Hecaton (7.102).

126. The charge that the Epicureans identified the τέλος with 'pleasure' is discussed at length by Diogenes Laertius (10, 6 and 9). On Stoics attacking Epicureans, Gellius records Taurus (*NA* 9.5) as being fond of quoting a saying of the Stoic Hierocles: 'Pleasure the τέλος: a harlot's creed!' (Dillon, p. 242). However, according to another tradition Epicurus had really taught that 'one must look for καλόν and the virtues if lust permits it, otherwise one must let it go' (*Fr.* 70, 123; *Fr.* 68, 121 Usener). According to others, Epicurus counted the joys of the soul higher than those of the body (D.L. 10.137; cf. 132, 140). It is nevertheless clear that for the Epicureans virtues were only pursued because of the benefits they produce, not because of any intrinsic worth (*ibid.*, 138). See further Delling, 'Telos-Aussage', p. 32 n. 21.

127. Epict. *Diss.* 3.24.37; Stob. *Ecl.* 3.6.57 (p. 300, 13-16).

128. Lucr. *Rer. Nat.* 4.822-42; 5.195-234; cf. Long, pp. 40-41.

129. The importance of this question can be seen from the fact that most of the Stoic masters wrote specific treatises περὶ τέλους. See D.L. 10.27, and especially Clem. Al. *Strom.* 2.127-33, where more than thirty philosophical definitions of τέλος from about thirty Greek philosophers, most of them Stoics and Neoplatonists, are given.

130. Gal. *Nat. Fac.* 1.12. At the basis of Stoicism is the acceptance of the existence of πρόνοια in nature (φύσις), understood as 'the power which moves matter' (Stob. *Ecl.* 1.5.15, pp. 78.18-20), 'the soul of the cosmos' (Plu. *Comm. Not.* 36.1077 D; cf. Philo, *Aet.* 47), or κοινὸς λόγος, the operating force of the universe (Cleanth. *Hymn.* 12-13).

131. For the Stoics nature not only works purposefully but also loves the beautiful. Every existing being is useful or beautiful, and often both. For example, the peacock exists 'for the sake of its tail' (Plu. Stoic. *Repugn.* 21, 1044 C).

132. M. Aurel. 5.16.5; 7.55.2.

133. Porph. *Abst.* 3.20. The principle that everything exists for the sake of man led to statements of the kind that 'bugs are useful because they wake us up in the morning, and mice because they help us to be careful with our storage systems!' (Plu. Stoic. *Repugn.* 21, 1044 D).

134. See list of τέλος definitions and teleological discussion by Zeno and disciples in SVF, I, *Zeno et Zenonis Discipuli*, pp. 45-47, 125-27; cf. III, pp. 3-9, 218-19, 252-53.

135. D.L. 7.87; cf. Cic. *Fin.*; Stob. *Ecl.* 2.76; Luc. *Comm.* 2.380.

136. D.L. 7.87; Gal. *Hippocr.* 6.468.

137. M. Aurel. 2.16.6; 7.55.1. In the Stoa the same φύσις or Λόγος which governs nature should govern the actions of man. Cf. Michel Spanneut, *Permanence du Stoïcisme* (Gembloux: Duculot, 1973), pp. 36-38.

138. Clem. Al. *Strom.* 2.129.4.

139. Cleanth. *Hymn.* 11-21 (SVF, I, p. 537). Cf. Rom 10.5 (Lev 18.5).

140. D.L. 7.86, 88.

141. Stob. 1.1.12 (pp. 25-27 W). See further in W. Wiersma, 'Τέλος und Καθῆκον in der alten Stoa', pp. 219-28. For other definitions of τέλος see SVF, IV, p. 169; cf. pp. 143-44.

142. See Porph. *Abst.* 3.20. Even Philo contested the opinion that nature was meant for the sake of man. For him to say that the cosmic order was created *in nostram utilitatem* or *commodum hominum* was a 'sin of pride' (*Provid.* 2.70-71); moreover, many things in nature are not only not useful but harmful (*ibid.*, 87-88, 92-94). However, despite his rebuttal, Philo clung to the teleological destiny of creation, even if he could not put every datum in connection with it (*ibid.*, pp. 99-112). Cf. Eus. *PE* 8.14.43-72.

143. Dillon, pp. 43-44.

144. *Ibid.*, p. 10. See further R.T. Wallis, *Neoplatonism* (New York: Scribner's, 1977), ch. 6.

145. Cic. *Leg.* 1.22. This providence was understood by Antiochus as the activity of God's Logos, expressed in the world through the natural laws. Since man has a share in the Logos (because endowed by God with reason), Logos is the bond between God and Man. And since right reason (ὀρθὸς λόγος) is expressed through Law (Νόμος), we must believe that we share in the divine Law and Justice (δικαιοσύνη), which are always God's (*ibid.*, 1.23; cf. Dillon, p. 80).

146. For references and discussion, see Dillon, p. 70; and Long, pp. 225-26.

147. Dillon, p. 44.

148. The underlined part corresponds to Antiochus' addition (Cic. *Fin.* 5.26-27). This 'external aid' needed by man to fulfill his τέλος is provided by the Torah in Judaism, and by Jesus Christ in Christianity; cf. Spanneut, pp. 130-38.

149. Cic. *Fin.* 5.71.

150. Plut. *De Sera* 550 D (Dillon, p. 192). Cf. Plut. *Treatise* 221 (catalogue of Lamprias, translated by Dillon, pp. 187-88). On Plutarch's use of τέλος see especially *De Is. et Os.* 352 A: '(λατρείας) . . . ὧν τέλος ἐστίν ἡ τοῦ πρώτου καὶ κυρίου καὶ νοητοῦ γνῶσις ('the aim [of the mystery of Osiris] is the knowledge of Him who is the first, the Lord of all, the Ideal One') (see commentary in *Plutarch's Ethical Writings and Early Christian Literature*, ed. H.D. Betz [Leiden: Brill, 1978], p. 40); and *De def. or.* 410 B, where Plutarch exposes the interesting idea of philosophy having its τέλος in θεολογία (see further Betz, p. 137). For other occurrences of τέλος in Plutarch, see *Plutarch's Theological Writings and Early Christian Literature*, ed. H.D. Betz (Leiden: Brill, 1975), pp. 99-101.

151. See Nicomachus of Gerasa (AD 50–150), *Ar.* 25.7; Gaius and his School, *An. Tht. Com.* 7.14; D.L. 3.67-109 (a whole summary of Platonic τέλος-definitions as 'likeness to God'); cf. Alb. *Eisagoge* 28.

152. See especially Hippol. *Haer.* 17 (cf. Dillon, p. 413).

153. The principle of εἷς σκοπός, that is, 'the principle of unity and consequence', is found already in Pl. *Phd.* 264 C.

154. This discussion was alive for centuries. Gregory of Nyssa still recalls it and argues that, in his own opinion, the σκοπός of the Law was to help Israel to abstain from evil. φημὶ τοίνυν ἐγὼ πάσης νομοθεσίας τῆς θεόθεν γεγενημένης ἕνα σκοπὸν εἶναι . . . ' (*In Ecclesistem hom.* 7, PG 44, 716 AB). Cf. Kerrigan, p. 93, n. 2.

155. Cicero adopted an eclectic philosophical position. In his concept of τέλος one can see the influence of the Platonists (especially Carneades) and the Stoics. H. Rackham, *Cicero: De Finibus Bonorum et Malorum with an English Translation* (London: W. Heinemann, 1931), p. vii.

156. *Ibid.*

157. Independently of trends and formulations, the τέλος (either related to the purpose of the cosmos or to the goal of human existence) continued to be looked for in the immanent world. Only some philosophers within the Platonist and hermetic circles seem to have sought for a transcendent τέλος. Cf. Proph. *Sent.* 32.3 (p. 19, 3-7 Mommert); *id. Abst.* 1.57; *Corpus Herm.* 1.26 A. See Delling, 'Telos-Aussagen', p. 34.

158. The value of these etymological possibilities is, of course, limited. Etymological determination is very seldom—if ever—unquestionable and always a risky enterprise. The etymological criteria can only be considered of auxiliary value. The principles stated by J. Barr in 'Etymology and the Old Testament', in *Language and Meaning. Studies in Hebrew Language and Biblical Exegesis*, ed. J. Barr et al. (Leiden: Brill, 1974), pp. 1-28, are also applicable here. On 'the root fallacy', see also *The Semantics of Biblical Language* (Oxford: University Press, 1961), pp. 158-60.

159. The most commonly recurrent are: the verb τελέω, found more than thirty times translating eight Hebrew different terms, but most frequently the verbs כלה (as in Ruth 2.21; 3.18) and שלם (as in Neh 6.15): 'to perform', 'to carry through', 'to complete', 'to actualize', 'to fulfill', 'to conclude', 'to deal with' (see Delling, 'Τέλος', pp. 58-59); with the sense of performing religious rites it translates the Hebrew קדש (as in Hos 4.14); τέλειος (twenty times), mainly as a translation of the Hebrew roots שלם and תמים, with the meaning of 'complete' and 'perfect'. The verb τελειόω is attested twenty-five times, with the meaning of 'being perfect or whole' (translating generally the hithpael of תמם), but also with the meanings of 'completing' and 'consecrating to the cult'. The noun τελείωσις occurs sixteen times translating מילוים, with the meaning of 'consecration' (to the cultus). The term τελειοτής occurs only five times translating forms of the root תם indicating 'perfection' and related concepts. Cf. Schippers, pp. 60-61.

160. See E. Hatch and H.A. Redpath, *A Concordance to the Septuagint and the Other Greek Versions of the Old Testament* (Graz: Akademische Druck, 1954), pp. 1344-45. Besides these 160 times, τέλος occurs also nine times as a subscription at the end of the following books: Exod (τέλος τῆς ἐξόδου, Num (τέλος τῶν ἀριθμῶν), Deut (τέλος τοῦ δευτερονομίου), Judg (τέλος τῶν κριτῶν), Ruth (τέλος τῆς Ῥούθ), 2 Chr (τέλος τῶν παραλειπομένων), Jdt (τέλος τῆς Ἰ.), Esth (τέλος τῆς Ἐσθήρ), Dan (τέλος Δαν. προφήτου).

161. Some give as the closest parallel to τέλος the rabbinic concept of כלל; cf. M. Jastrow, *A Dictionary of the Targumim, The Talmud Babli and Yerushalmi, and the Midrashic Literature*, 2 vols. (New York: Title Publishing Co., 1943), I, p. 644; cf. K. Barth, *Church Dogmatics*, II, p. 245; translated *perfectio* in Gesenius, *Thesaurus*, p. 688. The only Hebrew parallel to the use of τέλος in Rom 10.4 registered by Str-B (III, p. 277) is *b Bab Mez* 85b-86a, where it is said: 'Rabbi and R. Nathan are the end of the Mishnah (סוף משנה), R. Ashi and Rabina are the end of the teaching (סוף הוראה)

[Gemara?]'. Rabbi I. Epstein interprets this statement as 'they edited the Talmud' (*Baba Mezia, The Babylonian Talmud*, XXIV [London: Soncino Press, 1935], p. 493 n. 6). The formal parallelism of the Talmud statement with Rom 10.4 is striking: Both sentences speak of somebody as being 'the end' of a sacred legal code. The meaning of the Talmud statement is that the mentioned Rabbis gave the last, definitive, and normative form to the sacred traditions. Comparing this sentence with Rom. 10.4 Str-B say: 'Diese Worte bedeuten aber nicht—u. darin liegt ihr Unterschied von Röm 10,4—, dass die Mischna u. Gemara mit den gennanten Autoren aufgehoben şei, sondern vielmehr, dass sie mit ihnen zum Abschluss gekommen sei, so dass weiteres Material nicht mehr eingefugt werden darf' (III, p. 277). In spite of being the most close parallel to Rom 10.4 in rabbinic literature, the date of the document is too late to be relevant to the Pauline usage.

162. Delling, 'τέλος', p. 52.

163. In *Gesenius' Hebrew Grammar*, enlarged by E. Kautzsch, 2nd English edition trans. and revised by A.E. Cowley (Oxford: Clarendon Press, 1910), p. 342, we read that 'the infinitive absolute used before the verb' is used 'to strengthen the verbal idea, i.e. to emphasize in this way either the certainty or the forcibleness and completeness of an occurrence'. Amos 9.8 is quoted as 'an especially typical' instance. Cf. M. Johannessohn, *Der Gebrauch der Präpositionen in der Septuaginta* (Berlin: Weidmann, 1925), p. 303.

164. The root כלה has a semantic range of significations overlapping many of the basic meanings of τέλος: 'accomplish, cease, consume, determine, end, finish'. See J.N. Oswalt, 'כלה', *TWAT*, I, pp. 439-40; cf. G. Gerleman, 'כלה', *THAT*, I, cols. 831-33.

165. Du Plessis, p. 59.

166. Jdt 7.30; 14.13; Ps Sol 1.1; 2.5; Sir 12.11; 2 Macc 8.29 with the formula εἰς τέλος; 4 Ezra 3.13 with διὰ τέλους; Wis 16.5 and 19.1 with μέχρι τέλους.

167. See the titles of Ps 4; 5; 6; 8; 9; 10(11); 11(12); 12(13); 13(14); 17(18); 18(19); 21(22); 29(30); 30(31); 35(36); 36(37); 38(30); 39(40); 40(41); 41(42); 42(43); 44(45); 45(46); 46(47); 47(48); 48(49); 49(50); 50(51); 51(52); 52(53); 53(54); 55(56); 56(56); 57(58); 58(59); 59(60); 60(61); 61(62); 63(64); 64(65); 65(66); 66(67); 67(68); 68(69); 69(70); 74(75); 75(76); 76(77); 79(80); 80(81); 83(84); 84(85); 87(88); 108(109); 138(139); 139(140).

168. Aquila translated למנצח (a piel infinitive) as a personal participle: τῷ νικοποιῷ ('to the triumphant one'), followed by Jerome (Vg. *victori*); Theodoretus preferred the neuter form εἰς τὸ νῖκος, and Symmachus the more classical term ἐπινίκιος. But the LXX chose the enigmatic form εἰς τὸ τέλος. See Robert Devreesse, *Les anciens commentateurs grecs des Psaumes* (Città del Vaticano: Bibliotheca Apostolica Vaticana, 1970), *in loc.* Cf. J. Wellhausen, *The Book of Psalms*, trans. H.H. Forness (London: J. Clarke, 1898), p. 165.

169. This interpretation, already found in Eusebius, Theodoret, and especially in Augustine became traditional in the Catholic church. Probably this interpretation had its origin in a reading of לנצח as למנצח. This eschatological interpretation has been almost universally rejected in modern scholarship. However, it was still defended by K. Bornhauser, 'Das Wirken des Christus', *BFCT* 2 (1924), pp. 212-14.

170. The traditional Hebrew reading of this formula has been למנצח, a form from the root נצח, 'to be strong', in the piel, 'to have the mastery'. This form is translated in 2 Chr 2.17 in the general sense of 'leader'. Therefore, the translation 'for the Precentor', or leader of the temple choir is highly probable. For discussion, see J.W. Thirtle, *The Titles of the Psalms* (London: Morgan & Scott, 1916), pp. 6-19. This interpretation may be supported by the Hebrew נצח, which may have the meaning of 'to have authority' and 'to be permanent'. For a full discussion on this possibility, see B.D. Eerdmans, *The Hebrew Book of Psalms* (Oudtestmentische Studien, 4; Leiden: Brill, 1947), p. 54, and H.-J. Kraus, *Psalmen* (BKAT, 15, Neukirchen: Neukirchener Verlag, 1961), I, p. 5; M. Manatti and E. de Solms, *Les Psaumes*, I (Paris: Desclée de Brower, 1966), p. 20.

171. This possibility is supported by A.A. Anderson, *The Book of Psalms* (London: Oliphants, 1972), I, p. 48; Delling, 'τέλος', p. 52; Schippers, p. 60.

172. 4 Kgdm 8.3 (μετὰ τὸ τέλος τῶν ἑπτὰ ἐτῶν); cf. 2 Esdr 23.6 (μετὰ τέλος ἡμερῶν); Dan 1.15 and 4.34 (Θ), where the form קצה is translated by μετὰ τέλος.

173. Dan 11.13 (Θ) (εἰς τὸ τέλος τῶν καιρῶν ἐνιαυτῶν). Exceptionally קץ is translated by εἰς τέλος in 4 Kgdm 19.23 with the sense of 'spatial limit', because governed by the word μέρος.

174. Flückiger, pp. 153-54. Cf. G. von Rad, *Wisdom in Israel* (New York: Abingdon Press, 1972), pp. 138-43 ('The Doctrine of the Proper Time'); and pp. 263-83, Excursus: 'The Divine Determination of Times'. In 1QpHab 7.13 we read: 'All the times of God will come to their [appointed] measure'. Cf. Wis 8.8, and 1 Cor 10.11.

175. Delling, 'τέλος', p. 52.

176. Job 14.20; 20.7; 23.7; Ps 9.7, 19a, 32(10.11); 43.23(24); 48.9(19); 51.5; 67.16; 73.1, 10, 19; 76.8(9); 78.5; 88.46(47); 102.9; Hab 1.4.

177. Ps 12.2; 15.11; 73.3. In this last occurrence the LXX has changed the Hebrew text and εἰς τέλος may be understood either as 'for ever' or 'constantly'.

178. 1 Chr 28.9; Ps 9.18b (in cods. A B S: εἰς τὸν αἰῶνα). In both instances the phrase could also be understood in the sense of 'completely'. For Delling, however, the meaning of τέλος here is 'primarily temporal' ('τέλος' p. 51).

179. The expression תמיד ('continuation') is translated by διὰ παντός in Exod 25.29; 27.20; 28.26, etc.; by δι' ὅλου in 3 Kgs 10.8 and Ezek 38.8. It is translated by διὰ τέλους only in Isa 62.6. See further Johannessohn, p. 237. In Ps 9.6-7 the expressions εἰς τὸν αἰῶνα and εἰς τέλος are used in parallel:

the former is used for 'eternity' and the latter for the absolute destruction of enemy weapons.

180. Delling 'τέλος', p. 51 n. 51. Cf. Johannessohn, pp. 236-37.

181. Cf. Ps 13.2; 15(16).11; 51(52).7, 10, 11; 67(68).17, 34; 73(74).1, 3; 76(77).8; 78(79).5; 88(89).47. Du Plessis says that 'in none of these passages can we exclude the idea of totality' (p. 60).

182. Delling ('τέλος', p. 51 n. 15) notes that τέλος is never used in the LXX for the Hebrew אחרית though this term can mean 'the end that overcomes someone' (as in Deut 32.20; Ps 73.17; Lam 1.9; etc.) and 'the issue of a matter' (as in Isa 41.22; 46.10; 47.7; Eccl 7.8). אחרית is generally translated by ἔσχατα (with exception of Prov 14.12, where it is rendered τελευταῖα). However, τέλος is used, as we have already seen, for the end of other periods of time (cf. Wis 11.14; 3 Macc 3.14; 4.15; 5.19; 5.49).

183. Delling, 'τέλος', p. 52; cf. Schippers, pp. 60-61.

184. As a translation of מכסה the phrase τὸ τέλος τῆς τιμῆς should mean 'the levy of the value' or a similar expression (so Du Plessis, p. 57). However, the meaning of τέλος for 'fullness' is so dominant that some translators render the mentioned phrase in Lev 27.23 by 'the full valuation' (so Bagster, p. 168).

185. C. Thomson, *The Septuagint Bible* (Indian Hills, Col.: Falcon's Wing Press, 1954), translates 'and come to an issue' (p. 849).

186. The phrase ἐπὶ τέλει τῶν ἐκβάσεων ἐθαύμασαν makes better sense in its context when translated 'they marvelled at the events which had come to pass' (keeping the strength of τέλος as *nomen actionis*) than when translated 'at the end of the events they marveled at him' (NOABA).

187. Delling ('τέλος', p. 52) gives to τέλος in these two passages the meaning of 'cessation'. But in Bar 3.17, the translation 'there is no limit to their possessions' (JB) is preferable. 'Cessation' for τέλος in Wis 14.14 would be possible logically, but the translation 'their speedy end has been planned' (JB) seems more accurate.

188. In the three instances τέλος translates the term סוף, which like τέλος means at the same time 'end', 'conclusion', and 'sum'; cf. F. Brown, S.R. Driver, and C.A. Briggs, *A Hebrew and English Lexicon* (Oxford: Clarendon Press, 1979), p. 693.

189. The choice of words in the LXX translation of Qoheleth seems to betray that the translator was very aware of Hellenistic philosophy (cf. R. Gordis, *Qoheleth. The Man and His World* [New York: Jewish Theological Seminary of America, 1951], p. 28). By the use of specific technical terms (τέλος is just one of them) the translator of Ecclesiastes seems to have tried to put his translation both in dialogue and in opposition with these trends: against skepticism and cynicism, which pretended that man could never fathom the meaning of life (cf. 1.18; 2.11, 14-20; 4.2, 3; 6.12; 7.1-3, 27, 28; 9.11), Epicureanism, which preached pleasure as the *summum bonum* of existence (cf. 9.4-12), and even Stoicism, which had popularized the

Aristotelian ethical principle of the *aurea medriocritas* (7.15-25). On the relation of Ecclesiastes with contemporary thought, see further Gordis (p. 112), and G. von Rad, for whom 'that Qoheleth turns against the prevailing teachings is beyond doubt' (p. 233).

190. See Du Plessis, p. 62.

191. *Ibid.*, p. 63, emphasis his.

192. Von Rad, pp. 228-29. Qoheleth usually refers to this phenomenon by the neutral word 'time': God himself determines the 'appropriated times' (7.14; 4.14; cf. 3.1-8, 17; 8.6; 9.11-12).

193. Note the series of seven utterances in 7.1-14, each of which begins with the word טוב ('good'). See Gordis, pp. 164-65.

194. 'The conclusion of the whole matter' (KJV); 'Here is my final conclusion' (LB); 'To sum up the whole matter' (JB).

195. For Gordis, 'fear the Lord' means already 'fulfilling His purpose' (p. 169).

196. The pregnant idiom זה כל האדם, very characteristically Hebrew as a recapitulative, concrete formula, in its Greek form puts πᾶς in parallelism, almost as a synonym of τέλος. Cf. Sir 43.27.

197. The whole conclusion is usually considered the addition of an editor (see Gordis, pp. 190-91). However, A. Barucq has shown that vv. 13-14 are an integral part of the original text and are fully understood within the context of the whole book (*Ecclesiaste* [Verbum Salutis, Ancien Testament, 3; Paris: Beauchesne, 1968], pp. 196-97). Verses 9-12 could more likely be considered as a posterior addition.

198. E. Beaucamp, *Man's Destiny in the Books of Wisdom*, trans. J. Clarke (Staten Island, N.Y.: Alba House, 1970), p. 87 (emphasis his). Beaucamp sees here an intentional apologetic purpose, against the cyclical and meaningless conceptions of life and history among the Babylonians, Egyptians, and Greeks.

199. Von Rad, p. 229.

200. *Ibid.*, p. 235.

201. Cf. Acts 17.24-31; Rom 1.20-23; Jas 2.10-12.

202. Du Plessis, p. 64. According to G. von Rad (p. 235) 'not often in ancient Israel has the question of salvation been posed so inescapably to a single individual as was the case with Qoheleth'.

203. Probably in repudiation of certain antinomian tendencies the 'wisdom circles' came to identify 'Wisdom' and 'Torah' (Sir 24.23) and at the same time, in an effort to make 'Torah' acceptable for the Hellenistic mind, they came to express Torah-wisdom in terms of Greek philosophy (J.M. Reese, *Hellenistic Influence in the Book of Wisdom and Its Consequences* [Rome: Biblical Institute Press, 1970], pp. 50-61). In the ethical realm, the Jewish wisdom writers came very near to many of the ideas of popular Stoicism, as can be especially seen in Ben Sira (R. Pautrel, 'Ben Sira et le Stoicisme', *RSR* 51 [1963], pp. 535-49).

204. Winston, pp. 206-207.

205. Hengel, pp. 144-47. C. Larcher, *Etudes sur le livre de la Sagesse* (Paris: Gabalda, 1969), p. 202, says that Ben Sira 'semble au courant des speculations sur le *télos* de la vie humaine'. Cf. pp. 296-97.

206. 'Everything has a purpose given by God' (Sir 16.26-30); 'Everything has been created for its use' (39.21); God has a plan in history and reveals what is to be (16.17; 39.16-36; 42.19).

207. Trans. Hengel, p. 144. The term used here for *purpose* in the original is the Aramaic צורך, 'goal, need, use', a *hapax legomenon* in the OT (2 Chr 2.15), but a quite frequent term in Sirach.

208. Hengel, p. 145.

209. See U. Wilkens, 'Σοφία', *TDNT*, VII, p. 499.

210. Cf. Eccl 12.13; Jer 23.24; Ps 139.7-12; and Rom 11.36.

211. Du Plessis, p. 66.

212. References taken from R.H. Charles, *Th Greek Versions of the Testaments of the Twelve Patriarchs* (Oxford: University Press, 1960, reprint of 1908). For a complete list of τέλος references, see p. 322 (Index).

213. R.H. Charles, *The Apocrypha and Pseudepigrapha of the Old Testament*, 2 vols. (Oxford: Clarendon Press, 1913), II, pp. 631-32, quotes, as parallel constructions, 2 Chr 12.12; 31.1; and 1 Thess 2.16. The same phrase is used in 2.5 in the sentence 'I was *utterly* dishonoured'. In 3 Bar 13.2 the idea of intensification seems appropriate: 'In order that the enemy may not *utterly* prevail (εἰς τὸ τέλος)'. This seems to be also the intention of τέλος in εἰς τέλος δελεάσαι in Ap Mos 19, for intensifying the action of *strongly* luring or enticing. See also TLev 6.11, ἔφθασε δὲ αὐτοὺς ἡ ὀργὴ τοῦ θεοῦ εἰς τέλος ('but the wrath of the Lord came upon them to the uttermost') and TLevi 5.6, where εἰς τέλος is added for intensification in the *b* and *d* variants.

214. Note the similarity of construction with Rom 10.4. Even the word order is identical: τέλος followed by a noun in genitive modified by a phrase introduced with εἰς. The variant A of this passage reads in a way even closer to Rom 10.4, because instead of ἔρχεται it has ἐστι. For a similar occurrence, see TAsh 1.9. On textual variants, see Charles, *Testament of the Twelve Patriarchs*, p. 174.

215. See a similar use in ApMos, τὸ τέλος αὐτοῦ ὡσηλευτῆς (variant addition), in *Apocalypses Apocryphae*, ed. K. von Tischendorf (Hildesheim: Georg Olms, 1886, reprint 1966), p. 3.

216. This passage registers several variant readings: ἐπὶ τέλει (*b*); τὸ τέλος (*e*); συντελέια (*f*); τέλος (*g*). See further Charles, *Testament of the Patriarchs*, p. 55.

217. See *APOT*, II, p. 575.

218. For Bring ('Paul and the OT', pp. 40-42), the Semitic background for τέλος is to be found in the Hebrew roots סוף and קץ 'to bring something to a

conclusion', and the Aramaic כלל 'summation'. These terms are the common ones in apocalyptic literature.

219. TLevi 16.3; TGad 8.2 *b*; and TJos 8.2.

220. See J. Geffcken, *Die Oracula Sibyllina*, in GCS (Leipzig: J.C. Hinrichs, 1902), p. 59.

221. Cf. TSol 4.6 (D); 4.8; 8.2; *PJ* 9.15.

222. In a very cursory way, the teleological content of the Pseudepigrapha may be summarized as follows: God has a plan and a purpose for all his creatures (4 Ezra 4.41-49) and especially for man (8.4-15); the times of human history are divinely pre-determined according to God's purposes (4.35-50; cf. *APOT*, II, p. 567, notes on vv. 36-37); God's plans are inscrutable for human beings (4.1-11; 5.35-36); all the things that now we do not understand also fit in God's plans but will be known by humans only in the New Age (4.22-32); God's purpose will be finally executed (2 Bar 22-23; 4 Ezra 8.14-15, 42-54). The inference that because there is no word for τέλος this concept was unknown to the Hebrews would be completely unwarranted, for an idea may be operating in a thinking community without any single and specific word available to express it. Cf. Barr, *The Semantics of Biblical Language*, pp. 21-45.

223. The book of Jubilees is a defense of the absolute supremacy of the Law and its everlasting validity (*APOT*, II, p. 6). Since of all divine interventions in history the most important was considered the giving of Torah, the law is unanimously described in the Pseudepigrapha as eternal (1 En 99.2; 4 Ezra 9.28-37), everlasting (Jub 33.17; PsSol 10.5), and imperishable (Jub 12; 4 Ezra 9.37).

224. *APOT*, II, p. 88.

225. See particularly the ingenious interpretation of the laws related to unclean food, and the allegorical explanation given to the 'cloven hoof' and 'chewing the cud' (150-56). However, it must be noticed, with M. Hadas, that 'the allegorical interpretation of the Law contains no hint that its observance can be dispensed with or need be apologized for; but it is made clear that observance of the ritual is not for its own sake but for the sake of a higher religious view of life which ritual observances symbolize and protect' (*Aristeas to Philocrates* [New York: Harper & Brothers, 1951], p. 62).

226. H.G. Meecham, *The Letter of Aristeas. A Linguistic Study with Special Reference to the Greek Bible* (Manchester: University Press, 1935), p. 180, translates this phrase 'he brought to completion', and gives the following parallels: 1 Chr 29.19; 3 Macc 3.14; Plb. 3.5.7 (τὴν πρόθεσιν ἐπὶ τέλος ἀγαγεῖν).

227. Forms of the verb συντελέω are used twelve times, the verb τελέω three times, τελειόω four times, τελείωσις two times, the phrase τελεία ψυχῇ once, and τελευτᾶν once. See references in A. Pelletier, *Lettre d'Aristée à Philocrate. Introduction, texte critique, traduction et notes, avec index complet des mots grecs* (Paris: Editions du Cerf, 1962), pp. 310-311.

228. Cf. 2 Macc 3.8; Acts 9.23; cf. Meecham, p. 180. Pelletier, p. 193, translates 'le plus avantageux pour la vie', while H. St.J. Thackeray, *The Letter of Aristeas* (New York: Macmillan, 1918), p. 62, translates 'the highest good for his life'.

229. Günter Mayer, *Index Philoneus* (Berlin, New York: W. de Gruyter, 1974), pp. 275-76. Of these 204 instances, one (*Somn.* 2.250) is only attested in some manuscripts, and another comes in *Apol. Jud.* 8.6.6. Beside these, the verb τελέω is attested twenty-five times, the verb τελειόω fifty-four, the noun τελειοτής thirty-five, the emphatic form τελείωσις thirty-two, and the adjective τέλειος more than 400.

230. Only in three instances is τέλος used in uncommon ways: in *Migr.* 103 τέλος is used in a local sense, referring to the end of the high priest's garment (ἐπὶ τοῦ τέλους τοῦ ὑποδύτου). In *Spec. Leg.* 1.143 τέλος (in fact τέλη) is used in the sense of 'dues'. And in *Ebr.* 115 τέλος seems to have been used in its military sense in the phrase δυσὶν ἀντιτεταγμένους τέλεσιν ('two battalions of the enemy'), though combined with this particular sense there is perhaps the thought of the philosophical sense of 'purposes' or 'motives' (cf. n. 115, p. 504).

231. For Philo's use of the teleological and cosmological arguments to demonstrate the existence and providence of God, see *Spec Leg.* 187-89; *Praem.* 41-42; *Dec.* 60; *Abr.* 71; *Leg. All.* 3.97-103; *Quaes. Gen.* 2.34; *Fuga* 12; *Post.* 28, 167; *Mut.* 54. See further in Ursula Früchtel, *Die kosmologischen Vorstellungen bei Philo von Alexandrien* (Leiden: Brill, 1968), pp. 144-71; and Georgios D. Farandos, *Kosmos und Logos nach Philon von Alexandria* (Amsterdam: Rodopi, 1976), pp. 292-96.

232. Philo devoted himself to the task of reinterpreting the Torah in terms of Platonic idealism. In order to convince the educated Hellenists of the high philosophical and ethical value of the Jewish laws, he applied to the Hebrew Scriptures the allegorical techniques of interpretation which were common among Greek philosophers for reinterpreting the texts of Homer and ancient Greek mythology. His concern was to prove that the laws of Moses were reasonable, purposeful and philosophically superior to Hellenistic wisdom. Behind the letter—which Philo never rejected—the important meaning of the ancient Hebrew texts is to be found in the moral and philosophical ideas which God had conveyed through them. Cf. E. Bréhler, *Les idées philosophiques et religieuses de Philon d'Alexandrie* (Paris: Librairie Philosophique J. Vrin, 1950), p. 11.

233. In *Op.* 133-34 we read that '(the wise and righteous man) . . . taking the good runner as his example, finishes the race of life without stumbling, when he has reached the end (πρὸς τὸ τέλος ἐλθών) he shall obtain crowns and prizes as a fitting guerdon. Are not the crowns and prizes just this, not to have missed the end of his labours (μὴ ἀτυχῆσαι τοῦ τέλους τῶν πονηθέντων), but to have obtained those final aims of good sense that are so hard of attainment? What, then, is the end of right-mindedness (τί οὖν φρονεῖν

ὀρθῶς ἐστι τέλος)? . . . to hold that we know nothing, He alone being wise, who is alone God'; cf. *Plant.* 76.

234. In *Conf.* 144 those who run after many goals (πόλλα τέλη) at the same time are described 'like bowmen, whose shots roam from mark to mark' and who never take a skillful aim at a single point'. In *Vit. Mos.* 2.151 τέλος is treated as a synonym of σκοπός in the sense of 'target of life'.

235. Thus, in *Agr.* 5 it is said that 'the worker has but one end (ἕν τέλος) in view, his wages'. Cf. *Post.* 80. On 'reaching the goal' see *Leg. All.* 3.47; *Migr.* 225; *Somn.* 1.8, 16, 171, 230; *Sacr.* 125; *Plant.* 82; cf. 90, 99, 161; *Abr.* 49; 177; *Heres.* 246; *Vit. Mos.* 1.151, 329; *Dec.* 123; *Spec. Leg.* 1.333, 344; *Praem.* 24, 28; *Ebr.* 202; *Agr.* 91, 125, 126, 173; *Post.* 152, 157, 174; etc.

236. Philo defines each one of the arts as 'a system of conceptions coordinated to work for some useful end (πρός τι τέλος εὔχρηστον' (*Congr.* 141).

237. The culminating character of τέλος is better rendered some times in verbal sentences or periphrasis such as 'the success which crowned his career' (*Jos.* 1.246), or the circumstances that 'crowned them (τέλος προσέθηκαν) with impiety' (*Spec. Leg.* 2.125), or 'before he had consummated (τέλος ἀγαγεῖν) or carried out his plans' (*Gaium* 25).

238. Cf. *Heres.* 172; *Leg. All.* 2.73; *Sacr.* 113.

239. The LCL translates the phrase οἱ ἐν τέλει: 'The highly placed' (*Abr.* 93; *Gaium* 110); 'the chief men of the country' (*Abr.* 260); 'the dignitaries' (*Jos.* 98); 'the chiefs' (*Jos.* 250); 'the nobles' (*Vit. Mos.* 1.91); 'those in authority' (*ibid.*, 122; *Flacc.* 4); 'the men of rank' (*Vit. Mos.* 1.168); 'the chieftains' (*ibid.*, 221); 'the magnates' (*Spec. Leg.* 13; *Gaium* 108, 222, 303); 'persons of authority' (*Quod. Omn.* 127; *Gaium* 300); 'persons in high position' (*Flacc.* 141); '(persons) of high rank' (*ibid.*, 183; *Gaium* 252); 'the chief officials' (*ibid.*, 26); 'those in great position' (*ibid.*, 144).

240. Thus, he agrees with the Epicurean that 'every living creature hastens after pleasure as its most necessary and essential end (ὑπ' ἀναγκαιότατον καὶ συνεκτικώτατον τέλος ἡδονήν) and man above all' (*Op.* 162), but emphatically condemns those 'who regard pleasures as the end and aim of life' (τέλος τὰς ἡδονάς) because they follow 'ends for which they were not born' (*Quod Deus* 98). In *Conf.* 144 Philo compares those who have pleasure as their τέλος with the builders of Babel; cf. *Conf.* 146; *Congr.* 12; *Leg. All.* 3.37; *Cher.* 91; *Op.* 158.

241. In those who have many aims in life (πολλὰ τέλη τοῦ βίου) the divine Spirit does not remain (*Gig.* 53), they are drawn hither and thither (*Somn.* 2.11), cf. *Migr.* 153.

242. So, 'the knowledge of God is the best goal (τὸ ἄριστον τέλος) and the primal and most perfect good' (*Dec.* 81; *Spec. Leg.* 1.345; cf. *Dec.* 65-81). This is why, for Philo, 'the unbeliever misses the goal of life (ὁ ἄθεος ἀτυχεῖ τοῦ τέλους)' (*Quod Det.* 114; *Quod Deus* 100; *Plant.* 80). Even when Philo names the τὸ κατ' ἀρετήν ('life according to virtue', *Virt.* 15) as the τέλος

which is given to man in the law, he does not understand 'virtue' in the Greek classical way, but as θεραπεύειν, as a life of service to God (*Abr.* 130).

243. Philo's θεοῦ ἐξομοίωσις is primarily to be understood as an ethical attitude, but it may also mean a mystical experience (cf. *Dec.* 73; *Spec. Leg.* 4.188; *Virt.* 8).

244. *Migr.* 128 and 131, in connection with Gen 12.4, 26.5, and Deut 13.50.

245. *Gig.* 14; *Vit. Mos.* 1.327; *Mut.* 102.

246. *Plant.* 93: τὸ ἀρχὴν τε καὶ τέλος τῶν ἀπάντων εἶναι θεόν; cf. *Heres.* 120; *Leg. All.* 3.205.

247. *Fuga* 171, 172; *Op.* 44; on the philosophical relationship between ἀρχή and τέλος see *Op.* 82, *Heres.* 121; 122; *Vit. Mos.* 1.251; *Spec. Leg.* 1.266, 188; 2.142, 157; *Dec.* 35; cf. 51; in the sanctuary decoration the represented fruits were nuts signifying perfect virtue 'for just as in a nut beginning and end are identical, beginning represented by seed and end by fruit, so it is with the virtues' (*Vit. Mos.* 2.181); in fact, Philo identifies ἀρχή and τέλος: ἡ ἀρχή σου καὶ τὸ τέλος ἕν καὶ ταυτόν ἐστιν ('your origin and your end are one and the same', *Leg. All.* 3.253).

248. The relation τέλος-ἀρχή seems to consider τέλος as a turning point rather than as a terminal point: 'for the endings are the beginnings of other things, as the end of day is the beginning of night' (*Leg. All.* 1.6); ἀρχή and τέλος are not set against each other as an antithesis, but as completing of a cycle (*Quod Det.* 88); cf. *Abr.* 46; *Praem.* 23.

249. We find sometimes the expression κεφαλὴ καὶ τέλος used in a similar way; cf. *Sacr.* 115; 53. In *Spec. Leg.* 2.38 the service of God is called ἀρχὴ καὶ τέλος of happiness; cf. *Praem.* 142.

250. So, ἐπὶ τοῦ τέλους (*Leg. All.* 1.89) is translated 'at the last'; εἰς τέλος, translated in *Sac.* 21 (quoting Gen 46.4) by 'at last', and in *Apol. Jud.* 8.6.6 'to the end'; πρὸς τέλος in the phrase ἐαν δὲ βελτιούμενος ἀεὶ πρὸς τέλος ἀφίκῃ (*Sacr.* 42), 'if your life to the end be a progress to the better'.

251. In LCL, I, p. 476 n. 102, it is supposed that the reference is to the climax of a process, since the common word in Philo (and contemporary Greek) for *terminus* was ὅρος.

252. See *Dec.* 73, τέλος εὐδαιμονίας τὴν πρὸς θεὸν ἐξομοίωσιν 'the highest happiness is to become like God'; cf. *Plant.* 49; *Mot.* 216.

253. So Jos 43, προτεθείμενοι τέλος (γάμου) οὐχ ἡδονὴν ἀλλὰ γενησίων παιδῶν σποράν ('considering the end of our marriage not pleasure but begetting of legitimate children').

254. This is probably an allusion to Num 31.28; cf. a similar reference to that text in *Somn.* 2.29.

255. In *Vit. Mos.* 2.290 the phrase τέλος τῶν ἱερῶν γραμμάτων is referred to the conclusion of the Pentateuch. But this τέλος is said 'to stand to the whole law-book as the head to the living creature' in a strange phrase referring to the miraculous fact that in this end 'Moses prophesied about his

own end (death)'. The conclusion of the Pentateuch is called τέλος (apparently because it was viewed by Philo as a glorious culmination) while Moses' 'end' (death) is called τελευτή (*ibid.*, 292). For 'death' the usual term is τελευτή (fifty-five times), or a phrase with the verb τελευτάω (100 times). Probably the same sense of τέλος as culmination is to be seen in *Dec.* 121. The phrases for designating the 'cessation' or 'abrogation' of laws never contain the word τέλος or cognates, but τοῖς ἔθνεσι λύειν (*Migr.* 90), τὰ ... νομοθετηθέντα λύωμεν (*ibid.*, 91), and ἀνέλωμεν ... νόμον (*ibid.*, 92).

256. Τοῦτ' ἐστι τὸ τέλος τῆς ὁδοῦ τῶν ἐπομένων λόγοις καὶ προστάξεσι νομίμοις ('This is the [very] way of those who follow the words and injunctions of the law'). In LCL, IV, pp. 212-13, the phrase το τέλος τῆς ὁδοῦ is simply translated 'the way'.

257. *Leg. All.* 3.45. 'For the end of the Word is Truth, which casts a beam more far-reaching than light. To this it is the earnest endeavour of the Word to attain'. Notice the similarity of syntactical construction with Rom 10.4: Τὸ γὰρ τέλος τοῦ λόγου ἀλήθειά ἐστιν ἡ φωτός [τέλος γὰρ νόμου Χριστός] τηλαυγεστέρα εἰς ἣν σπουδάζει ὁ λόγος ἐλθεῖν [εἰς δικαιοσύνην].

258. Unfortunately Karl Heinrich Rengstorf's *Complete Concordance to Flavius Josephus* (Leiden: Brill, 1979–) is not yet fully printed. Only vols. I, II, and III are available (up to the letter π).

259. *AJ* 9.73: 'You shall see these things *come to pass* in this way' (ὄψεις τοῦτο λαμβάνοντα τὸ τέλος).

260. *AJ* 4.125: ' ... and from all these prophecies having received the fulfillment (ἐξ ὧν ἁπάντων τέλος ὅμοιον ...) which he predicted ... '; *AJ* 10.35; *BJ* 4.387; *AJ* 2.73.

261. 'Even our women and dependants would tell you that piety (εὐσέβειαν) must be the τέλος (motive, goal, or purpose) of all our occupations in life' (*Ap.* 2.181).

262. Cf. *Ap.* 2.190, where the formula takes the enlarged form of ἀρχὴ καὶ μέσα καὶ τέλος in the phrase 'He [God] is the beginning, the middle, and the end of all things'. On this triple formula see Hans Kosmala, 'Anfang, Mitte, und Ende', *ASTI* 2 (1963), p. 108-11. Cf. *AJ* 1.7.

263. *AJ* 17.185; *BJ* 7.155; *AJ* 4.331.

264. Thackeray translates 'the issue rested with God' (LCL, III, p. 345).

265. 'The troops, thereupon, rushed to the quarter of the city called "Delta" where the Jews were concentrated, and executed their orders (ἐτέλουν τὰς ἐντολάς) (tr. Thackeray, LCL, II, p. 515).

266. The usual terms are νόμου κατάλυσις (*BJ* 4.154, 233) and forms of λύω and καταλύω with νόμος (15.41; 18.55; 19.301).

267. In *Ap.* 2.277 Josephus said ὁ οὖν νόμος ἡμῖν ἀθάνατος διαμένει ('our laws remain immortal'); in 2.184 he adds that 'the Law cannot be improved', etc.; cf. 1.60; 2.173-78.

268. The main part of the *Antiquities* and *Contra Apion* are an apology on

the value of Israel's laws. In *AJ* 1.25 (and *passim*) Josephus mentions his plans of writing a whole book on the reasons and purposes of such laws: 'Should any further desire to consider the resons for every article in our creed, he would find the inquiry profound and highly philosophical; that subject for the moment I defer, but, if God grants me time, I shall endeavour to write upon it after completing the present work'.

269. Eighteen in the Pauline writings, fourteen in the Gospels, one in James, four in 1 Peter, and three in the book of Revelation. Some lists count forty-one times, including a variant reading of Rev 1.8 according to manuscripts N* 1, 1828, 1854, 2065, 2073, etc.

270. Delling, 'τέλος', p. 54.

271. *Ibid.*, p. 56.

272. Even BAG, which stresses the terminal signification of τέλος in most of the occurrences, acknowledges that here the meaning may be 'forever, through all eternity', or, rather 'decisively, extremely, fully' (p. 812).

273. Du Plessis translates it by 'full scope of hope' (p. 129).

274. 'τέλος', p. 55.

275. The verb βεβαιόω has a juridical usage, meaning 'to give acquittal in the face of accusation, or to give legal warranty', which seems to favor the understanding of τέλος as expressing totality ('full acquittal', or 'full warranty'); cf. Moulton–Milligan (pp. 107-108), s.v., for abundant examples of this use in the papyri. See further H. Schlier, 'Βέβαιος', *TDNT*, I, pp. 600-603.

276. BDF (p. 112) translates Luke 18.5: 'in order that she may not gradually (present ὑπωπιάζῃ) wear me out completely by her continual coming (present!)'. This use of τέλος for expressing duration is also found in the LXX; cf. pp. 57 above.

277. For Heinrich Ebeling, the right translation would be 'völlig, auf immer' (*Griechische-Deutsches Wörterbuch zum Neuen Testament* [Hannover: Hannsche, 1913], p. 395). BDF, p. 88, translates 'he gave them the perfect love-token'.

278. This stereotyped formula appears also in some variant readings of Rev 1.8, added to the statement Ἐγώ εἰμι τὸ Ἄλφα καὶ τὸ Ὦ.

279. Parallel expressions, like A/Ω (1.8) and πρῶτος/ἔσχατος, do not always facilitate the interpretation of ἀρχὴ καὶ τέλος. On the monogram A/Ω, see N. Müller, 'A-Ω', *RE* (1896), I, pp. 1-12. In theological-speculative cosmology A/Ω as divine attribute did not indicate the whole extent of the alphabet from A to Ω but the 'head', i.e. the superior being (see Du Plessis, pp. 146-47); cf. Col 1.18; 2.10, 19; Eph 1.22; 4.15; 5.25, where Christ is called ἡ κεφαλὴ τῆς ἐκκλησίας. R.H. Charles, however, sees here a Greek rendering of a Hebrew expression, like 'Lord of Hosts' (*A Critical and Exegetical Commentary on the Revelation of St. John* [ICC; Edinburgh: T. & T. Clark, 1920; repr. 1959], II, p. 230); but in the light of Greek influence on Judaism Du Plessis's hypothesis is more probable (cf. pp. 147, 152). On

πρῶτος/ἔσχατος see Isa 44.6 (cf. 48.12), where it appears not as a formula of eternity, but as a statement of monotheism, meaning 'the One and Only' (*ibid.*, 151).

280. Against Delling, 'τέλος', p. 55 n. 45. If the terminal meaning were to prevail this expression would run counter to the idea of God's eternity.

281. Du Plessis, p. 122; cf. a similar constrction in Pl. *Lg.* 6.768 B.

282. Delling, 'τέλος', p. 56.

283. See BDF, p. 88; cf. pp. 85-86; A.T. Robertson, *A Grammar of the Greek New Testament in the Light of Historical Research* (Nashville: Broadman, 1934), pp. 486-88. See further Selwyn, p. 188.

284. F.C. Burkitt proposed ('On 1 Corinthians XV 26', *JTS* 17 [1915], pp. 384-85), an adverbial reading of τὸ τέλος. According to it, the passage would run: ' . . . But every one in his own order: Christ as first fruits, then those that are Christ's at his coming, then *finally* . . . when he has abolished all rule and all authority and power . . . death will be abolished as the last enemy.' For Burkitt τὸ τέλος in v. 24 'is definitely not "the End", since there are further events to come' (p. 384). Cf. K. Barth (*Die Auferstehung der Toten. Eine akademische Vorlesung über I Kor. 15* [Zollikon-Zürich: Evangelischer Verlag, 1953], p. 94): 'Then, *finally* . . . θάνατος will be destroyed'. Delling, however, rejects the adverbial interpretion ('τέλος', p. 55). J. Héring does not reject it but prefers the eschatological one ('Saint Paul a-t-il enseigné deux resurrections?', *RHPR* 12 [1932], p. 306). Some interpreters have proposed the translation of τέλος in 1 Cor 15.24 by 'the remnant' (A. Oepke, H. Bietenhard et al.). This translation has been first advocated by Johannes Weiss (*Commentary on First Corinthians* [Meyer's Commentary on the NT, 10th edn], p. 358) and H. Lietzmann (*An die Korinther I. II.* [Handbuch zum Neuen Testament, 9; 2nd edn; Tübingen: Mohr, 1931], p. 81) on the basis of their interpretation of τέλος in Isa 19.15 (LXX) and Arist. *GA* 1.18 (725 B 8). But these passages are not convincing and do not prove that τέλος might ever mean 'remnant'. In Isa 19.15 τέλος is used in the classical expression of totality (κεφαλὴ καὶ οὐρὰ καὶ ἀρχὴ καὶ τέλος), and in Aristotle, the phrase τὸ ἐκ τῆς τροφῆς γινόμενον τέλος referring to the animal σπέρμα does not denote in the context a mere *residuum* but rather the *supreme* secretion of the body. For Héring 'τέλος a donc bien ici le sens téléologique' (p. 305); see Cerfaux, *The Christian in the Theology of St. Paul*, pp. 208-209. For Schippers (p. 62) τέλος means here 'the conclusion of the eschatological events', 'the point of time when Christ hands over the kingdom to his Father'. Cf. W.G. Kümmel, *An die Korinther I-II* (Tübingen: Mohr, 1969), p. 193; for Davies, τὸ τέλος means here also 'the final consummation' (*Paul*, p. 299).

285. Twice in Rom 13.7 and once in Matt 17.25 (cf. v. 24, where τελέω means 'to pay').

286. Delling translates 'what concerns me must actually be carried out'

('τέλος', p. 54); and the LB 'everything written about me by the prophets will come true'.

287. In spite of the contextual evidence some commentators have stuck to their principle of absolute consistency, translating τέλος always by *end* (terminal-temporal) and have interpreted this verse as a premonition of Christ's life needing to come to a close (cf. especially T. Zahn and F. Hauck, *Der Brief des Paulus an die Römer* [Leipzig: A. Reichert, 1925], p. 475, and T. Zahn, *Das Evangelium des Lucas* [Leipzig: A. Reichert, 1913], p. 686). Du Plessis translates: 'What is written must be fulfilled in me, for the written word has *final authority*' (p. 137). He supports his interpretation by the fact that often τέλος ἔχειν is used as a stereotyped idiom to relate the validity or sanction of decrees or ordinances, and quotes A. *Pr.* 13: ἐντολὴ Διὸς ἔχει τέλος ('the order of Zeus has final authority'). A particularly interesting interpretation has been suggested by Günther Schwarz and Sankt Hulfe in 'Κυριε, ἰδου μαχαιραι ὧδε δυο", *BN* 8 (1979), p. 22. According to these authors the Aramaic word ספיא would have been used by Jesus for τέλος, and since that word meant both 'end' and 'sword' it would explain the perplexing reference to the μάχαιραι δύο made by the disciples in v. 38.

288. Dibelius, *A Commentary on the Epistle of James* (Philadelphia: Fortress, 1976), p. 247 n. 33; cf. BAG, p. 811; Schippers, p. 62; Robinson, p. 715.

289. So Augustine, *Ep.* 140.10; A. Bishoff, 'Τὸ τέλος κυρίου', *ZNW* 7 (1906), pp. 274-79.

290. See R.P. Gordon, 'KAI TO TELOS KYRIOU EIDETE (Jas 5.11)', *JTS* 26 (1975), pp. 19-95. Cf. M. Dibelius, *James*, pp. 246-48.

291. *James*, pp. 246-47. 'Perhaps the proper meaning of τέλος is "purpose" or "aim" in this genitive construction' (p. 246).

292. Against Delling, 'τέλος', p. 54.

293. Note the similarity of structure of this statement and Rom 10.4a.

294. H.A.W. Meyer argues that 'τὰ τέλη τῶν αἰώνων is identical with ἡ συντέλεια τῶν αἰώνων' (*Critical and Exegetical Handbook to the Epistles to the Corinthians* [New York: Funk & Wagnalls, 1884], p. 225); and Hans Conzelmann, *1 Corinthians* (Hermeneia; tr. J.W. Leitch; Philadelphia: Fortress, 1975), p. 168.

295. '1 Corinthians 10:11. A Suggestion', *ExpT* 67 (1955-56), pp. 246-47.

296. Delling, 'τέλος', p. 54. The notion of times having a specific 'aim' is biblical (Acts 17.26) and well attested in intertestamental literature; cf. Wis 8.8 and 1QpHab 7.13: 'All the times of God will come to their (appointed) measure'.

297. He translates this verse in the sense that 'the goal of faith in Christ is eschatological salvation' ('τέλος', p. 54).

298. Cf. Wis 3.19; 2 Macc 6.15.

299. Du Plessis argues that even in these cases 'it would be out of keeping

with the whole structure to consider τέλος as a termination of a blind alley' (p. 164), because τέλος is to be understood here in its primitive sense of 'turning point'. The eschatological end is the turning point between the rabbinic עולם הבא and עולם הזה as the hinge between the present and the future aeons or worlds (Str-B, VII, pp. 99-976).

300. Cf. Matt 13.39, 40, 49; 24.3; 28.20; Heb 9.26. A. Feuillet considers both terms absolutely synonymous ('Le sens du mot Parousie dans l'évangile de Matthieu. Comparaison entre Matth. 24 et Jac. 5,1-2', in *The Background of the New Testament and Its Eschatology: Studies in Honour of C.H. Dodd*, ed. W.D. Davies and D. Daube [Cambridge: University Press, 1956], p. 271). In spite of the similar use, it is obvious that συντέλεια, as a compound of τέλος and the preposition σύν, is strongly expressive of perfective activity, and therefore it is normal that it became the most common word for the eschatological end. The fact that this term is always used in the NT with αἰών emphasizes the notion of completion of an existing phase. Cf. 1 Cor 15.24 and 1 Pet 4.7.

301. See for example, C.K. Barrett, *A Commentary on the Second Epistle to the Corinthians* (HNTC; New York: Harper & Row, 1973), p. 119; J. Carmignac, 'II Corinthiens iii.6, 14 et le début de la formation du Nouveau Testament', *NTS* 24 (1977-78), pp. 384-86; F.J. Collange, *Enigmes de la deuxième Epitre de Paul aux Corinthiens. Etude exégétique de 2 Cor 2.14–7.4* (New York: Cambridge University Press, 1972), p. 97; J.D.G. Dunn, '2 Corinthians iii 17—"The Lord is the Spirit"', *JTS* 21 (1970), p. 311; C.J.A. Hickling, 'The Sequence of Thought in II Corinthians, Chapter Three', *NTS* 21 (1974-75), pp. 390-91; J. Jeremias, 'Μωϋσῆς', *TDNT*, IV, pp. 869-70; P.R. Jones, 'L'Apôtre Paul: un second Moïse pour la communauté de la Nouvelle Alliance: une étude sur l'autorité apostolique paulinienne', *FoiVie* 75 (1976), p. 49; E. Richard, 'Polemics, Old Testament, and Theology. A Study of II Cor. iii,1–iv,6', *RB* 80 (1981), pp. 354-59; Martin H. Scharlemann, 'Of Surpassing Splendor. An Exegetical Study of 2 Corinthians 3.4-18', *ConcJ* 4 (1978), pp. 108-17; H. Schlier, 'La notion de *doxa* dans l'histoire du salut d'après Saint Paul', in *Essais sur le Nouveau Testament* (Lectio Divina, 46; Paris: Editions du Cerf, 1968), pp. 379-91; H. Ulonska, 'Die Doxa des Mose. Zum Problem des Alten Testaments in 2 Kor. 3,1-16', *EvT* 26 (1966), p. 386; W.C. van Unnik, 'With Unveiled Face, an Exegesis of 2 Corinthians iii 12-18', *NovT* 6 (1963), pp. 153-69.

302. The participle καταργουμένου can be either masculine or neuter, while δόξα can only be feminine. If καταργουμένου had referred to δόξα it would have taken the feminine form, as it does in v. 7 (καταργουμένην).

303. First of all one wonders what the 'concealing of the end of the glory' has to do with the point of the passage. Why should the children of Israel particularly not look upon the end of that brightness, since—according to Exod 34.29-35—the very purpose of the veil was to relieve them from the

unbearable sight of that brightness? Moreover, if the glory was only to come to an end hundreds of years after Moses' time—as Hanson has so rightly observed—'there would have been no need for a veil during Moses' lifetime' (A.T. Hanson, 'The Midrash in II Corinthians 3: A Reconsideration', *JSNT* 9 [1980], p. 16). As W.C. Kaiser, Jr, has observed, 'τέλος here cannot mean the termination or full stop, for the Mosaic and Jewish administration was just beginning and there was no danger of the people gazing on it right up to the end of its duration' ('The Weightier and Lighter Matters of the Law: Moses, Jesus and Paul', in *Current Issues in Biblical and Patristic Interpretation. Studies in Honor of M.C. Tenney Presented by his Former Students*, ed. G.F. Hawthorne [Grand Rapids: Eerdmans, 1975], p. 190). It is also hard to accept that for Paul the aim of the veil was to hide the temporary nature of the old covenant because that would imply making Moses responsible for keeping the Israelites unaware of the fact that τοῦ καταργουμένου was destined to be superseded, and therefore, the Jews could not be blamed for 'keeping their eyes fixed on Moses' as their one and definitive Revelator, covenant-mediator, and law giver.

304. Héring translates τέλος as 'but', 'raison d'être', and 'signification profonde' (*La seconde épitre de Saint Paul aux Corinthiens* [Neuchâtel: Delachaux & Niestlé, 1958], p. 38).

305. See LSJ, p. 269; cf. Acts 1.10; 7.55.

306. Du Plessis, p. 141; he hesitates, however, between 'the crown' and 'the transience of a passing glory' (cf. p. 140).

307. G. Abbott-Smith, *A Manual Greek Lexicon of the New Testament* (Edinburgh: T. & T. Clark, 1937), p. 443. 'By metonymy, also of one who makes an end' (quoting Rom 10.4).

308. Cf. BAG, p. 811; Delling, 'τέλος', p. 56. As we have already seen, some (e.g. BAG, p. 812) interpret the expression εἰς/ἕως τέλος ('to the end') in Heb 6.11; Rev 2.26; 1 Cor 1.8; and 2 Cor 1.13 as 'to the end—until the parousia' rather than 'fully' or similar expressions of totality.

309. This phrase seems to translate a Hebraism, according to A. Plummer (*A Critical and Exegetical Commentary on the Gospel According to St. Luke* [ICC; Edinburgh: T. & T. Clark, 5th edn, 1956], p. 24).

310. For discussion of interpretations see J. van der Ploeg, 'L'exégèse de l'Ancien Testament dans l'épître aux Hébreux', *RB* 54 (1947), p. 217.

311. Cf. 7.3, 8, 17, 20, 24-28.

312. The NT concepts of eternity and time are somehow difficult to grasp. For O. Cullmann, *Christ and Time. The Primitive Christian Conception of Time and History* (tr. F. Filson; SCM, 1951), pp. 19-62, eternity in the NT is expressed in categories of time. For G. Delling, *Das Zeitverständnis des Neuen Testaments* (Gütersloh: Bertelsmann, 1940), p. 157, eternity and time are not metaphysical categories in the NT, and they are only contemplated from their religious and moral perspective (cf. pp. 106-21).

313. Xavier Jacques, *List of New Testament Words Sharing Common Elements. Supplement to Concordance or Dictionary* (Rome: Biblical Institute Press, 1969), pp. 108-109.

314. So Schippers, p. 62. But Delling prefers the translation 'to bring to perfection' ('τέλος', p. 59).

315. Luke 12.50; 18.31; 22.37; John 19.28, 30; Acts 13.29; Rev 10.7; 11.7; 17.17.

316. The stereotyped formula καὶ ἐγένετο ὅτε ἐτέλεσεν ὁ Ἰησοῦς τοὺς λόγους τούτους is used in Matt for concluding five sermon complexes. On redactional conclusions based on this formula, see K. Stendahl, 'The School of St. Matthew', *ASNU* 30 (1954), pp. 24-27.

317. On the debated meaning of this verse, see E. Bammel, 'Mt 10.23', *ST* 15 (1961), p. 92.

318. This expression is found only in Matthew (13.39, 40, 49; 24.3; 28.20). See Feuillet, 'Le sens du mot Parousie dans l'Evangile de Matthieu', pp. 269-72.

319. See Delling, 'συντέλεια', *TDNT*, VIII, pp. 64-66.

320. See Delling, 'τελείωσις', *TDNT*, VIII, pp. 84-86.

321. Cf. the use of τέλος with τὴν ἐντολήν in Hes. 5.2.4.; and with τὰς ἐντολάς in Jos. *BJ* 2.495; cf. BAG, p. 811.

322. Rom 6.21, 22; Rom 10.4; 1 Cor 10.11; 2 Cor 3.13; 11.15; Phil 3.19; 1 Tim 1.5; Heb 6.8; Jas 5.11; 1 Pet 1.9; 4.7; 4.17. It is noteworthy that nine out of that thirteen instances are found in Pauline writings.

323. Cf. 1 Cor 10.11; 2 Cor 11.15; Phil 3.19; Heb 6.8; 1 Pet 4.7, 17. Robinson had already observed that 'Τέλος with genitive of person or thing means the end, the final lot, the ultimate end' (p. 715).

324. Cf. a parallel construction in Rom 13.10: πλήρωμα οὖν νόμου ἡ ἀγάπη.

325. So Collange gives to τέλος the meaning of 'évanouissement' ('vanishing') in 2 Cor 3.13 arguing that 'c'est aussi le sens général des 13 emplois pauliniens du terme' (p. 96 n. 3).

326. Luz, *Geschichtsverständnis Paulus*, p. 140.

327. *The Epistle to the Romans* (NICNT; Grand Rapids: Eerdmans, 1959), II, p. 49, quoting Rom 6.21; 1 Cor 1.8; 15.24; 2 Cor 1.12 (should be 1.13); 3.13; 11.15; Phil 3.19. For discussion, see Toews, p. 239.

328. Some scholars interpret all these texts (except 1 Tim 1.5) temporarily. For a defence of a teleological interpretation of Rom 6.21, 22 and 2 Cor 3.13, see Bartsch, 'Paul's Letter to the Romans', p. 39; cf. Bring, 'Gerechtigkeit Gottes', p. 48; and Peter von der Osten-Sacken, *Römer 8 als Beispeild paulinischer Soteriologie* (Göttingen: Vandenhoeck & Ruprecht, 1975), p. 262.

329. With Toews, pp. 239-40.

1. Käsemann, *Romans*, p. 253, says that 'probably no larger portion of Paul's writings can be said to have had a history of exposition which is more a suffering course of misunderstanding, acts of violence, and experimentation with shifting methods and themes'. Cf. H.E. Weber, *Das Problem der Heilsgeschichte nach Römer 9–11* (Leipzig: A. Deichert, 1911), pp. 10-12.

2. W.S. Campbell, 'Christ the End of the Law', p. 73.

3. As a working hypothesis, the 'law statements' of the passage are taken at their face value: Rather than working on the assumption that Paul was guilty of a 'fundamental misapprehension' of Judaism in its teachings about the law (cf. Schoeps, *Paul*, pp. 213-18), it seems hermeneutically preferable to assume that he understood the doctrine of the law both in Judaism and in Christianity at least as well as do his modern critics.

4. One γάρ attaches it to what precedes (Τέλος γάρ νόμου . . . , v. 4) and another γάρ attaches it to what follows (Μωϋσῆς γάρ γράφει . . . , v. 5).

5. For discussion and bibliography, see S. Lyonnet, 'Note sur le plan de l'épître aux Romains', *RSR* 39 (1951-52), pp. 301-16; J. Dupont, 'Le problème de la structure littéraire de l'épître aux Romains', *RB* 62 (1955), pp. 365-97. Today it is generally agreed that 1.1-17 includes the epistolary opening formula and the theological theses of the epistle; that the main parts of Romans are 1.18–8.39, 9.1–11.36, and 12.1–15.13; and that 15.14 onward is a continuation of 1.8-15 on Paul's personal relations with the Roman church. It is also agreed that 1.18–8.39 contains two main divisions, but there is no consensus as to where the break between the two divisions comes. See further in Cranfield, *Romans*, I, p. 27.

6. The break marked by the 'therefore' (οὖν) in 12.1 is so evident that the epistle has been traditionally divided into two main parts: (1) the 'theological' (chs. 1–11) and (2) the 'ethical' (chs. 12–16). See Sanday–Headlam, *Romans*, pp. xlvii-l.

7. A three-part division is accepted today by the majority of commentators. It is also agreed that these parts deal, respectively: (1) with justification by faith (chs. 1–8); (2) with the fate of Israel (chs. 9–11); and (3) with ethical teachings (chs. 12–16). See further W.G. Kümmel, *Introduction to the New Testament* (17th edn; Nashville: Abingdon, 1975), pp. 306-307. For a detailed study of the plan of Romans, according to a threefold division, see L. Ramaroson, 'Un "nouveau plan" de Rom 1.16–11.36', *NRT* 94 (1972), pp. 943-58; and especially Philippe Rolland, '"Il est notre justice, notre vie, notre salut". L'ordonnance des thèmes majeurs de l'épître aux Romains', *Bib* 56 (1975), pp. 394-404.

8. A. Nygren divided Romans into four main parts: (1) 'He who through faith is righteous' (chs. 1–4); (2) 'He who through faith is righteous shall live' (chs. 5–8); (3) 'The righteousness of faith is not against the promise of God'

(chs. 9–11); (4) 'The life of him who through faith is righteous' (chs. 12–15) (pp. i-v). The same plan with slightly different titles is followed by Cranfield, *Romans*, I, pp. 28-29. Käsemann offers a fivefold division (*Romans*, pp. ix-xi).

9. The unity of chs. 9–11 is so evident that some scholars have considered this section as an independent literary unit, included later in the epistle as an *addendum* with no connection with the rest of Romans (so Dodd, *Romans*, pp. 163-64); see further W.G. Kümmel, 'Die Probleme von Römer 9–11 in der gegenwärtigen Forschungslage', in *Israelfrage*, pp. 13-56.

10. See K.P. Donfried (ed.), *The Romans Debate* (Minneapolis: Augsburg, 1977); H. Gamble, *The Textual History of the Letter to the Romans* (Studies and Documents, 43; Grand Rapids: Eerdmans, 1977), pp. 132-37; J.W. Drane, 'Why Did Paul Write Romans?', in *Pauline Studies. Essays Presented to Professor F.F. Bruce On His 70th Birthday*, ed. D.A. Hagner and M.J. Harris (Grand Rapids: Eerdmans, 1980), pp. 208-27; W.S. Campbell, 'The Romans Debate', *JSNT* 10 (1981), pp. 19-28; F.F. Bruce, 'The Romans Debate—Continued', *BJRL* 64 (1982), pp. 334-59.

11. For discussion and survey of positions, see Mary Ann Getty, 'Structure and Interpretation of Romans 9–11. State of the Question' (Unpublished dissertation presented for the degree of Licentiate in Theology, Catholic University of Louvain, 1971); 'Christ Is the End of the Law', pp. 7-127; and R.B. Corley, 'The Significance of Romans 9–11: A Study in Pauline Theology' (Th.D. dissertation, Southwestern Baptist Theological Seminary, 1975): cf. K.H. Rengstorf, 'Das Ölbaum-Gleichnis in Röm ii,16ff.', in *Donum Gentilicium: New Testament Studies in Honour of David Daube*, ed. by E. Bammel, C.K. Barrett and W.D. Davies (Oxford University Press, 1978), pp. 127-64.

12. With Donfried, 'False Presuppositions in the Study of Romans', in *The Romans Debate*, pp. 122-23; Beker, pp. 66, 74; against K. Barth, *Römerbrief*, p. 5; Nygren, p. 7. Cf. G. Bornkamm, 'The Letter to the Romans as Paul's Last Will and Testament', in *The Romans Debate*, pp. 17-31; cf. A. Wikenhauser, *New Testament Introduction* (tr. J. Cunningham; New York: Herder & Herder, 1958), p. 406.

13. For discussion on Paul's logical inconsistency, see R. Bultmann, 'History and Eschatology in the New Testament', *NTS* 1 (1954), p. 12; *Theology of the NT*, I, pp. 329-30; Minear, *The Obedience of Faith: The Purposes of Paul in the Epistle to the Romans* (London: SCM, 1971), p. 81; H. Räisänen, 'Paul's Theological Difficulties with the Law', pp. 301-20; cf. Davies, *Paul*, pp. 75-76; Dodd, *Romans*, pp. 43, 183; H.H. Graham, 'Continuity and Discontinuity in the Thought of Paul', *ATR* 38 (1956), pp. 137-46.

14. So Michel, p. 210: 'der jüdische Gegner'; Sanday–Headlam, p. 257: 'a definite opponent, a typical Jew'; Dodd, p. 155: 'his Pharisaic opponents'.

15. See J.H. Ropes, 'The Epistle to the Romans and Jewish Christianity',

in *Studies in Early Christianity*, ed. S.J. Case (New York, London: The Century Co., 1928), pp. 360-61.

16. Stendahl, 'Foreword', to Munck, *Christ and Israel*, p. ix.

17. See 2.1-11, 17-29; 3.1-8, 9-20; 4.1; 7.1, 4-6). Cf. Suggs, 'The Word is Near', p. 298. Nowhere does Paul exalt his 'kinsmen' (9.1-5; 10.1; 11.15-21, 26-28), the law, and Judaism (3.31; 6.15; 7.7, 12, 16; 8.3-4; 9.31–10.4; etc.), more than in Romans.

18. On the problem of the composition of the Roman church, see W. Schmithals, *Der Römerbrief als historisches Problem* (Gütersloh: Gütersloher Verlagshaus Mohn, 1975), pp. 10-94, but particularly pp. 83-91. Beker explains the great familiarity of the addressees of Romans with Jewish questions by supposing that many of the Gentile Christians had been 'God-fearers' or proselytes who had recently abandoned the synagogue (p. 76). Cf. Romano Penna, 'Les Juifs à Rome au temps de l'apôtre Paul', *NTS* 28 (1982), pp. 321-47. It is worthy of notice that among the twenty-six persons to whom Paul sends greetings in 16.3-16 there are several whom Paul calls his 'kinsmen' (οἱ συγγενεῖς μου; cf. vv. 7, 11, and 21). One may well suppose that at least these were Jews. Cf. Minear, *The Obedience of Faith*, pp. 1-35.

19. Beker, pp. 71-72; cf. Ropes, p. 361.

20. Only by discarding ch. 16 as spurious can one pretend that Paul was ignorant of the situation, composition, and problems of the church of Rome. But if ch. 16 is taken seriously—and there are thus far no sufficiently convincing reasons for rejecting its authenticity—one has to accept that Paul had in Rome enough friends, disciples, and acquaintances to keep him informed of the situation there. See K.P. Donfried, 'A Short Note on Romans 16', in *The Romans Debate*, pp. 50-60. Cf. Halvor Moxnes, *Theology in Conflict. Studies in Paul's Understanding of God in Romans* (Leiden: Brill, 1980), p. 34.

21. Unless Romans is understood as the beginning of Paul's work in Rome (cf. 15.15-18). See further H.W. Bartsch, 'The Historical Situation of Romans', *Encounter* 33 (1972), pp. 329-39.

22. Wolfgang Wiefel argues that this anti-Jewish attitude might have been the effect of the so-called edict of Claudius of c. AD 49 and the wave of anti-Semitism it caused in the city of Rome. See 'The Jewish Community in Ancient Rome and the Origins of Roman Christianity', in *The Romans Debate*, pp. 100-19; cf. C. Muller-Duvernoy, 'L'Apôtre Paul et le problème juif', *Judaica* 15 (1959), pp. 65-91; Marxsen, *Introduction to the NT*, pp. 95-104; Gamble, pp. 136-57.

23. Getty, 'Christ is the End of the Law', pp. 25-26.

24. This intriguing question has fascinated recent scholarship: Bruce, basing his argument on the great importance of the Roman church, says that 'if the Jerusalem leaders could be given to understand (tactfully) that Rome was being kept in the picture, this might have influenced their reception of Paul and his Gentile friends' ('The Romans Debate', p. 357); Ernst Fuchs

describes Romans as a 'hidden letter to Jerusalem' in which Paul rehearses
before the Roman church the impending dialogue with Jerusalem (*Hermeneutik*
[Bad Cannstatt: R. Müllerschön, 1958], p. 191); for M.J. Suggs, Romans 'is a
brief drawn up by Paul in anticipation of the renewed necessity of defending
his gospel in Jerusalem' on the occasion of the collection ("The Word Is Near
You": Rom 10.6-10', in *Christian History and Interpretation*, ed. W.R.
Farmer, et al. [Cambridge: University Press, 1967], p. 295); J. Jervell says
that 'Paul is writing Romans mainly for himself, and, thereby, on behalf of
the entire Gentile Christian churches which he is hoping to present to God
as a sacrifice' ('The Letter to Jerusalem', *The Romans Debate*, p. 74; cf.
pp. 61-74). See further Antonio Ambrosiano, 'La "colletta paolina" in una
recente interpretazione', *AnBib* 17-18 (1963), II, pp. 591-600.

25. It has been argued that for Paul the acceptance by the Jewish sector of
the church of the collection offered by Gentile congregations had a great
eschatological and ecclesiological significance. It represented the consummation of his apostolic mission, a sign of the fulfillment of God's design
concerning the eschatological unity of Jews and Gentiles in the Christian
church. See O. Cullmann, *Christ and Time: The Primitive Christian
Conception of Time and History* (3rd edn rev.; tr. F.V. Filson; London: SCM,
1962), p. 162; and *Salvation in History* (tr. S.G. Sowers; New York: Harper
& Row, 1967), pp. 248-68; Munck stresses the *heilsgeschichtlich* role of this
event in *Christ and Israel*, pp. 68, 122-23, and in *Paul and the Salvation of
Mankind*, p. 40. Since the conversion of the Gentiles would finally bring
about the salvation of Israel, and this was to be the supreme event of
Heilsgeschichte, Munck argues that for Paul the collection was an eschatolo-
gical sign: the fact that Gentiles of several countries traveled with him to
Jerusalem bringing their gifts was the fulfillment of Isa 2.2-4 and Mic 4.1-4
(*Christ and Israel*, pp. 11-12). See further K.F. Nickle, *The Collection: A
Study in Paul's Strategy* (Studies in Biblical Theology, 48; Naperville: A.R.
Allenson, 1966), pp. 129-42.

26. Rom 11 and 15 seem to indicate that Paul felt the whole collection
enterprise endangered by Jewish-Gentile tensions. He knew that the success
of his visit to Jerusalem depended on whether he could define his position
vis-à-vis Israel and the law in such a way that the unity symbolized by the
offering would be protected from Gentile animosities and Jewish suspicions.
This probably explains why the question of the relation between Jews and
Gentiles in God's plan of salvation and in God's community—which is
precisely the theme of chs. 9–11—is so central in Romans. In the interest of
this cause Paul wrote this epistle, a document intended to be—in the words
of Suggs—'a review of areas of prior dissension and a projection of solutions
to possible future conflicts' (pp. 311-12). See further Antionio Ambrosiano,
'La "colletta paolina" in una recente interpretazione', pp. 591-600.

27. Nils Alstrup Dahl says that 'The inner unity of Paul's mission and
theology is nowhere more obvious than in Rom 9–11' ('The Missionary

Theology in the Epistle to the Romans', in *Studies in Paul* [Minneapolis: Augsburg, 1977], p. 86); cf. pp. 70-94; see also Etienne Trocmé, 'L'Epître aux Romains et la méthode missionaire de l'apôtre Paul', *NTS* 7 (1961), pp. 148-53; cf. Kümmel, *Introduction to the NT*, pp. 220-22; Michel, *Römer*, p. 4.

28. On the conciliatory character of Romans, see Bartsch, 'The Historical Situation of Romans', pp. 329-39; 'Die Empfänger des Römerbriefes', *ST* 25 (1972), pp. 81-89; cf. Minear, *Obedience of Faith*, pp. 8-20; D.W.B. Robinson, 'The Salvation of Israel in Rom 9–11', *RTR* 26 (1967), pp. 81-96.

29. See Beker, *Paul*, pp. 87-89. Arguing on the basis of the historical fact that the gospel was preached 'to the Jew first' (Rom 1.1-5, 16-17; 2.9-10; 3.9; 3.21-31; 10.12), Paul shows to the church in Rom 9–11 its responsibility vis-à-vis Israel, for not only had God not rejected the Jews (11.1) nor ever will reject them (11.29), but their entrance within the church depends somehow on the attitude of (Gentile) Christians towards them (11.11-15).

30. O. Michel, *Römer*, p. 192: 'Redet als *Jude* über Gottes Handeln aus Israel' (emphasis his).

31. J.M. Osterreicher, 'Israel's Misstep and Her Rise', *AnBib* 17-18 (1963), pp. 318.

32. G. Eichholz, *Die Theologie des Paulus im Umriss* (Neukirchen: Neukirchener Verlag, 1972), p. 296.

33. See Béda Rigaux, *The Letter of St. Paul: Modern Studies* (tr. S. Yonick; Chicago: Franciscan Herald Press, 1968), pp. 3-31; W.G. Kümmel, *The New Testament: The History of the Investigation of its Problems* (tr. S. McLean Gilmour and H.C. Kee; Nashville: Abingdon, 1972), pp. 162-84; and especially R.B. Corley, 'The Significance of Romans 9–11: A Study in Pauline Theology', pp. 1-63; and Getty, 'Christ the End of the Law', pp. 7-127; cf. Beker, *Paul*, pp. 64-74; and Käsemann, *Romans*, pp. 253-56.

34. The view of Augustine prevailed until the Reformation (see Wiles, *The Divine Apostle*, pp. 97-98); Calvin read into it the doctrine of double predestination (*Institutes*, 3.23.7 [LCC, 21.955]); and K. Barth the doctrine of eternal *Erwählung* (*Dogmatik*, II/2, pp. 101-214). The predestinarian interpretation of Rom 9–11 has been strongly challenged by Munck in *Christ and Israel*, pp. 75-79. For further discussion and bibliography, see also Cranfield, *Romans*, II, pp. 445-51, and Käsemann, *Romans*, pp. 253-57.

35. So for Schmithals (*Der Römerbrief als historisches Problem*, p. 210) Rom 9–11 is 'an appendix or an afterthought'; so Sanday and Headlam, p. 225; for Dodd, it is a separate treatise (*Romans*, p. 148); for F.W. Beare (*St. Paul and His Letters* [New York: Abingdon, 1962], it is 'a kind of supplement' which does not form 'an integral part of the main argument', and where 'we cannot feel that the apostle is at his best'; and for R. Bultmann, it is just the fruit of Paul's 'speculative fantasy' (*Theology of the NT*, II, p. 132). Stendahl, in the 'Foreword' to Munck, *Christ and Israel*, p. viii, deplores this general attitude.

36. F.C. Baur considered Rom 9–11 as 'the most radical and thorough-going refutation of Judaism' and a 'systematische Streitschriftgegen des Judenchristentum' (*Paul: The Apostle of Jesus Christ* [tr. E. Zeller; London: Williams and Norgate, 1873], I, p. 349); for survey of similar positions see Corley, pp. 27-37.

37. See the full survey of positions in Getty, 'Structure and Interpretation of Romans 9–11. State of the Question', pp. 1-73. Cf. B. Noack, 'Current and Backwater in the Epistle to the Romans', *ST* 19 (1965), pp. 155-66. W.S. Campbell speaks of 'a Scandinavian interest' in Rom 9–11 ('Romans III as a Key to the Structure and Thought of the Letter', *NovT* 23 [1981], p. 23) represented among others by K. Stendahl, *Paul among Jews and Gentiles and Other Essays* (Philadelphia: Fortress, 1976), and Munck, *Paul and the Salvation of Mankind*; *Christ and Israel*, etc.

38. Campbell, 'Romans III', p. 27. At the two extreme positions on the importance of Rom 9–11, we have, supporting the centrality of this section, Munck, *Paul and the Salvation of Mankind*, pp. 36-86; and arguing that chs. 9–11 is a secondary theme, Dodd, *Romans*, pp. xxx-xxxi, 148-50.

39. K. Stendahl, 'The Apostle Paul and the Introspective Conscience of the West', *HTR* 56 (1963), p. 205. A. Maillot, 'Essai sur les citations vétéro-testamentaires contenues dans Romains 9 à 11, ou Comment se sevir de la Torah pour montrer que le "Christ est la fin de la Torah"', *ETR* 57 (1982), p. 56; Pierre Benoit calls this section 'l'aboutissement, le sommet, la conclusion de tout ce qui précède' ('Conclusion par mode de synthèse', in *Israelfrage*, p. 218). F.C. Baur regarded these chapters as 'the kernel out of which the entire letter emerged' (*Paul: His Life and Works* [tr. A. Menzies; Theological Translation Fund Library, 1876], p. 315); and Leenhardt called them 'the touchstone of interpretation for Romans' (*Romans*, pp. 19-23).

40. L. Goppelt, *Jesus, Paul and Judaism* (New York: Nelson & Son, 1964), p. 153.

41. K.H. Rengstorf, quoted in H.L. Ellison, *The Mystery of Israel* (Grand Rapids: Eerdmans, 1966), p. 11.

42. See J. Dupont, W. Vischer, F. Smyth-Florentin, S. Frutiger, J.-P. Gabos, 'Diversité d'options exégétiques et théologiques concernant Israel', *FoiVie* 66/5 (1967), pp. 55-84; Wilhelm Vischer, 'Le mystère d'Israel. Une exégèse des chapîtres IX, X, XI de l'épître aux Romains', *FoiVie* 6 (1965), pp. 421-87; A.T. Davies, *Anti-Semitism and the Christian Mind* (New York: Herder and Herder, 1969), p. 149; J. Parkes, *The Foundation of Judaism and Christianity* (London: Vallentine Mitchell, 1960), pp. 195-206; A.R. Eckard, *Elder and Younger Brothers: The Encounter of Jews and Christians* (New York: C. Scribner's Sons, 1967), pp. 66-70; R.R. Ruether, *Faith and Fratricide. The Theological Roots of Anti-Semitism* (New York: Seabury, 1974), pp. 137-65; L. De Lorenzi (ed.), *Die Israelfrage nach Röm 9–11* (Rome: St. Paul Abbey, 1977), *passim*.

43. W.D. Davies, *The Gospel and the Land* (Berkeley: California University Press, 1974), p. 171; cf. Käsemann, *Romans*, p. 256. Out of the twelve occurrences of the word 'people' (λαός) in the Pauline epistles eight appear in the book of Romans, and six of them are used in Rom 9–11 (9.25-26; 10.21, 11.1-2); cf. *Computer Konkordanz zum Novum Testamentum Graece*, ed. H. Bachmann and W.A. Slaby (Berlin: W. de Gruyter, 1980), pp. 1108-11.

44. Munck rightly says that 'as long as Rom 9–11 is regarded as an isolated point of view peculiar to Paul, out of touch with the main line of Christian thought, it is difficult to understand the separate parts of the whole. But if we regard the questions that Paul answers, and the problems that he takes up and discusses, as burning questions among Christians of Jewish as well as of Gentile origin, the line of thought becomes clearer . . . ' (*Paul and the Salvation of Mankind*, p. 44).

45. Noack, p. 165.

46. Moxnes argues that the statements such as 'God shows no partiality' (2.7-11), 'Let God be true' (3.1-8), etc., show that '*the question raised is nothing less than the question of the credibility of God*' (p. 38, emphasis his), in the sense that either the OT is a false witness or else that God has not been faithful to his word (cf. 2.17-29; 3.1-2; 9.4-6); cf. L. Goppelt, *Christentum und Judentum im ersten und zweiten Jahrhundert: Ein Aufriss der Urgeschichte der Kirche* (Gütersloh: C. Bertelsmann, 1954), p. 113; Cranfield, *Romans*, pp. 176-77; Nygren, p. 354; for G. Schrenk, however, Rom 9–11 is an apologetic explaining Paul's missionary failure among Jews (*Die Weissagung über Israel im Neuen Testament* [Zürich: Gotthelf, 1951], p. 25).

47. Out of only seven occurences of ἐκλογή in the NT, five are used by Paul, and four of them in Rom 9–11 (9.11; 11.5, 7, 28); cf. *Computer Konkordanz*, p. 591.

48. C. Gore, 'The Argument of Romans ix–xi', *Studia Biblica et Ecclesiatica. Essays in Biblical and Patristic Criticism*, ed. S.R. Driver (Oxford: Clarendon Press, 1891). Cf. M. Zerwick, 'Drama populi Israeli secundum Rom 9–11', *VD* 46 (1968), pp. 321-38.

49. In doing this Paul seems to put Israel's rejection of Christ on a similar level to the Gentiles' rejection of God in the days of their disobedience (Rom 1.18-32). Cf. Gore, p. 43; Rhyne, p. 98. See further Fischer, 'Dissent within a Religious Community', pp. 105-10.

50. C. Senft, 'L'élection d'Israel et la justification', in *L'Evangile hier et aujourd'hui. Mélanges offerts à Franz-J. Leenhardt* (Geneva: Labor et Fides, 1968), pp. 131-42. Cf. Dahl, 'The Doctrine of Justification', p. 87.

51. For Käsemann Rom 9–11 shows that 'Israel too falls under the justification of the ungodly' ('Justification and Salvation History in the Epistle to the Romans', in *Perspectives on Paul*, p. 75); cf. C. Müller, *Gottes Gerechtigkeit und Gottes Volk. Eine Untersuchung zu Römer 9–11* (Göttingen: Vandenhoeck & Ruprecht, 1964), pp. 93-99. For an emphatic defense of the

connection between Rom 9–11 and the theme of the epistle see Bruce, *Romans*, pp. 181-84.

52. On the social and corporate dimensions of 'the righteousness of God' in Rom 9–11, see N.A. Dahl, 'The Doctrine of Justification, Its Social Function and Implication', in *Studies in Paul*, pp. 95-120; Stendahl, *Paul among Jews and Gentiles*, pp. 26-29. Cf. P. Minear, *The Obedience of Faith. The Purposes of Paul in the Epistle to the Romans* (London: SCM, 1971), pp. 97, 90; M. Barth, 'Jews and Gentiles. The Social Character of Justification in Paul', *JES* 5 (1968), pp. 241-67; P. Bonnard, 'La justice de Dieu et l'histoire (selon les épîtres pauliniennes)', *Cahiers de la RTP* 3 (1980), pp. 169-76. Moxnes calls attention to the fact that every time that Paul deals with the question of 'the righteousness' of God, he shows its implications for Israel and the Gentiles (p. 33). Cf. Gaston, 'Paul and Torah', pp. 52, 69; Howard, 'Christ the End of the Law', p. 335; Leenhardt, *Romains*, p. 10; Munck, *Paul and the Salvation of Mankind*, pp. 247-81; Oesterreicher, p. 320; P. Stuhlmacher, *Gerechtigkeit Gottes bei Paulus* (Göttingen: Vandenhoeck & Ruprecht, 1965), pp. 91-99; Ziesler, *The Meaning of Righteousness in Paul*, pp. 164-71. For emphasis on individual salvation, see E. Dinkler, 'The Historical and Eschatological Israel in Romans, chapters 9–11. A Contribution to the Problem of Predestination and Individual Responsibility', *JR* 36 (1956), pp. 123-24; and Luz, *Geschichtsverständnis des Paulus*, pp. 294-95, 395-97. For discussion see H. Conzelmann, *Outline*, pp. 248-52; C. Plag, *Israels Wege zum Heil: Eine Untersuchung zu Römer 9 bis 11* (Stuttgart: Calwer, 1969), pp. 41-48.

53. See X. Léon-Dufour, 'Juif et gentil selon Romains 1–11', *Studiorum Paulinorum Congressus*, II, pp. 309-15.

54. Dahl, 'The Doctrine of Justification', p. 119.

55. See C. Muller-Duvernoy, 'L'apôtre Paul et le problème juif', *Judaica* 15 (1959), pp. 65-91; H. Schlier, 'La notion paulinienne de la Parole de Dieu', in *Littérature et théologie pauliniennes*, ed. A. Descamps et al. (Louvain: Desclée de Brouwer, 1960), pp. 127-41.

56. Campbell, pp. 37-38.

57. Beker, p. 73; cf. R. Jewett, *Paul's Anthropological Terms: A Study of Their Use in Conflict Settings* (Leiden: Brill, 1971), pp. 41-48.

58. See Munck, *Christ and Israel*, pp. 8, 14; *Paul and the Salvation of Mankind*, pp. 148-50.

59. As J.J. Collins says: 'Suddenly the reader comes upon something entirely unexpected, an abrupt digression of a confusing tangent' ('Chiasmus: The "ABA" Pattern and the Text of Paul', *AnBib* 17-18 (1963), II, p. 575). Paul has the tendency—extremely common in Jewish literature—to digress at a word. See further J.A. Fischer, 'Pauline Literary Forms and Thought Patterns', *CBQ* 39 (1977), pp. 209-23.

60. M.-J. Lagrange, *L'évangile de Jésus-Christ* (Paris: Gabalda, 1928), p. 169.

61. See J. Nelis, 'Les antithèses littéraires dans les épîtres de saint Paul', *NRT* 70 (1948), pp. 36-87.

62. See Osterreicher, pp. 319-20.

63. Fischer, 'Dissent within a Religious Community', p. 106.

64. See Feuillet, 'Les attaches bibliques des antithèses pauliniennes dans la première partie de l'épître aux Romains (1–8)', in *Mélanges Bibliques en Hommage au R.R. Béda Rigaux*, ed. A. Descamps (Gembloux: Duculot, 1970), p. 524. For other examples of parallelism see 1.24-26, 28; 2.1-2, 3-4, 5-11; 3.22-23, 24-26; 6.5-11; 7.14-20; 8.5-17; 14.1-12.

65. Collins, 'Chiasmus', p. 579.

66. Osterreicher p. 320. Paul exposes his arguments in successive retakings—*à plusieures reprises*—i.e. in ever new ways and from different perspectives. Torti defines, quite accurately, this approach as 'graduale e ciclico insieme' (p. 20). Some of the more obvious 'retakings' in our section are the following: the permanence of election (9.4-5, 11-21 = 11.28-29); the partiality of Israel's failure (9.6-8 = 11.25); the mercy of God, who has the power and the right to reject, but still calls (9.17-22 = 10.21 = 11.22-23); the paradoxical character of Israel's failure (9.25-26 = 9.30-33 = 11.16-24); the permanence of a remnant (9.26 = 11.16); Israel's rejection of Christ (9.31-33 = 11.7-10); Paul's concern for the salvation of his kinsmen (9.1-3 = 10.1 = 11.14); salvation by grace, not by merits (10.5-12 = 11.6); the role of Gentiles in the salvation of Israel (10.19 = 11.11-14), etc. (see further Rolland, *Romains*, p. 6).

67. See example on p. 96 below.

68. 'Thus', says Gore, 'St. Paul, less than almost any other author, admits of being used as a repertory of detached texts' (p. 37).

69. Collins, 'Chiasmus', p. 579.

70. For the chiastic structure of Rom 9–11, see pp. 94-95 below.

71. A. Sabatier (*The Apostle Paul: A Sketch of the Development of His Doctrine* [tr. A.M. Hellier; London: Hodder & Stoughton, 1906], pp. 89-90) ranks Paul with the great dialecticians of all time—with Plato, Augustine, Calvin, and Hegel.

72. Cf. 5.9-21 for a whole series of examples. This device, common in the Stoic-Cynic diatribe, is also the rabbinic procedure of *qal wahomer* (for further discussion and examples, see Str-B, III, pp. 223-26).

73. Cf. Feuillet, 'Le plan salvifique', pp. 344-45.

74. See R. Scroggs, 'Paul as Rhetorician: Two Homilies in Rom 1–11', in *Jews, Greeks and Christians. Essays in Honor of W.D. Davies*, ed. K. Hamerton-Kelly and R. Scroggs (Leiden: Brill, 1976), pp. 271-98. Cf. Dahl, 'The Future of Israel', p. 140.

75. On this question contemporary scholarship has been heavily dependent on R. Bultmann, *Der Stil der paulinische Predigt und die kynisch-stoische Diatribe* (FRLANT, 13; Göttingen, 1910). See the enlightening criticism of E.A. Judge, 'St. Paul and Classical Society', *JAC* 15 (1972), p. 33; and

especially *Diatribe in Ancient Rhetorical Theory* (The Center for Hermeneutical Studies in Hellenistic and Modern Culture; Protocol series, 22; Berkeley, 1976); and S.K. Stowers, *The Diatribe and Paul's Letter to the Romans* (SBL Dissertation Series, 57; Chico: Scholars Press, 1981). Stowers says that there must be a reason for Paul's use of the diatribe in Romans, for in his other writings the diatribe style occurs only in 1 Cor 15.35 and Gal 2.17; 3.21; however in Romans it occurs at least fifteen times (3.1, 3, 5, 9, 27, 31; 4.1-2; 6.1, 15; 7.7, 13; 9.14, 19; 11.1, 19). Stowers's thesis is that Paul presents himself in Romans as a teacher. He addressed this letter to his 'school' to serve as a kind of prolepsis to his future teaching in Rome (p. 182). The former 'students' of Paul now in Rome are the core of his 'school' (p. 183). This understanding—says Stowers—helps to explain, on the one hand, why the letter is something like a theological treatise, and, on the other hand, why such a treatise would be sent to Rome (p. 181).

76. Paul consistently uses abrupt questions as transitional devices at major divisions of the passage: τί οὖν ἐροῦμεν . . . (9.14, 33); Ἐρεῖς μοι οὖν, τί . . . (9.19); πῶς οὖν . . . (10.14); Λέγω οὖν . . . (11.1, 11), accompanied sometimes by the Pauline deprecation μὴ γένοιτο (9.14; 11.1, 11). Cf. C.F.D. Moule, *An Idiom Book of New Testament Greek* (Cambridge: University Press, 1953), p. 163. On Paul's rhetoric devices, see BDF, pp. 252-63.

77. Collins states that 'the apparent disorder of the thought may at times be a proof not of an interpolation but of the original text sequence' (p. 583). Cf. T. Boman, *Hebrew Thought Compared with Greek* (tr. J.L. Moreau; Philadelphia: Westminster, 1960), pp. 134-35; Dahl, 'The Future of Israel', p. 143.

78. Dahl, 'The Future of Israel', *Studies in Paul*, p. 138 (cf. p. 142), points out that though the literature on Rom 9–11 has become lately very abundant, there are still at least two aspects which have not yet received the attention they deserve: the formal analysis of Rom 9–11 (composition and structure of this section) and Paul's use and view of the OT there.

79. A. Maillot, 'Essai sur les citations vétéro-testamentaires contenues dans Romains 9 à 11', pp. 55-57. Cf. E.E. Ellis, *Saint Paul's Use of the Old Testment* (Grand Rapids: Eerdmans, 1957), pp. 11, 22-25, 160-70.

80. The contrast becomes very impressive when we notice that in Rom 5–8 there are only two quotations. For other observations on Paul's use of the OT in 9–11, see Harrisville, *Romans*, pp. 260-61 n. 51; cf. C.J. Costello, 'The Old Testment in St. Paul's Epistles', *CBQ* 4 (1942), pp. 141-45.

81. Cf. Maillot, pp. 57-58.

82. The books of the prophets and the *Ketubim* were understood in classical Judaism as little less than commentaries on Torah. See further D. Patte, *Early Hermeneutic in Palestine* (SBL Dissertation Series, 22; Philadelphia: Society of Biblical Literature, 1975), p. 119.

83. See J. Coppens, 'Les arguments scripturaires et leur portée dans les lettres pauliniennes', *AnBib* 17-18 (1963), II, pp. 243-53. The prominence of

Isaiah may come from the fact that he is the prophet of the 'remnant' and of the 'return'; cf. Maillot, p. 58. Even Getty, who interprets τέλος as 'termination', concedes that 'the successive quotations of and allusion to the law (cf. Rom 10.5ff., 19), the prophets (Rom 10.11, 13, 15f., 20f.), and Psalms (Rom 10.18) possibly reveal the traditional Jewish tripartite division of the Scriptures (cf. also 11.8-10)' ('Christ Is the End of the Law', pp. 102-103).

84. For examples and discussion, see Getty, 'Christ Is the End of the Law', pp. 67-69; cf. Hanson, *Studies in Paul's Technique and Theology* (Grand Rapids: Eerdmans, 1974), pp. 145-59.

85. So Paul quotes Moses by name two times (plus one more time indirectly), Isaiah five times, David, Hosea, Elijah, ὁ λόγος (9.9), and 'righteousness of faith' (10.6-7) once each.

86. For A. Maillot all this arrangement proves is that the passage had been very carefully worked by Paul as a kind of *testimonium* (p. 73). Rafael Vicent takes the whole section as a 'homily' on the theological signification of the history of Israel, based formally on the synagogue lectionary. See 'Derash Homilético en Romanos 9–11', *Salesianum* 42 (1982), pp. 751-78. Cf. R. Scroggs, 'Paul as Rhetorician', pp. 271-98.

87. Cf. Ellis, *Paul's Use of the OT*, p. 122.

88. Rolland, following Bengel (*Gnomon Novi Testamenti* [Tübingen, 1742], II, pp. 7-8), takes the plan of Romans from the programmtic statement in Rom 1.16-17, in the following way: (1) 'sur la justification par la foi (Rom 1–4, annoncé par 1.17a)'; (2) 'sur la vie dans l'Esprit (Rom 5–8, annoncé par 1.17b)'; (3) 'sur le salut offert à tous (Rom 9–11 annoncé par 1.16b)' (p. 3). See also 'L'ordonnance des thèmes majeurs de l'épître aux Romains', pp. 394-404; cf. Feuillet, 'Le plan salvifique le Dieu', p. 489.

89. On this problem see Barrett, 'Romans 9.30–10.21: Fall and Responsibility of Israel', pp. 99-127.

90. See Getty, pp. 26-35 and 64-72.

91. See Collins, 'Chiasmus', pp. 576-78; cf. A. Feuillet, 'La citation d'Habacuc ii.4 et les huit premiers chapîtres de l'epître aux Romains', *NTS* 6 (1959), p. 71; idem, 'Le plan salvifique de Dieu', pp. 336-87, 489-529; A. Brunot, *Le génie littéraire de Saint Paul* (Paris: Editions du Cerf, 1955), pp. 41-51. L. Cerfaux, in his *Théologie de l'église suivant Saint Paul* (Paris: Editions du Cerf, 1948), p. 32, had already seen the ABA' pattern in Rom 9–11. Cf. also A. Descamps, 'La structure de Rom 1–11', *AnBib* 17-18 (1963), I, pp. 3-14; J. Jeremias, 'Chiasmus in den Paulusbriefen', *ZNW* 49 (1958), pp. 145-56.

92. See F.F. Bruce, 'Promise and Fulfilment in Paul's Presentation of Jesus', in *Promise and Fulfilment. Essays Presented to Professor S.H. Hooke*, ed. F.F. Bruce (Edinburgh: T. & T. Clark, 1964), pp. 36-50.

93. Benoit, *Israelfrage*, p. 219. Cf. Barrett, 'Romans 9.30–10.21', p. 104.

94. Throughout this chapter Paul shows how the fate of Israel and the fate of the church are bound together (see especially 11.25-32). The differences in

God's way of dealing with Jews and Gentiles in the two main periods of history are here summed up as parts of God's plan of salvation. See further, Moxnes, p. 52; Eichholz, *Die Theologie des Paulus im Umriss*, pp. 284-301. For discussion on recent interpretation, see P. Stuhlmacher, 'Zur Interpretation von Römer 11.24-32', *Probleme biblischer Theologie. G. von Rad zum 70. Geburtstag*, ed. H.W. Wolff (Munich: C. Kaiser, 1971), pp. 555-70.

95. Via considers Rom 9.30–10.21 'a self-contained text' ('A Structural Approach'), p. 206. So do Dodd, *Romans*, p. 161; Feuillet, 'Le plan salvifique', p. 497; Cranfield, *Romans*, p. 503; Käsemann, *Romans*, p. 276.

96. So Aland, *Greek NT*, p. 556; Käsemann, *Romans*, p. 289; Kuss, *Römer*, p. 748; Munck, *Christ and Israel*, p. 79.

97. So Barrett, *Reading through Romans*, p. 53.

98. So Bruce, *Romans*, p. 203; Cranfield, *Romans*, p. 515; Getty, 'Christ Is the End of the Law', p. 1; Rhyne, p. 103.

99. Only in chs. 9–11 does Paul explain what he meant by expressions such as 'to the Jews first' (1.16), 'in everything God works for good with those . . . who are called according to his purpose' (8.28), or 'Who shall bring any charge against God's elect?' (8.32), etc.

100. Getty, p. 109.

101. See Wiles, *Paul's Intercessory Prayers*, pp. 253-58.

102. See Str-B, III, pp. 261-67; cf. L. Cerfaux, 'Le privilège d'Israël selon saint Paul', in *Recueil Lucien Cerfaux* (Gembloux: Duculot, 1954), I, pp. 339-64.

103. Obviously the word of God spoken in Scripture; cf. Barrett, 'Fall and Responsibility of Israel', p. 124.

104. See Str-B, III, pp. 268; cf. Moxnes, pp. 46-47; *Tg. Yer. I* on Exod 33.19 'mercy to him who is worthy'. See further B.W. Helfgott, *The Doctrine of Election in Tannaitic Literature* (New York: King's Crown Press, 1954).

105. On the tension between election and freedom see G. Maier, 'Mensch und freie Wille nach den jüdischen Religionsparteien zwischen ben Sira und Paulus', *WUNT* 12 (1972), pp. 382-92.

106. The frequency of the scheme οὐ μόνον . . . ἀλλά in Romans (cf. 9.24 and 4.12, 16) points to a situation of conflict. See further Moxnes, pp. 48-49.

107. In Rom 9.14 Paul addresses the issue of God's justice in his dealing with Israel. Whether God's justice is seen as an expression of fidelity to the covenant (as 9.6-13 and 25-27 seem to show) or of his fidelity to creation (as 9.19-24 would seem to indicate) Paul insists in ch. 9 that any infidelity or injustice cannot be attributed to God. See Getty, 'Christ Is the End of the Law', p. 110. Cf. Dahl, 'The Future of Israel', p. 86.

108. The theme of 'mercy' is basic to Rom 9–11, as the use of ἐλεέω and ἔλεος indicates. Out of twelve uses of ἐλεέω by Paul six appear in Rom 9–11 (*Computer Konkordanz*, p. 601); and out of three uses of ἔλεος in Romans, two appear in Rom 9–11 (*ibid.*, p. 602). Cf. 9.15, 18; 11.30, 31, 32; 9.23. The passage obviously refers to God's mystery of choice, but, as

Cranfield says, 'we shall misunderstand these chapters if we fail to recognize that their key-word is mercy' (*Romans*, p. 448). Cf. M. Barth, *Paulus— Apostat oder Apostel?*, pp. 45-134. The key word ἔλεος needs to be understood against its OT background, as חסד, the term for God's faithfulness to his covenant promise. Cf. R. Bultmann, 'ἔλεος', *TDNT*, II, pp. 474-82; W. Zimmerli, 'χάρις', *TDNT*, IX, pp. 379-81; Dodd, *The Bible and the Greeks*, p. 61. According to Gaston, what Paul wants to say here to his Roman audience is that 'Israel's election depends solely on God's mercy because their own election depends on the same mercy. This is the point of the whole chapter' ('Paul's Enemies', p. 416). Cf. Munck, *Christ and Israel*, p. 77.

109. This anticipates the idea that even the hardening of Israel is used by God for the salvation of the Gentiles (11.12-15, 28-32).

110. R.E. Clements, "A Remnant Chosen by Grace" (Romans 11.5): The Old Testament Background and Origin of the Remnant Concept', in *Pauline Studies. Essays Presented to Professor F.F. Bruce on His 70th Birthday*, ed. D.A. Hagner and M.J. Harris (Exeter: Paternoster, 1980), p. 106; on the remnant motif in Rom 9–11, see G. Schrenk, 'λεῖμμα, κτλ', *TDNT*, IV, pp. 209-14; cf. G.F. Hasel, 'Remnant', *IDBSup*, p. 736; T.W. Manson, *The Teaching of Jesus* (Cambridge: University Press, 1963), p. 181, sees the remnant concept in Paul as a 'saved few' and a 'saving few'.

111. The theme of the divine purpose is very Pauline and may be found in other places. But nowhere else does Paul expose so clearly his teleological view of history and Scripture. See further Stauffer, 'ἵνα und das Problem des teleologischen Denkens bei Paulus', pp. 232-57; and Delling, 'Zur paulinischen Teleologie', pp. 705-10.

112. Cranfield, 'Some Notes on Romans 9.30-33', in *Jesus und Paulus. Festschrift für Werner Georg Kümmel zum 70. Geburtstag*, ed. E.E. Ellis and E. Grässer (Göttingen: Vandenhoeck & Ruprecht, 1975), p. 35.

113. This kind of question generally serves to introduce major issues (cf. 9.30 with 9.14; 11.1, 11; 3.31; 4.1; 6.1, 15; 7.7) See further Campbell, 'Romans 3', p. 32.

114. It is significant that of nineteen uses of the word Ἰσραήλ in the Pauline writings, thirteen belong to Rom 9–11.

115. W. Gutbrod, 'Ἰσραήλ', *TDNT*, III, p. 380.

116. This race imagery looks back to the τρέχοντος of 9.16. See Barrett, 'Romans 9.30-33', p. 106. On the race imagery, see V.G. Pfitzner, *Paul and the Agon Motif. Traditional Athletic Imagery in the Pauline Literature* (NovTSup, 16; Leiden: Brill, 1967), p. 140. Cf. Meyer, 'Romans 10.4', p. 62.

117. A. Oepke, 'διώκω', *TDNT*, II, p. 230; cf. G. Stahlin, 'προσκόπτω', *TDNT*, IV, p. 755; A. van Veldhuizen, 'Rom 9.30-33', *TSK* 29 (1911), p. 439. On διώκειν δικαιοσύνην (רדף צדק), see Isa 51.1 and Prov 15.9; cf. Rom 12.13; 14.19; 1 Cor 14.1; 2 Tim 2.22; Heb 12.14; cf. 2 Clem 10.1; the verbs διώκω and καταλαμβάνω ('pursuing and overtaking') are used together in Exod 15.9; Sir 11.10; 27.8; Phil 3.12-14.

118. G. Delling, 'λαμβάνω' *TDNT*, IV, p. 10.

119. G. Fitzer, 'φθάνω', *TDNT*, IX, pp. 88-92.

120. G. Stahlin, 'προσκόπτω', *TDNT*, VI, p. 746.

121. See BAG, p. 410.

122. LSJ, p. 1774.

123. Toews, p. 130, says that Israel is described in these terms because of its character of 'intensely goal-oriented people'.

124. See R. Bultmann, 'ΔΙΚΑΙΟΣΥΝΗ ΘΕΟΥ', *JBL* 83 (1964), pp. 12-16; E. Käsemann, 'God's Righteousness in Paul', *JTC* 1 (1965), pp. 100-10; Bo Reicke, 'Paul's Understanding of Righteousness', in *Soli Deo Gloria*, ed. J.M. Richards (Richmond: J. Knox, 1968), pp. 37-49; S.K. Williams, 'The "Righteousness of God" in Romans', *JBL* 99 (1980), pp. 241-90; cf. R.F. Surburg, 'Justification as a Doctrine of the Old Testament: A Comparative Study in Confessional and Biblical Theology', *CTQ* 46 (1982), pp. 129-46.

125. See G. Schrenk, 'δικαιοσύνη', *TDNT*, II, pp. 192-210; Hill, *Greek Words*, pp. 82-162; Barrett, *Romans*, p. 193; Ziesler, *Righteousness in Paul*, pp. 206-207; Nygren, *Romans*, p. 98.

126. L.E. Keck, *Paul and His Letters* (Philadelphia: Fortress, 1979), pp. 118-23.

127. The term δικαιοσύνη cannot mean 'moral righteousness' here for Paul speaks about it as something which Gentiles did not seek but received as a pure gift (κατέλαβον)—the prefix κατά stressing either the suddenness or the definitiveness of the attainment (cf. Delling, 'λαμβάνω', *TDNT*, IV, p. 10). K. Barth (*Dogmatics*, II, p. 241) defines 'righteousness' in Rom 9.30 as 'God's mercy'.

128. Bo Reicke, 'Paul's Understanding of Righteousness', pp. 37-49.

129. The traditional interpretation refers ἐκ πίστεως to the Gentiles' faith; so Cranfield, 'Some Notes on Rom 9.30-33', p. 35; cf. G.M. Taylor, 'The Function of PISTIS CHRISTOU in Galatians', *JBL* 85 (1966), pp. 58-76; G. Howard, 'On the Faith of Christ', *HTR* 60 (1967), pp. 459-84; 'The Faith of Christ', *ET* 85 (1974), pp. 212-15; J.J. O'Rourke, 'Pistis in Romans', *CBQ* 35 (1973), pp. 188-94. On our passage in Romans 9.30-33: F.-W. Marquardt, *Die Juden im Römerbrief* (Zurich: Theologischer Verlag, 1971), p. 39. However, Gaston ('Abraham and the Righteousness of God', *HBT* 2 [1980], p. 54), from a stimulating study of the Pauline use of the phrase ἐκ πίστεως, and πίστις τοῦ θεοῦ (cf. Rom 3.3; Gal 3.7), concludes that this phrase refers to the 'faithfulness of God', and that God's faithfulness needs to be understood in the sense of reliability (p. 66 n. 60).

130. So Sanday and Headlam, *Romans*, p. 279, and Murray, *Romans*, II, p. 43, who endeavor to interpret νόμος as 'principle' or 'rule'.

131. See Wilson, '*Nomos*: The Biblical Significance of Law', pp. 36-48; Démann, 'Moïse et la loi dans la pensée de Saint Paul', pp. 189-242; Cranfield, 'St. Paul and the Law', pp. 43-68; Ladd, 'Paul and the Law',

pp. 50-67; Gaston, 'Paul and the Torah', pp. 48-71; Feuillet, 'Loi de Dieu, loi du Christ', pp. 29-65; Fuller, *Gospel and Law*, pp. 73-81.

132. J.A. Sanders, 'Torah and Paul', pp. 136-38.

133. See Barr, *Semantics of Biblical Language*, p. 237; Hill, *Greek Words*, p. 17.

134. See C.H. Dodd, *The Bible and the Greeks* (London: Hodder & Stoughton, 1935), p. 25; Wilson, 'Nomos: The Biblical Significance of Law', pp. 38-39; Bring, 'Paul and the Old Testament', p. 22; and BAG, p. 542; L. Monsengwo Pasinya argues that '*Nomos* ne signifie donc pas la Révélation divine en tant qu'elle ordonne ou commande mais en tant qu'elle enseigne et instruit' (*La notion de* νόμος *dans le pentateuque grec* [AnBib, 52; Rome: Biblical Institute Press, 1973], p. 203.

135. Sanders, 'Torah and Paul', p. 138. νόμος in many passages of the LXX and Pseudepigrapha, and in the NT, maintains the Torah connotations of *revelation* and *covenant* rather than of a mere legal code. See further Gaston, 'Paul and the Torah', p. 59, and especially Monsengwo Pasinya, *La notion de Nomos dans le pentateuque grec*, p. 203. H. Hummel, in 'Are Law and Gospel a Valid Hermeneutical Principle?', p. 183, argues that 'it is especially for Lutherans to remember that *exegetically* the dynamic equivalent of "*Torah*" is more nearly "Gospel" than "law"' (emphasis his). Cf. G. Siegwalt, *La Loi chemin du salut* (Neuchâtel, Paris: Delachaux et Niestlé, 1971), pp. 25-26, 75-77.

136. This expression appears also once in the LXX (Wis 2.11). See M.J. Suggs, 'Wisdom of Solomon 2.10-15: A Homily on the Fourth Servant Song', *JBL* 76 (1957), p. 26.

137. So Williams, 'Righteousness of God', p. 283. Cf. BDF, p. 90; Moule, *An Idiom Book of NT Greek*, pp. 39-40.

138. So Barrett, 'Romans 9.30', p. 108, who gives as controlling parallels Rom 7.12 (νόμος ἅγιος) and Rom 8.4 (δικαίωμα τοῦ νόμου).

139. Huby, *Romains*, p. 360; Lagrange, *Romains*, p. 249; Zahn, *Römer*, p. 471; cf. T. Aquinas, *Super Epistolas S. Pauli Lectura I*, p. 148, second alternative.

140. The JB translates: 'a righteousness derived from law'; Luz, *Geschichts-verständnis*, p. 157, corrects the text from νόμον δικαιοσύνης to δικαιοσύνη ἐκ νόμου to make it say 'die Gerechtigkeit des Gesetzes'. This modification had already been supported by Calvin, *Romans and Thessalonians*, p. 217; Bengel, *Gnomon Novi Testamenti*, p. 544. For bibliography and discussion, see Wang, 'Paul's Doctrine of the Law', p. 143; Rhyne, p. 99 n. 35; Barrett, *Romans*, p. 193.

141. See Käsemann, *Romans*, p. 277-78; cf. Williams, 'Righteousness of God', p. 283; Cranfield, 'Romans 9.30-33', pp. 37-39. Rhyne has observed that every time that νόμος is used in Romans with qualifying genitives as here, the connotations are positive and that there is no indication in 9.30-33 to understand νόμος δικανοσύνης in a negative way. The Jews are not

faulted for pursuing the law of righteousness but only for the way they pursued it (pp. 99-100).

142. Müller corrects Paul, translating εἰς νόμον οὐκ ἔφθασεν by 'they did not attain *righteousness*', making him say 'righteousness' where he says 'law' (*Gottes Gerechtigkeit*, p. 96, emphasis ours). Barrett, from a different viewpoint, also sees that εἰς νόμον οὐκ ἔφθασεν 'can hardly mean anything other than that Israel failed to achieve the *righteousness* that the law required' ('Rom 9.30-33', p. 198, emphasis ours).

143. With Meyer, 'Rom 10.4', p. 63; cf. p. 68.

144. See Fitzer, 'φθάνω', pp. 88-92; cf. Max Zerwick, *A Grammatical Analysis of the Greek New Testament*, (Rome: Biblical Institute Press, 1976), II, p. 481. Cf. 1 Thess 4.15, where φθάνω is used in a very similar sense.

145. Käsemann, *Romans*, p. 272, also sees here the image of the contest.

146. Flückiger, p. 154, hints at this conclusion. Cf. Rhyne, p. 100.

147. Käsemann, *Romans*, p. 277, interpolates the verb 'to live'. Barrett, *Romans*, p. 193, substitutes δικαιοσύνη for νόμος.

148. So Cranfield, 'Rom 9.30-33', p. 38; Meyer, 'Rom 10.4', p. 63.

149. Against Muller-Duvernoy, 'Problème', p. 75. Cf. Käsemann, *Romans*, p. 277.

150. Against Dülmen, *Gesetzes*, p. 125.

151. Barrett says: 'Israel's fault is that they have pursued the right law in the wrong way ... This means that the right response to the Law of Moses was not works but faith' ('Rom 9.30-33', pp. 110-11). For further discussion see J.B. Tyson, 'Works of Law in Galatians', *JBL* 92 (1973), pp. 423-31.

152. Cf. Meyer, 'Rom 10.4', p. 68.

153. So, when in 9.11 Paul says that the election does not depend ἐξ ἔργων ἀλλ' ἐκ τοῦ καλοῦντος, he means that God does not choose men *on the basis of their merits or performance* but on the basis of God himself. Similarly in 11.6 ἐξ ἔργων is put in contrast with χάριτι to show that election does not depend on human merits but on divine grace. The context of this last reference is very illuminating for our understanding of Rom 9.30-32, for it clearly shows that the issue is election or 'status' within the people of God. Thus 11.7, explaining 11.6, says: 'That which Israel is seeking for, it has not obtained, but *those who were chosen* obtained ...'—referring obviously to the Gentiles who became part of the Christian church.

154. The use of ὡς is common in ellipses and subjective sentences. Cf. BAG, p. 897.

155. See L. Sabourin, *The Bible and Christ. The Unity of the Two Testaments* (Staten Island, N.Y.: Alba House, 1980), p. 141. J.A. Sanders argues that 'The frustration for Paul did not stem so much from a lack of affirmation of Christ by the majority of Jews of his day, but that he could not get them to read the Torah and the Prophets correctly, that is, in the way he read them' ('Torah and Christ', p. 379). 'It was Paul's conviction that if one read the Torah story, emphasizing it as a story of *God's* works of salvation

and righteousness for ancient Israel, then one could not escape seeing that God had wrought another salvation, and committed another righteousness, in Christ just like the ones of old but an even greater one' (p. 380, emphasis his). 'Paul says that if all Jews would read the Torah in that way, concentrating on God's mighty acts, then they could clearly see that "Christ is the climax of the Torah for all who believe in the righteousness of God"'.

156. Cf. Cranfield, 'Rom 9.30-33', p. 41.

157. The most likely possibilities are: (1) to put a comma after ἔργων and supply διώκοντες, so that everything from ὅτι right to the end of v. 33 is the answer of διὰ τί. Thus the text would read: 'Because pursuing it not out of faith but as out of works, they stumbled against the stone of stumbling . . . ' It is also possible (2) to put a period after ἔργων and supply ἐδίωξαν, so that only the phrase from ὅτι to ἔργων is the answer to διὰ τί; and (3) to put a comma after ἔργων and supply ἐδίωξαν, so that the whole sentence is the answer to διὰ τί. This is the punctuation preferred here, although (1) would be equally acceptable.

158. Stahlin, 'προσκόπτω', p. 746. It suggests the image of 'the stone as it trips one who runs his own course mindless of what had been done by the one who placed the stone' (Giblin, p. 282).

159. Isa 28.16 refers to the foundation stone of the new temple; therefore λίθος has soteriological connotations (J. Jeremias, 'λίθος', *TDNT*, IV, p. 276); cf. F.F. Bruce, 'New Wine in Old Wine Skins, III. The Corner Stone', *ExpTim* 84 (1973), pp. 233-34.

160. Cranfield says that the asyndeton at the beginning of 32b stresses the Scriptural character of the reference, adding to the whole sentence 'a certain tone of solemnity' ('Rom 9.30-33', p. 41).

161. On the possibility of a pre-Pauline interpretation of the 'stone' here in a messianic way, see Jeremias, 'λίθος', pp. 272-73; Stahlin, 'προσκόπτω', pp. 754-56; 'σκάνδαλον', *TDNT*, VII, pp. 352-54; Käsemann, *Romans*, pp. 278-79; Rhyne, p. 101. For full bibliography and discussion, see Karlheinz Müller, *Anstoss und Gericht: Eine Studie zum jüdischen Hintergrund des paulinischen Skandalon-Begriffs* (SANT, 19; Munich: Kösel, 1969), pp. 75-78. Cf. J.R. Harris, *Testimonies* (Cambridge: University Press, 1916-1920), I, pp. 18-17; C.H. Dodd, *According to the Scriptures. The Substructure of the New Testament Theology* (London: Nisbet, 1965), pp. 42-43.

162. Toews, p. 146 (emphasis ours); cf. Meyer, 'Rom 10.4', p. 64: 'There is nothing in the antecedent context, in the whole chapter 9 or all of Romans before it to suggest anything else [than the Law]'. Toews rejects any possibility of comparison of Rom 9.32-33 with 1 Pet 2.6-8, where the same quotations are applied to Christ. Λίθος refers to the Law—according to Toews—for three main reasons: (1) the context is a law context: Christ only enters as a factor in the discussion in 10.4; (2) the stone is the law because this was its current meaning in Judaism; and (3) Paul never used the image

of the stone messianically (pp. 147-204). This is the central point of Toews's thesis.

163. The immediate context of Isa 8.14 (namely, v. 16) suggests that the recalcitrant persons are those who will not accept Torah (חתום תורה בלמדי; LXX οἱ σφραγιζόμενοι τὸν νόμον τοῦ μὴ μαθεῖν). Cf. Barrett, 'Rom 9.30–10.21', p. 112.

164. So Rhyne, p. 102, and Cranfield, 'Rom 9.30-33', pp. 42-43. However, Meyer, in spite of Rom 10.13, qualifies the messianic interpretation of Rom 9.33 as an 'example of a crucial exegetical decision made on grounds extrinsic to the text itself' (p. 64). Paul also uses a stone image (πέτρα) in reference to Christ in 1 Cor 10.4; Isa 8.14 and 28.16 were already understood messianically in Tg. Isaiah; cf. the messianic interpretation of Isa 8.14 in *Sanh.* 38a; in favor of a messianic interpretation of this text in the time of Paul, see Str-B, II, pp. 139-40 and Jeremias, 'λίθος', p. 277; against, Barrett, 'Rom 9.30–10.21', pp. 111-12; and Toews, p. 192.

165. *Dogmatics*, II, p. 242. Barth recalls that the stone of Isa 28.16 'constitutes the centre of Zion, the foundation of all its temple cultus and service of the Law, of the whole life of the holy people as such . . . This stone and rock, Israel's foundation and support, is God's free mercy which wills to be apprehended as a promise, the fulfilment of which is according to its content to be looked for from God alone, and towards which, therefore, it is impossible to push on by means of any human willing and running' (pp. 241-42).

166. Gore, 'The Argument of Romans ix–xi', p. 41, says 'Thus the Christ, who should have been the goal of all their efforts, became only the occasion of their rejection'.

167. Toews claims that ἐπ' αὐτῷ is not a masculine but a neuter (p. 202), something that cannot be grammatically demonstrated, since both forms are identical. The point he wants to make is that the stumbling block of the Jews was not Christ (against the whole context of Rom 9–11) but the law itself. 'The Law was given to them as an occasion for faith but they stumbled and thus missed their goal' (p. 203). What Paul stresses, concludes Toews, is that 'faith is the only way to run the race . . . whether faith in God via the law or via Christ' (p. 204). This would obviously imply two-parallel-ways-of-salvation.

168. Meyer, 'Rom 10.4', p. 63.

169. The verb καταισχύνω means 'the shame and disappointment that comes to one whose faith or hope is shown to be vain' (BAG, p. 410; cf. LSJ, p. 892); see the use of this same term in Luke 13.17, where καταισχύνω also refers to the shame of the loser in a public 'contest'.

170. Cranfield, 'Rom 9.30-33', p. 41.

171. Rhyne, p. 101.

172. Toews, pp. 202-204.

173. Today very few (like Kühl, *Römer*, p. 347, and Dahl, 'The Future of Israel', p. 143 n. 24) contend that 10.1 starts a new theme, somehow unrelated to the preceding. The unity of 9.30–10.21 has imposed itself on the majority of scholars. The loose connection between 9.33 and 10.1 is common in Paul and does not necessarily mean a break (BDF, p. 242).

174. Meyer, 'Rom 10.4', p. 65.

175. Barrett, 'Rom 9.30–10.21', p. 113. This prayer of Paul has been compared with a similar petition made by Moses to God in behalf of Israel in Ex 32.32; but a closer parallel may be Esth 4.17 (LXX).

176. The word σωτηρία occurs in Rom 9–11, three of the five times in Romans (10.1, 10; 11.11); the verb σώζω five of the eight times in Romans (9.27; 10.9, 13; 11.14, 26); cf. *Computer Konkordanz*, pp. 1767, 1760.

177. BDF, p. 232 n. 447.

178. Barrett, 'Rom 9.30–33', p. 104. It must be said, *en passant*, that this prayer of hope discards by itself as wrong any predestinarian interpretation of ch. 9. Had Paul advocated a deterministic theology of salvation this prayer would have been automatically excluded. Cf. Leenhardt, *Romans*, p. 264.

179. A. Stumpff, 'ζῆλος', *TDNT*, II, p. 877; cf. BDF, p. 90 n. 163; Moule, *Idiom Book*, pp. 39-40.

180. See the use of this phrase in 1 Macc 2.44-45; 1QS 2.15; 4.4, 10, 17; 1QH 1.5; 2.15, 31; 4.23; 9.3; 14.14; and Str-B, III, p. 3277. See further Hengel, *Judaism and Hellenism*, I, pp. 287-309.

181. So R.E. Picirelly, 'The Meaning of Epignosis', *EvQ* 47 (1975), p. 91; R. Bultmann, 'γινώσκω, γνῶσις', *TDNT*, I, p. 703; K. Sullivan, '*EPIGNOSIS* in the Epistles of St. Paul', *SPC*, II, pp. 405-16.

182. So Moulton–Howard, II, p. 314; Boman, *Hebrew Thought Compared with Greek*, pp. 200-201.

183. Cf. Rom 1.28 and 3.20, where the word is used. A good pointer may be 1 Pet 3.7, where ἐπίγνωσις means, according to Barrett, 'a sensible and correct appreciation of the situation' ('Rom 9.30-33', p. 114).

184. Godet, *Romans*, p. 375; cf. J. Dupont, *Gnosis: La connaissance religieuse dans les épîtres de Saint Paul* (Paris: Gabalda, 1960), p. 6; Rom 10.17-18 proves that the issue is not involuntary ignorance but refusal to listen and obey.

185. Cf. S. Zedda, 'L'uso di ΓΑΡ in alcuni testi di San Paolo', *SPC*, I, pp. 445-56.

186. K. Barth puts it this way: 'They do not accept this God for what He is, namely, the One who wills and acts for them' (*Dogmatics*, II, p. 243); on the signification of the ἀγνοεῖν formulae in Paul, see I.T. Blazen, 'Death to Sin According to Romans 6.1-14 and Related Texts; An Exegetical-Theological Study with Critique of Views' (Ph.D. dissertation, Princeton University, 1979), pp. 221-29.

187. See Delling, 'τάσσω ... ὑποτάσσω ... ', *TDNT*, VIII, p. 42.

188. For survey on different trends, see S.K. Williams, 'The "Righteous-

ness of God" in Romans', *JBL* 99 (1980), pp. 241-90; for a contextual interpretation of τοῦ θεοῦ δικαιοσύνη here, see Bo Reicke, 'Paul's Understanding of Righteousness', pp. 37-49.

189. See E.D. Burton, *New Testament Word Studies* (Chicago: University of Chicago Press, 1927), p. 19; cf. Ziesler, *The Meaning of Righteousness in Paul*, pp. 205-206; for an existential viewpoint, see Bultmann, 'ΔΙΚΑΙΟΣΥΝΗ ΘΕΟΥ', pp. 12-16.

190. Käsemann defines the 'righteousness of God' in terms of 'the redemptive activity of God' and of 'a power which establishes salvation' ('God's Righteousness in Paul', pp. 103-10); cf. K. Kertelge, *'Rechtfertigung' bei Paulus. Studien zur Struktur und zum Bedeutungsgehalt des paulinischen Rechtfertigungsbegriffs* (Munich: Aschendorff, 1967), pp. 95-99; M. Barth, *Justification. Pauline Texts Interpreted in the Light of the Old and the New Testaments* (tr. A.M. Woodroff; Grand Rapids: Eerdmans, 1971), pp. 30-32; Dahl, 'The Doctrine of Justification', p. 97; Müller, *Gottes Gerechtigkeit*, pp. 72-75; Stuhlmacher, *Gerechtigkeit Gottes*, p. 93; Williams, 'The Righteousness of God in Romans', pp. 241-43; Barrett, *Romans*, pp. 196-97; Lietzmann, *Römer*, p. 95; Michel, *Römer*, p. 223.

191. M. Zerwick has called the attention of scholarship not only to the difficulty but also to the arbitrariness of these distinctions and has proposed being cautious in unnecessarily narrowing the interpretations of what he calls the 'general genitive' (*Biblical Greek Illustrated by Examples* [tr. J. Smith; Rome: Pontifical Biblical Institute, 1963], pp. 12-13, vis. 36-38).

192. B. Reicke, insisting on the importance of looking at Paul's concept of δικαιοσύνη in continuity with the OT concept of 'the righteousness of God', says that 'Paul's conviction of being an honest reproducer of given traditions is a historical factor more important than any modern construction of a logical development' ('Paul's Understanding of Righteousness', p. 42). For J. Piper, the righteousness of God here is 'God's unwavering commitment always to act for his own name's sake' ('The Demonstration of the Righteousness of God in Rom 3.25-26', *JSNT* 7 (1980), p. 2. S. Lyonnet describes δικαιοσύνη θεοῦ as 'salvifica Dei activitas' ('De Iustitia Dei in Epistola ad Romanos 10.3 et 3.5', *VD* 25 [1947], p. 118). Descamps defines it as 'le ferme attachement de Dieu à l'alliance' ('La justice de Dieu dans la Bible grecque', in *Studia Hellenistica*, 5, ed. L. Cerfaux and W. Peremans [Leiden: Brill, 1948], p. 90); cf. Käsemann, 'God's Righteousness', p. 109; Williams, 'Righteousness of God in Romans', p. 283.

193. W.R. Schoedel, 'Pauline Thought: Some Basic Issues', in *Transitions in Biblical Scholarship* (Essays in Divinity, 6; ed. J. Coert Rylaarsdam; Chicago: University of Chicago Press, 1968), p. 283 (cf. 263-86). The contrast presented in this verse between τοῦ θεοῦ δικαιοσύνην and τὴν ἰδίαν (δικαιοσύνην) has been commonly interpreted from the viewpoint of the antithesis 'faith'—'works of the law' in Phil 3.9. In spite of all the invoked

convergences in terminology these two passages do not say the same thing. Phil 3.9 belongs to an autobiographical context completely alien to the theme and concern of Rom 10.3. Paul does not describe in Rom 10.3 Israel's own 'righteousness' (τὴν ἰδίαν δικαιοσύνην) in terms of ἐκ νόμου, as he does—in a pejorative sense—in Phil 3.9. On the contrary he endeavors to prove that 'the righteousness of God' is precisely the righteousness promised in the law (cf. 9.30; 10.5-8; 3.21-22), or in other words, that the righteousness which God promised in Scripture he has realized in Christ. For a defense of Israel's doctrine of justification, see L. Gaston, 'Paul and the Torah', pp. 48-71. For a brief but substantial review and evaluation of Paul's view of the law vis-à-vis Judaism, see J.A. Sanders, 'Torah and Paul', pp. 132-40.

194. Gaston explains this verse by saying that 'Israel as a whole interpreted the righteousness of God as establishing the status of righteousness for Israel alone, excluding the Gentiles from election' ('Paul and the Torah', p. 66), while God manifested his righteousness by keeping his promise to Abraham and justifying all peoples by their faith in Christ (cf. 3.26). Therefore, 'God's righteousness' is God's fidelity to his promises in the OT that all nations will be blessed in Abraham's seed (cf. Gen 12.3 and Gal 3.13). Salvation both for Israel and the nations is called 'righteousness of God' in Neh 9.3-8 and Sir 44.19-21. Cf. 'Abraham', p. 55; R.B. Hays, 'Psalm 143 and the Logic of Romans 3', *JBL* 99 (1980), pp. 107-15. For Howard 'to establish their own righteousness' in 10.3 means that the Jews pretended to be the only depositaries of the benefice of a *collective* righteousness to the exclusion of the Gentiles ('Christ the End of the Law', p. 336).

195. Rhyne, p. 103. Cf. Barrett, 'Rom 9.30-33', p. 114.

196. K. Kertelge (*Rechtfertigung bei Paulus*, p. 98) and Leenhardt (*Romans*, p. 265) see Christ here as the personified 'righteousness of God' which Israel rejected.

197. Cf. Gaston, 'Paul and the Torah', p. 67.

198. Leenhardt, *Romans*, p. 265.

199. F. Rienecker, *A Linguistic Key to the Greek New Testament* (Grand Rapids: Zondervan, 1980), II, p. 24.

200. Dahl, 'The Future of Israel', p. 155.

201. Cranfield, p. 43.

202. Howard, 'Christ the End of the Law', p. 336.

203. Reicke, 'Paul's Understanding of Righteousness', p. 43.

204. 'The Righteousness of God in Romans', pp. 254-55.

205. C.H. Giblin, *In Hope of God's Glory. Pauline Theological Perspectives* (New York: Herder & Herder, 1970), p. 279.

206. Ibid., p. 281.

207. Ibid., p. 283.

208. So Μαρτυρῶ γάρ . . . (v. 2), ἀγνοοῦντες γάρ . . . (v. 3), τέλος γάρ . . . (v. 4), and Μωϋσῆς γάρ (v. 5).

209. According to BAG, p. 152, when γάρ is repeated it is intended to

introduce 'several arguments for the same assertion' where 'one clause confirms the other', or 'to have various assertions of one and the same sentence confirmed one after the other'.

210. This obvious connection has been, however, largely overlooked. It has been claimed that Rom. 10.4 inaugurates a new section about the end of law-righteousness (only slightly related to 9.30–10.1-3). For discusssion, see Flückiger, p. 155. For emphasis in the connective intention of these occurrences of γάρ, see Kuss, *Römer*, p. 748.

211. BDG, p. 70 n. 127.

212. Ibid., p. 248 n. 472. 'The predicate very commonly comes first simply because, as a rule, the predicate is the most important thing of the sentence' (Robertson, *Grammar of the Greek New Testament*, p. 417).

213. So Cranfield, *Romans*, II, p. 519. Against this possibility Sanday and Headlam already observed that 'if τέλος were taken to mean "goal" then Χριστός would become the predicate' (p. 285).

214. The emphasis on τέλος νόμου is so great that J.C. O'Neill has assumed that Χριστός was not in the original text (*Paul's Letter to the Romans* [London: Penguin, 1975], p. 169). Rewriting the text independently of any supporting textual evidence, O'Neill suggested that Rom 10.4 should read: τέλος νόμου εἰς δικαιοσύνην . . . and should be translated: 'The end of the law is righteousness . . .', τέλος meaning aim or goal, and the word Χριστός being 'a late interpolation representing a marginal gloss' (*ibid.*).

215. See N.A. Dahl, 'The Messiahship of Jesus in Paul', in *The Crucified Messiah and Other Essays* (Minneapolis: Augsburg, 1974), pp. 37-47; S. Garofalo, 'Il messianesimo di San Paolo', *AnBib* 17 (1963), pp. 31-34; M. de Jonge, 'The Word "Anointed" in the Time of Jesus', *NovT* 8 (1966), pp. 133-42.

216. So J.B. Lightfoot, *The Epistle of St. Paul to the Galatians* (New York: Macmillan, 1980), pp. 118-19; Gifford, *Romans*, pp. 41-48. Cf. Slaten, 'The Qualitative Use of Νόμος', pp. 213-19. For related conclusions, see Sanday and Headlam, pp. 284-85; Denney, *Romans*, II, p. 669; Murray, *Romans*, II, p. 51; Burton, *Galatians*, pp. 449-60.

217. 'Predicate nouns as a rule are anarthrous' (BDF, p. 143 n. 273).

218. See Walter Grundmann, 'Χρίω, Χριστός, κτλ', *TDNT*, IX, p. 527. Of a total of sixty-five occurrences of Χριστός in Romans, fifty-five times it is used without an article. Cf. A.Q. Morton, S. Michaelson, and J.D. Thompson, *A Critical Concordance to the Letter of Paul to the Romans* (The Computer Bible, 13; Biblical Research Associates, 1977), pp. 150-51.

219. See Gutbrod, 'νόμος', *TDNT*, IV, p. 1070; Longenecker, *Paul*, pp. 118-119. Cf. BDG, pp. 134-35 n. 258.

220. See, for example, Rom 2.17, 25, 27; 4.14, 15; 7.1; 13.8, 10; Gal 3.17, 18, 23, 24.

221. Longenecker, *Paul*, p. 118.

222. Even Sanday and Headlam, *Romans*, p. 80, who advocated the

interpretation of νόμος in Rom 10.4 as 'law as a principle', acknowledged that the absence of the article before νόμου is not a reliable criterion. However their interpretation would not fit their purpose, for what they want to be finished in' Christ is precisely the Mosaic law and not 'law' in the ethical sense. Today there is a growing consensus for interpreting νόμος here as the Mosaic law. See, for example, Taylor, *Romans*, p. 79; Lagrange, *Romans*, p. 253; Leenhardt, *Romans*, pp. 265-68; O'Neill, *Romans*, p. 168; Munck, *Christ and Israel*, pp. 83-84; Longenecker, *Paul*, p. 144; Schneider, p. 420.

223. Rhyne, p. 103.

224. In the Hellenistic world, 'νόμος is by its very nature righteousness' (H. Kleinknecht, 'νόμος', *TDNT*, IV, p. 1026). So, Plutarch says: δίκη μὲν οὖν νόμου τέλος ἐστίν (*Princ. Inerud.* 3 [*Moralia* 780E]), a statement which stands in amazing parallel with Rom 10.4 and shows how the relationship between the law and righteousness might be understood in the first century in a τέλος νόμου phrase. The relation between νόμος (*Torah*) and δικαιοσύνη was even more positive in Judaism (Str-B, III, pp. 160-64). F. Nötscher shows that in Qumran 'law' (תורה) and 'righteousness' (צדק) are often used as virtually synonymous (*Zur theologischen Terminologie des Qumran Textes* [BBB, 10; Bonn: Hanstein, 1956], pp. 133, 186); cf. 1QS 1.26; CD 1.1; 9.37. The brilliant idea of Paul was to relate both concepts (νόμος and δικαιοσύνη) to Christ. See further S.H. Blank, 'The Septuagint Rendering of the OT Terms for Law', *HUCA* 7 (1930), pp. 259-83; E.L. Copeland, 'Nomos as a Medium of Revelation—Paralleling Logos—in Ante-Nicene Christianity', *ST* 27 (1973), pp. 51-61.

225. According to Rhyne, 'In Christ the Law in its promises of righteousness reaches its goal' (p. 104); according to G.E. Ladd, 'righteousness was the goal of the law' (*The Presence of the Future* [Grand Rapids: Eerdmans, 1974], p. 142).

226. Démann rejects the temporal interpretation of this phrase arguing that 'La construction de la phrase s'accorderait mal avec ce dernier sens, et surtout, on ne voit pas bien ce que la phrase ainsi entendue viendrait faire dans ce context' ('Moïse et la loi', p. 235).

227. The Hellenistic search for the τέλος was paralleled in the Jewish milieu by related concerns, such as the purpose of the laws (cf. Aristeas) or the concept of כלל; Barth, *Dogmatics*, II, pp. 245-47, argues for the practical identity of the concepts of כלל, τέλος, and ἀνακεφαλαίωσις; cf. H. Schlier, 'ἀνακεφαλαίομαι', *TDNT*, III, pp. 681-82.

228. See Stauffer, '"Ἵνα und das Problem des teleologischen Denkens bei Paulus', pp. 232-57; Delling, 'Zur paulinischen Teleologie', pp. 706-10. According to J. Jeremias, 'the *terminus technicus* among early Christians for the eschatological goal was the word *télos*' (*New Testament Theology. The Proclamation of Jesus* [New York: Scribner's, 1971], p. 208).

229. For reference see LSJ, p. 1774.

230. Toews, p. 240.

231. There is unanimous agreement in construing the dative participle with the prepositional phrase and not with the main clause. Meyer analyzes the possibility of construing παντὶ τῷ πιστεύοντι with the main clause. This would give the following translation: 'For every believer ("in the judgment of every believer") Christ has become the end of the law (as a way) to righteousness'. Although this constuction might be acceptable in classical Greek (R. Kühner–B. Gerth, *Ausführliche Grammatik der griechischen Sprache* [Leverkusen: Gottschalk, 1955], I, p. 421), Meyer rejects any possibility of such a subjective statement in the actual context ('Rom 10.4', p. 74 n. 8). In any case this interpretation would need to prove that τέλος means 'end', in order to justify all the other words supplied for the sake of the meaning.

232. The importance of this phrase has been emphasized by Howard: 'The words "*Christ is the* τέλος *of the Law*" cannot be understood alone. The whole phrase must be taken together, for the key to its proper understanding appears in the last words: "to everyone who believes".' The Torah promised God's righteousness to whoever would accept the Messiah. Israel's hostility to the Gentiles (2 Thess 2.15-16) has caused them to miss the point of the Law itself, i.e. 'that its very *aim* and *goal* was the ultimate unification of all nations under the God of Abraham according to the promise' ('Christ the End of the Law', p. 336); cf. Moule, 'Obligation', p. 402; Longenecker, *Paul*, p. 144; and Barrett, *Romans*, pp. 197-98.

233. This is obviously a dative of interest, indicating the beneficiaries of δικαιοσύνη; cf. BDF, p. 101 n. 188.

234. So Gaugler, *Römer*, II, p. 94; cf. O'Neill, *Romans*, p. 169.

235. So Murray, *Romans*, II, p. 50. Both translations (1) and (2) are given in the NEB: (1) in the text and (2) in the margin.

236. Cranfield, *Romans*, II, p. 520.

237. BAG, p. 228; Zerwick translates εἰς in Rom. 10.4 'to bring' (*Grammatical Analysis of the NT*, II, p. 482).

238. So RSV; Cranfield, *Romans*, II, p. 504; cf. p. 519: 'The εἰς is consecutive'. For Toews εἰς here expresses 'the result which flows from the achievement of the goal pursued from 9.30ff.', which he understands as 'the consequence of Christ's fulfillment of the law' (p. 241).

239. Ladd explains the meaning of this statement saying that 'the law is not in itself abolished, but it has come to its end as a way of righteousness, for in Christ righteousness is by faith, not by works' ('Law', p. 502). Not satisfied with this explanation, Ladd himself proposes an alternative option: 'Christ has brought the law to its end in order that righteousness based on faith alone may be available to all men' (*ibid.*). Cf. Moule, 'Obligation', pp. 402-3; A.T. Robertson, *Grammar of the Greek NT*, pp. 591-96.

240. See further R. Bultmann, 'πιστεύω', *TDNT*, VI, p. 203; cf. D.H. van Daalen, '"Faith" According to Paul', *ExpTim* 87 (1975), pp. 83-85.

241. Cf. Flückiger, pp. 153-56; cf. Howard, 'Rom 10.4', pp. 331-37; Bring, 'Rom 10.4', pp. 35-72; and Bandstra, *Law*, p. 101.

242. Ladd, *Theology of the NT*, p. 505; cf. Cranfield, *Romans*, II, p. 519; Rhyne, p. 169 n. 67.

243. So Luther: 'everything (in Scripture) points to Christ' (*Romans*, p. 131); Cerfaux: 'the Jews . . . have not understood the essence of the law, which was that it led them to Christ' (*Christ in the Theology of Paul*, p. 221); 'Christ was in mind when God set up the system of the law, and the whole of the old law was directed towards him, as much by its prophecies as by its economy' (p. 496).

244. Knox, *Romans*, p. 554.

245. Phillips, *NT*, p. 336.

246. See Flückiger, pp. 154-55; and Rhyne, p. 96.

247. Barth, *Romans*, p. 375.

248. Cranfield, *Romans*, p. 520; cf. Barrett, 'Rom 9.30-33', p. 101.

249. Cranfield, p. 519.

250. C P⁴⁶ D* G K P 33* 88 et al.; cf. Aland et al., *The Greek NT*, p. 557.

251. B.M. Metzger, *A Textual Commentary on the Greek New Testament* (New York: United Bible Societies, 1971), pp. 524-25.

252. In spite of all the problems mentioned, this reading has been preferred by Metzger (*ibid.*); cf. BDF, p. 241 n. 474.

253. Metzger (p. 525) argues that these substitutions 'appear to be scribal emendations prompted because the context contains no antecedent to which the plural may be referred'. It may also be perfectly argued that the most common reading may be a scribal emendation intended to quote the OT more literally.

254. ℵ* A D* 33* 81, et al. It must be said that the basic meaning of the sentence is not affected by either construction.

255. Käsemann, *Romans*, p. 285.

256. Of the twenty-three uses of the verb ποιέω in Romans, there is only one other instance of ποιέω related to νόμος, and it appears in 2.14, where Paul speaks of the Gentiles who have not the law, but 'do by nature what the law requires'. Notice that Paul himself in Rom 2.13 does not take 'doing the law' (οἱ ποιηταὶ νόμου) and 'being justified' (δικαιωθήσονται) as opposites, for he states that only 'the doers of the law will be justified' (NASB). The opposition is not between 'doing the law' and 'having faith', but between 'doing' and just 'hearing' (οἱ ἀκροαταί).

257. With Bandstra, 'Law and the Elements', p. 104; Bartsch, 'Lectures on Romans', p. 40; and Toews, p. 253.

258. See his use of Ps 143.2 in Rom 3.20 and Gal 2.16.

259. Against an exegesis of Rom 10.5 (Lev 18.5) through Gal 3.12 see H. Hübner, 'Gal 3.10 und die Herkunft des Paulus', *KD* 19 (1973), p. 217; cf. Toews, pp. 271-82, 102-104. See also D.P. Fuller, 'Paul and the Works of the Law', *WTJ* 38 (1975), pp. 28-42.

260.   See on the problems of this passage, W.J. Kaiser, Jr, 'Leviticus 18.5 and Paul: "Do This and You Shall Live" (Eternally?)', *JETS* 14 (1971), pp. 19-28.

261.   Bandstra, *Law and the Elements*, pp. 102-10; cf. Cranfield, *Romans*, p. 521.

262.   Bring, 'Gerechtigkeit Gottes', pp. 45-54.

263.   *Commentary on Galatians* (tr. E. Wahlstrom; Philadelphia: Muhlenberg Press, 1961), p. 139; cf. Bandstra, *Law and the Elements*, pp. 102-104; Toews, p. 234.

264.   On the meaning of ζήσεται here (middle form in the future), see Zerwick, *Biblical Greek*, p. 72 n. 226.

265.   See Str-B, III, pp. 277-78.

266.   Dittmar, p. 297, lists more than forty instances in both the OT and the NT where this passage is quoted or paraphrased.

267.   In Lev 18.5 those *things* which Israel was to do were the ways of the Lord as contrasted with the customs of the Egyptians and Canaanites (W. Kaiser, 'Lev 18.5', p. 24). The passage begins and ends (Lev 18.1, 30) with the covenant statement, 'I am the Lord your God'. This shows that lawkeeping was not presented there as the condition for salvation, for the Lord was their God already. Furthermore, the text does not say that the keeping of the law acquires or earns eternal life. It simply states that the keeping of the law is the way of life for the believer. And one of the ways of 'doing' the law was to recognize, by the performance of sacrifices, the necessity for atonement and forgiveness (*ibid.*, p. 25). Already Calvin, writing on Lev 18.5 in Rom 10.5, said: 'Obedience of the law is the way of life (Lev 18.5; Ezek 18.9; Gal 3.12; Rom 10.5; Lk 19.28), transgression of the law, death (Rom 6.23; Ezek 18.4, 20)' (*Institutes*, 3.4.28).

268.   W. Eichrodt says that 'here following the law means reaching out spontaneously and taking an inestimable gift which makes possible a life full of strength and joy . . . It is a point of view which cannot be made a target of any of the customary rebukes against nomism and legalism' (*Ezekiel. A Commentary* [OTL; London: SCM, 1970]). Barrett comments that 'the law thus provided an instrument by which the purpose of God operated among the Israelites. Through the law God was always offering life to his people' ('Fall and Responsibility', p. 119). 'The law was a pointer directing this people on the way of faith' (*ibid.*, p. 125); cf. Amiot, *Key Concepts of St. Paul*, p. 155 n. 5.

269.   D.N. Freedman, 'The Chronicler's Purpose', *CBQ* 23 (1961), pp. 440-42.

270.   *b.Yoma* 85a-b; *Sipra* 86b; *b.Sanh.* 74a; *b.Abod. Zar.* 54a; *Eccl. R.* 1.8.3.

271.   *b.Mak.* 23b; and *m.Mak.* 3.15.

272.   *b.Sanh.* 59a; cf. *B. Qam.* 38a; *b.Abod. Zar.* 3a; *Num. R.* 13.15-16; *Midr. Ps.* 1.18.

273. Toews, pp. 269, 283. Howard, 'Christ the End of the Law', p. 334.

274. O'Neill, basing his argumentation on the variant reading of manuscript A, which has instead of τὲν δικαιοσύνην τὴν ἐκ τοῦ νόμου the reading τὴν δικαιοσύνην τήν ἐκ πίστεως, proposes a new translation: 'For Moses writes that he who practices the righteousness which is of faith shall live by that faith'. O'Neill's thesis is that Paul was quoting Hab 2.4 instead of Lev 18.5, but the text was corrupted by a scribal error. This interpretation resolves, indeed, most of the problems of the passage. But it is based on such hypothetical grounds that it cannot be considered as a valid explanation (pp. 169-72).

275. Munck, *Christ and Israel*, p. 84; the antithesis between 'law righteousness' and 'faith righteousness' as an explanation of Rom 10.5-8 was already proposed by Calvin, who interpreted this passage through Phil 3.8-9 (*Institutes*, 3.11.18); cf. also Althaus, *Römer*, p. 98; Barrett, p. 198; Bläser, *Gesetz*, p. 180; Bruce, *Romans*, p. 201; Dodd, *Romans*, p. 177; Ellis, *Paul's Use of the OT*, p. 123; Godet, *Romans*, pp. 376-78; Hodge, *Romans*, p. 337; Käsemann, *Romans*, p. 286; Knox, *Romans*, p. 556; Lagrange, *Romains*, p. 254; Lietzmann, *Römer*, p. 97; Michel, *Römer*, p. 246; Murray, *Romans*, II, p. 51; Nygren, p. 389; Sanday and Headlam, p. 285; Taylor, *Romans*, p. 80; Zahn and Hauck, *Romans*, pp. 477-80. Against, see Cranfield, *Romans*, II, pp. 520-23; Howard, 'Rom 10.4', pp. 335-37; Rhyne, p. 96; Toews, pp. 250-70.

276. Murray, *Romans*, II, pp. 249-51. Hodge says that 'there is nothing in the language of the apostle to require us to understand him as quoting Moses in proof of his doctrine' (p. 340).

277. Käsemann, *Romans*, p. 284. Jeremias argues that 'Moses' stands often for 'the law' ('Μωϋσῆς', p. 864).

278. *Ibid.*, pp. 286-87.

279. 'We stand here at the commencement of a theologically reflected Christian hermeneutics. Its mark is that it is not satisfied with the "It is written". It demands critical exposition, with the message of justification as the decisive criterion. Only when this message is brought to light does Scripture become a word that is near . . . ' (*ibid.*, p. 287). Cf. 'The Spirit and the Letter', p. 155.

280. Käsemann, *Romans*, p. 284.

281. Käsemann, 'Spirit and Letter', p. 156; *Romans*, p. 284.

282. 'Very frequently [δέ is used] as a transitional particle pure and simple without any contrast intended' (BAG, p. 170). 'When there is no preceding μέν . . . then δέ is used merely to pass from one thing to another' (LSJ, p. 175). An antithetical relation would require the μέν–δέ construction rather than γάρ–δέ. The γάρ–δέ construction is used conjunctively by Paul in other places where similar concepts are discussed (cf. Rom 3.21, 22; Gal 3.10-12). See Howard, 'Christ the End of the Law', pp. 335-36; Kaiser,

'Leviticus 18.5', p. 27. Cf. Campbell, 'Christ the End of the Law', p. 78; Wang, pp. 151-53; Flückiger, p. 155.

283.   As R.O. Zorn observes, 'To quote in one breath Moses as stating the way of justification by keeping the law, and then in another give a totally different way of justification by means of faith but still in the language of Moses could seem only to the Jews to be making Moses contradict himself' ('The Apostle Paul's Use of the OT in Rom 10.5-8', *Gordon Review* 5 [1959], p. 31).

284.   It should be noticed that in Romans Paul repeatedly states that the gospel had been announced by the law and the prophets: 1.1-6; 3.21-22, 31; 16.25-26. Cf. Flückiger, p. 155.

285.   Hanson has challenged Käsemann's identification of Paul's designation of Scripture as 'Moses' with the idea of 'letter', showing that of the four uses of Μωϋσῆς λέγει in Paul (Rom 9.15; 10.5, 19; and 1 Cor 9.9) none may be proved as emphasizing the concept of 'letter' as Käsemann understands it (*Paul's Technique*, pp. 139-49). P. Richardson has also refuted the thesis of Käsemann showing that the pair γράμμα/πνεῦμα suggests continuity rather than the radical discontinuity claimed by Käsemann ('Spirit and Letter: A Foundation for Hermeneutics', *EvQ* 45 [1973], pp. 208-18). And D.O. Via has demonstated the lack of solid ground for the hermeneutics of 'letter/spirit' applied by Käsemann to Paul in the exegesis of Rom 9.30–10.21, a passage where neither of the two expressions is ever used ('Structuralist Approach', pp. 208-209).

286.   See Matt 18.16; 2 Cor 13.1; 1 Tim 5.19; Heb 10.28; cf. Deut 17.6; 19.15; Str-B, I, pp. 790-91.

287.   Thus, Targum Pseudo-Jonathan paraphrases Lev 18.5 saying: 'And you shall keep my *covenant* and the order of my laws which if a man performs them he shall live by them eternal life, and his portion shall be among the *righteous*' (Diez Macho, *Neofiti I*, p. 501; cf. pp. 374-95).

288.   See A. Festorazzi, 'Coherence and Value of the Old Testament in Paul's Thought', in *Paul de Tarse, apôtre de notre temps*, ed. L. De Lorenzi (Rome: S. Paolo, 1979), pp. 165-73.

289.   Murray, who ends up saying that Lev 18.5 is quoted in Rom 10.5 as a 'definition of the principle of legalism' (*Romans*, II, p. 251) acknowledges that 'the problem that arises from this use of Lev 18.5 is that the latter text does not appear in a context that deals with legal righteousness as opposed to that of faith. Lev 18.5 is in a context in which the claims of God upon his redeemed and covenant people are being asserted and urged upon Israel. In this respect Lev 18.1-5 is parallel to Exod 10.1-17; and Deut. 5.6-21. The preface is "I am the Lord your God" (Lev 18.2) and corresponds to the preface of the ten commandments. The whole passage is no more "legalistic" than are the ten commandments. Hence the words "which if a man do, he shall live in them" (v. 5) refer not to the life accruing from doing in a

legalistic framework but to the blessing attendant upon obedience in a redemptive and covenant relationship to God' (p. 249).

290. Zorn, p. 33.

291. See J. Schmid, 'Die alttestamentlichen Zitate bei Paulus und die Theorie von sensus plenior', *BZ* 3 (1959), pp. 159-73.

292. See H. Renard, 'La lecture de l'Ancien Testament par Saint Paul', *AnBib* 17-18 (1961), pp. 207-15; Hanson, 'Paul's Technique and Theology', pp. 136-37, 182.

293. O'Neill solves the problem by arguing that most of the claimed quotation in Rom 10.6-8 is non-Pauline. Only v. 6a can be authentic. The rest is the work of a later redactor, who corrected Paul here as he did already in v. 5, making Paul quote Lev 18.5 instead of Hab 2.4. For O'Neill, Paul simply said that 'the righteous man is the one who practices righteousness by faith and lives by faith' (*Romans*, pp. 165-73). This interpretation has to be discarded for lack of textual support (for refutation, see Toews, pp. 309-10).

294. H. Windisch, *Paulus und das Judentum* (Stuttgart: Kohlhammer, 1935), p. 70; F. Prat, *Théologie de Saint Paul* (8th edn; Paris: Beauchesne, 1920), I, p. 45; M. Black, 'The Christological Use of the Old Testament in the New Testament', *NTS* 18 (1981), p. 8.

295. J.A. Beet, *A Commentary on St. Paul's Epistle to the Romans* (New York: Thomas Whittaker, 1892), p. 285.

296. R. Le Déaut, *The Message of the New Testament and the Aramaic Bible (Targum)* (tr. S.F. Miletic; Rome: Biblical Institute Press, 1982), p. 29.

297. Godet, *Romans*, p. 378; M.J. Hughes, 'Romans x,6-8', *ExT* 19 (1907f.), p. 524; Lagrange, *Romains*, p. 256; Moule, *Romans*, p. 180; A.T. Robertson, *Word Pictures in the New Testament* (Nashville: Broadman Press, 1931), IV, p. 388.

298. For Käsemann Paul quoted Deut 30.12-14 just for the purpose of stressing the antithetic contrast with Lev 18.5. Lev 18.5 represents the 'gramma' of the OT while Deut 30.12-14 represents the 'pneuma'. The first stands for the 'law' while the last stands for the 'gospel'. Thus for Käsemann the use of Deut 30.12-14 in Rom 10.6-8 reflects Paul's creative and dialectic hermeneutic. Although Leviticus and Deuteronomy belong to the same Torah, Paul's hermeneutic requires their separation. This is why, explains Käsemann, Paul ascribes Lev 18.5 to 'Moses' (mediator of the 'letter') while he ascribes Deut 30.12-14 to 'the righteousness of faith' (personification of the '*spirit*') ('Spirit and Letter', p. 155). Maillot, p. 72, calls also the 'justice-par-la-foi' of Rom 10.6 'la nouvelle quille hermeneutique de la Torah'; cf. Althaus, *Römer*, p. 98; Bläser, *Gesetz bei Paulus*, p. 179; Bruce, *Romans*, pp. 203-205; Dodd, *Romans*, p. 177; Ebeling, 'Doctrine of the Law', p. 266.

299. Barrett, *Romans*, p. 129; Davies, *Paul and Rabbinic Judaism*, pp. 153-55; Knox, *Romans*, p. 556; Longenecker, *Biblical Exegesis*, pp. 114, 121; Sanday and Headlam, p. 289.

300. R.M. Grant, *The Spirit and the Letter* (London: SPCK, 1957), p. 51: 'This is pure allegorization'. Cf. Barclay, *Romans*, p. 148; Kirk, *Romans*, p. 225; Meyer, *Romans*, p. 406; Nygren, *Romans*, p. 38.

301. See J.A. Fitzmyer, 'The Use of Explicit Old Testament Quotations in Qumran Literature and in the New Testament', *NTS* 7 (1961), pp. 297-333.

302. See J. Bonsirven, *Exégèse rabbinique et exégèse paulinienne* (Paris: Beauchesne, 1939), pp. 307-309; M. McNamara, *The New Testament and the Palestinian Targums to the Pentateuch* (AnBib, 27; Rome: Pontifical Biblical Institute, 1966), p. 72; Suggs, 'The Word Is Near You', pp. 301-302; Longenecker, *Biblical Exegesis*, p. 123.

303. Bonsirven, *Exégèse*, pp. 340-42; Suggs, pp. 301-302.

304. Suggs, p. 301.

305. Hanson, *Paul's Technique*, p. 147.

306. For discussion, see Suggs, 'The Word is Near', pp. 299-301.

307. For a comparison between Paul and the rabbinic haggadists, see D. Windfuhr, 'Der Apostel Paul als Haggadist', *ZAW* 44 (1926), pp. 328-30; cf. K. Stendahl, *The School of Matthew and Its Use of the Old Testament* (Philadelphia: Fortress, 1968), p. 216; for comparison of Paul with the *midrashim* and the Qumran *pesher*, see Hanson, *Paul's Technique*, p. 143; B. Lindars, *New Testament Apologetic. The Doctrinal Significance of the Old Testament Quotations* (Philadelphia: Westminster, 1961), pp. 240-48; Bruce, *Romans*, p. 204; Käsemann, *Romans*, pp. 160-66; Munck, *Christ and Israel*, p. 85; for the possible influence of *targums*, see R. Le Déaut, 'Traditions targumiques dans le corpus paulinien?', *Bib* 42 (1961), pp. 28-28; McNamara, *NT and Palestinian Targums*, pp. 70-81; A. Díez Macho, 'Targum y Nuevo Testamento', in *Mélanges Eugène Tisserant*, ed. P. Henniquin (Rome: Vatican Press, 1964), pp. 153-85.

308. T. Arvedson, *Das Mysterium Christi. Eine Studie zu Mt 11.24-30* (Uppsala: Wretmanns, 1937), p. 216; U. Wilckens, *Weisheit und Torheit* (Tübingen: J.C.B. Mohr, 1959), pp. 97-99; id., 'σοφία', *TDNT*, VII, pp. 496-526; H. Conzelmann, 'Paulus und die Weisheit', *NTS* 12 (1966), pp. 236-44; Feuillet, *Le Christ, Sagesse de Dieu*, pp. 321-27; Suggs, pp. 304-306.

309. Suggs, pp. 309-11. On the personification of 'the Word' as Wisdom, see H. Cazelles, *Le Deutéronome* (Paris: Editions du Cerf, 1950), p. 122.

310. Suggs, p. 309.

311. 'And thereby rescue his gospel from the stigma of absolute opposition to the Law' (*ibid.*, p. 31).

312. For discussion of the problem, see A. van Roon, 'The Relation between Christ and the Wisdom of God according to Paul', *NovT* 16 (1974), pp. 226-27; cf. Davies, *Paul and Rabbinic Judaism*, p. 154, and Toews, pp. 292-95, who categorically rejects this hypothesis.

313. E.E. Ellis, 'Midrash, Targum and New Testament Quotations', in *Neotestamentica et Semitica*, ed. E.E. Ellis and M. Wilcox (Edinburgh: T. &

T. Clark, 1969), pp. 61-69; M.P. Miller, 'Targum, Midrash and the Use of the Old Testament in the New Testament', *JSS* 2 (1971), pp. 29-82.

314. Translation of McNamara, *Neofiti I. Targum Palestinense, ms. de la Biblioteca Vaticana, Deuteronomio*, ed. Alejandro Diez Macho (Madrid: CSIC, 1978), pp. 553-54.

315. McNamara and S. Lyonnet are the chief advocates of this view. See S. Lyonnet, 'Saint Paul et l'exégèse juive de son temps. A propos de Rom 10.6-8', *Mélanges Bibliques rédigées en l'honneur d'André Robert* (Paris: Bloud & Gay, 1956), pp. 494-506.

316. McNamara, *NT and Palestinian Targums*, pp. 74-78. Cf. Roger Le Déaut, 'Targumic Literature and NT Interpretion', *BTB* 4 (1974), pp. 253-54; cf. A. Jaubert, 'Symboles et figures christologiques dans le Judaïsme', *RevScRel* 47 (1973), p. 379.

317. Review of *The New Testament and the Palestinian Targum to the Pentateuch*, by M. McNamara in *TS* 29 (1968), pp. 322-25. The present copy of Targum Neofiti comes from the sixteenth century, and though some parts of the text can be traced back to the second century AD, it has not yet been proved that this Targum existed prior to the time of Paul. Moreover, nothing in the context of Rom 10.6-8 (or in the whole context of Romans) suggests the influence of a Moses/Jonah typology related to the incarnation, death, resurrection and ascension of Jesus.

318. Käsemann cites the Targum, but considers 1 Baruch a more probable source for Paul's interpretation (*Perspectives*, pp. 160-61). A. Goldberg thinks that Paul did not use Targum Neofiti but was familiar with the tradition underlying the Targum: 'Torah aus der Unterwelt? Eine Bemerkung zu Rom 10.6-7', *BZ* 14 (1970), pp. 127-31; Black supports the McNamara thesis ('Christological Use', p. 9); so does Hanson (*Paul's Technique*, pp. 146-94); Le Déaut insists that the typology Moses/Jesus is essential for the understanding of Rom 10.6-8 ('Targumic Literature', pp. 252-55).

319. Dittmar gives as allusions to Deut 30.12-14 the following: Amos 9.2; Ps 46.6; 68.19; 107.26; 139.8; Prov 30.4; Job 11.18; Bar 3.29, 30; Sir 16.18; 24.5; 4 Ezra 4.8 (cf. Ps 71.20); John 3.13; 6.62; Acts 2.33; Rom 10.6-9; Eph 4.9-10; cf. Philo, *Post.* 84; *Mut.* 236; *Virt.* 183; *Quod Omn.* 68.

320. *b.Tem.* 16a; *b.Besa* 59b; *Erub.* 54a; *Deut. Rab.* 8.6 (cf. 8.2). For commentaries, see Str-B, III, pp. 278-82; cf. McNamara, *NT and Palestinian Targum*, pp. 74-76.

321. See 'Pseudo-Jonathan Parallels to Deuteronomy', on 30.14, in Diez Macho, *Neofiti I, Deuteronomy*, p. 616.

322. This very text used by Paul in order to prove that the Word of God had been made near in Christ was used in later Judaism against the Christian claim that Jesus was the eschatological prophet and brought a new revelation (cf. *Midr. Deut. Rab.* 8.6).

323. A possibility already suggested by Lyonnet, 'Saint Paul et l'exégèse

juive', p. 499. On the earliest Christian interpretations of this passage, see T.F. Glasson, 'The Gospel of Thomas, Saying 3, and Deuteronomy xxx.11-14' (*ExpT* 78 [1976-77], pp. 151-52).

324. Cranfield, *Romans*, p. 522.

325. R. Bultmann, *Der Stil der paulinischen Predigt und die kynisch-stoische Diatribe* (Göttingen: Vandenhoeck und Ruprecht, 1910), pp. 87-88.

326. So Suggs, 'The Word Is Near', p. 301.

327. 'Structuralist Approach', p. 212; cf. 201-10.

328. Hanson, *Paul's Technique*, p. 148.

329. Lyonnet, 'Saint Paul et l'exégèse juive de son temps', pp. 505, 497; cf. F.F. Bruce, *Biblical Exegesis in the Qumran Texts* (Grand Rapids: Eerdmans, 1959), pp. 66-77.

330. See Leenhardt, *Romains*, p. 152.

331. Feuillet, 'Le Christ, Sagesse de Dieu', pp. 323-24.

332. For P.C. Craigie Deut 30.12-14 describes 'the very essence or purpose of the law (*The Book of Deuteronomy* (NICOT; Grand Rapids, Eerdmans, 1976), p. 365; cf. S.R. Driver, *Deuteronomy* (ICC; Edinburgh: T. & T. Clark, 3rd edn, 1902), p. 330; Lagrange, *Romains*, p. 81.

333. Hanson, *Paul's Technique*, p. 195.

334. Hanson (*ibid.*, p. 182) rightly argues against Bultmann that Paul does not interpret Deut 30.12-14 as 'a prophecy of justification by faith' (R. Bultmann, 'Prophecy and Fulfillment', in *Essays in Old Testament Hermeneutics*, ed. C. Westermann [Richmond: John Knox, 1963], pp. 51-52) but as a *statement* of justification by faith: there was no need to prophesy about it, for it was already God's way of salvation.

335. Cf. Murray, *Romans*, II, pp. 52-54.

336. Via suggests that the old terms like 'righteousness', etc., are given a new meaning within Paul's kerygma, but they always retain their old basic significance. The very fact of retaining the basic meaning is what made possible their transformation. 'The apostle', says Via, 'was intuitively following the rule of compatibility: no proclamation will reach anyone if it cannot make some contact with the hearer's preunderstanding. The new meaning system cannot be so incompatible with the hearer's frame of reference' (p. 220).

337. *Targum Neofiti I*, V, p. 555.

338. In the Deuteronomy context, obedience to God's word is a response to his love, a reflection of his holiness, not a condition for or a means of acquiring life or merits. This obedience, which is the appropriate response for the gift of life, is seen by Paul as synonymous with 'righteousness by faith'. So, although Paul interpreted 'word' in Deuteronomy to mean 'kerygma' when it actually meant 'law', he was not misinterpreting the OT text or offering an eisegesis, for his 'overall understanding' of the passage was correct. Paul's thought and the Deuteronomy expressions, while worded

differently, belonged, in the words of Via, to the same 'epistemological field' (p. 219). 'Paul thus would be saying that Moses had this in mind in the broad context of the passage Paul utilizes, but because he has broadened it, Paul appropriately lets "the righteousness of faith" speak instead of Moses, though it was Moses himself who said it and meant such by it' (Zorn, p. 33). The context of the law was the covenant. Israel was constituted God's people not because of merit gained by obedience to the law, but because of God's free election (Walter Eichrodt, *Theology of the OT* [London: SCM, 1961], I, ch. 2); cf. Knight, *Law and Grace*, pp. 25-26; Kleinknecht, 'νόμος', p. 1035. The reward of obedience to the law was preservation of the positive relationship with Yahweh. This is the meaning of Lev 18.5, that the man who obeys the law shall live, i.e. enjoy the blessings of God (the primary concept of 'life' in the OT is not eschatological). Therefore, life was not a reward earned by good works; it was itself God's gift (cf. Deut 30.15-20). Life or death are determined by whether or not Israel chooses to follow the word of God. 'Only by faith, i.e. by cleaving to the God of salvation, will the righteous have life (Hab 2.4; Amos 5.4, 14; Jer 38.20); it is obvious that life is here understood as a gift' (G. von Rad, 'ζάω', *TDNT*, II, p. 845; cf. *Old Testament Theology* (Edinburgh: Oliver and Boyd, 1965), II, pp. 388-409. As Ladd has put it, 'the obedience demanded by the law could not be satisfied by a mere legalism, for the law itself demanded love for God (Deut 6.5; 10.12) and the neighbor (Lev 19.18). Obedience to the law of God was an expression of trust in God' ('Paul and the Law', p. 52).

339. See Cranfield, *Romans*, pp. 523-24.

340. Many scholars suggest that this change is due to the influence of Ps 107.26, which reads: ἀναβαίνουσιν ἕως τὸν οὐρανῶν καὶ καταβαίνουσιν ἕως τῶν ἀβύσσων. Paul wants to juxtapose ἀναβήσεται/καταβήσεται and εἰς τὸν οὐρανόν/εἰς τὴν ἄβυσσον. W. Bieder, however, rejects this possible influence in *Die Vorstellung von der Höllenfahrt Jesu Christi* (ATANT, 19; Zürich: Zwingli, 1949), pp. 71-72. See further J. Heller, 'Himmel- und Höllenfahrt nach Römer 10.6-7', *EvT* 32 (1972), p. 481; and Goldberg, 'Torah aus der Unterwelt', pp. 129-30: cf. G. von Rad, *Deuteronomy* (OTL; Philadelphia: Westminster, 1966), p. 184. For Heller the 'ascending–descending' imagery betrays a certain influence from the mythology of the Gilgamesh Epic, as well as a polemic against a religious-mystical ideology which made divine revelation accessible only through 'trips' to the heavens and the underworld (p. 480).

341. Roon, 'Relation between Christ and Wisdom', p. 225.

342. The foot-race imagery seems to go through until 11.12, where Paul describes the failure of the Jews by means of the terms παράπτωμα ('a misstep') and ἔπταισαν ('they tripped'). See Lyonnet, *Galates et Romains*, p. 110; Oesterreicher, 'Israel's Misstep', p. 322; and K.L. Schmidt, 'πταίω', *TDNT*, VI, pp. 883-84.

343. See Delling, 'Nahe ist dir das Wort', *TLZ* 99 (1974), cols. 401-12.

344. See B.M. Newman and E.A. Nida, *A Translator's Handbook on Paul's Letter to the Romans* (Stuttgart: United Bible Societies, 1973), p. 200.

345. G.R. Beasley-Murray, 'Righteousness of God in the History of Israel and the Nations: Rom. 9–11', *RevExp* 73 (1976), p. 445. It has been suggested that the reference to Christ as 'near' was apologetic. Paul wanted to make clear something about the 'absence' of Jesus the Messiah: He is not any more in the realm of death, nor forever absent up in heaven. The exalted Christ (like the Word of Torah) is *near* and always present in the Christian proclamation. See Fibling, p. 287. J.A.T. Robinson explains this passage in the following terms: 'The Christ presence is not now something remote or speculative. "There is no need for you to say: Who will go up into heaven? Heaven has come down to you; Christ has come and lived among men. There is no need to search the hidden places of the deep. Christ has risen. There is not need to seek the living among the dead" or, as Dodd puts it, "Christ is not an inaccessible heavenly figure (like the apocalyptic Messiah of Judaism) nor yet a dead prophet (as the Jews thought), but the living Lord of his people, always near"' (*Wrestling with Romans*, p. 123).

346. So Rhyne, p. 97; Bläser, *Gesetz*, p. 179; Wang, 'Law', p. 146.

347. Cf. Heb 4.2, where it is said that the gospel was already proclaimed to those who fell in the wilderness; Acts 7.17 and 13.21, where it is a question of 'the promise made to the Fathers'; called 'the Gospel' in Rom 1.12 and 10.14-15. See further W. Kaiser, 'The Eschatological Hermeneutics of Evangelicalism: Promise Theology', *JETS* 13 (1970), pp. 91-100. Vicent says: 'La Palabra de Dios se cumple ("*qayyem*") en Cristo, que es su plenitud, su *télos*' (p. 780). Cf. T.W. Manson, 'The Argument from Prophecy', *JTS* 46 (1945), pp. 129-36.

348. According to Käsemann τὸ ῥῆμα τῆς πίστεως is 'the faith which is believed' (*fides quae creditur*), i.e. the gospel (*Romans*, p. 290); cf. Cranfield, *Romans*, II, p. 526. The gospel is described in Rom 1.16 as 'the righteousness of God'; cf. P.E. Langevin, 'Le salut par la foi, Rom 10.8-13', *AssSeign* 14 (1973), pp. 47-53.

349. Käsemann insists that 'the element of divine giving is unmistakably stressed'. The only human participation is response to the divine proclamation (*ibid.*, p. 289).

350. Kaiser, 'Leviticus 18.5', p. 27; cf. Campbell, p. 78; Bring, p. 49; Suggs, p. 301.

351. Cazelles sees in Deut 30.14 'une des sources de la théologie du Verbe telle qu'elle s'exprime dans le prologue du quatrième évangile, après avoir été murie dans les livres de la Sagesse' (*Le Deutéronome*, p. 117 n. b). Both terms, λόγος and ῥῆμα, are used to refer to the revelation which God has granted to man. B.F. Westcott makes the distinction that ὁ λόγος τοῦ Θεοῦ

is 'the whole message of the Gospel' while Θεοῦ ῥῆμα is 'some special utterance . . . such as that which marks the confession of faith, apprehended in its true character as an utterance of God: Rom 10.8; Eph 5.26' (*The Epistle to the Hebrews* [2nd edn; New York: Macmillan, 1892], p. 149). Cf. Steward Custer, *A Treasure of New Testament Synonyms* (Greenville, S.C.: Bob Jones University Press, 1975), p. 82.

352. Pierre Benoit explains Israel's misstep in the following terms: 'Looking in the Torah for what man can do many in Israel did not see in it what God wanted to do, nor in Christ what God has already done' ('Conclusion par mode de synthèse', in *Die Israelfrage in Rom. 9–11*, p. 226. Zorn comments: 'Had the Jews really heard and followed Moses and the prophets they would have been led to this as Paul here so plainly shows. For he was simply preaching what they had announced and what God had fulfilled in Christ. Whether it were the Jews of their time, or the Jews and Gentiles of Paul's day, the principle of justification was the same; namely, righteousness to be imputed by faith in God's Redeemer' (p. 34). Cf. Fuller, *Gospel and Law*, p. 86.

353. Cranfield, *Romans*, p. 524.

354. Vv. 9-11 by Isa 28.16; v. 12 by Joel 2.32; vv. 14-15 by Isa 52.7; v. 16 by Isa 53.1; vv. 17-18a by Ps 19.4; v. 19b by Deut 32.21 and Isa 65.1-2.

355. ὅτι, v. 9; γάρ, vv. 10, 11, 12, 13; οὖν v. 14; δέ, vv. 15, 20, 21; ἄρα, v. 17; ἀλλά, vv. 16, 18, 19.

356. Giblin, pp. 287-88.

357. The order of the two conditional clauses (ἐὰν ὁμολογήσῃς . . . ἐὰν πιστεύσῃς), putting *confession* before *belief*, does not seem to have any particular significance, since it is reversed in the next verse. It certainly depends on the order given in Deut 30.14, where the 'mouth' precedes the 'heart'.

358. See V.H. Neufeld, *The Earliest Christian Confessions* (Grand Rapids: Eerdmans, 1963), pp. 13-20, 42-51.

359. See P.E. Langevin, 'Sur la christologie de Rom 10.1-13', *LTP* 35 (1979), pp. 39-42.

360. Bultmann, *Theology of the NT*, I, pp. 18, 312.

361. The verb ὁμολογέω generally designated the binding public declaration which definitively orders a relation with the legal power. See Michel, 'ὁμολογέω', *TDNT*, V, pp. 199-220; cf. Cranfield, *Romans*, p. 529. It is not probable that confession before the authorities is here in view, so Munck, *Christ and Israel*, p. 89; O. Cullman, *The Earliest Christian Confession* (tr. J.K.S. Reid; London: Lutterworth, 1949), pp. 27-28; rejected by Käsemann, *Romans*, p. 291.

362. Notice that these two parallel clauses are precisely linked by γάρ . . . δέ, like vv. 5-6, for indicating a simple juxtaposition. Notice also that δικαιοσύνη and σωτηρία are used almost as synonymous. For describing

God's actions for the salvation of mankind, there is a certain shift of terms: the section starts and ends with emphasis on ἔλεος (9.15, 16, 18, 23; 11.30, 31, 32); in the central section (9.30–10.21), the predominant terms are δικαιοσύνη (9.30, 31; 10.3, 4, 5, 6, 10), and σωτηρία (9.27, 10.1, 9, 10, 13; 11.11, 14, 26).

363. Bultmann shows that δικαιοσύνη can be both a precondition of salvation and also an equivalent of salvation (*Theology of the NT*, I, pp. 270-85); cf. Cranfield, *Romans*, p. 531.

364. Against Toews, p. 327. It is not only improbable that Paul had two different objects in mind for the same quotation, in the same context, but the context proves that 'faith in Christ' was intended in both instances.

365. The insistence on πᾶς in 10.4-13 was probably intended to show that the gospel call included also the Jews. See further Oscar Cullmann, 'Le caractère eschatologique du devoir missionaire et de la conscience apostolique de S. Paul. Etude sur le κατεχον (-ων) de II Thess 2.6-7', *RHPR* 16 (1963), pp. 210-45.

366. Käsemann, 'The Spirit and the Letter', pp. 163-64.

367. Id., *Romans*, p. 292.

368. Cranfield, *Romans*, p. 531.

369. Against Toews, who claims that Paul here 'is speaking theologically rather than christologically' (p. 230).

370. See further in P.-E. Langevin, 'Ceux qui invoquent le nom du Seigneur', *Sciences Ecclésiastiques* 19 (1967), pp. 393-407; 21 (1969), pp. 71-122; cf. 'Sur la christologie de Romains 10.1-13', *LTP* 35 (1979), pp. 35-43; and 'Le salut par la foi (Rom 10.8-13)', *Ass Seign* 14 (1973), pp. 47-53.

371. See O. Cullmann, 'All Who Call on the Name of Our Lord Jesus Christ', *JES* 1 (1964), pp. 1-21; cf. Käsemann, 'The Spirit and the Letter,' p. 164.

372. J.A. Sanders, 'Torah and Christ', *Int* 29 (1975), pp. 384-85. Paul's reference to Ps 19.4 is less arbitrary than it sems at first glance. Ps 19 is an exaltation of the transforming power of the God's Torah (cf. Ps 19.7-14). Paul just claims for the gospel what contemporary Jewish thought claimed for the Torah; cf. Hanson, *Paul's Technique*, p. 155.

373. Sanders, 'Torah and Christ', p. 389.

374. Barrett, 'Fall and Responsibility', p. 119.

375. Barrett, 'Rom. 9.30–10.21', p. 104.

376. Later Paul says that this perplexing situation of Israel reduced by its unbelief to a little remnant (9.25-29; 11.1-5) is the same situation which happened in the time of Elijah (11.2-5).

377. Barth, *Shorter Commentary on Romans*, p. 134. Maillot comments on this verse in the following terms: 'Paul, comme à son habitude, va montrer que le refus humain ne fait que rendre le "Oui" de Dieu plus grand et le filet de la miséricorde divine plus vaste et plus serré' (p. 56).

378. Getty, 'Christ Is the End of the Law', p. 99. According to Getty, 'Paul is still responding to the implied question of Rom 9.6' (*ibid.*).

379. Cambier calls Rom 10.21 'un résumé d'évangile' (*L'Evangile de Dieu*, p. 185; cf. p. 193).

380. Paul says in ch. 11 that, if indeed the gospel has been better received by the Gentiles, this is only due to God's mercy, and therefore, through the Christian mission to Israel, the Gentile Christians have to show mercy to Israel (11.31). If the church has problems with the Jews, this is not a reason to reject or despise them, for, although 'from the standpoint of the gospel they are enemies for your sake, from the standpoint of God's choice they are beloved for the sake of the fathers' (11.28, NASB). If 'a partial hardening has happened to Israel', it is just 'until the fulness of the Gentiles has come in, and then all Israel will be saved' (11.25, NASB).

381. Rolland rightly says that Paul's aim would not be reached at all if he leaves his readers with the impression that God had rejected Israel or that Israel's rejection of Christ is definitive. That would mean to ignore 'the riches of God's goodness and forbearance and longsuffering . . . ' (2.4; cf. 11.33). God cannot abandon the people who are the depository of his promises (3.2; 4.16; 9.4) for God cannot abandon anybody. God will not stop calling Israel and Gentiles to conversion until 'the πλήρωμα of Israel and the nations will be saved' (11.25; cf. 11.12). The very existence of a remnant (λεῖμμα, 11.5) to which Paul belongs (11.1) is already a guaranty that God 'had not rejected his people' (11.1, 26); his aim is that they also be saved (10.1). This same attitude of concern for the salvation of Israel is what Paul sought to find in the Christian community, in Rome, and elsewhere ('Il est notre justice', p. 403).

382. Barrett, 'Rom 9.30–10.21', p. 99.

383. So Scroggs argues that in Rom 1–11 there are two independent homilies: one formed by 1–4 and 9–11 and the other by 5–8 ('Paul as Rhetorician', p. 297).

384. Dahl observes that 'Several times Paul introduces a theme and appears to leave it undeveloped only to take it up again later in the letter (3.1-8; 4.15-16; 5.20). He raises objections to his own arguments and discusses them in sections which seem to interrupt the main line of argumentation but which enrich and deepen it . . . ' ('The Future of Israel', *Studies in Paul*, p. 139). This may be the answer to Scroggs.

385. Feuillet has emphasized the importance of this passage, saying that it 'exprime la pensée dominante de l'apôtre en ces chapîtres et est presque comparable en importance à 1.16-17' ('Le plan salvifique', p. 491).

386. See, for example, Isa 55.11: 'So shall my word (Λόγος) be which goes forth from my mouth; it shall not return to me empty, without accomplishing what I desire, and without succeeding in the matter for which I sent it'. Cf. other passages where it is explicitly said that the word of certain prophets 'did not fail' (πίπτω): 1 Sam 3.19; Jos 21.43; 23.14; 1 Kgs 8.56; 2 Kgs 8.10.

The words in 9.28, 'God will execute his word upon the earth', recall Isa 55.11 and are the specific answer to 9.6.

387. For full discussion, see Campbell, 'Romans iii as the Structural Centre of the Letter', pp. 24-39.

388. For Campbell, 'The centre of Paul's argument in the letter is iii,21-26 and its climax is chs. ix-xi' (*ibid.*, p. 39).

389. Rhyne, p. 114.

390. So O. Michel, quoted by Campbell, p. 307.

391. Rhyne, p. 116.

392. Barr argues that 'quite the reverse' is true (*Semantics*, p. 2); cf. P.R. Ackroyd, 'Meaning and Exegesis', in *Words and Meaning. Essays Presented to David Winton Thomas on His Retirement*, ed. P.R. Ackroyd and B. Lindars (Cambridge: University Press, 1968), pp. 3-4.

393. Barr, *Semantics*, p. 233, discusses the notion of 'new content' and warns against an indiscriminate use of such an exegetical criterion; see further pp. 206-62.

394. 'Old Testament Exegesis and the Problem of Ambiguity', *ASTI* 5 (1967), p. 14.

395. According to Meyer, Rom 9–11 is the place in Paul's writings where 'he grapples most directly with the question whether God's purposes and judgments are sustained in the history of his people or whether that history shows God's word instead to have failed' ('Rom 10.4', p. 60); cf. A.E. Martens, *God's Design. A Focus on Old Testament Theology* (Grand Rapids: Baker, 1981), pp. 256-58; cf. Stendahl, *Paul among Jews and Gentiles*, p. 27; Jeremias, *New Testament Theology*, p. 208; cf. Benoit, *Exégèse et Théologie*, II, pp. 38-39.

396. Jeremias observes that 'in the New Testament it is particularly the coming of Christ that cannot be understood save in reference to teleological questions' (*NT Theology*, p. 208).

397. Notice that Paul preaches from the OT even in his preaching to Gentiles. For him, the OT is also their only Bible, and, therefore, only the biblical texts can be the basis of his argument (cf. O. Michel, *Paulus und seine Bibel* [Darmstadt: Wissenschaftliche Buchgesellschaft, 1972]), pp. 122-29; cf. Vicent, p. 751. Costello explains this fact by saying: 'The use of Scripture was not, however, without effect on the Gentiles, for St. Paul knew that they at least could understand from the inspired records that the religion of Christ had been in times past foretold, prefigured, and prepared' ('The OT in St. Paul's Epistles', p. 142).

398. Rhyne, pp. 120-21 (quoting Mussner, 'Rom 10.4', p. 37, and Dülmen, *Gesetzes*, p. 126).

399. See R. Martin-Achard, 'Brèves remarques sur la signification théologique de la loi selon l'Ancien Testament', *ETR* 57 (1982), pp. 342-59. Cf. L. Gaston, 'Abraham and the Righteousness of God', p. 59.

400. Bruce, *Biblical Exegesis in the Qumran Texts*, p. 68; cf. Vicent, 'Derash', p. 781.

401. Jeremias, *NT Theology*, p. 208.

402. Whatever may be the judgment of the contemporary exegete on Paul's hermeneutics—whether related to Palestinian or Diaspora rabbinism, or related to the targumic or midrashic traditions—it is always possible to see the apostle go to the heart of the problem through these approaches, going far deeper than mere dialectical or exegetical virtuosity. In any case, Paul is not 'suspending dogmatic mountains on textual hairs' (Costello, p. 144). His topics are the essential ones. As G. Vermes says, Paul's hermeneutic is 'organically bound to the Bible' and 'its spirit and method are of biblical origin' ('Bible and Midrash: Early Old Testament Exegesis', *CHB*, I, p. 220). Behind Paul's hermeneutic there is his 'pre-understanding' that the OT authors would concur in his interpretation of the OT texts (Getty, 'Christ Is the End of the Law', p. 76); cf. P. Grech, 'The "Testimonia" and Modern Hermeneutics', *NTS* 19 (1972-73), p. 320; Ellis, *Paul's Use of the OT*, p. 85.

403. The typological and the 'promise–fulfillment' approaches may become reductionistic when they are understood as if only parts of the OT are deemed worthy of attention for the Christian exegete. Paul's teleological view of the OT included, because of its Messianic nature, the Christological and the eschatological categories.

404. It seems that Paul's teleological understanding of the relation of Christ to the law does not differ from the view that Christ himself had of that relationship acording to the gospels (cf. Matt 5.17; Luke 24.44-46; John 5.39, 46, 47; etc.). Cf. Ladd, *The Presence of the Future* (Grand Rapids: Eerdmans, 1974), p. 284; Feuillet, 'Habacuc 2', p. 78. See further Démann, 'Moïse et la loi', p. 238; Kaiser, 'Leviticus 18.5', p. 26; Cerfaux, *La Théologie de l'église suivant S. Paul* (Paris: Editions du Cerf, 1965), pp. 39-40; Amiot, *L'Enseignement de Paul*, I, p. 100.

405. Bonsirven, *Exégèse rabbinique et exégèse paulinienne*, p. 384.

406. Garofalo, pp. 42-43; cf. B. Rigaux, 'L'interprétation du paulinisme dans l'exégèse recente', in *Littérature et théologie pauliniennes*, p. 45.

BIBLIOGRAPHY

Achtemeier, Elizabeth R. *The Old Testament and the Proclamation of the Gospel.* Philadelphia: Westminster, 1973.

Ackroyd, Peter R. 'The Vitality of the Word of God in the Old Testament.' *Annual of the Swedish Theological Institute* 1 (1962), pp. 7-23.

Aldrich, Roy L. 'Has the Mosaic Law Been Abolished?' *Bibliotheca Sacra* 116 (1959), pp. 322-35.

Althaus, Paul. *Der Brief an die Römer.* Vol. 6. Das Neue Testament Deutsch. Edited by P. Althaus and G. Friedrich. Göttingen: Vandenhoeck and Ruprecht, 1959.

— *The Divine Command: A New Perspective on Law and Gospel.* Facet Books, Social Ethics Series 9. Philadelphia: Fortress Press, 1966.

Amiot, François. *L'enseignement de Saint Paul.* Paris: Gabalda, 1938.

— *The Key Concepts of St. Paul.* New York: Herder & Herder, 1962.

Bammel, Ernst. 'Νόμος Χριστοῦ.' *Studia Evangelica* 3 in *Texte und Untersuchungen,* 88. Edited by F.L. Cross. Berlin: Akademie Verlag, 1964, pp. 120-28.

Bandstra, Andrew John. *The Law and the Elements of the World. An Exegetical Study in Aspects of Paul's Teaching.* Kampen: J.H. Kok, 1964.

Baker, D.L. *Two Testaments—One Bible: A Study of Some Modern Solutions to the Theological Problem of the Relationship between the Old Testament and the New Testament.* Downers Grove, Ill.: InterVarsity Press, 1976.

Banks, Robert. 'The Eschatological Role of the Law in Pre- and Post-Christian Jewish Thought.' In *Reconciliation and Hope.* Edited by R. Banks. Exeter: Paternoster, 1974, pp. 173-85.

Barclay, William. 'Law in the New Testament.' *Expository Times* 86 (1974-1975), pp. 100-103.

Barr, James. *Old and New in Interpretation: A Study of the Two Testaments.* New York: Harper and Row, 1966.

Barrett, Charles Kingsley. *A Commentary on the Epistle to the Romans.* London: Adam & Charles Black, 1957.

— 'The Interpretation of the Old Testament in the New.' In *Cambridge History of the Bible.* Vol. 1. Edited by P.R. Ackroyd and C.F. Evans. Cambridge: University Press, 1970, pp. 377-411.

—*Reading Through Romans*. Philadelphia: Fortress, 1977.

—'Rom 9.30–10.21: Fall and Responsibility in Israel.' In *Die Israelfrage nach Rom 9–11*. Edited by L. De Lorenzi. Rome: Abbazia S. Paolo, 1977.

Barth, Karl. *The Epistle to the Romans*. Oxford: University Press, 1933.

—*A Shorter Commentary on Romans*. Richmond, Va.: John Knox Press, 1959.

Barth, Markus. 'Jews and Gentiles. The Social Character of Justification in Paul.' *Journal of Ecumenical Studies* 5 (1968), pp. 241-67.

—*Justification. Pauline Texts Interpreted in the Light of the Old and the New Testaments*. Grand Rapids: Eerdmans, 1971.

—'Die Stellung des Paulus zu Gesetz und Ordnung.' *Evangelische Theologie* 33 (1973), pp. 496-526.

—'Das Volk Gottes—Juden und Christen in der Botschaft des Paulus.' In *Paulus—Apostat oder Apostel?*. Edited by M. Barth et al. Regensburg: Pustet, 1977, pp. 45-234.

—'St. Paul—A Good Jew.' *Horizons in Biblical Theology* 1 (1980), pp. 7-45.

Bartsch, Hans Werner. 'Paul's Letter to the Romans.' Unpublished lectures. Bethany Theological Seminary, Oak Brook, Illinois, 1967.

—'The Concept of Faith in Paul's Letter to the Romans.' *Biblical Research* 13 (1968), pp. 41-53.

—'Die Empfänger des Römerbriefes.' *Studia Theologica* 25 (1971), pp. 81-89.

—'The Historical Situation of Romans.' *Encounter* 33 (1972), pp. 329-39.

Baules, Robert. *Commentaire de l'Epître aux Romains*. Paris: Cerf, 1968.

Beare, Francis Wright. *St. Paul and His Letters*. New York: Abingdon Press, 1962.

Beasley-Murray, George Raymond. 'The Righteousness of God in the History of Israel and the Nations: Romans 9–11.' *Review and Expositor* 73 (1976), pp. 437-50.

Beet, Joseph Agar. *A Commentary on St. Paul's Epistle to the Romans*. 7th edn. New York: Thomas Whittaker, 1892.

Beker, Johan Christiaan. *Paul the Apostle: The Triumph of God in Life and Thought*. Philadelphia: Fortress Press, 1980.

Benoit, Pierre. 'La loi et la croix d'après Saint Paul.' *Revue Biblique* 47 (1983), pp. 481-509.

—*Exégèse et Théologie*. Vol. 2. *La Théologie de St. Paul*. Paris: Editions du Cerf, 1961.

Best, Ernest. *The Letter of Paul to the Romans*. Cambridge Bible Commentary. Cambridge: University Press, 1967.

Black, Matthew. 'The Chronological Use of the Old Testament in the New Testament.' *New Testament Studies* 18 (1971), pp. 1-14.

—*Romans*. New Century Bible. London: Oliphants, 1973.

Blank, Sheldon Haas. 'The Septuagint Rendering of the Old Testament Terms for Law.' *Hebrew Union College Annual* 7 (1930), pp. 259-83.

Bläser, Peter. *Das Gesetz bei Paulus*. Neutestamentliche Abhandlungen, 19. Münster: Aschendorffsche Verlagsbuchhandlung, 1961.

Boman, Thorlief. *Hebrew Thought Compared with Greek*. Philadelphia: Westminster Press, 1960.

Bonsirven, Joseph. *Exégèse rabbinique et exégèse paulinienne*. Bibliothèque de Théologie Historique. Paris: Beauchesne et Fils, 1939.

Bornkamm, Günther. *Das Ende des Gesetzes*. Beiträge zur evangelischen Theologie, 16. Munich: Kaiser Verlag, 1961.

—*Paul*. New York: Harper and Row, 1971.

—'The Revelation of Christ to Paul and Paul's Doctrine of Justification and Reconciliation.' In *Reconciliation and Hope. New Testament Essays on Atonement and Eschatology*. Edited by R. Banks. Exeter: Paternoster, 1974.

Bornkamm, Heinrich. *Luther and the Old Testment*. Phildelphia: Fortress Press, 1969.

Bousset, Wilhelm. *Kyrios Christos*. New York: Abingdon Press, 1970.

Bover, José María. *Teología de San Pablo*. 4th edn. Madrid: Biblioteca de Autores Christianos, 1967.

Bring, Ragnar. 'Die Erfüllung des Gesetzes durch Christus.' *Kerygma und Dogma* 5 (1959), pp. 1-22.

—'Das Gesetz und die Gerechtigkeit Gottes. Eine Studie zur Frage nach der Bedeutung des Ausdruckes *télos nómou* in Rom. 10.4.' *Studia Theologica* 20 (1966), pp. 1-36.

—'Die Gerechtigkeit Gottes und das alttestamentliche Gesetz: Eine Untersuchung von Rom 10.4.' In *Christus und das Gesetz: Die Bedeutung des Gesetzes des Alten Testaments nach Paulus und sein Glauben an Christus*. Leiden: Brill, 1969.

—'Paul and the Old Testament: A Study of the Ideas of Election, Faith, and Law in Paul, with Special Reference to Rom. 9.30–10.13.' *Studia Theologica* 25 (1971), pp. 21-60.

Bruce, Frederick F. *The Epistle of Paul to the Romans*. Grand Rapids: Eerdmans, 1963.

—'Promise and Fulfillment in Paul's Presentation of Jesus.' In *Promise and Fulfillment. Essays Presented to Professor S.H. Hooke*. Edited by F.F. Bruce. Edinburgh: T. & T. Clark, 1964.

—'Paul and the Law of Moses.' *Bulletin of the John Rylands University Library* 57 (1975), pp. 259-79.

—'The Romans Debate—Continued.' *Bulletin of the John Rylands University Library* 64 (1982), pp. 334-59.

Brunner, Emil. *The Letter to the Romans. A Commentary*. Philadelphia: Westminster Press, 1959.

Brunot, Amédée. *Le génie littéraire de Saint Paul*. Paris: Les Editions du Cerf, 1955.

Bugge, Christian A. 'Das Gesetz und Christus nach der Anschauung des ältesten Christengemeinde.' In *Zeitschrift für die neutestamentliche Wissenschaft* 4 (1903), pp. 89-110.

Bultmann, Rudolf K. 'Christ the End of the Law.' In *Essays Philosophical and Theological*. New York: Macmillan, 1955, pp. 36-66.

—'Prophecy and Fulfillment.' In *Essays on Old Testament Hermeneutics*. Edited by Claus Westermann. Richmond: John Knox Press, 1963, pp. 50-75.

—'ΔΙΚΑΙΟΣΥΝΗ ΘΕΟΥ.' *Journal of Biblical Literature* 83 (1964), pp. 12-16.

Calvin, John. *Commentaries on the Epistle of Paul to the Romans*. Edited by J. Owen. Grand Rapids: Eerdmans, 1947.

—*The Epistles of Paul the Apostle to the Romans and to the Thessalonians*. Edited by David W. Torrance and Thomas F. Torrance. Edinburgh: Oliver and Boyd, 1961.

Cambier, Jules. *L'Evangile de Dieu selon l'épître aux Romains: Exégèse et Théologie Biblique*. Louvain: Desclée de Brouwer, 1967, vol. 1, pp. 184-93.

Campbell, W.S. 'Christ the End of the Law: Romans 10.4.' In *Studia Biblica 1978: III. Papers on Paul and Other New Testament Authors. Sixth International Congress on Biblical Studies. Oxford, April 1978*. Edited by E.A. Livingstone. Journal for the Study of the New Testament Supplement Series, 3. Sheffield: JSOT Press, 1979, pp. 173-81.

—'The Romans Debate.' *Journal for the Study of the New Testament* 10 (1981), pp. 19-28.

—'Romans III as a Key to the Structure and Thought of the Letter.' *Novum Testamentum* 23 (1981), pp. 22-40.

Cerfaux, Lucien. 'Le Privilège d'Israël selon Saint Paul.' In *Recueil Lucien Cerfaux*. 2 vols. Gembloux: Duculot, 1954, pp. 339-64.

—*Christ in the Theology of St. Paul*. New York: Herder & Herder, 1958.

Collins, John J. 'Chiasmus. The ABA Pattern and the Text of Paul.' *Studiorum Paulinorum Congressus Internationalis Catholicus 1961*. 2 vols. Rome: Pontifical Biblical Institute, 1963, vol. 2, pp. 575-83.

Conzelmann, Hans. *An Outline of the Theology of the New Testment*. New York: Harper and Row, 1969.

Copeland, E.L. 'Nomos as a Medium of Revelation—Paralleling Logos—in Ante-Nicene Christianity.' *Studia Theologica* 27 (1973), pp. 51-61.

Coppens, Joseph. 'Les arguments scripturaires et leur portée dans les lettres pauliniennes.' *Studiorum Paulinorum Congressus Internationalis Catholicus 1961*. Rome: Pontifical Biblical Institute, 1963, vol. 2, pp. 243-53.

Corley, Russell Bruce. 'The Significance of Romans 9–11: A Study in Pauline Theology.' Th.D. Dissertation, Southwestern Baptist Theological Seminary, 1975.

Costello, C.J. 'The Old Testament in St. Paul's Epistles.' *Catholic Biblical Quarterly* 4 (1942), pp. 141-45.

Cranfield, Charles E.B. 'St. Paul and the Law.' *Scottish Journal of Theology* 17 (1969), pp. 43-68.

—'Some Notes on Rom. 9.30-33.' In *Jesus und Paulus. Festschrift W.G. Kümmel.* Edited by E.E. Ellis and F. Grässer. Göttingen: Vandenhoeck and Ruprecht, 1975.

—*A Critical and Exegetical Commentary on the Epistle to the Romans in Two Volumes.* 2 vols. ICC. Edinburgh: T. & T. Clark, 1979.

—'Romans 9.30–10.4.' *Interpretation* 34 (1980), pp. 70-74.

Cullman, Oscar. *Christ and Time. The Primitive Christian Conception of Time and History.* London: SCM, 1951.

Daalen, D.H. van. 'Faith According to Paul.' *Expository Times* 87 (1975), pp. 83-85.

Dahl, Nils Alstrup. 'The Messiahship of Jesus in Paul.' In *The Crucified Messiah and Other Essays.* Minneapolis: Augsburg Publishing House, 1974.

—*Studies in Paul: Theology for the Early Christian Missions.* Minneapolis: Augsburg Publishing House, 1977.

Davies, William David. *Paul and Rabbinic Judaism. Some Rabbinic Elements in Pauline Theology.* London: SPCK, 1948.

—*Torah in the Messianic Age and the Age to Come.* Philadelphia: Society of Biblical Literture, 1952.

—'Law in the New Testament.' *Interpreter's Dictionary of the Bible.* Edited by G.A. Buttrick et al. New York: Abingdon Press, 1962.

—*The Gospel and the Land.* Berkeley: University Press, 1974.

Delling, Gerhard. 'Telos-Aussagen in der griechischen Philosophie.' *Zeitschrift für die neutestamentliche Wissenschaft* 55 (1964), pp. 26-42.

—'Nahe ist dir das Wort.' *Theologische Literaturzeitung* 99 (1974), pp. 401-12.

De Lorenzi, Lorenzo, ed. *Die Israelfrage nach Röm 9–11.* Rome: St. Paul's Abbey, 1977.

—*Paul de Tarse: Apôtre de notre temps.* Rome: St Paul's Abbey, 1979.

Démann, Paul. 'Moïse et la loi dans la pensée de Saint Paul.' In *Moïse, l'homme de l'alliance.* Paris: Desclée, 1955.

Descamps, Albert. 'La Structure de Rom 1–11.' *Studiorum Paulinorum Congressus Internationalis Catholicus 1961.* Rome: Pontifical Biblical Institute, 1963, 1.3-14.

—et al. *Littérature et théologie pauliniennes.* Louvain: Desclée de Brower, 1960.

Dibelius, Martin, and Kümmel, Werner Georg. *Paul.* Philadelphia: Westminster Press, 1953.

Díez Macho, Alejandro. 'Çesará la Tora en la Edad Mesiánica?' *Estudios Biblicos* 12 (1953), pp. 115-58; 13 (1954), pp. 5-51.

Dodd, Charles Harold. *Gospel and Law: The Relation of Faith and Ethics in Early Christinatiy.* New York: Columbia University Press, 1951.

—*The Epistle of Paul to the Romans.* London: Hodder & Stoughton, 1954.

—*The Old Testament in the New.* Philadelphia: Fortress, 1963.

Donfried, Karl P. 'False Presuppositions in the Study of Romans.' *Catholic Biblical Quarterly* 36 (1974), pp. 332-55.

—ed. *The Romans Debate.* Minneapolis: Augsburg, 1977.

Doulière, Richard F. *L'Epître aux Romains.* Neuchâtel: Imprimerie Nouvelle, 1975.

Drane, John W. *Paul: Libertine or Legalist? A Study in the Theology of the Major Pauline Epistles.* London: SPCK, 1975.

—'Why Did Paul Write Romans?' In *Pauline Studies. Essays Presented to Professor F.F. Bruce on His 70th Birthday.* Edited by D.A. Hagner and M.J. Harris. Grand Rapids: Eerdmans, 1980.

Dülmen, A. van. *Die Theologie des Gesetzes bei Paulus.* Stuttgarter Biblische Monographien, 5. Stuttgart: Katholischer Bibelwerk Verlag, 1968.

Du Plessis, Paul Johannes. *Teleiosis: The Idea of Perfection in the New Testament.* Kampen: J.H. Kok, 1959.

Dupont, Jacques. 'Le problème de la structure littéraire de l'Epître aux Romains.' *Revue biblique* 62 (1955), pp. 365-97.

Ebeling, Gerhard. 'Reflections on the Doctrine of the Law.' In *Word and Faith.* Philadelphia: Fortress Press, 1963.

Efird, J.M., ed. *The Use of the Old Testament in the New and Other Essays.* Durham: Duke University Press, 1972.

Eicholz, Georg. *Die Theologie der Paulus im Umriss.* Neukirchen: Neukirchener Verlag, 1972.

Ellis, Edward Earle. *Saint Paul's Use of the Old Testament.* Grand Rapids: Eerdmans, 1957.

—'Midrash, Targum and New Testament Quotations.' In *Neotestamentica et Semitica.* Edited by E.E. Ellis and M. Wilcox. Edinburgh: T. & T. Clark, 1969.

Fesperman, Francis Irving. *Freedom from the Law: Paul's Doctrine and Its Role in the Early Church.* Ph.D. Dissertation, Vanderbilt University, 1968.

Festorazzi, A. 'Coherence and Value of the Old Testament in Paul's Thought.' In *Paul de Tarse, apôtre de notre temps.* Edited by L. De Lorenzi. Rome: S. Paolo, 1979, pp. 165-73.

Feuillet, André. 'Le plan salvifique de Dieu d'après l'Epître aux Romains.' *Revue Biblique* 57 (1950), pp. 336-87, 489-529.

—'Loi de Dieu, loi du Christ et loi de l'Esprit d'après les épîtres pauliniennes.' *Novum Testamentum* 22 (1980), pp. 29-65.

Fischer, James A. 'Pauline Literary Forms and Thought Patterns.' *Catholic Biblical Quarterly* 39 (1977), pp. 209-23.

—'Dissent within a Religious Community: Romans 9–11.' *Biblical Theology Bulletin* 10 (1980), pp. 105-10.

Fitzmyer, J.A. 'The Letter to the Romans.' In *The Jerome Biblical Comment-*

ary. Edited by R.E. Brown, J.A. Fitzmyer, R.E. Murphy. Englewood Cliffs: Prentice-Hall, 1968.

—'Paul and the Law.' In *A Companion to Paul.* Edited by M.J. Taylor. New York: Alba House, 1975.

Flückiger, Felix. 'Christus des Gesetzes τέλος.' *Theologische Zeitschrift* 11 (1955), pp. 153-57.

Forde, Gerhard O. *The Law-Gospel Debate: An Interpretation of Its Historical Development.* Minneapolis: Augsburg, 1969.

Friedländer, M. 'The Pauline Emancipation from the Law a Product of the Pre-Christian Jewish Diaspora.' *Jewish Quarterly Review* 14 (1901-1902), pp. 265-301.

Fuller, Daniel P. 'Paul and the Works of the Law.' *Westminster Theological Journal* 38 (1975), pp. 28-42.

—*Gospel and Law. Contrast or Continuum? The Hermeneutics of Dispensationalism and Covenant Theology.* Grand Rapids: Eerdmans, 1980.

Furnish, Victor Paul. *Theology and Ethics in Paul.* New York: Abingdon, 1968.

Gamble, Harry. *The Textual History of the Letter to the Romans.* Grand Rapids: Eerdmans, 1977.

Garofalo, Salvatore. 'Il Messianesimo di San Paolo.' In *Studiorum Paulinorum Congressus Internationalis Catholicus 1961.* Rome: Pontifical Biblical Institute, 1967.

Gaston, Lloyd. 'Paul and the Torah.' In *Antisemitism and the Foundations of Christianity.* Edited by A. Davies. New York: Paulinist Press, 1979.

—'Abraham and the Righteousness of God.' *Horizons in Biblical Theology* 2 (1980), pp. 39-68.

Getty, Mary Ann. 'Structure and Interpretation of Romans 9–11. State of the Question.' Dissertation presented for the degree of Licentiate in Theology, Catholic University of Louvain, 1971. (Unpublished).

—'Christ Is the End of the Law: Rom 10.4 in Its Context.' Th.D. dissertation, Katholieke Universitaet Leuven, 1975. (Unpublished)

Godet, Fréderic. *Commentary on St. Paul's Epistle to the Romans.* Edinburgh: T. & T. Clark, 1892: reprint edn, Grand Rapids: Zondervan, 1956.

Godsey, John D. 'The Interpretation of Romans in the History of the Christian Faith.' *Interpretation* 34 (1980), pp. 3-16.

Goldberg, A.M. 'Torah aus der Unterwelt?' *Biblische Zeitschrift* 14 (1970), pp. 126-31.

Goldstain, J. *Les valeurs de la loi, la Thora lumière sur la route.* Théologie historique, 56. Paris: Beauchesne, 1980.

Goppelt, Leonhard. *Jesus, Paul and Judaism.* New York: Nelson and Sons, 1964.

Gore, Charles. 'The Argument of Romans ix–xi.' In *Studia Biblica et Ecclesiastica: Essays in Biblical and Patristic Criticism.* Edited by S.R. Driver et al. Oxford: Clarendon Press, 1891.

Grafe, E. *Die paulinische Lehre von Gesetz nach den vier Hauptbriefen.* Freiburg: J.C.B. Mohr, 1884; revised edn, 1893.

Graham, Holt H. 'Continuity and Discontinuity in the Thought of Paul.' *Anglican Theological Review* 38 (1956), pp. 137-46.

Grelot, Pierre. *Sens chrétien de l'Ancien Testament.* Paris: Desclée, 1962.

Grundmann, Walter. 'The Teacher of Righteousness of Qumran and the Question of Justification by Faith in the Theology of the Apostle Paul.' *Paul and Qumran.* Edited by J. Murphy-O'Connor. London: Geoffrey Chapman, 1968.

Gulin, E.E. 'The Positive Meaning of the Law According to Paul.' *Lutheran Quarterly* 10 (1958), pp. 115-28.

Günther, Agnes. 'Endziel der Gesetzes ist Christus (Rom. 10.4). Zur heutigen innerkirchlichen Gesetzeskrise.' *Erbe und Auftrag* 43 (1967), pp. 192-205.

Hahn, Ferdinand. 'Das Gesetzesverständnis im Römer- und Galaterbrief.' *Zeitschrift für die neutestamentliche Wissenschaft* 67 (1976), pp. 29-63.

Hanson, Anthony Tyrrell. *Studies in Paul's Technique and Theology.* Grand Rapids: Eerdmans, 1974.

Harrisville, Roy A. *Romans.* Augsburg Commentary on the New Testament. Minneapolis: Augsburg, 1980.

Haufe, C. von. 'Die Stellung des Paulus zum Gesetz.' *Theologische Literaturzeitung* 91 (1966), 171-78.

Hellbardt, Hans. 'Christus, das Telos des Gesetzes.' *Evangelische Theologie* 3 (1936), pp. 331-46.

Heller, J. 'Himmel- und Höllenfahrt nach Römer 10.6-7.' *Evangelische Theologie* 32 (1972), pp. 478-86.

Holtzmann, Oskar. *Der Römerbrief.* Das Neue Testament. 2 vols. Giessen: Alfred Töpelmann, 1962.

Howard, George E. 'Christ the End of the Law: The Meaning of Romans 10.4ff.' *Journal of Biblical Literature* 88 (1969), pp. 331-37.

Hübner, Hans. *Das Gesetz bei Paulus: Ein Beitrag zum Werden der paulinischen Theologie.* Forschungen zur Religion und Literatur des Alten und Neuen Testaments, 119. Göttingen: Vandenhoeck & Ruprecht, 1978.

Huby, Joseph. *Saint Paul: Epître aux Romains.* Edited by S. Lyonnet. Paris: Beauchesne, 1957.

Hughes, Meredith J. 'Romans x.6-8.' *Expository Times* 19 (1907-1908), pp. 524-25.

Hummel, Horace. 'Are Law and Gospel a Valid Hermeneutical Principle?' *Concordia Theological Quarterly* 46 (1982), pp. 181-208.

Jeremias, Joachim. 'Chiasmus in den Paulusbriefen.' *Zeitschrift für die neutestamentliche Wissenschaft* 49 (1954), pp. 145-56.

—*New Testament Theology: The Proclamation of Jesus.* New York: Scribner's, 1971.

Jewett, Robert. *Paul's Anthropological Terms: A Study of Their Use in Conflict Settings*. Leiden: Brill, 1971.

—'Major Impulses in the Theological Interpretation of Romans Since Barth.' *Interpretation* 34 (1980), pp. 17-31.

Jones, Peter Ronald. 'The Apostle Paul: A Second Moses According to II Corinthians 2.14–4.7.' Ph.D. dissertation, Princeton Theological Seminary, 1973.

Kaiser, Walter C., Jr. 'Leviticus 18.5 and Paul: Do This and You shall Live (Eternally?)' [Rom. 10.4–5]. *Journal of the Evangelical Theological Society* 14 (1971), pp. 19-28.

Käsemann, Ernst. 'God's Righteousness in Paul.' *Journal for Theology and the Church* 1 (1965), pp. 100-10.

—'Sentences of Holy Law in the New Testament.' *New Testament Questions of Today*. London: SCM, 1969.

—*Perspectives on Paul*. Philadelphia: Fortress, 1974.

—*Commentary on Romans*. Grand Rapids: Eerdmans, 1980.

Keck, Leander E. *Paul and His Letters*. Philadelphia: Fortress, 1979.

Kertelge, Karl. *Rechtfertigung bei Paulus. Studien zur Struktur und zum Bedeutungsgehalt des paulinischen Rechtfertigungsbegriffs*. Münster: Aschendorff, 1967.

—*The Epistle to the Romans*. New York: Herder and Herder, 1972.

Kevan, Ernest F. *The Grace of Law: A Study in Puritan Theology*. Grand Rapids: Baker, 1965.

Kirk, Kenneth E. *The Epistle to the Romans*. The Clarendon Bible. Edited by B. Stroup and B. Wild. Oxford: Clarendon Press, 1937.

Knight, George Angus Fulton. *Law and Grace*. London: SCM, 1962.

Knox, John, and Cragg, Gerald R. 'Romans.' *The Interpreter's Bible*. New York: Abingdon Press, 1954, vol. 9, pp. 355-668.

Kühl, Ernst. *Der Brief des Paulus an die Römer*. Leipzig: Quelle und Meyer, 1913.

Kümmel, Werner Georg. *The Theology of the New Testament According to Its Major Witnesses Jesus–Paul–John*. London: SCM, 1974.

—'Die Probleme von Römer 9–11 in der gegenwärtigen Forschungslage.' In *Israelfrage Rom 9–11*. Edited by L. De Lorenzi. Rome: St Paul's Abbey, 1979.

Kuss, Otto. '*Nomos* bei Paulus.' *Münchener Theologische Zeitschrift* 17 (1966), pp. 173-227.

—*Der Römerbrief: übersetzt und erklärt (Rom. 8.19–11.36)*. Regensburg: F. Pustet, 1978.

Ladd, George Eldon. 'Paul and the Law.' In *Soli Deo Gloria: New Testament Studies in Honor of W.C. Robinson*. Edited by J.M. Richards. Richmond: John Knox, 1968.

Lagrange, Marie Joseph. *Saint Paul. Épître aux Romains*. Paris: Gabalda, 1915 (1950).

Langevin, Paul E. 'Le Salut par la foi. Rom. 10.8-13.' *Assemblées du Seigneur* 14 (1973), pp. 47-53.

—'Sur la christologie de Romains 10.1-13.' *Laval Théologique et Philosophique* 35 (1979), pp. 35-54.

Larcher, C. *L'actualité chrétienne de l'Ancien Testament d'après le Nouveau Testament* Paris: Cerf, 1962.

Le Déaut, Roger. 'Traditions targumiques dans le corpus paulinien?' *Biblica* 42 (1961), pp. 28-48.

Lee, Edwin Kenneth. *A Study in Romans*. London: SPCK, 1962.

Leenhardt, Franz J. *The Epistle to the Romans*. London: Lutterworth Press, 1961.

Léon-Dufour, X. 'Juif et gentil selon Romains 1-11.' *Studiorum Paulinorum Congressus Internationalis Catholicus 1961*. Rome: Pontifical Biblical Institute, 1963, vol. 1, pp. 309-15.

Liddon, Henry P. *Explanatory Analysis of St. Paul's Epistle to the Romans*. Grand Rapids: Zondervan, 1961.

Lietzmann, Hans. *Einführung in die Textgeschichte der Paulusbriefe an die Römer*. Tübingen: J.C.B. Mohr, 1919.

Lindars, Barnabas. *New Testament Apologetics. The Doctrinal Significance of the Old Testament Quotations*. Philadelphia: Westminster Press, 1961.

Longenecker, Richard N. *Paul, Apostle of Liberty*. New York: Harper and Row, 1964.

Lowy, M. 'Die paulinische Lehre von Gesetz.' *Monatsschrift für Geschichte und Wissenschaft des Judentums* 47 (1903), pp. 322-39, 417-33, 534-44; 48 (1904), pp. 268-76, 321-27, 400-16.

Luther, Martin. *Commentary on the Epistle to the Romans*. Grand Rapids: Zondervan, 1959.

—*Lectures on Romans*. Library of Christian Classics, vol. 15. Edited by W. Pauck. Philadelphia: Westminster Press, 1961.

Luz, Ulrich. *Das Geschichtsverständnis des Paulus*. Beiträge zur evangelischen Theologie, 49. Munich: Kaiser Verlag, 1968.

Lyonnet, S. 'De Justitia Dei in Epistola ad Romanos 10.3 et 3.5.' *Verbum Domini* 35 (1947), pp. 118-21.

—'Saint Paul et l'exégèse juive de son temps. A propos de Romans 10,6-8.' *Mélanges Bibliques redigées en l'honneur de André Robert*. Travaux de l'Institut Catholique de Paris, IV. Paris: Bloud & Gay, 1957.

—*Les Epîtres de Saint Paul aux Galates et Romains*. La Sainte Bible. Paris: Les Editions du Cerf, 1959.

—*Quaestiones in Epistulam ad Romanos*. 2 vols. Rome: Pontificio Istituto Biblico, 1962.

Maillot, Alphonse. 'Essai sur les citations vétérotestamentaires contenues dans Romains 9 et 11, ou Comment se servir de la Torah pour montrer que le "Christ est la fin de la Torah".' *Etudes Théologiques et Religieuses* 57 (1982), pp. 55-73.

Manson, Thomas Walter. 'Jesus, Paul, and the Law.' In *Judaism and Christianity*. 3 vols. London: Sheldon Press, 1937-1938.

Marin, Francisco. 'Matices del término ley en las cartas de San Pablo.' *Estudios Eclesiásticos* 49 (1974), pp. 19-46.

Marquardt, Fredrich Wilhelm. *Die Juden in Römerbrief*. Zürich: Theologischer Verlag, 1971.

Martin, Brice L. 'Matthew and Paul on Christ and the Law: Compatible or Incompatible Theologies?' Ph.D. dissertation, McMaster University, Canada, 1977.

Maurer, Christian. *Die Gesetzeslehre des Paulus nach ihrem Ursprung*. Zürich: Evangelischer Verlag, 1941.

Meyer, Heinrich August Wilhelm. *Critical and Exegetical Handbook to the Epistle to the Romans*. New York: Funk and Wagnalls, 1884.

Meyer, Paul W. 'Romans 10.4 and the End of the Law.' In *The Divine Helmsman: Studies on God's Control of Human Events, Presented to Lou H. Silberman*, pp. 59-78. Edited by James L. Crenshaw and Samuel Sandmel. New York: Ktav, 1980.

Michel, Otto. *Der Brief an die Römer*. Kritisch-exegetischer Kommentar über Neue Testament, 12. Göttingen: Vandenhoeck & Ruprecht, 1963.

—*Paulus und seine Bibel*. Darmstadt: Wissenschaftliche Buchgesellschaft, 1972.

Minear, Paul S. *The Obedience of Faith: The Purposes of Paul in the Epistle to the Romans*. London: SCM, 1971.

Monsengwo Pasinya, Laurent. *La notion de nomos dans le Pentateuque grec*. Analecta Biblica, 52. Rome: Biblical Institute Press, 1973.

Moule, Charles F.D. 'Fulfilment Words in the New Testament: Use and Abuse.' *New Testament Studies* 14 (1968), pp. 293-320.

Moule, Handley C.G. *The Epistle of St. Paul to the Romans*. The Expositor's Bible. New York: Hodder & Stoughton, 1893.

Moxnes, Halvor. *Theology in Conflict. Studies in Paul's Understanding of God in Romans*. Supplements to Novum Testamentum, 53. Leiden: E.J. Brill, 1980.

Müller, Christian. *Gottes Gerechtigkeit und Gottes Volk. Eine Untersuchung zu Römer 9–11*.

Muller-Duvernoy, C. 'L'apôtre Paul et le problème juif.' *Judaica* 15 (1959), pp. 65-91.

Munck, Johannes. *Paul and the Salvation of Mankind*. Richmond: John Knox Press, 1959.

—*Christ and Israel. An Interpretation of Rom. 9–11*. Philadelphia: Fortress, 1967.

Murray, John. *The Epistle to the Romans*. 2 vols. Edited by F.F. Bruce. Grand Rapids: Eerdmans, 1959 (1965).

Mussner, Franz. 'Christus (ist) des Gesetzes Ende zur Gerechtigkeit für jeden, der glaubt (Röm 10.4).' In *Paulus—Apostat oder Apostel? Jüdische und Christliche Antworten.* Regensburg: Verlag Friedrich Pustet, 1977.

Nelis, J. 'Les Antithèses littéraires dans les épîtres de saint Paul.' *Nouvelle Revue Théologique* 4 (1948), pp. 360-87.

Nygren, Anders. *Commentary on Romans.* Philadelphia: Muhlenberg Press, 1949.

O'Neill, J.C. *Paul's Letter to the Romans.* London: Penguin Books, 1975.

Osten-Sacken, Peter von der. 'Das paulinische Verständnis der Gesetzes im Spannungfeld von Eschatologie und Geschichte.' *Evangelische Theologie* 47 (1977), pp. 549-87.

Oesterreicher, J.M. 'Israel's Misstep and Her Rise.' In *Studiorum Paulinorum Congressus Internationalis Catholicus 1961.* Rome: Pontifical Biblical Institute, 1963, vol. 1, pp. 317-27.

Pedersen, Sigfred, ed. *Pauline Literature and Theology.* Göttingen: Vandenhoeck & Ruprecht, 1980.

Pfitzner, Victor C. *Paul and the Agon Motif. Traditional Athletic Imagery in the Pauline Literature.* Supplements to Novum Testamentum, 16. Leiden: Brill, 1967.

Philippi, F.A. *Commentary on St. Paul's Epistle to the Romans.* 2 vols. Edinburgh: T. & T. Clark, 1879.

Plag, Christoph. *Israels Wege zum Heil. Eine Untersuchung zu Römer 9 bis 11.* Arbeiten zur Theologie, 40. Edited by A. Jepsen, O. Michel, T. Schlatter. Stuttgart: Calwer Verlag, 1969.

Pohlenz, Max. *Paulus und die Stoa.* Darmstadt: Wissenschaftliche Buchsgesellschaft, 1964.

Prat, Ferdinand. *The Theology of St. Paul.* 2 vols. London: Burns, Oates and Washbourne, 1945.

Räisänen, Heikki. 'Paul's Theological Difficulties with the Law.' *Studia Biblica* 3 (1978), pp. 301-20.

Ramaroson, Leonard. 'Un nouveau plan de Rom. 1.16–11.36.' *Nouvelle Revue Théologique* 94 (1972), pp. 943-58.

Reicke, Bo. 'The Law and This World According to Paul.' *Journal of Biblical Literature* 70 (1951), pp. 259-76.

—'Paul's Understanding of Righteousness.' *Soli Deo Gloria.* Edited by J.M. Richards. Richmond: John Knox Press, 1968.

Rhyne, Clyde Thomas. *Faith Establishes the Law: A Study on the Continuity between Judaism and Christianity, Romans 3.31.* SBL Dissertation Series, 55. Missoula: Scholars Press, 1981.

Ridderbos, Herman N. *Paul: An Outline of His Theology.* Grand Rapids: Eerdmans, 1975.

Rigaux, Beda. 'L'interprétation du paulinisme dans l'exégèse récente.' In *Littérature et théologie pauliniennes.* Louvain: Desclée de Brouwer, 1960.

—*The Letters of St. Paul.* Chicago: Franciscan Herald Press, 1968.

Robinson, D.W.B. 'The Salvation of Israel in Rom. 9–11.' *Reformed*

Theological Review 26 (1967), pp. 81-96.

Robinson, John A.T. *Wrestling with Romans*. London: SCM Press, 1979.

Rolland, Philippe. 'Il est notre justice, notre vie, notre salut. L'ordonnance des thèmes majeurs de l'épître aux Romains.' *Biblica* 56 (1975), pp. 394-404.

—*Epître aux Romains. Texte grec structuré*. Rome: Institut Biblique Pontifical, 1980.

Ryrie, Charles Caldwell. 'The End of the Law (Rom. 10.4).' *Bibliotheca Sacra* 124 (1967), pp. 239-47.

Sabourin, Leopold. *The Bible and Christ. The Unity of the Two Testaments*. Staten Island: Alba House, 1980.

Sand, Alexander. 'Gesetz und Freiheit. Vom Sinn des Pauluswortes: Christus, des Gesetzes Ende.' *Theologie und Glaube* 61 (1971), pp. 1-14.

Sanday, William, and Headlam, Arthur C. *A Critical and Exegetical Commentary on the Epistle to the Romans*. ICC. Edinburgh: T. & T. Clark, 1958.

Sanders, E.P. *Paul and Palestinian Judaism: A Comparison of Patterns of Religion*. Philadelphia: Fortress Press, 1977.

—'On the Question of Fulfilling the Law in Paul and Rabbinic Judaism.' In *Donum Gentilicium, New Testament Studies in Honor of David Daube*. Edited by E. Bammel, C.K. Barret, and W.D. Davies. Oxford: Clarendon Press, 1978.

Sanders, James A. 'Torah and Christ.' *Interpretation* 29 (1975), pp. 372-90.

—'Torah and Paul.' In *God's Christ and His People: Studies in Honour of Nils Alstrup Dahl*. Edited by Jacob Jervell and Wayne A. Meeks. Oslo: Universitetsforlaget, 1977.

Sandmel, Samuel. *The Genius of Paul*. New York: Farrar, Straus, and Cudahy, 1958.

Schelkle, Karl Hermann. *Paulus Lehrer der Väter. Die altkirchliche Auslegung von Römer 9–11*. Düsseldorf: Patmos Verlag, 1956.

Schlatter, Adolf. *Gottes Gerechtigkeit: Ein Kommentar zum Römerbrief*. Stuttgart: Calwer Verlag, 1962.

Schlier, Heinrich. *Der Römerbrief*. Freiburg: Herder, 1977.

Schmithals, Walter. *Paul and the Gnostics*. Nashville: Abingdon Press, 1972.

—*Der Römerbrief als historisches Problem*. Gütersloh: Gütersloher Verlagshaus Mohn, 1975.

Schneider, Erwin E. 'Finis legis Christus, Rom. 10.4.' *Theologische Zeitschrift* 20 (1964), pp. 410-22.

Schoedel, William R. 'Pauline Thought: Some Basic Issues.' In *Transitions in Biblical Scholarship*. Essays in Divinity, 6. Edited by J. Coert Rylaarsdam. Chicago: University of Chicago Press, 1968.

Schoeps, Hans Joachim. *Paul: The Theology of the Apostle in the Light of Jewish Religious History*. Philadelphia: Westminster, 1961.

Schrenk, Gottlob. *Die Weissagung über Israel im Neuen Testament*. Zürich: Gotthelf Verlag, 1951.

Schweitzer, Albert. *The Mysticism of Paul the Apostle*. New York: Macmillan, 1956.

Scroggs, Robin. 'Paul as Rhetorician: Two Homilies in Romans 1–11.' *Jews, Greeks and Christians. Essays in Honor of W.D. Davies*. Edited by K. Hamerton-Kelly and R. Scroggs. Leiden: Brill, 1976.

Senft, Christoph. 'L'élection d'Israël et la justification.' In *L'Evangile hier et aujourd'hui. Mélanges offerts au professeur Franz-J. Leenhardt*. Geneva: Labor et Fides, 1968.

Siegwalt, Gerard. *La loi chemin du salut*. Neuchâtel, Paris: Delachaux et Niestlé, 1971.

Slaten, Arthur W. 'The Qualitative Use of νόμος in the Pauline Epistles.' *American Journal of Theology* 23 (1919), pp. 213-19.

Sloyan, Gerhard S. *Is Christ the End of the Law?* Philadelphia: Westminster, 1978.

Stauffer, Ethelbert. 'Ἵνα und das Problem der teleologischen Denkens bei Paulus.' *Theologische Studien und Kritiken* 102 (1930), pp. 232-57.

Stendahl, Krister. 'The Apostle Paul and the Introspective Conscience of the West.' *Harvard Theological Review* 56 (1963), pp. 199-215.

—*Paul among Jews and Gentiles and Other Essays*. Philadelphia: Fortress Press, 1976.

Stowers, Stanley Kent. *The Diatribe and Paul's Letter to the Romans*. SBL Dissertation Series, 57. Chico: Scholars Press, 1981.

Stuart, Moses. *Commentary on Romans*. Andover: Gould N. Newman, 1832/1835.

Stuhlmacher, Peter. *Gerechtigkeit Gottes bei Paulus*. Göttingen: Vandenhoeck and Ruprecht, 1965.

—*Das paulinische Evangelium: I. Vorgeschichte*. Göttingen: Vandenhoeck and Ruprecht, 1968.

—'Das Ende des Gesetzes: Über Ursprung und Ansatz der paulinischen Theologie.' *Zeitschrift für Theologie und Kirche* 67 (1970), pp. 14-39.

—'Zur Interpretation von Römer 11.25-32.' In *Probleme biblischer Theologie. G. von Rad zum 70. Geburtstag*. Edited by H.W. Wolff. Munich: C. Kaiser Verlag, 1971.

—'Das Gesetz als Thema biblischer Theologie.' *Zeitschrift für Theologie und Kirche* 75 (1978), pp. 251-80.

Suggs, M. Jack. 'The Word Is Near You: Rom. 10.6-10 within the Purpose of the Letter.' In W.R. Farmer et al., *Christian History and Interpretation*. Cambridge: University Press, 1967, pp. 289-312.

Teeple, Howard M. *The Mosaic Eschatological Prophet*. Philadelphia: Society of Biblical Literature, 1957.

Toews, John E. 'The Law in Paul's Letter to the Romans. A Study of Romans 9.30–10.13.' Ph.D. dissertation, Northwestern University, 1977.

Tholuck, F. August G. *St. Paul's Epistle to the Romans*. Philadelphia: Sorin and Ball, 1824/1844.

Torti, Giovanni. *La Lettera ai Romani*. Studi Biblici, 41. Brescia: Paideia, 1977.

Trocmé, Etienne. 'L'Epître aux Romains et la méthode missionnaire de l'apôtre Paul.' *New Testament Studies* 7 (1961), pp. 148-53.

Unnik, Willem van. 'La conception paulinienne de la Nouvelle Alliance.' In *Littérature et théologie pauliniennes*. Edited by A. Descamps et al. Louvain: Desclée de Brouwer, 1969.

Veldhuizen, A. Van. 'Romans 9.30-33.' *Theologische Studien und Kritiken* 29 (1911), p. 439.

Verweijs, Pieter G. *Evangelium und Neues Gesetz in der ältesten Christenheit bis auf Marcion*. Studia Theologica Rhenotraiectiva, 5. Utrecht: V.H. Kemink en Zoon, 1960.

Via, Dan O. 'A Structuralist Approach to Paul's Old Testament Hermeneutic.' *Interpretation* 28 (1974), pp. 201-20.

Viard, André. *Saint Paul. Epître aux Romains*. Paris: Gabalda, 1975.

Vicent, Rafael. 'Derash homilético en Romanos 9–11.' *Salesianum* 47 (1980), pp. 751-88.

Wagner, Günter, ed. *Exegetical Bibliography on the Epistle to the Romans*. Bibliographical Aids, 3. Rüschlikon-Zürich: Baptist Theological Seminary, 1973.

Wallis, Gerhard. 'Torah und Nomos: Zur Frage nach Gesetz und Heil.' *Theologische Literaturzeitung* 105 (1980), pp. 321-32.

Walvoord, John F. 'Law in the Epistle to the Romans.' *Bibliotheca Sacra* 94 (1937), pp. 15-30, 281-95.

Wang, Joseph S. *Pauline Doctrine of Law*. Ph.D. dissertation. Emory University, 1970.

Weber, Hans Emil. *Das Problem der Heilsgeschichte nach Römer 9–11*. Leipzig: A. Deichert, 1911.

Westermann, Claus, ed. *Beginning and End in the Bible*. Philadelphia: Fortress, 1972.

Wilckens, Ulrich. *Der Brief an die Römer*. Neukirchen: Neukirchener Verlag, 1980.

—'Zur Entwicklung des paulinischen Gesetzesverständnis.' *New Testament Studies* 28 (1982), pp. 154-90.

Wiles, Maurice F. *The Divine Apostle: The Interpretation of St. Paul's Epistles in the Early Church*. Cambridge: University Press, 1967.

Williams, Sam K. 'The Righteousness of God in Romans.' *Journal of Biblical Literature* 99 (1980), pp. 241-90.

Williams, Norman Powell. 'The Epistle to the Romans.' *A New Commentary on Holy Scripture*. Edited by C. Gore, H.L. Goudge, and A. Guillaume. London: SPCK, 1928.

Wilson, R. McL. 'Νόμος: The Biblical Significance of Law.' *Scottish Journal of Theology* 5 (1952), pp. 36-48.

Windisch, Hans. *Paul und das Judentum*. Stuttgart: W. Kohlhammer, 1935.

Wrede, William. *Paul*. Lexington: American Theological Library Association, 1962.

Wuellner, Wilhelm. 'Paul; Rhetoric of Argumentation in Romans: An Alternative to the Donfried–Karis Debate over Romans.' *Catholic Biblical Quarterly* 38 (1976), pp. 330-51.

Wyschogrod, Michael. 'The Law: Jews and Gentiles—A Jewish Perspective.' *Lutheran Quarterly* 21 (1969), pp. 405-15.

Zahn, Theodor, and Hauck, F. *Der Brief des Paulus an die Römer.* Kommentar zum Neuen Testament. Edited by P. Bachmann et al. Leipzig: A. Deichert, 1925.

Zahn, A. *Das Gesetz Gottes nach der Lehre und der Erfahrung des Apostel Paulus.* Halle: Ebend, 1876.

Zerwick, Max. 'Drama populi Israeli secundum Rom. 9–11.' *Verbum Domini* 46 (1968), pp. 321-38.

Ziesler, J.A. *The Meaning of Righteousness in Paul: A Linguistic and Theological Inquiry.* Cambridge: University Press, 1972.

Zorn, Raymond O. 'The Apostle Paul's Use of the Old Testament in Romans 10.5-8.' *Gordon Review* 5 (1959), pp. 29-34.

INDEXES

INDEX OF BIBLICAL REFERENCES

INDEX OF AUTHORS

DATE DUE

MAY 30 '86			
OCT 23 86			
NOV 20 '86			
18 '86			
28			
EB 1 '89			
MY 1 '96			
DE 21 '96			
AP 1 2 97			
OC 4 97			
SE 25 '98			